EMPIRE'S EAGLES

The Fate of the Napoleonic Elite in America

THOMAS E. CROCKER

 Prometheus Books

Lanham • Boulder • New York • London

Ⓟ Prometheus Books

An imprint of The Rowman & Littlefield Publishing Group, Inc.
4501 Forbes Boulevard, Suite 200, Lanham, Maryland 20706
www.rowman.com

Distributed by NATIONAL BOOK NETWORK

British Library Cataloguing in Publication Information Available

Library of Congress Cataloging-in-Publication Data

Names: Crocker, Thomas E., author.
Title: Empire's eagles : the fate of the Napoleonic elite in America / Thomas E. Crocker.
Other titles: Fate of the Napoleonic elite in America
Description: Lanham, MD : Prometheus Books, [2021] | Includes bibliographical references and index. | Summary: "The never-before told story of how Napoleon's top brass escaped to America after Waterloo"— Provided by publisher.
Identifiers: LCCN 2020037551 (print) | LCCN 2020037552 (ebook) | ISBN 9781633886544 (hardback) | ISBN 9781633886551 (ebook)
Subjects: LCSH: French—United States—History—19th century. | Exiles—France—History—19th century. | Napoleonic Wars, 1800–1815. | Aristocracy (Social class)—France—History—19th century. | French Americans—History—19th century. | United States—Emigration and immigration—History—19th century.
Classification: LCC E184.F8 C76 2021 (print) | LCC E184.F8 (ebook) | DDC 973/.0044109034—dc23
LC record available at https://lccn.loc.gov/2020037551
LC ebook record available at https://lccn.loc.gov/2020037552

For Beth

Contents

List of Illustrations and Maps

Color Insert

Preface

THIS IS A STORY ABOUT IMMIGRANTS TO THE UNITED STATES OF America. It starts with one man, Napoleon Bonaparte, who almost fled to America aboard a Baltimore privateer with the secret collaboration of a freelancing American consul. It tells the little-known story of the hundreds of marshals of France, generals, and other senior Bonapartists who sought asylum in the United States, especially Philadelphia, after Napoleon's last stand at Waterloo. Finally, it examines the 200-year-old mystery of whether one particular Bonapartist immigrant was in fact Marshal Michel Ney, the "Bravest of the Brave" and the hero of the retreat from Moscow, whom history says was executed for treason by a firing squad in Paris.

More ink has been expended writing on the Napoleonic saga than probably any period in history, starting with the memoirs of the participants in it seeking to justify their actions. The purpose of this book is not to rewrite what has already been written but to tell a story of which most Americans are unaware, drawing on a variety of sources, some of which have never appeared in English or even in print before.

Many of the persons described in this book had lengthy and confusing names. In the interests of simplicity and clarity, the author has in most cases used the first and last name, with titles as appropriate. That should allow the curious reader to explore further the full biographies of these persons.

Little Drummer Boy

THE GLORY THAT WAS FRANCE LAY STREWN ACROSS THE UNDULATING fields of Waterloo in Brabant as far as the eye could see when dusk crowded in late that mid-June day: thousands of human bodies, spread-eagled in the mud, crumpled in heaps, or sitting upright with arms outstretched as if to cry "*Vive l'Empereur!*," the latest of more than 5 million dead across Europe; horses flat on their sides twitching or with legs akimbo; steel cuirasses punctured by cannonballs; plumed helmets dented and discarded in flight; wooden gun carriages shattered and listing; bright and shiny 12-pound cannon—known affectionately to their crews as "*les belles filles de l'Empereur*"—lying upended in the muck; General Jacquinot's nine-foot-long lances snapped like toothpicks—all compressed into a two-and-a-half-mile-square patch of rich gently rolling farmland turned for the day of June 18, 1815, into a battlefield on which close to 200,000 men fought; the air still choked and girdled with black powder smoke and cordite that stung the nose, watered the eyes, and cauterized any taste left in the parched mouth, an assault on the senses so presumptuous and complete that it rendered the survivors something less than human—and all the while the sounds: the moans and cries of the wounded begging for water, the pistol shots as the Prussian pursuers picked off stragglers and plundered gold, watches, and rings from the dead and dying, they only the first wave of scavengers soon to be followed in the darker shades of night by a lower order in the hierarchy of degradation, the Belgian peasants, many of them black-shawled crones, who would strip the bodies of whatever plunder the Prussians left behind—boots, pants, shirts, anything—leaving the bodies naked to greet the rising sun: the final verdict of St. Michael the Archangel, Commander of the Heavenly Host, who had hovered over the French all that morning and through much of the day, only to switch sides as the British squares held and Field Marshal von Blücher's black-clad uhlans appeared from the woods—and to bestow Victory.

The emperor Napoleon turned his back on Waterloo. He put the Duke of Wellington's "near run thing" behind him as he gripped the blue and gold lacquered door of his campaign coach with bright red wheels and bulletproof glass and heaved himself inside to flee south on the main road to Paris. Napoleon's valet Marchand had already locked and loaded onto another vehicle the imperial *nécessaire* containing 100,000 francs in gold and three times that in banknotes. In Napoleon's coach and others in the imperial baggage train were hidden bags of precious gems, including a fortune in diamonds. Soon after departing, the advancing and marauding Prussians, who were in close pursuit, set fire to the farm and barns at Le Caillou from which the baggage train had started, burning alive all the French wounded who had sought shelter within.[1] Everywhere, Prussian pursuers ran amok in a paroxysm of bayoneting and shooting to death prisoners who surrendered: no quarter given.

According to Clausewitz, the Prussian general commanding the van of the pursuit ordered his unit's drummer to beat "incessantly, intending by this sign of his troops' approach to strike terror into the hearts of the fleeing enemy on all sides, and to keep them in continuous flight."[2]

As the imperial coach accompanied by a guard of the 1/1st Chasseurs slowly made its way along the road clogged with fleeing troops just ahead of the pounding Prussian drum, Napoleon had time to replay the battle in his mind, as he was often to do in his remaining years. Why had Marshal Emmanuel Grouchy, after being commanded to find and intercept the Prussian force before the battle and having failed to do so, not returned to the field of battle to reinforce Napoleon even though he was in audible range of the fighting? Where was Grouchy? Why had Marshal Michel Ney, whom Napoleon had placed in overall charge of the battle, wasted the French cavalry on repeated futile charges against the British squares? Why had Ney bungled his command? Other participants in the battle had different questions, many centered on Napoleon himself, but these were the questions beginning to form in Napoleon's mind.

The clogged road made for slow progress. At Genappe, the road passed over a one-lane bridge that became a scene of abandoned artillery as crews unhitched their horses and fled on them. As the village began to burn to the sound of the beating Prussian drum, Napoleon abandoned his coach and continued on horseback. Shortly afterward, a Prussian major found himself in possession of Napoleon's sword, medals, and hat, as well as a purse filled with diamonds, mere afterthoughts as the emperor panicked and abandoned his coach.[3]

Once the Prussian pursuers themselves cleared Genappe they paused to sing a hymn of praise and thanksgiving and then continued the chase in the black of the night.

The van of the Prussians now reached the rear of the imperial baggage train, abandoned in the middle of the road and with its horses still harnessed. Even as their officers urged them forward, the uhlans fell on the wagons and plundered them, filling their pockets with precious gems and other booty. The following day, an officer wrote, fusiliers were selling diamonds as big as peas for a few francs.[4]

The retreat turned into a rout as the Prussian cavalry now joined the chase and fell on and looted the wagon carrying the imperial *nécessaire* and the vehicles of the marshals of France and general staff. Accompanied by a handful of aides and surrounded by his fleeing troops, Napoleon managed to keep just a few steps ahead of his pursuers. It would by now have been clear that the sole option was *sauve que peût*—in whatever form that might take. For Napoleon, this meant one last effort to regroup and, failing that, flight from France. For the marshals of France and other senior generals, it meant whatever they could devise. What were they to do—where were they to go before the Allies captured them and the restored Bourbons unleashed the hounds of retribution?

CHAPTER 2

Bonaparte's Retreat

SHORTLY AFTER HE RETURNED TO PARIS FROM THE DISASTROUS Russian campaign in 1812, Napoleon reportedly placed a large map of the United States on a table and said to his older brother, "Joseph, it is very probable that the time is not distant when you and I will be forced to seek an asylum in the United States. Come, let us look out the best spot."[1]

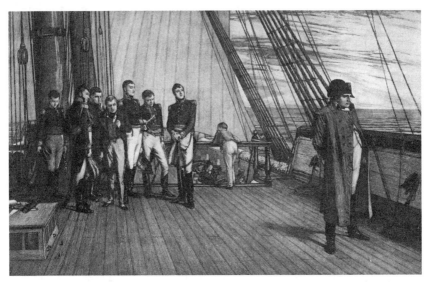

Figure 2.1. Napoleon on board *Bellerophon*. *Pictures of Travel* by Heinrich Hein (1797–1856), Charles Godfrey Leland (1824–1903), and Charles Harvey Genung (New York: D. Appleton), 1898, based on oil painting by same title by Sir William Quiller Orchardson (1832–1910), ca. 1880. Tate Gallery, London, UK. WIKIMEDIA COMMONS.

The place they selected lay north of the Delaware River near Philadelphia: New Jersey. The choice proved prophetic in terms of what Napoleon sought and what Joseph achieved.

—◦—

Napoleon pushed straight for Paris following the debacle at Waterloo. Traveling on horseback and by mail coach, he was determined to arrive in the capital ahead of the bad news and the Allies in order to rally a renewed defense. His motivations were thus political as well as military, to which was added a strong dose of self-preservation, for he feared that the Prussians would execute him if they captured him, which indeed they were most assiduously seeking to do.

Marshal Emmanuel Grouchy had escaped Waterloo with his corps intact, and Napoleon believed that if he could unite Grouchy's forces with other scattered units, stragglers, the national guard, garrison soldiers, and new conscripts, he could make another stand. But first he had to shore up his political support in the legislature, which was meeting at the Palais Bourbon across the Seine on the Left Bank.

Napoleon entered Paris at 7:00 a.m. on Wednesday, June 21, the summer solstice and longest day of the year. From then on, Napoleon found himself on a rapidly shrinking chess board.

Wednesday, June 21: On reaching his residence at the Elysée Palace near the Place de la République (today's Place de la Concorde), Napoleon summoned his family (as usual) and top ministers, pausing only to take his first bath in days. Napoleon originally had thought to head straight for the legislature dirty and dressed in his battle uniform to make an impassioned, patriotism-infused appeal for support. He still wished to go, even after bathing. The idea gained the support of some of his ministers but not the majority, who judged the ploy to be too dangerous. Instead, he sent a note to the legislature stating that he had returned to Paris "to consult with my ministers about measures of national salvation"[2] and dispatched his eloquent younger brother Lucien as his surrogate to speak for him. It was a maneuver reminiscent of his successful coup d'état on 18 Brumaire 1799 that ended the Directory.

But he was too late. The Marquis de Lafayette had already appointed five deputies to assume ministerial functions, thus effectively staging a parliamentary coup d'état. Napoleon's erstwhile chief of police Joseph Fouché and his agents also had been hard at work shaping parliamentary sentiment against the emperor.[3] Fouché, whom Napoleon had ennobled in 1809 as the Duke of Otranto, was the head of the provisional government. The exchanges between Lucien Bonaparte and the Marquis de Lafayette were pointed. Lucien took the podium in the Chamber of Deputies and spoke:

> It is not Napoleon that is attacked; it is the French people. And a proposition is now made to this people, to abandon their Emperor; to expose the French nation before the tribunal of the world, to a severe judgment on its levity and inconstancy.

Lafayette responded directly to Lucien:

> Who shall dare to accuse the French nation of inconstancy to the Emperor Napoleon? That nation has followed his bloody footsteps through the sands of Egypt and through the wastes of Russia; over fifty fields of battle; in disaster as faithfully as victory; and it is for having thus devotedly followed him that we now mourn the blood of three millions of Frenchmen.[4]

Lucien left empty-handed. Both the Chamber of Deputies and the Chamber of Peers called for Napoleon's abdication.

Napoleon was later to regret his decision not to appear personally at the Palais Bourbon, speculating that had he appeared, he would have cut off Lafayette's head.[5] He also was later to regret his failure to appreciate fully at the time the implications of the absence from his hastily summoned conclave of ministers of Joseph Fouché, who was widely known never to be on the losing side.

Thursday, June 22 through Saturday, June 24: Bereft of political support, with the legislature calling for his abdication and with even his loyal ministers advising capitulation, Napoleon abdicated at noon on June 22 and appointed his four-year-old son the king of Rome as Napoleon II. Two days later, Fouché, as head of the provisional government, accepted Napoleon's abdication. The king of Rome's "reign" was to last a short 15 days.

That evening Napoleon sent a message to the Ministère de la Marine (minister of the navy) requesting that two French naval frigates in the roadstead of the port of Rochefort on the west coast of France stand by to evacuate him to America. The two ships, *Saale* and *Méduse*, were the only two naval vessels reachable and ready to sail. The naval minister Denis Decrès responded that he would be pleased to do so as soon as he received orders from the provisional government, led by Fouché. The following day, Napoleon repeated the request to Lieutenant General Henri Count Bertrand, marshal of France, and also directed him to apply to Fouché for passports.[6]

Those surrounding Napoleon commented on his calm demeanor, as he studied reports of troop movements and, ever the autodidact, languished in his bath reading Alexander von Humboldt's diaries on his travels in the Americas. Napoleon still hoped to command French forces under the provisional government in resistance to the invading Allies, but, if not, he told his aide-de-camp Antoine Chamans Count Lavalette that he hoped to live as a private citizen in the United States—if he could get there.[7] On June 23, Lavalette discussed the options with Napoleon, who had been soaking for two hours in his bath:

> [Napoleon] spoke of the United States. I rejected the idea without reflection, and with a degree of vehemence that surprised him. "Why not America?" he asked.[8]

The idea was not a stretch: the United States had just concluded the bitter War of 1812 with Napoleon's archenemy Great Britain, and thus there was a certain "my enemy's enemy must be my friend" psychology at play. America also had an ambiguous fascination with Napoleon. He had, after all, ended the atrocities of the French Revolution and sold America vast western lands under advantageous terms in the Louisiana Purchase.

Moreover, Napoleon would not have been the first Bonaparte to settle in America. His youngest brother, Jérôme, had gone to Maryland and in 1803 married a Baltimore belle Elizabeth ("Betsy") Patterson from a prominent family. Napoleon, who could not abide his brother's marriage to an American and a commoner, disapproved of the marriage even though Betsy was soon pregnant with a child. In a coldhearted series of maneuvers, Napoleon refused to recognize the marriage or allow their son to be born on French soil. He eventually annulled the marriage himself when the pope refused to do so.

The flirtation between America and Napoleon was therefore of the one-sided, unrequited kind: more a matter of convenience than of conviction for Napoleon as his options dwindled.

Sunday, June 25: Since Napoleon's arrival at the Elysée Palace, crowds of supportive Parisians had surrounded the building and cheered Napoleon whenever he appeared in public. It is unclear whether these crowds made Fouché sufficiently uneasy to ask Napoleon to leave Paris or whether Napoleon had begun to perceive that Fouché needed to deliver him up to save his own skin with the Bourbons. Either way, Napoleon began to plan his departure from Paris.[9] He left the city for the last time on Sunday, June 25, as the Prussians and Allies pressed toward the capital. He was accompanied by his family, aides, a battalion of infantry, and about 100 of his loyal dragoon guards. His destination was the late empress Josephine's former home Malmaison, some 14 kilometers west of Paris. There he would await the passports.

On arrival, he conferred further with his entourage of family and friends. Many urged him to escape immediately, but Napoleon appeared to be in no hurry to flee farther for the moment. The imperial treasurer Guillaume Baron de Peyrusse remarked on Napoleon's calm when he learned that the first English and Prussian skirmishers had been spotted. The emperor "continued to read a work by M. de Humboldt on America."[10]

While at Malmaison, Napoleon's dream of a new life in America evolved. In his abdication message he had said that his "political life was over." In its place, Napoleon envisioned a new role for himself in America: that of a scholar and savant surrounded by his family. He would devote himself to his avocations of geography, science, and mathematics. This too was not a stretch, as Napoleon had long harbored serious interests in these subjects, and he was proud of his valid credentials as an intellectual (he often wore the uniform of the prestigious Institut de France, to which he had been elected). As for his family, he even went so far as to summon to Malmaison his two illegitimate children, his son the future count Léon and his other son Alexandre by Marie Walewska, with the intent that they accompany him to the United States. He ordered more concrete steps put into motion as well. He directed the imperial treasurer Baron de Peyrusse to transfer 3 million francs in gold to the banker Jacques Laffitte (not to be confused with the pirate Jean Lafitte, who comes later in the story) for transmittal to the United States. He directed his aide General Henri Bertrand to organize transportation to America of most of the imperial library and sufficient china, linens, and furniture from Malmaison to furnish both a large town house and a country estate. Twenty hunting guns were not neglected. He ordered his groom with 15 stable boys, horses, saddles, and equipment to sail for America. Subscriptions were even taken out for various Parisian newspapers to be delivered to Bertrand in care of general delivery, New York.[11]

Monday, June 26: The provisional government, which at this point wanted Napoleon out of France, decreed that "two frigates in the port of Rochefort may be armed for the purpose of transporting Napoleon Bonaparte to the United States." However, there was a catch: the frigates were not to "leave the roadstead of Rochefort until the passes shall have arrived."[12]

The same day, Napoleon sent his aide Lieutenant General René Savary, the Duke of Rovigo, to ask Fouché for the passports. According to Savary, Fouché in turn asked him,

"Where does the Emperor intend to go?"

"Where else can he go," I resumed, "but to America? I thought you were aware of it."

. . . Fouché [responded], "this is the first time the subject is mentioned to me. He is quite right; but I will not take upon myself to let him depart without adopting every precaution for his safety: otherwise, I should be blamed if any accident were to happen to him. I will apply to Lord Wellington for passports for him, as it behooves me to protect my individual responsibility in the eyes of the nation. I should never be forgiven for acting without the requisite precaution."[13]

Fouché's disingenuousness about his knowledge of Napoleon's destination and false solicitousness of Napoleon's safety and not-so-false concern for his own position betray further end games: passing off his own responsibility for issuing the passports and tipping off the British about Napoleon's plan of escape in order to curry favor. Fouché's position was also legally disingenuous because the provisional government of France, not Wellington, had jurisdiction over Napoleon and should have been the only authority empowered to issue the passports. The provisional government had not yet surrendered to the Allies, entered into a peace treaty, or abdicated in a way that would bestow sovereign authority over a French citizen on a foreign power. Clearly, Fouché's calculations were dictated by realpolitik rather than legal niceties, even when those niceties supported the sovereign integrity of the French state.

Napoleon's plan to emigrate to America resonated with his immediate family. On June 26, his brother Lucien, then at the Château de Neuilly, wrote their sister Pauline, "You will have known of the recent disaster to the Emperor, who has just abdicated in favor of his son. He will depart for the United States of America, where all of us will join him. I shall try to join my family in Rome in order to conduct them to America."[14]

Tuesday, June 27: General Nicolas Becker, whom Napoleon knew from previous campaigns (in fact, he had sacked him when he was aide-de-camp to Marshal André Masséna), arrived at Malmaison and reported to Napoleon that he "had been ordered to watch over his safety." He explained that he had received orders from the minister of war, no doubt acting at the behest of Fouché, to "take command of the troops entrusted to protect him and to answer for his person to the provisional government." This move immediately made Napoleon and his aides suspicious. They feared that Becker was the unwitting stalking horse for separating the emperor from whatever troops remained at his disposal and that once Napoleon relinquished command, another, even less sympathetic officer would replace Becker. As Napoleon said to Savary, "This proceeding savours much more of the revolutionary committee than of a noble-minded government."[15]

Napoleon was now more determined than ever to make his exit, and he directed Savary to approach Fouché a second time to demand the passports. Meanwhile, the provisional government, acting through the Ministère de la Marine, sent conflicting signals to Napoleon at Malmaison, once telling him he was free to leave without the passports and then countermanding that direction the following day.

Wednesday, June 28: Not surprisingly, and almost certainly as anticipated by Fouché, the Duke of Wellington responded to Fouché that he had "no authority from his government, or from the Allies, to give any answer to the demand of a passport and assurances of safety for Napoleon Buonaparte and his family to pass to the United States of America."[16]

Wellington's carefully worded response was legally correct: he had no authority to issue a passport for a French citizen. It was also practically and politically motivated: he could not ensure Napoleon's safety when in fact the Allies sought his capture. It appears that Wellington forwarded the request to the government in London. To complete his duplicity, also on June 28, Fouché secretly transmitted a message to Wellington via a British agent. The British agent reported to Wellington, "Every possible concession that a free nation [France] will make can be granted; and the Duc d'Otrante [Fouché, as head of the provisional government], in the name of the French government, pledges himself to deliver up Buonaparte in any way that may be most suitable to the views of the British government."[17]

London's response was a denial of the request for passports, as made clear in orders shortly thereafter passed down to the British naval squadron blockading France and actively seeking to intercept Napoleon in any effort to escape: "Government received, on the night of the 30th, an application from the rulers of France, for a passport and safe conduct for Buonaparte to America, which had been answered in the negative, and, therefore, directing an increase of vigilance to intercept him: but it remains quite uncertain where he will embark."[18]

Despite the responses of Wellington and subsequently London, the provisional government directed Napoleon to proceed to Rochefort to await the passports. Fouché, acting through the Ministère de la Marine, passed the lie to Napoleon that the passports were in transit and would be available to him aboard one of the British naval vessels patrolling off Rochefort. Napoleon still sought a way to avoid exile; he offered the provisional government to stay to fight the Allies under the authority of his son Napoleon II. Fouché ignored his offer.

Thursday, June 29: With the advancing Prussian columns closing in on him at Malmaison, Napoleon had to make a quick exit. He bade farewell to his mother and stepdaughter/sister-in-law Hortense de Beauharnais Bonaparte and (in a particularly poignant gesture) visited one last time the room at Malmaison in which the love of his life, the empress Josephine, had died the previous year.

Savary describes the departure:

His suite was divided into two parties. The first consisted of several carriages, in which were Madame Bertrand and her children, M. and Madame de Montholon with their child, M. de Las Cases and his son, as well as several orderly officers who had requested leave to accompany the Emperor. All those carriages were to take the road to Orléans, pass by Châteauroux, and reach Rochefort on an appointed day.

The second convoy consisted of a single summer calash containing the Emperor, General Bertrand, General Becker, and myself. The Emperor's valet was on the calash-box, and a courier proceeded half a league before us in order that we might find horses in readiness on our arrival at every post station.

The Emperor was dressed like ourselves, in a plain frock, without any mark of distinction. We carried no luggage with us; and the calash had no appearance of being intended for a long journey. We were merely provided with every kind of arms.

The Emperor's effects were in another carriage containing two seats. General Gourgaud was in this carriage, which kept at the distance of two hours' journey behind us. All the carriages came up to the portico of the palace, with the exception of the calash, which remained in the court-yard that divides the castle from the kitchens. The Emperor over took it with us through the winding walks of the garden, whilst the other persons I have mentioned stepped into the carriages drawn up under the portico.

The calash was the first to depart through one of the walks of the park. As it was less conspicuous in appearance than the others, the public attention was not directed to it, but was fixed on the carriages of the other convoy, to which the picket stationed at the iron gate opening on the high road presented arms, under the impression that the Emperor was in one of them. It had not discovered that he had already passed.[19]

As Napoleon departed for Rochefort, he still was confident that the passports would be issued.

Monday, July 3: After a four-day journey from Malmaison on the outskirts of Paris, Napoleon arrived at Rochefort at about 9:00 a.m. accompanied by General Becker, his aides, and some 60 guards. The emperor's party had attempted to travel incognito but was recognized and, in general, warmly greeted by the populace along the way. Despite several close calls with patrolling soldiers, they arrived at Rochefort, where they took up residency in the Maritime Prefecture. The passports of course had not arrived. However, the two French frigates, *Saale* and *Méduse*, were on station and ostensibly prepared to sail, but neither the British nor the weather was cooperative. Indeed, the Maritime Prefect at Rochefort Baron de Bonnefoux—and thus Napoleon's party—was convinced that a full Royal Navy squadron was blockading Rochefort, making escape all but impossible. In fact, at this time only one third-rate British ship of the line, the redoubtable 74-gun HMS *Bellerophon* (in Greek mythology, Bellerophon was the son of Poseidon and a renowned slayer of monsters), known affectionately to her crews as *Billy Ruffian*, was doing picket duty off Rochefort. Her commander, Captain Frederick Lewis Maitland, had earlier detached her consorts for duty elsewhere.

Tuesday, July 4: While en route, General Becker had written the provisional government renewing Napoleon's offer to fight the Allies and requesting instructions. The response, written by Fouché on July 4 but received some days later by Becker, made clear that (1) the provisional government declined the offer and wanted Napoleon to exit the country as quickly as possible and that (2) no passports would be issued:

> Paris, 4th of July, 1815.
>
> General Becker,
>
> The commission of government has received the letter you have written to it from Niort under date of the 2nd of July. Napoleon must embark without delay. The success of the negotiations mainly depends upon the positive assurance the allied powers wish to receive of his actual embarkation; and you are not aware to what extent the safety and repose of the state are compromised by this procrastination. . . . The commission therefore places the person of Napoleon under your responsibility; you must employ every measure of coercion you may deem necessary, without failing in the respect due to him. Accelerate his arrival at Rochefort, and make him instantly embark. As to his offer of services, our duties towards France and our engagements towards foreign powers do not allow us to accept of them; and you must no longer mention the matter to us. Lastly, the commission conceives it to be inexpedient that Napoleon should communicate with the English squadron. It cannot grant the permission which is asked on that subject,
>
> Accept, &c.
>
> (Signed) The Duke of Otranto.[20]

The letter can be read in several ways. The more cynical interpretation is that it was an attempt to hasten Napoleon into the hands of the British, which would have been consistent with Fouché's machinations. A more charitable view is that the provisional government simply wanted Napoleon out of the country so as not to complicate its negotiations with the advancing Allies, which was consistent with the provisional government's expressed views from the start (but at odds with Fouché's June 28 secret message to Wellington). Perhaps most tellingly, by obliquely warning

Napoleon not to contact the British naval vessels because they carried no passports, the message was giving him the favor of honest advice even if the gravamen of that advice was that he must leave at once and that he was on his own. As it turned out, the admonitions were inapposite, for Napoleon lingered at Rochefort, and he was not on his own because a brave French naval captain and an official of the United States had his escape covered—if he were willing to avail himself of it.

However, at the same time, on July 4, Paris ordered an "embargo" prohibiting all ships from leaving France. It is unclear if Napoleon knew of the embargo, which was to last until July 13. From their ensuing actions, it appears that Napoleon and his entourage were ignorant of it.

During the course of the day on July 4 Napoleon and his aides met with the Maritime Prefect at Rochefort and tried to devise alternative means of eluding the British blockade. In order to understand what ensued, it is first necessary to understand the geography. Rochefort, on the River Charente, is a port on the western coast of France. Some 163 kilometers by land to the south is the larger port of Bordeaux, situated on the River Garonne near its confluence with the River Dordogne. Just northwest of Bordeaux, the two rivers flow into the Gironde Estuary, a long and broad arm of the sea bounded by a peninsula on its western shore and the French mainland on its eastern shore (see figure 2.2).

The town of Royan sits at the mouth of the Gironde Estuary on the mainland and is only 41 kilometers by land from Rochefort, easily facilitating communication from Rochefort to the Gironde Estuary. Opposite Royan, on the tip of the peninsula and also at the mouth of the Estuary, is the town of Verdon-sur-Mer. All of these places were to play critical roles in what transpired.

Savary relates the discussion at the meeting between Napoleon and the Maritime Prefect:

> The Saale and Méduse frigates were those which were appointed to convey us to America.[21] There were in the same road two other ships of war, which were placed at the prince's disposal; a brig, and the corvette La Bayadère, the latter in the direction of the Gironde [near Bordeaux]. The two frigates were quite new. The

Méduse carried eighteen-pounders, and had already made an excursion in which it was found to be a very superior sailer. The Saale was of a rather larger class; nevertheless, I could not affirm that it carried heavier guns than eighteen pounders; this was her first attempt at sailing; but all were agreed in opinion that she would also prove an excellent sailer. The crews of both were composed of old seamen who had returned from the prisons of England since the peace of 1814.

During the five or six days which the Emperor had passed at Rochefort, a small Danish vessel then in port had been prepared for sea, and fully provisioned: a secret recess had even been contrived in it, in the event of its being visited by the English cruisers. It was proposed to the Emperor that he should proceed in this vessel to America; but he refused, and declined running

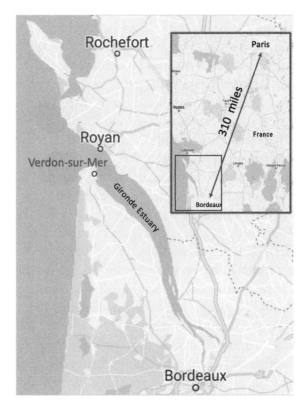

Figure 2.2. Map of Rochefort, Bordeaux, and the Gironde Estuary. COURTESY OF ROGER WILLIAMS.

a risk which might be attended with unpleasant consequences. Nevertheless, he made this small vessel proceed into the road, reserving to himself the power of afterwards considering what course it might be most advantageous for him to adopt.[22]

The alternatives boiled down to three possibilities. First, the badly out-gunned and outclassed *Méduse* could distract *Bellerophon* in a single ship combat while *Saale* slipped out with Napoleon for America—not an attractive option. Alternatively, Napoleon might board the French naval corvette *Bayadère* (a *bayadère* is a Hindu temple dancer) near Bordeaux (Gaspard Baron Gourgaud, who was involved in the discussions, stated that she "lay off Bordeaux" in the Gironde Estuary)[23] and try to elude the British patrols.

The commander of *Bayadère*, Charles Baudin (see insert, illustration 1), was no ordinary captain. In 1804 he had sailed as a midshipman on *Géographe*'s scientific/espionage expedition to Australia, subsequently lost an arm in combat, became an ardent Bonapartist (he was a Huguenot), and went on in later years to rise to full admiral. Captain Baudin was willing but feared his vessel was not sufficiently fast. The third alternative, which Captain Baudin suggested, was to place the former emperor and his dwindling entourage aboard one of two American ships in the Gironde Estuary near Bordeaux, *Pike* and *Ludlow*, and make a dash for it, with *Bayadère* and its consort, the 380 ton transport brig *Infatigable*, running interference against *Bellerophon*.

Just as Captain Baudin was no ordinary captain, *Pike* and *Ludlow* were not ordinary merchantmen. Emmons's List of U.S. privateers during the War of 1812 contains entries for a 275-ton Baltimore schooner named *Pike* as well as a Kennebec-based *Ludlow*.[24] *Pike* is of particular interest. Even though Emmons describes her as a schooner, other references call her a brig. Either way, she was special. She was built in Baltimore in 1813 and was owned by a consortium of four owners, all from Baltimore: Peter Arnold Karthaus, his son-in-law Ferdinand Hurxthal,[25] Frederick Wae-sche, and (most important to this story) Joel Vickers, a working captain who had moved into an ownership role beginning about 1808 and had interests in four armed Baltimore privateers: *Garonne*, *Lawrence*, *Revenge*, and *Pike*.[26] After *Pike*'s successful initial trading voyage to France under

Captain Henry Bolton on which she carried letters of marque but took no prizes, her owners converted her into a privateer and upped her armament from one long 12-pound cannon, three long 9-pound cannon, and two 12-pound carronades to one long 9-pounder and 12 12-pounder carronades.[27] They also increased her crew from 37 to 120 men, which was typical of a privateer. She then went on a spree, taking 13 prizes, including a British brig also named *Pike*, which she captured and burned. In terms of prize taking, she was not in the top tier of Baltimore privateers, such as *Chasseur*, *Comet*, *Surprise*, or *Amelia*, but she was in the very respectable second echelon.[28] Baltimore privateers like *Pike* were renowned at the time for their speed. With their raked masts, topmasts, topsail yards, and topgallant yards, Baltimore privateers, also known as Baltimore Flyers, used the wind more efficiently than other ships. Handled properly, they could cruise at speeds of 11 or 12 knots versus 5 or 6 for ordinary warships. On the rare occasions that the British captured them during the War of 1812, they proved virtually useless because only their specialized Baltimore crews knew how to handle them.[29]

Baudin's exact words, written partially in the third person, describe his proposal:

> At this moment the Bayadère, detached at the opening of the Gironde, was afloat on the road of Verdon. The Emperor, already uncertain of the intentions of the provisional government, charged the maritime prefect of Rochefort, the Baron de Bonnefoux, to ask Captain Baudin if he would wish to undertake conducting him to the United States. The text of the response of the commander of the Bayadère deserves to be reproduced.
>
> "Baron," wrote Captain Baudin, "if it were only a question of myself, of my existence, of my own honor, I would not need a single instance of reflection to respond affirmatively to the question contained in your letter of last night. But it is a matter of saving a great man, France itself, from the humiliation that would result from failure. I have thus seriously considered the chances of the enterprise that you have proposed to me and I do not hesitate to say that I believe it possible and easy, that I am ready to take it on.

"Neither the Bayadère nor the Infatigable which are here under my orders have the greatest speed but happily by chance *I have at my disposition* [emphasis added] two magnificent American ships—the Pike and the Ludlow—which because of the recently concluded peace [between America and Great Britain] find themselves at my sides in the bottom of the Gironde, all ready to sail to the United States. Both have, by their extraordinary speed, escaped, as corsairs, all the English cruisers, during the last war. I will take them with me, and if it works, I will put the Emperor aboard one of the two. In case of an encounter [with the British], I will sacrifice the Bayadère and Infatigable to block passage to the enemy: I am well certain of being able to stop them, however superior they might be. I have moreover a close to infallible means to divert the attention of the enemy cruiser[s] and to clear the mouth of the river: there exists but a single line of cruisers: this line once breached, we will have the open sea. The Emperor must hasten therefore to come, in the greatest secrecy, with the least suite and with the least baggage possible: I will take him to the United States. He can have confidence in me. . . . Signed the Bayadère, the roads of Verdon, July 4, 1815 4 o'clock in the morning."

This letter sent, Captain Baudin put into place the measures necessary to ensure the execution of his project.[30]

For Baudin, an active duty captain in the French navy, to state that he had "at my disposition" what were almost certainly American privateers, possibly operating under official U.S. letters of marque, suggests at least some degree of advance coordination with the U.S. government. Exactly what the two American ships were doing at Bordeaux is a subject of some mystery. On June 28, 1815, based on information that dated from before the Battle of Waterloo, the New York *Evening Post* reported that "the French have begun their preparations for private maritime hostility. Two armed ships, the one lately belonging to an American and American built, are now at Bordeaux, ready to take advantage of the first notice of a rupture, and to clear the mouth of the Garonne." Neither *Pike* nor *Ludlow* appears in previous lists of merchantmen plying the Bordeaux wine trade.

As discussed below, it is likely that the U.S. consul at Bordeaux, William Lee, was at least aware of (and perhaps had a hand in) the armed ships' presence for operations against the British and that, later, he helped coordinate the ships' availability to Captain Baudin for the express purpose of spiriting the emperor out of France.

For his part, Captain Maitland, although aware of the possibility of a breakout at Bordeaux, stated that "it was my decided opinion that Rochefort was much more likely to be the port where the trial would be made."[31] Captain Maitland and his superior officer Rear Admiral Sir Henry Hotham were well aware of the likelihood of Napoleon escaping aboard one of the two French naval frigates and debated between themselves how Maitland could stop them with only *Bellerophon* and no consort frigate. Thus, Maitland later wrote that

> there was little doubt of its being his intention to effect his escape, if possible, from that place [Rochefort], in the frigates . . . I anchored the Bellerophon as close to the French squadron as the batteries would permit. . . . I trained one hundred of the stoutest men, selecting them from the different stations in the ship; it being my intention to, after firing into and silencing one frigate, to run the Bellerophon alongside of her, throw that party in, and then, leaving her in charge of the first lieutenant, to have proceeded in chase of the other. [In other words, Maitland would take out one of the frigates, place a boarding party aboard her, and then pursue the remaining frigate.]

Hotham warned Maitland, "Although the force of the Bellerophon would be sufficient for the ships at Isle d'Aix, if they were to give you an opportunity of bringing them to action together, you cannot stop them both, if the frigates separate; I am, therefore, now anxious that you should have a frigate with you."[32]

Thus the British naval commanders opposing Napoleon were well aware of the difficulties posed by the French naval frigates, but at this point, they were unaware of Baudin's daring plan to use his own ship *Bayadère* as a shield for the actual means of Napoleon's escape: the American privateers.

The plan had a plausible chance of success because the attention of the British was directed toward the River Charente and Rochefort rather than the Gironde Estuary and Bordeaux. Moreover, the plan had the advantage of surprise, as the British at this juncture were focused exclusively on a breakout at Rochefort involving the two French naval frigates *Saale* and *Méduse* (and subsequently the Danish merchant ship when Maitland learned of it). The British at this point appear to have been entirely ignorant of *Bayadère* and the American privateers.

As noted by Baudin, the Road of Verdon is not more than 15 leagues from Rochefort. The same day that Baudin sent his letter the response from Baron de Bonnefoux arrived. The emperor approved the plan. All Captain Baudin had to do was wait.[33]

Napoleon envisioned a new, private life in America. One of his entourage, Gaspard Baron Gourgaud, explained, "[Napoleon] told me . . . that when he reached America he should live there as a private gentleman; that he should never return to France . . . that when he grew bored in the United States, he would take to his carriage, and travel over a thousand leagues, and that he did not think any one would suspect that he intended to return to Europe."[34]

Was his aspiration to a retired life genuine? Later, in exile on St. Helena, he mused, "If I had gone to America, we might have founded a state there."[35] Apparently, imperial ambition still fanned the emperor's heart and, as shall be seen, motivated some of his closest supporters when they eventually found refuge in the United States.

Wednesday, July 5 through Saturday, July 8: Napoleon tarried inexplicably at Rochefort, not taking advantage of any of the options at his disposal. Although both the provisional government and his advisers pressed him to depart, Napoleon dallied and offered up only excuses. He still held out an increasingly forlorn hope of receiving the passports. He was reluctant to depart without his entourage. The weather also played an important and maybe even critical role as his naval advisers waited in vain for a favorable wind.

In the meantime, the British augmented their blockade, and now the escape plan was complicated by the fact that the breakout would face hostile ships in addition to *Bellerophon*. As one British sailor put it, "nothing could escape our argus-eyes, eagerly looking into every rat-hole for 'Napoleon Le Grand.'"[36]

Finally, on July 8 the provisional government ordered Napoleon to leave Rochefort. He boarded *Saale* and proceeded to the roadstead of Île d'Aix, a nearby island just beyond the mouth of the River Charente. Napoleon remained on board the ship.

The same day, Admiral Hotham wrote to Captain Maitland, "I have no doubt that the two frigates at Isle d'Aix are intended for him . . . and I am sure you will use your utmost endeavors to intercept him." The letter also contained an order: "The Lords Commissioners of the Admiralty having every reason to believe that Napoleon Buonaparte meditates his escape, with his family, from France to America, you are hereby required and directed, in pursuance of orders from their Lordships, . . . to keep the most vigilant look-out for the purpose of intercepting him; and to make the strictest search of any vessel you may fall in with; and if you should be so fortunate as to intercept him, you are to transfer him and his family to the ship you command, and there keeping him in careful custody, return to the nearest port in England (going into Torbay in preference to Plymouth) with all possible expedition; and on your arrival you are not to permit any communication whatever with the shore . . . ; and you will be held responsible for keeping the whole transaction a profound secret, until you receive their Lordships' further orders."[37]

Sunday, July 9: Napoleon's situation grew more desperate by the day. Napoleon continued to consider escaping on one of the two French naval frigates or on a merchant ship. All options remained in play. In the absence of the promised passports, Napoleon was anxious to avoid a confrontation with the British patrols that he feared he may well lose.

Monday, July 10: To these ends and against the admonition from the provisional government to General Becker just days before, Napoleon sent Savary and his counselor of state, Emmanuel Count de Las Cases, under a flag of truce to feel out Captain Maitland of *Bellerophon* about his intentions if Napoleon were to depart. They bore a letter from Lieutenant General Henri Count Bertrand, marshal of France, explaining Napoleon's dilemma. The relevant portions of the conversation between the two emissaries and Captain Maitland, as recounted by Savary, are worth reading in full:

The Emperor has no wish to conceal his departure. He can have no personal motive for doing so, as is clearly demonstrated by the step which he has directed us to take. But in the event of the wind turning fair previously to his receiving your answer, and of his taking advantage of it and sailing out with his suite in the frigates or brigs, what course would you pursue?

If instead of setting sail in the frigates, he were to put to sea in a French trading vessel, how would you act?

And lastly, if instead of proceeding in the above vessels, he should sail out in a neutral vessel, an American ship for instance, what would you do in that case?

Captain Maitland replied as follows: "If the Emperor sails out with the frigates, I will attack, and if possible capture them. The Emperor would, in this case, become a prisoner.

"If he sails in a French trading vessel, as we are at war, I will capture it; and in this case also the Emperor would become a prisoner.

"If he sails in a neutral vessel, and I should search it, I will not take upon myself to suffer him to proceed. I will detain the vessel, and refer the matter to my admiral, who will determine the question."

It was then observed to him, that in this case also he would no doubt make him a prisoner. "Not at all," said Captain Maitland, with warmth; "but I will not take upon myself to decide the matter. This is a question of so extraordinary a nature, that I shall leave the responsibility to my admiral."

Demonstrating considerable quick thinking, Captain Maitland followed up on this last question by penning a response to Marshal Bertrand, while the two emissaries stood in his cabin talking, to the effect that he would have to raise the matter with Rear Admiral Hotham, "hoping, by that means, to induce Napoleon to remain for the Admiral's answer, which would give time for the arrival of reinforcements."[38]

Savary's narrative continues:

This explanation was followed by many details respecting the Emperor's position. Captain Maitland said to us in the course of conversation—

"The Emperor acts very properly in demanding passports, in order to avoid misunderstandings, which would be of daily occurrence at sea. But I do not think that our government would suffer him to proceed to America."

"Where then," said we to Captain Maitland, in return, "would it be proposed to him that he should fix his residence?"

"I am at a loss to form an idea on the subject," rejoined the captain; "but I am almost certain of what I tell you. What repugnance could he feel in coming to England? He would thereby solve all difficulties."

M. de Las Cases answered, that we were not empowered to discuss this question; personally speaking, he was of opinion the Emperor had not entertained that idea, as he perhaps apprehended the effects of a resentment, which was the natural consequence of the long misunderstanding subsisting between him and the English government. On the other hand, he had a predilection for mild climates, and especially for social intercourse; both which advantages he might find in America, without apprehending any harsh treatment from any one.

Captain Maitland replied, that it was a mistake to suppose the English climate was damp or unhealthy. In some counties, the county of Kent for instance, it was as mild as in France. As to the enjoyments of a social life, they were incomparably superior in England to any thing the Emperor might find in America.

"As for the resentments he might apprehend," said the captain, "his coming to England would be the surest means of extinguishing them. Residing in the midst of the nation, placed under the protection of its laws, he will be protected from every danger, and render the efforts of his enemies altogether powerless." He observed, that if even the [Bourbon] ministers were to attempt to molest him, a circumstance which he doubted, they would not do so, because with us, he added, the government is not of an arbitrary character; it is obedient to the laws.

"I dare say," continued Captain Maitland, "that the government will adopt towards him every measure of precaution calculated to secure his repose, as well as that of the country where he may reside; such precautions, for instance, as it adopted in respect to his brother Lucien: but I cannot imagine that any other course would be adopted, because, as I repeat, ministers have no right to do so, and the nation would not suffer it."

M. de Las Cases again observed to Captain Maitland, that he was not empowered to discuss that subject; but he had not lost one word of his conversation, and would report it to the Emperor; and if this prince should determine upon proceeding to England, he should let him know. He then put this question to him:

"In the event of the Emperor's adopting the idea of going to England—an idea which I shall do all in my power to promote—may he depend upon being admitted on board of your ship, as well as those who accompany him? for such a supposition no longer admits of a passage on board the frigates."

Captain Maitland replied that he would instantly address a dispatch to his admiral on the subject; but that if the Emperor should request a passage on board of his ship previously to his receiving a reply, he should at once admit him.[39]

Thus, the seed of the idea of seeking asylum in England was germinated and began to grow in Napoleon's mind when his two emissaries reported back on the afternoon of July 10, but that option was by no means a foregone conclusion. In the middle of the night, Napoleon summoned Savary and instructed him to order the captain of *Saale* to set sail immediately for America. The captain refused the request on the grounds that his secret orders from Paris were not to sail if doing so would endanger the ship. Both Savary and Napoleon viewed that argument as an excuse and that in fact Fouché had never intended for the frigates to sail unless it were to deliver Napoleon straight into the hands of his enemies. They both blamed Fouché for the secret orders. This episode proved to Napoleon that escape by the French frigates was no longer an option. All that remained were *Bayadère* and the American privateers or a third-country ship.

Tuesday, July 11: Meanwhile, as instructed by Baron de Bonnefoux and with the embargo still in place, Captain Baudin had waited for eight days aboard *Bayadère* in the Gironde Estuary. On July 11, Napoleon dispatched his highly trusted aide, Lieutenant General Charles Baron Lallemand (illustration 2), to visit Captain Baudin aboard *Bayadère*. Lallemand traveled overland, and, because the surrounding country was largely royalist, he traveled in disguise as a merchant marine officer on the supposition that such a person would pass unnoticed in that maritime region. Lallemand later reported finding four American ships (evidently two unnamed vessels beyond *Pike* and *Ludlow*) that "had near them a French corvette [presumably *Bayadère*] which was anchored at the mouth of the river."[40] The two unnamed ships he saw were probably part of the trio of American merchantmen *Belle*, *Clotilda*, and *Almeda*, which ultimately joined *Pike* and *Ludlow* on their return voyage to America.[41] The reference to the mouth of the river appears to be a misnomer, understandable for an army officer, for the mouth of the Gironde Estuary. The fact that Napoleon entrusted such a risky mission to so senior a general attests to the seriousness with which he viewed the American option.

The exact nature of Lallemand's July 11 mission and the American role in it have long been shrouded in mystery. Lallemand's conversation with Captain Baudin was recounted by the latter in his handwritten memoirs, written partly in the third person and published here in English translation for the first time:

> The following morning as I landed ashore at Verdon I encountered, directing itself toward the Bayadère, a fishing vessel carrying a naval officer. This officer was none other than General Lallemand in disguise. . . .
> General Lallemand's mission was to study afresh the chances of an evasion by the Gironde. . . . "Can you, would you still undertake what you had proposed eight days ago?" asked the general of the captain. "I still would, responded the captain of the Bayadère, only I find it less easy than yesterday. It is at the invitation of the

Emperor that I am diminished in the means on which I counted to favor his break out; I was going to go to Bordeaux to create some others. May the Emperor therefore come! But he must come without that entourage of forty persons who follow after him. He must come with one suitcase, one chamber valet, one or two friends, men of head and of heart. He must arrive in a small post carriage, tomorrow morning, without noise."

General Lallemand returned overland to Rochefort. Captain Baudin went immediately to Bordeaux to the house of General [Bertrand Count] Clausel, who commanded about 4,000 to 5,000 troops loyal to Bonaparte in that city. At two o'clock in the morning, the Captain and the General transported themselves to the home of the American consul, Mr. [William] Lee. In a few words, Baudin explained the reason for his visit: he came to ask the consul to assist him in his enterprise. In response, Mr. Lee threw his arms around him. An American ship was in the port; he immediately summoned the captain: that he appear without losing a moment and go to the road of Verdon to be put under the disposition of the commander of the Bayadère.[42]

The fact that Baudin and Clausel called on Lee at 2:00 a.m. and that Lee's response was immediate, forthcoming, and understanding of the context suggests not only familiarity but also a prior course of conduct involving efforts to remove Napoleon from France. The unnamed American ship to which Lee referred may have been a different one from *Pike* or *Ludlow*, about which Baudin already knew. However, such an interpretation makes little sense. More likely, the ship was *Pike*, and Lee was activating and ordering its involvement.

Also on July 11, an informant advised Maitland that "a message had been sent from Île d'Aix, early that morning, for a man who was considered the best pilot on the island for the Mamusson passage, being the only person who had ever taken a frigate through; that a large sum of money had been offered to him to pilot a vessel to sea from that passage, and that it certainly was Buonaparte's intention to escape from thence; either in the corvette, which had moved down some days before, or in a Danish brig, which was then lying at anchor near the entrance."[43]

Clearly, Maitland continued to focus on the two French naval ships and the Danish brig (*Magdeleine*, commanded by a Frenchman named Besson) and remained ignorant of the planned role for *Bayadère* and the American privateers.[44] Maitland, now reinforced, promptly ordered the frigate *Myrmidon* to block the entrance to the Gironde Estuary.

But he was too late: *Pike* and *Ludlow*, accompanied by *Belle*, *Clotilda*, and *Almeda*, sailed that very day. However, Napoleon was not on board. What transpired is described by Baudin:

> . . . forty ships were bottled up by the [British] embargo, the English cruiser[s] gathered strength all the time: the commander of the Bayadère thought it necessary to send a courier to Rochefort. In response he received an invitation to lift the embargo. On July 11 at sunset, the wind was favorable to leave by three passages in the south, the west and the north, the signal which freed the merchant fleet from any constraints was hoisted. The forty ships unfurled their sails: each making way for its destination, they soon found themselves dispersed like a fan. The Bayadère got under way last. No obstacle on the horizon . . . the sea was free: the English cruiser[s] showed themselves to be scattered, running, to visit them, one ship after another. The Bayadère succeeded in passing the blockade![45]

Wednesday, July 12: Napoleon and his entourage disembarked at the Île d'Aix to await Lallemand's return. By then, Louis XVIII had regained the throne and was soon to impose royalist control over Rochefort and its region. Because of the prospects for vengeance, this was a greater concern to Napoleon than the British or even the Prussians. The former emperor's options were rapidly dwindling.

Thursday, July 13: Baron Gourgaud, who was present, reported that "at nine o'clock [in the morning] General Lallemand returned from his visit to Bordeaux and the corvette, etc. He held many mysterious talks with different persons."[46] Gourgard's statement raises the possibility that Lallemand in fact went to Bordeaux and met with the U.S. consul, William Lee, even though Baudin's memoirs suggest he went straight back to Rochefort after visiting *Bayadère*. A detour to Bordeaux appears unlikely, as Lallemand was dispatched on July 11, arrived at Verdon the morning of July 12, met all day with Baudin, and then traveled back to Île d'Aix near Rochefort by night, arriving early on July 13. A detour to Bordeaux would have taken longer.

Napoleon's older brother Joseph, the king of Spain, himself en route to Bordeaux to flee France, joined Napoleon on the Île d'Aix. Joseph, who bore a strong resemblance to Napoleon, gallantly offered to disguise himself as Napoleon and remain on the island while his brother escaped to the United States. Napoleon did not wish to endanger his brother and declined the offer, all the while urging Joseph to hasten to Bordeaux and escape before the royalists exerted control.

A young American, James Carret from New York State, who spoke French and was traveling as part of the king of Spain's entourage, quickly ingratiated himself with Napoleon, who peppered him for information about America. As related in Carret's "Recollections of 1815,"

> That day the Emperor kept me a long time, walking about with his hands behind him, and I following. When he turned at the end of the room, my arms sometimes touched his, and he often stopped, looking in my face, asking me questions, and then resumed his walk. His tone was neither abrupt nor rough, and I soon felt quite at ease with him. The conversation turned entirely on the United States. The Emperor inquired into the details of the powers of the governors of the different States, both civil and military; about the army, the militia, the distances between the large towns, the state of the roads, the breeds of horses, the population of New York and of Philadelphia. As I was speaking warmly of New York—"I should prefer Baltimore," said he; and I supposed that his brother Jerome had commended it to him, having resided in that town, and married an American lady there, in 1805. I ventured to speak to the Emperor, also, of M. LeRayde Chaumont's

lands in the State of New York, my father and brothers having resided there for ten years. The Emperor rejected that overture, saying, "No, no; that is too near the English, and I want to travel some time before establishing myself"; and then he began again his questions on the roads and the horses, and seemed in great haste to set off.[47]

At the same time, Maitland rode at anchor offshore, watching. "On the 13th of July ... [w]e could plainly perceive, that the frigates, from whom we were distant about three miles, were perfectly ready to put to sea, should an opportunity offer; having their sterns covered with vegetable[s], their top-gallant yards across, studding sail gear rove, and numerous boats passing between them and the island the whole day:—all indications, well known to professional men, of preparing for sea."[48]

Napoleon considered slipping out hidden in the Danish merchant-man, which had been specially fitted with a secret compartment to hold him, and made a few tentative efforts to put the plan into motion. However, the plan did not advance far because Napoleon did not want to leave his aides and retainers behind because if he were captured, he would be held prisoner and because something about the pathetic furtiveness of the plan offended him.

Friday, July 14: Napoleon called a meeting of his advisers to decide what he should do. Lallemand, back on Île d'Aix and almost certainly aware of the departure of *Bayadère* and the American ships from the Gironde Estuary on the evening of July 11, reported favorably on the exit strategy involving them and argued for Napoleon to flee to the United States. Napoleon's first valet recalled the discussion:

Before reaching a final decision, the Emperor wished to have the advice of the people around him: he gathered them together, and submitted to their deliberation whether he should surrender to the British; several opinions were given. One of the witnesses told me that Count de Las Cases, the Duke of Rovigo (Savary), and Count Bertrand ... thought His Majesty would be greeted in England with all the respect due adversity. The others, Generals

Lallemand, Montholon, and Gourgaud, did not share that opinion: less confident of British hospitality, they advised against it and begged His Majesty not to come to such a decision. General Lallemand . . . said that there were in the Bordeaux River several vessels . . . that had offered their services, and stated they would escape the British cruisers: all vied for the honor of saving the Emperor and taking him to America. . . . [T]he Emperor could easily reach them by land; it only required tricking the surveillance around us by pretending to be ill. . . . This plan was disputed, the opposition won out, and the Emperor returned to his room, saying to the grand marshal who accompanied him: "Bertrand, it is not without danger to place oneself in the hands of one's enemies, but it is better to risk trusting their honor than to fall into their hands as a rightful prisoner."[49]

Another eyewitness, the American Carret accompanying Napoleon's brother Joseph, both of whom who remained with Napoleon at Île d'Aix, recalled that Lallemand reported that several towns through which they would have to pass to reach Royan and the waiting American ships had fallen into royalist hands and that Napoleon would therefore have to make his escape in disguise. The emperor felt that this, like the surreptitious escape aboard the Danish merchantman, was beneath his dignity. That value judgment may well have been the deciding factor in his not acting on the American option.[50]

Although Napoleon continued to contemplate living the life of a "private gentleman" in America and never returning to France, he came increasingly to focus on England as an alternative if he could not reach America. In what was surely an exercise in self-delusion, Napoleon imagined himself renouncing his political life and living on a country estate ten or twelve leagues out of London. That day he even penned and dispatched a short but remarkable letter to the prince regent, whom he did not know but whose "noble character" he esteemed: "I come, like Themistocles, to throw myself upon the hospitality of the English people. I put myself under the protection of their laws; which I claim from your Royal

Highness, as the most powerful, the most constant, and the most generous of my enemies." Napoleon was right: he did not know the prince.

Napoleon then sent Lallemand and Las Cases, again under a flag of truce, to Captain Maitland aboard *Bellerophon* to ascertain whether he would accept him aboard his ship for a voyage to England. Maitland politely assured them he would.

The same day a warrant for Napoleon's arrest issued by King Louis XVIII was delivered to General Becker, who immediately conveyed it to Napoleon and, in a noteworthy gesture, undertook to delay its implementation for a few hours to allow Napoleon to escape. Bonaparte embarked in the French war brig *L'Épervier* to approach *Bellerophon*.

Saturday, July 15: At 5:00 a.m., Napoleon and a handful of aides boarded *Bellerophon*, where they were received by Captain Maitland as guests, not prisoners, and were afforded every courtesy. On the ensuing voyage to Torbay, Napoleon generally had the run of the ship and engaged daily with its officers and men in a friendly, intellectually curious way. He became popular with both the officers and the crew and did not in the least suspect the fate that was awaiting him.

Napoleon remained aboard *Bellerophon* once it reached Torbay. Local officials called on him, and crowds of small boats with curious onlookers thronged the ship while it lay at anchor awaiting instructions on the next steps. So much for "profound secrecy." Those orders eventually came from London: Napoleon was to be treated as a prisoner of war, and he was to be immediately transferred to HMS *Northumberland* to be conveyed into exile on St. Helena. Shocked, his newfound friends among the officers of *Bellerophon* urged him to resist the order. Napoleon protested mightily but in vain.

Napoleon had been betrayed not only by Fouché but also one final time by Perfidious Albion. He died six years later, the victim of a fogbound existence at Longwood House on St. Helena, the assiduous attentions of Sir Hudson Lowe, and either stomach cancer or arsenic, depending on one's affinity for conspiracy theories.[51]

Why did *Bayadère* and the American privateers depart on July 11 before Napoleon could make a decision on his escape? Where did they go? Were they in fact no longer an option after July 11, or were they lingering offshore awaiting the emperor's pleasure? Perhaps we shall never know, but at least three documents suggest they were in play right up until Napoleon boarded *Bellerophon* on July 15.

First, in a letter to the U.S. consul at Bordeaux, William Lee, written on July 16, 1815, from *Bayadère* off Blaye, Captain Baudin advised,

> Sir,
> All our efforts to save Napoleon from the humiliation of falling into the hands of the English are now to no purpose; for he has on the 15th instant, delivered up himself, with the whole of his attendants and baggage, to the English squadron off Rochefort."

On the outside of the letter, which still exists, written in English and in Baudin's distinctive backward-sloping handwriting but with one corner and some text missing, Lee wrote a note in his own hand: "Letter from Capt [Baudin?] of the French navy for Bordeaux to [Rochefort?] save Napoleon—see the plan agreed on between Count Clausel, the Genl & Com: in chief & myself—we were one hour too late."[52]

The "plan agreed on" appears to be lost. It is not among the Lee papers, nor is it mentioned in an apologia written in the following year by Clausel.[53] Nonetheless, it is possible to piece together the outlines of the plan based on Baudin's writings and several other sources.

Second, and importantly, Lallemand kept a diary. In it he stated in relevant part, "Above all, the preparations at the mouth of the Gironde showed a chance of success." In describing the debate and his actions leading up to the July 14 conference, Lallemand went on to write,

> Struck by the truths demonstrated to me by the sailors with whom I had undertaken the means of ensuring the departure of the Emperor, I alone insisted, but I insisted strongly, on the project to make the Emperor depart from the mouth of the Gironde, and on the necessity of occupying ourselves with the greatest

activity [with it]. They [the other aides] answered me only with objections to the execution and doubts as to the certainty of the means. All I could say was that at least we should not neglect a plan that could save the Emperor. All I could do was to go myself to make sure of the truth on the spot. I went there by Royan, and it was easy for me to convince myself of the solidity of the plan. I made sure it was easy to get from the designated point. The wisest arrangements had been made; *everything was ready for several days. The ships destined for the Emperor came out from there,* and several made their way without having been visited by the enemy, although they had scarcely tried to avoid it. [emphasis added] [54]

Third, there appears to have been at least some level of contemporary knowledge in Baltimore of the role played by *Pike* in this affair. On October 20, 1817, the French-language newspaper *L'Abeille Américaine* (The American Bee), published in Philadelphia, ran a satirical letter to the editor from a certain "A.B." in Baltimore on a hypothetical escape by Napoleon. It stated in relevant part, "On the Brig P . . . there was a brave superior artillery officer of the former [French] Army of Italy who was of distinguished and recognized merit" [coming to the United States].[55]

What if Napoleon had fled on one of the American ships? As reported in the New York *Evening Post* on August 18, 1815, the brig *Pike*, commanded by Captain Samuel [*sic*] Vickers, left the River Garonne on July 11.[56] As reported in *Niles' Weekly Register* on August 19, 1815, she arrived at Baltimore:

> The brig Pike has arrived at Baltimore from Bordeaux, but as she left that place with the Ludlow arrived a few days since at Boston we have little news of her. She was robbed of her latest Bordeaux paper by a British frigate, from which she was boarded to search for Bonaparte.[57]

What had happened to *Pike* and *Ludlow* after they got under way was in fact more dramatic. By this point, the British had gotten wind of a plot for Napoleon to escape on an American vessel (some historians have long suspected that Napoleon's entourage was penetrated by spies given the alacrity with which the Royal Navy continually learned of his evolving plans). The British patrol was now augmented to four frigates and five sloops of war that were intent on stopping and searching every American ship they could find. Captain Vickers of *Pike* provided the following report on his arrival in Baltimore:

> On getting out of the river, discovered 4 British frigates and three sloops of war cruising close in with the Cordovan light house— the commodore's ship hove out a signal for one of the frigates and a sloop of war to chase the Pike to the westward, which they had done after firing 18 or 20 shots at the Pike; she hove too, the frigate coming up—she proved to be the British frigate Hebros; sent her boat on board with 2 officers, 8 marines with the boat's crews armed, to search for Napoleon. On the boarding officer getting on board of the Pike he immediately enquired of the captain where was Napoleon Bonaparte, and said that he had orders to search the brig close for him, as it was expected that he would endeavour to make his escape in some American vessel for the United States. During this time the captain of the Hebros hailed the Pike, and ordered the captain to get his boats out immediately; otherwise he would fire into him, and sink him; and a short time after, hailed the boarding officer and ordered him to get the latest Bordeaux Newspaper that was on board of the brig and send it on board of the frigate, and he would pay him for it. The officer immediately applied to the captain of the Pike for a paper of the latest date, when the captain of the Pike informed him he would with pleasure send the paper to the captain of the frigate, and lay by him until he had perused it, praying it might be returned, as it was the only one on board of the brig that contained the news of Paris having capitulated with the allied armies on the 4th July, and the paper which contained the articles of capitulation, and that he would wish to carry it to the United States. Accordingly the officer took the paper and promised to return it, but in a short time after, being on board of the frigate, the captain of the frigate

hailed the brig and informed the captain that he was at liberty to make sail, keeping the paper. Then the ship Belle and the brig Ludlow, laying too under his lee, which he was about to board and no doubt to commit the same robbery, or a robbery of a similar nature, on board of each vessel [*sic*].[58]

The British not finding Napoleon aboard, *Pike* continued on her way, only to be chased on July 20 by "three large ships of war" that Vickers thought to be "Algerine corsairs." However, the "superior sailing of the *Pike* enabled her to get away."[59]

The British also boarded and searched *Ludlow*. A newspaper article published after her arrival in Boston reported,

Soon after sailing, Capt. Mudge was boarded from an English frigate, and demand made if Bonaparte was on board? Strict search was accordingly made over every part of the vessel;—but not finding him, the boarding officers proceeded to examine the phizes [faces] of every person on board, to see if there was not a Bonaparte among them. They stated that they believed he intended to make his escape in some American vessel, for this country; and that they would search every one they might fall in with, to find the ex-Emperor.[60]

It is evident that if Napoleon had sought his escape on one of the American ships, his chances might have been 50-50 or better. If Captain Baudin's *Bayadère* and *Infatigable* had run interference as planned, *Pike* likely would not have been caught and boarded, and the chances of success would have been even better. Moreover, when *Pike* was stopped and boarded it is likely that she acquiesced in such action because she was not carrying Napoleon. If she had been carrying him, she would have fled like the wind and outrun any British frigate.

CHAPTER 3

The Enabler

SOME OF THE ESCAPES FROM FRANCE TO AMERICA DID NOT HAPPEN spontaneously. They were aided and abetted by a crucial American on the ground in France: the U.S. consul at Bordeaux, William Lee.

Lee was a singular character. No relation to the Lees of Virginia, he was born in 1772 in Halifax, Nova Scotia, to a Yankee family with its origins on Cape Cod. His father had emigrated to Canada to work at the British Royal Navy yard at Halifax at the end of the Seven Years' War. Lee was thus a dual national at birth. However, Lee was educated at Philips Academy Andover, which he entered in 1785 at age 12, and claimed his American identity as a young man when he went to work as a commission merchant affiliated with the firm of Lyman & Williams in Boston. At age 22 he married Susan Palfrey, who was the daughter of William Palfrey, a Boston merchant who served as a patriot paymaster during the Revolution. Lee made his first voyage to France in 1796 at age 24. He stayed there two years, during which time he also visited England and the Netherlands.

At first, France scandalized his New England sensibilities. His initial observations in the diary he kept on his trip were not flattering:

> Last evening I went to the theatre. The house was crowded. There were a vast number of women of the loose sort. I am told no others frequent this place. It is a sink of debauchery. You pay but fourpence sterling for the best seat in the house. The lowness of the price permits all classes. There is no distinction of persons. You must sit down with a smutty rascal, who stinks of garlic

enough to knock a horse down, and who, if you do not look sharp, will pick your pockets. I begin to dislike this liberty and equality. I think myself superior to a bawd or a pickpocket.[1]

There also was a prudishness to his observations. Two days later he wrote,

Last evening I went to the Comedy. . . . The dress of the actresses I do not like. Their arms are generally uncovered and one of their breasts. There were a number of elegant dancers, but their figures disgusted me. . . . A silk net covered part of their arms, their breasts and the lower part of their bodies, of a flesh color so that at a distance I thought they were half naked; for this cobweb covering was drawn over them so tight that you could discover every muscle. They performed admirably, and displayed their hips at every move. Such indecent representations can never lead the mind to virtue. All the exhibitions I have been at appeared to me to be calculated only to inspire libidinous thoughts.[2]

But "indecent" or "libidinous" though he found it, he developed a habit for the theatre. More important, Lee began to establish critical relationships that were later to play pivotal roles in his life and activities. For example, he met and dined with U.S. Minister to France (and later Secretary of State and President) James Monroe as early as March 6, 1796, when his diary noted that he "[d]ined with the American minister, Mr. Monroe."[3] Eight months later President George Washington fired Monroe because of his excessively pro-French sentiments and activities.

Lee also made political observations that, though accurate, were largely critical of France and the Directory government in particular. "The present government," he wrote, "is as despotic as that of Algiers. It is supported by the sword entirely."[4] A visit to the lower body of the legislature, the Council of Five Hundred, proved (probably for good reason) disillusioning:

There is neither decency nor deliberation in their debates, and their language resembles flashes of lightning from a troubled sky. . . . There are here some of the most ill-looking dogs I ever saw:

men with short hair, beards which a razor has not touched for some weeks, clothes ragged and dirty and shirt collars open.[5]

Nonetheless, the charms of France slowly began to work their wiles on the young American and were brought home to him when he continued on an extensive trip to England and the Netherlands, both of which he compared unfavorably to France. One can almost see him sizing up and contrasting at every stop as he took in new sights:

"Seen nothing as yet in England equal to the delightful views in France. And as to climate, France is certainly preferable. If the people of France were honest, good fellows, what a charming good country it would be to live in! . . ." or "Disappointed in both [the theatres], as well as in Drury Lane Theatre, which is not so handsome as the Opera or Republique at Paris. . . . I never was in an American or English theatre in my life, when before the evening was half gone, I did not wish myself out. But in Paris one may sit forever."

Even the ecclesiastical architecture did not measure up: "St. Paul's is unquestionably one of the most magnificent buildings in Europe for loftiness, grandeur, beauty, design and harmony of parts; but certainly falls far short of the Pantheon at Paris in simplicity and elegance."

Finally this: "London, at this season of the year [February], is one of the worst places in the world to live in. You are choked with coal dust and enveloped with smoke, and do not see the sun once a week; and in some parts of the city people use candles [for a] great part of the day. The flat stones are so greasy that it is with difficulty you can walk, and the insolence of the lower class of people and the inconvenience of the Scotch mist are insupportable."[6]

Next he went to Brussels: "There are many parish churches, besides chapels, monasteries and convents. The people are Catholic, full of religion and superstition. The streets of the city are not very clean, and among other things are infested with priests. . . . You meet with saints and crucifixes in every street, and Virgins and little Jesuses at every corner."[7]

Although Lee admired the wealth and industry of the Netherlands, he found fault there too. On visiting the Jewish synagogue at Amsterdam, Lee recorded his reaction thus: "Strolled into the Jews' Synagogue. Such a collection of dirty, ill-looking thieves I never before beheld. Their ceremony was quite new and ludicrous." Nor did the ethnic Dutch fare much better: "That the species thrive better in England than in Holland, I believe, is true; though the Dutch certainly make the prettiest children, but the speaking of their horrible language distorts their features and renders them hideous before they grow up."[8]

Thus armed with a jaundiced and limited knowledge of Europe, Lee returned to America in 1798 and lobbied to be appointed U.S. consul at Bordeaux. Largely through the political influence of James Monroe, Elbridge Gerry (a Massachusetts politician subsequently famous for "Gerrymandering"), and several others, he received an appointment from President Thomas Jefferson on June 3, 1801 as "commercial agent" for the United States at Bordeaux.[9] Lee's predecessor, Isaac Cox Barnet, bitterly opposed his appointment and impugned his patriotism and lack of higher education in a letter to Secretary of State James Madison. However, his protestations fell on deaf ears, and Lee was to occupy his position as the chief American representative in the bustling port of Bordeaux for 15 years. Aside from his official duties, which paid only a modest stipend that was never enough for Lee to support his growing family, he occupied himself with an export–import business known as Perrot & Lee (such mixing of public and private business was common then).

As an American consul, Lee was authorized to wear a U.S. Navy uniform on state occasions. The only known portrait of Lee (figure 3.1), painted in 1812, shows Lee in a fancy modified naval uniform that he supposedly designed himself and that appears to have been influenced by the fashions of the Napoleonic court. His visage evidences a certain reserve and the doubting, penetrating eyes of a keen observer—good qualities for a diplomat then and now.

Most of his correspondence during his early years at Bordeaux was, as would be normal, with Secretary of State James Madison, and much of it dealt with shipping issues and frauds perpetrated by the French on Americans. American ships entering and clearing ports like Bordeaux

Figure 3.1. U.S. Consul in Bordeaux William Lee. MARY LEE MANN, ED., *A YANKEE JEFFERSONIAN: SELECTIONS FROM THE DIARY AND LETTERS OF WILLIAM LEE OF MASSACHUSETTS.* CAMBRIDGE, MA: HARVARD UNIVERSITY PRESS, 1958.

were required by U.S. law to present their papers to the U.S. consul,[10] who in turn had a detailed knowledge of the ships entering and leaving Bordeaux and their cargoes. Many of his official duties involved assisting destitute American sailors and generally representing the interests of the U.S. merchant community resident in Bordeaux. However, there was another dimension to the posting. Lee and Madison knew one another from at least as early as 1801, and it was clear that Lee was performing personal favors for both Jefferson and Madison almost from the start. Jefferson's Memorandum Books show that in 1803 Lee assisted Jefferson in the purchase of 1,050 francs worth of 150 bottles of Rausan Margaux 1798 and 150 bottles of Château Filhot Sauterne 1798.[11] Similarly, on April 20, 1804, Lee wrote to Madison concerning a shipment of wine he had procured for the secretary of state. In that letter, he also mentioned looming financial difficulties encountered by his mercantile firm Perrot & Lee that resulted in a default on its debts: "If the friends of those persons who may wish my place should exaggerate my misfortunes and attack my official character I trust you will do me the honour to support me near the President by recommending if necessary an enquiry into my official conduct."The same letter refers to a visit by James Monroe, with whom he met at Bordeaux.[12] In any event, Lee worked through his bankrupt firm's financial difficulties and dissolved the firm in 1805.[13]

In 1806, while Lee remained at his post in Bordeaux, Lee's wife took their children to Paris and enrolled their two daughters in a fashionable school maintained by Madame Campan in St. Germain. Fellow students included Napoleon's sister Caroline and the empress Josephine's daughter Hortense de Beauharnais. Mrs. Lee and, by implication, her husband began to mix in the top echelons of Napoleonic society. In 1808 the empress Josephine visited Bordeaux, where she received both Lee and his wife: "Mrs. Lee and myself were introduced to the Empress. . . . She received us with great kindness, made Mrs. Lee sit down by her, and conversed with her in the most familiar manner for half an hour."[14] The Lees were to remain in favor with the empress Josephine during the ensuing years, with, for example, Lee noting in his Memorandum Book that they dined with the empress at Malmaison on June 5, 1812, and again two weeks later on June 24, 1812 (Napoleon divorced Josephine in 1810, but she retained the title of empress; she died in 1814).

Lee's presence in the country gradually turned him into a self-confessed Francophile, although he continued to make astute observations in his correspondence ("These Frenchmen are the strangest compounds in nature. They mix business and pleasure and jumble everything together."). He also became an admirer of Napoleon, whom he termed "this wonderful man"[15] but about whom he also expressed exasperation at times ("No dependence can be placed on the Emperor. He acts entirely from the impulse of the moment, and without reflection.").[16] Still, Lee's relationship with the government was sufficiently close that he was asked to prepare memoranda on U.S.–French relations by the minister of the interior and the vice high constable of France—a rather unusual assignment for an American diplomat and seemingly a departure from protocol that would normally have had their own staff prepare such reports.

On July 8, 1810, Lee sailed for the United States, where he spent slightly over one year, mainly in New York and Washington. When in Washington he stayed with Joel Barlow at his estate "Kalorama" (site of the present-day Embassy Row). Barlow was a multifaceted individual—a poet, publicist, Revolutionary War chaplain, lawyer, dual French and American citizen, French National Assembly deputy, regicide, and Jefferson intimate. During this time, Lee sought to ingratiate himself with both Barlow and the new Madison administration. He succeeded. Building on his direct relationship with Madison when the latter was secretary of state, Lee was able to note on October 20, 1810,

> I am a constant visitor and favorite at the President's. The Government have a wish that I would take the general Consulate at Paris, but I have declined it, on the expectation that the revocation of the decrees will do something for me at Bordeaux [meaning his shipping interests]. I can have any appointment here that I please, suited to my talents; but the salaries are all low, and I had rather remain in France a few years longer on account of the education of our children.[17]

Lee also at this time acted as a purchasing agent for Dolley Madison, the president's wife. In a letter dated December 12, 1810, to his wife, Susan, who remained at Bordeaux, he instructed her to purchase certain unspecified goods spelled out in a memorandum for various people but noted that Mrs. Madison's "above all must not be neglected."[18] Later, in 1811 while Lee was posted in Paris, Dolley Madison sent a large order: "As you have everything that is beautiful; & we have nothing . . . send me by safe Vessels—Large Headdresses a few flowers, Feathers, gloves & stockings . . . or any other pretty thing, suitable to an Economist & draw on my Husband for the Amt." Lee studied French fashion magazines and then set off to "waddle round Paris" assembling her wardrobe. Madison must have balked at the $2,000 cost, a staggering sum at that time and about 8 percent of the president's annual salary.[19] This purchasing agency relationship for President and Mrs. Madison lasted throughout his tenure in France, as evidenced by a letter from Lee to President Madison dated September 6, 1815, in which he discusses a shipment of "wine, cordials &c" to Madison and "trifles I have occasionally sent to Mrs. Madison."[20] Even after Lee left Bordeaux for good, he was still writing Madison in

1818 trying to collect on old debts for "wine, sweet oil, vinegar and sundries" he had purchased for the then president in 1815.[21]

With the appointment of Joel Barlow as American minister to France in February 1811 (see appendix A for a summary chart of the principal U.S. officials responsible for France during this period), Lee's star was ascendant. The new minister asked him to be secretary of the American legation in Paris, although he would simultaneously keep the consulship at Bordeaux. That Lee thought this was an illegal and unconstitutional maneuver is revealed in his letter of March 6, 1811, announcing the appointment to his wife: "You [know] my angel friend, that according to the constitution of the United States a man cannot hold two offices; so keep to yourself my being Secretary of Legation. I shall do the business and have the emoluments without the character publicly." In the very next sentence of his letter Lee reminds his wife that "Mrs. Madison wishes her things."[22] Thus, no matter how one looks at the facts, it is inescapable that with the undoubted collusion of the Madison administration, a U.S. official who had sworn an oath of office to uphold and defend the Constitution willingly and knowingly thought he was violating the Constitution, and he sought to cover it up. What is more, he did it while running personal favors and errands for the president and his wife.

Lee's plotting only thickened before he left the United States to take up his new positions. Observing in March 1811 while in Washington that he was "much abused" in the papers, he also noted that James Monroe, whom he had known since 1796, was to be secretary of state and probably the next president "so that my standing will be kept up."

Lee at this time was surrounded by swirling controversy. The recently returned former American minister to France, General John Armstrong Jr., whose relationship with Lee had soured when both were at post, attacked Lee publicly and vice versa, resulting in Armstrong obtaining a warrant for Lee's arrest and suing him for defamation and seeking $100,000 in damages.[23] Lee literally fled the United States aboard USS *Constitution* for France one step ahead of the sheriff.[24] Nonetheless, one of his last dispatches from America to his wife positively gloated,

I receive from the President and Mrs. Madison daily marks of kindness. In short no one is more intimate there. They are the most amiable people on earth. It would amuse you to see how I get roasted in the papers. One party says I brought over my pockets full of licenses. Another says I have exclusive privileges to trade to France. Then again I have been treated with greater attention in France than even our minister, because I have been so useful to the Emperor &c. &c. &c.[25]

Lee accompanied Barlow to Paris, while Mrs. Lee remained at Bordeaux. On November 17, 1811, Barlow formally presented his credentials to the emperor, accompanied by Lee at least part of the way. Lee, whose role seemed like that of Polonius to "swell a scene or two," was at once impressed and amused by the pomposity of it all:

The ceremony of this presentation is very stiff. I conducted Mr. Barlow in my full dress to the *Salon des Ambassadeurs* [at St. Cloud], where he was visited by, and I was presented to Comte Segur and the Duke of Bassano, who left the Minister to learn the Emperor's pleasure, when two under *Maitres des Ceremonies* in their garbs and with their black velvet, ivory headed canes, threw open the doors and received from my hands the Minister. They conducted him to the head of the stairs, where he was received by the *Grand Maitre des Ceremonies*, who conducted him to the door of the Emperor's cabinet, where he was received by Prince Cambaceres, who presented him. The Minister made one bow on entering, another halfway of the room, and a third when he approached his Majesty. At this moment he addressed him in a very few words, much to the purpose, and the Emperor answered in a very flattering way, by saying he was gratified in receiving as Minister Plenipotentiary of the United States a character so highly distinguished, and whose opinions and writings were so friendly to France.[26]

Lee and Barlow spent subsequent days calling on Madame Mère (Napoleon's mother) and the empress Josephine. On December 2, Lee himself was formally presented to the emperor, and the two had a rather silly and meaningless exchange of pleasantries over the fancy consular uniform Lee was wearing. Lee lamented the fact that much of his and Barlow's days were consumed by pomp and circumstance and that they had to work by night, often getting little sleep. However, working at Barlow's side, Lee became directly involved in helping manage bilateral political issues and was privy to all confidential correspondence between the minister and the secretary of state. But Lee also opened his own direct channel to President Madison, reporting on political matters as early as January 1, 1812; whether Barlow knew of this back channel of his subordinate to the chief executive is unclear. It was and is a highly irregular diplomatic practice.[27]

Barlow died in Poland on December 26, 1812, while returning from an abortive trip to meet with Napoleon on his retreat from Russia. By January 1813 Lee was busy ingratiating himself with former (and future) foreign minister Charles Talleyrand by selling him Barlow's supply of Madeira wine.[28] In the meantime, David Bailie Warden, an Irish émigré in the U.S. diplomatic service and the U.S. consul at Paris, declared himself consul general and chargé d'affaires ad interim of the legation. Lee wanted the positions for himself, and he protested. Although eventually supported in his actions by Barlow's successor as minister, Lee nonetheless returned in March 1813 full-time to his consulship at Bordeaux. Still, he grumbled to Monroe in August of that year, "Every public man has his enemies, I know I have more than my share from the ardour of my character and the firmness with which I support my own rights and the warmth with which I espouse the cause of my friends."[29]

By March 1814, with Napoleon's power crumbling and allied Russian, Prussian, and Austrian armies advancing on Paris, the British seized Bordeaux. At the time, the United States was at war with the United Kingdom, and in his letters Lee referred to the invading British repeatedly as "the enemy." Lee perceived himself to be hated by the British because of his pro-French and pro-Bonapartist sympathies. But his troubles were not confined to the political. His business interests again failed and drew critical attention. On November 1, 1814, Barlow's successor as minister, William Harris Crawford, wrote to President Madison, "Mr. Lee's bankrupt circumstances and incorrect conduct in money transactions, I am informed, are spoken of all over Europe, without reserve. Mr. [Albert] Gallatin [until earlier that year secretary of the treasury] informed me, that he heard much of them wherever he had been."[30]

Lee exacerbated his situation in December 1814 by publishing in Bordeaux a 346-page screed in French titled *Les États Unis et L'Angleterre* (The United States and England), which blamed England for every aspect of the War of 1812.[31] He sent an unsolicited copy of the published book to Thomas Jefferson on December 20, 1814, under cover of a particularly obsequious letter (some eight months later Jefferson acknowledged its receipt in a letter to Lee). The book enjoyed considerable play[32] but did not sit well with the British, who, with their continental allies, had just ousted Napoleon and sent him into exile on Elba. Its publication was also poorly timed, as the United States and Britain signed the Treaty of Ghent on December 24, 1814, ending their war. Lee was later to write in a letter to Jefferson that the book was "the great cause of my abandoning a situation [meaning his consulship at Bordeaux] which was in every point of view agreeable to me."[33]

In short, Lee's financial affairs and diplomatic career began to crumble simultaneously and with mutually reinforcing effect. So apparently did his judgment. When Napoleon escaped from Elba and landed in southern France, Lee reported, without skepticism or qualification, to Secretary of State Monroe, "The English, who are detested on the continent, are suspected of being at the bottom of this affair, with a view to create a civil war in France."[34]

With the landing of Napoleon in southern France on March 1, 1815, and the Hundred Days culminating in the Battle of Waterloo and its aftermath, the historical record surrounding both Lee and the American legation in Paris grows strangely silent. The Lee-Palfrey Families Papers at the Library of Congress contain no correspondence from this period (with one exception: a letter that Lee wrote to try to induce Napoleon's minister of agriculture, commerce, and industry, Jean-Antoine Count Chaptal, to emigrate to America).[35] Lee's Memorandum Book has no entries from May 13, 1813, to February 4, 1816. Similarly, the papers of William Harris Crawford, the American minister in Paris who succeeded Barlow, also in the Library of Congress, are missing from May 12, 1815, to February 19, 1817. The set of Communications with the French Government in the Crawford collection stops at March 14, 1815, just after Napoleon's landing. This is perhaps not surprising, as Crawford left his post as American minister in Paris in April 1815, and it was not filled by Albert Gallatin until July 1816. During the interim, Henry Jackson, the secretary of the U.S. legation, acted as chargé d'affaires.[36] Notwithstanding Crawford's departure, these are rather strange hiatuses in the records for a period that shook the world. However, there are dispatches from Jackson, as chargé, to Secretary of State Monroe during this period in the National Archives. The corresponding instructions from Monroe to Jackson, if they ever existed, are missing.

With the abdication of Napoleon after Waterloo and the restoration of the Bourbons, Lee found himself increasingly the target of pro-British and royalist factions in Bordeaux. Among other things, a mob appeared at his residence and demanded that he remove the emblem of the American eagle over his door. He properly refused. Lee also became involved in an imbroglio over a demand that he fly the white royalist flag at the consulate, which he refused to do. He complained about it to the prefect of the Bordeaux region, and he became something of a lightning rod for controversy. The correspondence reached Jackson in Paris, who forwarded it to Monroe. Lee began to fear for his own and his family's safety. On February 16, 1816, he wrote to President Madison that "I feel my position so irksome that I have a great desire to return home." Two days later, he wrote Secretary of State Monroe requesting a "leave of absence for six months." He cited as his reasons "[h]aving a considerable amount to adjust with the UStates [United States] and some other concerns of moment which call for my attention." He went on to suggest Daniel Strobel, the underemployed U.S. consul at Nantes, "to fill my place during that time."[37]

What were these vague "concerns" and matters requiring adjustment? Lee admitted in correspondence at the time that he had given up trying to make a living as a merchant in Bordeaux because of his recurring financial difficulties, and he did not think he could make ends meet solely on his consular salary. He became increasingly interested in recruiting skilled manufacturers, such as silk weavers, for emigration to the United States. The U.S. side of that new line of business may have tempted him to take the leave of absence. However, he had not resigned his consular position, and by all appearances he intended to return to it. There was perhaps more to it. On September 28, 1815, former speaker of the U.S. House of Representatives (and youngest signer of the Declaration of Independence) Jonathan Dayton of Elizabeth, New Jersey, had written ominously to Lee,

> I think it proper to apprise you that attempts are intended to be made when Congress will be in session in the approaching winter to have you removed from the Consular office at Bordeaux in order to open the way for the appointment of another. This other person is Mr. Samuel Ogden, who contemplates a removal thither this autumn with his family. If therefore it be your interest and your wish to continue in the Consulate at that place it is proper that you immediately do apprise me that I may in season take the necessary measures and exert the necessary influence to prevent your being supplanted.[38]

Thus, as with his 1810–1811 leave of absence spent in Washington lobbying for a promotion, Lee may also have deemed it a propitious time to press the flesh once again in the capital to save his position.

On June 13, 1816, Lee sailed with his family for America aboard *Liguria* under Captain Norton, stopping in New York and Philadelphia. He brought with him 60 French cloth weavers, some 15 of whom traveled at his personal expense.[39] Meanwhile, Strobel, it turned out, was a striver. Four days after seeing Lee off at the docks, he wrote Secretary of State Monroe a long, fawning letter reassuring him that everything would be just right under his tenure and making no secret of his desire to be made consul permanently. He soon got his wish and held the position for 14 years.

How did this happen? Lee may have fallen victim to a game of diplomatic tit for tat. Lee arrived in New York on August 2. In the interim, at a July 4 celebration in Baltimore, Postmaster James Stuart Skinner had proposed a toast to "the exiled generals of France and the glory of their native land—they should not be dishonored by the denunciations of an imbecile tyrant!," and he referred to Marshal Grouchy as a "Marshal of France," a title not bestowed by the king. The newly arrived royalist French ambassador Jean-Guillaume Baron Hyde de Neuville was understandably upset and demanded that Secretary of State Monroe have Skinner removed from office. The demand touched a raw nerve on the American side and brought back memories of French interference in U.S. domestic affairs by Hyde de Neuville's decidedly unroyalist predecessor, Edmond-Charles "Citizen" Genêt. In fact, the matter escalated to the French foreign minister, festered throughout the autumn to the point that it caused a crisis in Franco–American relations, and was the subject of instructions on September 10, 1816, from Secretary of State Monroe to the new American minister in Paris, Albert Gallatin, and of further discussions between Monroe and Hyde de Neuville and additional instructions to Gallatin as late as November 1816.[40]

In any event, Monroe declined Hyde de Neuville's request to remove Skinner on the grounds that he was not responsible for the private opinions of government employees and that America was a country of free speech. In retaliation, the French government recalled its consul in Baltimore. In order to resolve the spat, the administration accepted the "resignation" of the pro-Bonaparte William Lee, whom Hyde de Neuville had accused of having earlier mentioned "patriotic exiles" in a certificate he issued in Bordeaux.[41]

On September 9 (the very day before Monroe issued his instructions to Gallatin), Lee wrote to President Madison from Philadelphia offering his "resignation," which the president immediately accepted. Proper protocol would have had the letter directed to the secretary of state, but Lee was using his back channel again. Whether Lee was fired or resigned is debatable. The fact is that he had already left his post and by then may have wanted out permanently, so his "dismissal" was a relatively painless way for the administration to offer up a concession to soothe ruffled French feathers.

The September 9 letter that Lee wrote to President Madison provides a little further color. After apologizing for not calling personally on the president because he had been so busy with the group of French manufacturers he had brought with him from France, Lee addressed his consulship, which was surrounded in controversy to its very end:

> Having taken the liberty some time before my departure from Bordeaux to write you on the subject of that consulate ... [illegible] time I wrote of forming a connection with Mr. Strobel under a conviction that through my influence in the UStates I should have it in my power to throw considerable immigrants into his hands, the profits of which, with his honorable principles & knowledge of business, would have been acceptable to both. But I had no sooner named him to take my place, until your pleasure should be known, than a report was circulated, that I had engaged to support him in his application for that office *on condition of my sharing the emoluments thereof* [emphasis in the original]. Though the fees of that office will not in times of peace pay house rent, and at no period since I held it would meet the expenses of a family living as a consul is obliged to live, which of itself is sufficient to show the absurdity of such a report. Still I feel it might produce some unpleasant consequences to me, and for that reason I abandoned all plans of continuing my commercial establishment at Bordeaux, leaving Mr. Strobel to struggle for himself, attaching myself to some manufacturing.... [illegible] Should therefore my letters on this subject have an insight in your mind, I beg leave to state, that in resigning that office as I now do, I have no further interest in the nomination of Mr. Strobel, than what his amiable qualities of numerous family [*sic*] inspires.
>
> I ought Sir to apologize for having from time to time occupied so many of your important moments on my private concerns. When a man turned of forty [*sic*] with a large family, has suffered commercially, and politically, so much as I have, it was with difficulty he can refrain from dwelling on a subject which

touches him so nearly but, as I have already experienced so much indulgence from the President, I hope in this case it will not be withdrawn.[42]

Lee's presence in Philadelphia at this time was hardly coincidental, as he was actively involved with the French community there in plans to support the emigration of skilled French artisans to America. He even wrote Jefferson about them in the hopes of settling some of them near Charlottesville, Virginia. In a lengthy letter to Jefferson dated October 25, 1816, he expounded on his views of the French, stating in relevant part, "Even the Dukes, Counts, and Generals, who were created by Napoleon, are very different men from most of those of the ancient French school. They rose by their merit, not by hereditary right. Having received their education in the walks of private life, we find them here returning with ease to the source from which they came, and to the dignity of useful citizens."

In the same letter, he stated that he hoped to "present my respects to you in person, and at the same time to present to you my friend and intimate Marshal Grouchy. I have taken the liberty to give to the celebrated *ex-legislateur*, M. Penières, a letter of introduction to you. He is one of the best informed men of the age." Lee neglected to tell Jefferson that Penières was also his business partner in the emigration scheme and a regicide with a death penalty hanging over his head.[43]

Lee's French emigration and resettlement plans came to naught. On November 17, 1816, after initially turning it down, Lee accepted an appointment from President Madison as an accountant at the War Department in Washington. Shortly thereafter, on March 16, 1817, the formerly bankrupt Lee, who had recently been accused of "incorrect conduct in monetary transactions," was appointed second auditor at the Department of the Treasury with responsibility for managing the furniture fund for refurbishing the White House after its burning at the hands of the British.[44] However, Lee's involvement with notable French émigrés did not end with his move to the Department of the Treasury, as we shall see.

Lee's 12 years as a treasury clerk were not happy ones. He constantly complained in correspondence with his family that Congress and the federal government were inhabited by people "from the verge of civilization." Actually, it got worse: "Now in this golgotha of numbskulls, where for six months in the year now is seen but worms of the desk creeping out on the commons, at stated hours, from those hospitals of incurables, the public offices, to their hog, hominy, and hemlock from the still, if one did not cherish such intellectual beings as Law and Cutting, one should have no amusement, and shortly should have as little wit as we have of the savoir faire."[45] Lee was eventually sacked by President Andrew Jackson, a victim of the spoils system. He complained bitterly about the loss of a job he hated.

But his ending was not so unhappy. His daughter Mary married the Russian baron of German extraction Johann Georg Friedrich Franz von Maltitz, who was in the tsar's diplomatic service. Lee initially opposed the marriage because the groom was not wealthy. But he came around when the baron achieved good postings like Berlin, London, and The Hague. Eventually, Maltitz served as the tsar's minister in Washington, D.C. At one time, Lee was pressed for funds, and the baron stepped forward with an offer to help. "This letter with the generous offer of assistance from the Baron made me weep with affection," Lee wrote his daughter.[46]

Finally, following the death of his beloved wife, Susan, Lee married a wealthy widow and moved to Boston. His financial problems were at long last over.

The question arises whether Lee's actions to try to save Napoleon and to assist other high-ranking Bonapartists in their escapes to America were officially authorized by higher authorities in the U.S. government, especially given Lee's channels of communication with both Secretary of State Monroe and President James Madison.

Monroe in particular had connections with France that make the question relevant. Monroe, secretary of state under President James Madison from April 2, 1811, to March 3, 1817, was an ardent Francophile who defended the French Revolution and its republican values. Having served as American minister in Paris from 1794 through 1796, he was intimately familiar with the country. Monroe first met Napoleon on May 1, 1803, when he was in Paris to negotiate the Louisiana Purchase. The context was a formal presentation to the then first consul. As with many of his American interlocutors, Napoleon grilled Monroe with staccato bursts of questions:

> When the Consul came round to me, Mr. Livingston presented me to him, on which the Consul observed that he was glad to see me. . . . "You have been here 15 days?" I told him I had. "You speak French?" I replied "A little." "You had a good voyage?" Yes. "You came in a frigate?" No in a merchant vessel charged for the purpose. Col. Mercer was presented; says he "He is Secretary of legation?" No but my friend. He then made enquiries of Mr. Livingston & his secretary how their families were, and then turned to Mr. Livingston & myself & observed that our affairs should be settled.
>
> We dined with him. After dinner when we retired into the saloon, the first Consul came up to me and asked whether the federal city grew much. I told him it did. "How many inhabitants has it?" It is just commencing, there are two cities near it, one above, the other below, on the great river Potomack, which two cities if counted with the federal city would make a respectable town, in itself it contains only two or three thousand inhabitants. "Well; Mr. Jefferson, how old is he?" About sixty. "Is he married or single?" He is not married. "Then he is a garcon." [meaning he is gay] No he is a widower. "Has he children?" Yes two daughters who are married. "Does he reside always at the federal city?" Generally. "Are the public buildings there commodious, those for the Congress and President especially?" They are. "You the Americans did brilliant things in your war with England, you will do the same again." We shall, I am persuaded, always behave well when it shall be our lot to be in war. "You may probably be in war with them again." I replied I did not know, that that was an important question to decide when there would be an occasion for it.[47]

Monroe again met with Napoleon on June 24, when he took his leave to accept an appointment as American minister to the United Kingdom.

The relationship between the two remained cordial, with Napoleon advising that he viewed President Thomas Jefferson as "a virtuous enlightened man, a friend of liberty and equality."

However, a dispute over Spanish Florida soon strained Napoleon's view of the United States. When in late 1804 Monroe and his wife sought to attend Napoleon's self-coronation in Nôtre Dame Cathedral, their names were initially struck from the invitation list. The Monroes protested, only to wind up shunted off in a gallery, largely out of sight. Monroe never forgot the insult.

By the time Monroe ascended to the office of secretary of state, relations between the United States and France had deteriorated significantly because of French depredations against neutral American shipping (the same was true of course as to Great Britain and for the same reason). Although Monroe had a high regard for France and acknowledged having received "much kindness & attention" from Bonaparte, he was clear-eyed as to the dangers France posed and to his duty to the United States.[48]

It therefore is instructive to view Lee's actions against the backdrop of official U.S. policy toward an ever-changing France as enunciated at the highest levels of the U.S. government. What becomes clear is that official U.S. policy was nuanced and principled, driven largely by the issue of American merchants' claims against seizure of vessels by the French, and was, at least after Waterloo, disappointed in Napoleon.

Both Monroe and Madison were alert to the desirability of a balance of power in Europe and therefore were not unhappy with Napoleon's first abdication. On learning of this event from American minister Crawford, Monroe wrote to Crawford on June 25, 1814 (a year before the Battle of Waterloo), "It is satisfactory to find, in regard to France herself, that the disposition manifested by the provisional government toward the United States indicates no change of an unfavorable nature. Its deportment towards you . . . breathe a spirit of amity, the sincerity of which there is no reason to doubt. It is even probable that our relations with France may be improved by this event."[49]

This reaction changed when Napoleon escaped from Elba and launched the Hundred Days. The view of Secretary of State Monroe to Napoleon's return was one of alarm. He wrote Madison of his concern about "the overweaning [*sic*] ambition & gigantic usurpations of Bonaparte," and he implored Madison to defer planned reductions in the army and call a special session of Congress. Madison judged these measures to be premature.

During the Hundred Days Monroe steered a clear public course of neutrality between Britain and France. For example, in his May 11, 1815, instructions to the newly appointed minister to Great Britain John Quincy Adams, Monroe took care to define U.S. policy: "It is the sincere desire of the United States to remain at peace equally with Great Britain and France, of which the President desires that you will give early and explicit assurance to the British government. No motive exists here to take any part in their contests."[50]

However, privately, Monroe was relieved when Napoleon was defeated at the Battle of Waterloo.[51] In his initial formal instructions to the new American minister to France, Albert Gallatin, dated April 15, 1816, Monroe made clear official U.S. dissatisfaction with the Napoleonic regime—despite the Louisiana Purchase—and its hopes for a better relationship with the restored Bourbons. It is worth quoting at length, as it is revelatory of hitherto unexpressed U.S. official thinking on Napoleon:

It has at all times since our Revolution been the sincere desire of this government to cultivate a good intelligence with France. The changes which have taken place in her government have never produced any change in this disposition. The United States have looked to the French nation, and to the existing government, as its proper organ, deeming it unjustifiable to interfere with its interior concerns. . . .

Cherishing these sentiments toward the French nation, under all the governments which have existed there, it has not been less a cause of surprise [*sic*] than of regret, that a corresponding disposition has not at all times been reciprocated by the French govt. towards the United States. The history of the last ten years is replete with wrongs received from that government, for which no justifiable pretext can be assigned. The property [meaning ships and cargoes seized] wrested, in that space of time, from our citizens, is of great value, for which reparation has not been obtained. These injuries were received under the late Emperor of France, on whom the demand of indemnity was incessantly made, while he remained in power. Under the sensibility thereby excited and the failure to obtain justice, the relations of the two countries were much affected ... now that the government appears to be settled, it is due to our citizens, who were so unjustly plundered, to present their claim anew to the French government. The President is aware of the delicate nature of this subject.[52]

A review of the diplomatic dispatches and instructions from the period 1815–1816 shows the senior U.S. foreign policy direction focused on an array of pressing issues, including the overwhelming matter of claims by U.S. merchants, the need for reciprocal trade relations and nondiscriminatory tariffs with France, managing the European reaction to the breakup of the Spanish Empire in Latin America, establishing correct relations with Great Britain following the Treaty of Ghent, settlement of boundaries with Great Britain in the American West, compensation for U.S. slaveholders whose slaves had sought refuge with British military forces in America, and on and on. Nowhere does the fate of Napoleon and his top generals figure in the agenda. Put simply, the world had moved on.

Thus, based on the available evidence, it appears that Lee acted on his own initiative in trying to assist Napoleon's escape to America and in offering assistance to other figures from the regime, such as Count Chaptal. None of the surviving presidential correspondence, Department of State instructions to U.S. ministers and ambassadors or U.S. consuls, or U.S. diplomatic dispatches from Bordeaux or Paris evidence any involvement by Monroe or Madison in the attempt to exfiltrate Napoleon or anyone else. Indeed, such an action would have been contrary to the official U.S. policy of strict neutrality in the conflict between Britain and France. It also would have been a feat of rapid communications. Given the facts that Napoleon's reign was only the proverbial Hundred Days and that it would have been prescient to have predicted his fall and flight from 3,000 miles away and send instructions across the Atlantic in time for the immediate aftermath of Waterloo, it is all but certain that neither Lee nor any other U.S. diplomat in France was operating under such instructions.

However, Monroe was informed of the possibility of Napoleon's coming to the United States, even though he learned of it after the opportunity had already passed. In a July 9, 1815, dispatch to Monroe marked "Private," Chargé Henry Jackson at Paris informed the secretary of state, "Napoleon has not yet embarked and is watched by two vessels of war. Unless therefore the English Government judge it prudent to grant him passports for the United States, he will have no alternative but to put himself at the head of the troops who would still arrange themselves with enthusiasm under his standard."[53]

When he wrote this dispatch, Jackson obviously was aware that Napoleon had requested passports from Fouché starting on June 23 and that Fouché had forwarded the request to Wellington and thence the British government. He also was aware that two British warships were attempting to block his exit, which was correct, as *Bellerophon* had just been reinforced at the time.[54] Jackson's reference in the dispatch to the request for passports from the British government is also diplomatically correct. He is deferring to the British government on their issuance, at least in the absence of their issuance by the French government. Only if they were issued would Napoleon legally and politically be able to depart for America. Jackson is not proposing to issue American passports or false passports or to surreptitiously assist in Napoleon's departure.

This posture stands in stark contrast to the actual actions of Consul William Lee in Bordeaux, who, knowing full well the British intent to stop Napoleon, nonetheless took affirmative actions to facilitate his departure for the United States, actions that could have resulted in a hostile naval engagement with the Royal Navy and the loss of life. Had this occurred, the negative effect on U.S. relations with Great Britain, with which the United States had recently concluded peace, would have been significant and possibly long lived. Moreover, it would have violated Monroe's profession of strict neutrality, and it also could have poisoned relations with the new government in France. Lee's position was foolhardy; Jackson's was nuanced and diplomatic.

This vignette illustrates the latitude and discretion with which diplomats worked in the early nineteenth century when communications were not as they are now. Today, the decision would have been made in Washington, most likely by the White House (not even the State Department), and communicated instantly for the in-country diplomats to execute. Diplomacy in the nineteenth century put a premium on the intelligence, character, and wisdom of the man on the scene.

As for émigrés beyond Napoleon, Monroe and Madison appear to have been ignorant of them until they started showing up on U.S. shores. Although Lee had open lines of communication with both Monroe and Madison and Chargé Jackson had an open and often-used line with Monroe, the subject of an exodus of political refugees was never broached in the in-clear communications that have survived. The closest Jackson came to noting it was his rueful comment in a September 27, 1815, dispatch to Monroe: "The applications of individuals who are desirous to emigrate to America are endless. Unfortunately they count on the assistance of the Government—artists of all kinds are among their numbers."[55]

Lee's surviving dispatches during the period of Napoleon's flight are nonexistent. In the period leading up to the events of 1815, he was a frequent reporter to both Monroe and Madison on political events and other matters. A hiatus then follows in the records, with his fulsome reporting picking up again only in October 1815. A letter dated July 1, 1815, to Monroe from Lee's assistant at the consulate, one Peters, may provide some insight:

> Mr. Lee having had the misfortune to dislocate his shoulder and break his right arm by a fall from his carriage is now confined to his bed where it is probable he will remain for some time which renders it impossible for him to write you by this opportunity. He therefore has instructed me to transmit to you by Captain Vickery of the Brig Pike a file of the Moniteur which will furnish you with all the extraordinary occurrences of the past month.[56]

The *Moniteur* is undoubtedly the "latest Bordeaux paper" that the British boarding party stole from *Pike* when they overhauled her en route home. One can only speculate what reports Lee might have written had he not broken his right arm—and why he did not dictate his reports to Peters for transmission to his superiors.

CHAPTER 4

The Hounds of Retribution

NAPOLEON'S CHANCE TO ESCAPE TO THE UNITED STATES ABOARD A Baltimore Flyer was a mere precursor to an unprecedented exodus by the Bonapartist leadership to America. The list of who made the journey, often in disguise and under duress, reads like a "who's who" of the top echelon of the leadership during the Hundred Days. Never before had so much of a nation's governing military or political class migrated en masse to the United States. It is probably impossible to make a comprehensive list of all Bonapartist political refugees who came[1] or even their exact numbers, but they surely would have run well into the hundreds, perhaps more when officers of lower rank and their families are included in the count. Napoleon himself, who followed such matters, estimated from St. Helena that 300 regime insiders had fled to the United States.[2] Of these, the successful flight of Joseph Bonaparte, Napoleon's older brother and the king of Spain, led the way. He was soon joined in America by a marshal of France and at least 10 generals, most of them regime insiders who were marked men in France. The exodus included prominent civilians as well, many of them subject to the Bourbon proscription as having been regicides or prominent in the regime during the Hundred Days. In many instances, they were spurred by being listed on the newly restored Bourbon government's proscription ordinance of July 24, 1815. This list, initially devised by Fouché (who then actually helped some of them escape so that they would be in his debt), consisted of several tiers of proscribed persons. The first tier included 12 generals and other officers who had rallied to Napoleon before dissolution of the royalist army during the Hundred Days. They were to be tried before a court-martial for treason, which was tantamount to a death sentence. The second tier consisted of persons ordered to confine themselves to specified rural areas until the authorities decided whether to try them in court or banish them. Many of these persons understandably did not want to wait around to find out. In addition, the royalist government issued a follow-on decree on January 12, 1816, targeting in particular regicides from the early days of the French Revolution who had played a role in supporting Napoleon's resumption of power.

A further category of émigrés consisted of many officers of lower rank from colonel on down who, though not proscribed, nonetheless feared the so-called White Terror of the newly restored Bourbons. There also were officers on half pay, or *demi-soldes*, of whom there were many following ensuing royalist purges of the military; a subset of these were Bonapartist dead-enders whose world no longer made sense and who were subject to varying degrees of psychological distress (they tended to congregate in the Marais district, where rents were cheap and hours could be spent in cafés). Beyond these, there was a large category of purely economic refugees from France who emigrated in the wake of the disruptions of the Napoleonic Wars. One estimate placed these at as many as 30,000.[3] All came to America.

To a remarkable degree, the émigrés regrouped in and about one city: Philadelphia, which soon became known for its glittering recreation of Parisian glamour. They were aided in this choice by three factors. First was Quaker Philadelphia's reputation as the most sophisticated and tolerant city in the United States. At the time, with more than 60,000 inhabitants, Philadelphia was the second-largest city in the United States after New York. In the words of one French visitor, its residents included the "inhabitants of every country, men of every class and of every degree of character—philosophers, priests, literati, princes, dentists, wits and idiots."[4] Second was the residence in Philadelphia of one of the wealthiest men in America, the French-born Stephen Girard, who not only financed the War of 1812 but also helped provide a safe haven for his fellow countrymen. Third was the presence in Philadelphia of a relatively large colony of white French-speaking Domingans who had fled the slave revolt of 1791 in what is now Haiti.[5] Mostly shopkeepers, artisans, and other petit bourgeoisie, they had little in common with the formerly powerful and cosmopolitan newcomers, but they nonetheless provided an established francophone community onto which the newcomers could graft themselves. There were of course other French-speaking communities in the United States at the time, including in New Orleans and to a lesser degree in New York City and Charleston, but Philadelphia became the lodestone.[6]

Philadelphia even boasted a weekly pro-Bonapartist French-language newspaper, *L'Abeille Américaine* (The American Bee), published from 1815 to 1821 by a Domingan exile, the educated, Swiss-trained watchmaker and Freemason Jean-Simon Chaudron. Its name was an allusion not only to Napoleon and industry (of which the bee was a symbol) but also to the Merovingian dynasty as an alternative to the detested Bourbons. The newspaper served to tie the community together, with its unerring format of an opening poem (often quite lengthy and of the epic variety), philosophy (quotations from Voltaire and Rousseau figure prominently), prolix essays comparing the exiled French to Coriolanus, news and rumors from France and Europe, fragmentary reports on Napoleon's health and spirits from St. Helena (e.g., the July 31, 1817, edition reported that "Bonaparte enjoys good health but . . . continues to show chagrined dispositions"), anti-British sentiment, lampoons of Louis XVIII and other Bourbons, outraged letters to the editor, and, as time went on, support for various grand projects conjured up by the Bonapartist elite in exile. It also did not lack for the quirky and eccentric, such as advertising and promoting "la liqueur vitale de Dr. J. Rucco" for sale at the newspaper's offices at 168 Spruce Street for two dollars a bottle.

The émigrés apparently included a surprising number of artists and musicians who must have emigrated fearing a loss of patronage. For example, in a letter dated April 23, 1816, Thomas Jefferson's former private secretary and U.S. diplomat William Short wrote from Philadelphia to Jefferson:

> Some very remarkable men of another description have also been thrown on our coast from France & who will more probably stay amongst us. They belonged to the conservatory of Music at Paris, an establishment created or perfectionned by the revolutionary

Governments of France. It seems now to be abolished—and its members are dispersed in various ways. . . . Three have come here—a performer & composer on the Piano, one on the Violoncello & another on the Hautboy—Performers of equal distinction have certainly never been heard in this country. They give public concerts & I hope will improve the taste & the talents of this country in this department.[7]

In a similar vein, *L'Abeille Américaine* reported the opening of a school of equitation by a Monsieur Sagnier at the corner of 9th and Walnut streets in Philadelphia.[8] This was part of a larger trend. A surprising number of the Napoleonic exiles remade themselves as educators in an America that provided limited opportunities for financially strapped persons without entrepreneurial skills.[9] In addition to riding masters, some veterans set themselves up as fencing instructors or gave French lessons, while others sought employment as tutors to the children of the wealthy or even, like a Monsieur de Perdreauville, who had trained pages for the courts of Marie Antoinette and Napoleon, established schools.[10]

THE KING OF SPAIN: JOSEPH-NAPOLEON BONAPARTE (1768–1844)

Napoleon's older brother Joseph Bonaparte (illustration 3) bore a strong physical resemblance to the emperor, but their personalities differed, a fact recognized by Napoleon when he was only 15 years old and wrote that his brother should not become a soldier: "the great Mover of all human destiny has [not] given him, as to me, a distinct love for the military profession," adding "he has not the courage to face the perils of action; his health is feeble . . . and my brother looks upon the military profession from only a garrison point of view." If, he suggested, Joseph had chosen to go into the Church, he would have gotten "a fat living and he would have been sure to become a bishop. What an advantage for the family!"[11]

As it was, Joseph became a lawyer, politician, and diplomat. He also was a Freemason. In 1799, he served as French ambassador to Rome. In 1800, he applied his diplomatic skills to negotiate an end to the Quasi-War between the United States and France to the benefit of both countries. The rising tide of his younger brother's fortunes inevitably lifted him to new heights, and in 1806, Napoleon installed him as king of Naples and Sicily. In the two years he held that position, he instituted a vigorous campaign of reform and modernization that won him plaudits in many quarters. In 1808, Napoleon crowned him king of Spain, but the country was already in revolt over French rule, and he never was able to rule effectively. Joseph asked to be relieved of the Spanish crown and to return to Naples, but Napoleon refused. He remained on the throne of Spain until the Allies defeated the French at the Battle of Vitoria in 1813, at which point he abdicated and returned to France. Throughout his tenure on the throne of Spain, he was little more than a puppet of his brother. The bluntness with which Napoleon used Joseph is illustrated by a letter he sent his older brother after the Battle of Vitoria: "France is invaded, all Europe is in arms against France, and above all, against me. You are no longer king of Spain. I do not want Spain either to keep or to give away."[12] In 1814, Joseph purchased a tract of land in upstate New York, thinking tentatively of emigration.

Joseph remained close to his brother throughout the latter's career, as evidenced by his offer to substitute for him in order to facilitate his escape from Île d'Aix—a move that almost certainly would have brought him a death sentence if the royalists had captured him. When Napoleon declined Joseph's offer, Joseph remained with him until he departed aboard *Bellerophon* on July 15. He then resumed his flight to escape France for America (he had earlier also considered flight to Switzerland). In his baggage he carried a fortune in jewels and possibly other movable items of value looted from Spain. His escape was recounted by the American James Carret, who took part:

> I remained with King Joseph, who conducted himself with prudence in order to escape from his enemies. . . . He trusted himself to M. Francis Pelletreau, a Rochefort merchant; but could remain no longer in that town, for the Bourbons were already at Paris. . . . M. Pelletreau had, near the aspen grove on the sea-coast, a small country-place, with some acres of land and a farmer; to which habitation King Joseph went, accompanied by two persons only, and remained there quiet and concealed for ten days,

leaving me at Rochefort, where, by his orders, I purchased several articles for the voyage we were about to undertake,—linen, plate, some books, French classics, the work of M. de la Rochefoucalt [*sic*] on the United States, &c. In this interval I went to see him twice, and learned from him that he had sent Pelletreau the son to Bordeaux, to freight an American vessel, who wrote that he had secured a brig going down to the mouth of the Gironde, where the Prince could embark, the little town of Royan being the nearest point to the river's mouth. King Joseph ordered me to go there, and warn him by express when the brig appeared. I had an American passport, which Mr. Jackson, charge d'affaires of the United States at Paris, had given me [Carret was an American citizen]. M. Dumoulin, established at Royan, exercised the office of consul of that nation. He was an obliging man, and endorsed my passport, adding, without much difficulty, the name of one of the persons going to America with King Joseph. During the three or four days that we sojourned at Royan, we had to be very circumspect. The commandant of the place lodged in the same hotel with us, and attracted there a great many officers and persons curious to be informed what was doing. The [royalist] white flag was already hoisted at Royan. The second day a superior officer arrived, post from Paris, his mission being to have the government of the Bourbons recognised everywhere. His conversation at table with the commandant and other military men was most revolting; but I had to swallow every thing in silence, in order not to betray myself. After meals, some officers, who had read in my face what was passing in my mind, took me aside, and testified to me their indignation at hearing our brave army treated with such injustice, and foreseeing the fate reserved for all who expressed any sympathy for the illustrious chief whom we had just lost for ever. At last I learned that the brig had anchored before Royan. M. Dumoulin showed her to me, and we agreed that a shallop should be ready at midnight to take us on board, with some friends whom I expected. I sent an express to King Joseph, who arrived in the night on foot, quietly, accompanied by M. Edward Pelletreau,

M. Unzaga [military aide], and young Maillard [secretary]. At twelve o'clock the bark had not yet come. We spent two or three hours of painful expectation. The commandant was in a room near us; the Prince might be recognised by some of the officers who were going and coming in the house; and we were relieved from a great weight, when they informed us that the bark was waiting. It was the 25th of July; the weather was beautiful; the moon shone on our embarkation, which was made cautiously. The tide being favorable, the anchor was raised and sails spread. The brig of two hundred tons, named the Commerce, was commanded by Captain Misservey, a man of about forty years of age, born in the island of Guernsey, but having inhabited the United States for a long time, at Charleston, where he was to return, after having transported us to New York. He did not know the illustrious passenger whom he received on board; thinking that we were persons of the Emperor's suite who were going to the United States.[13]

The ship left suddenly, in ballast and without its expected return cargo of cognac. The vessel was chartered for 18,000 francs. Joseph and his French traveling companions also bore bogus passports that were erroneously reported as having been arranged by Henry Jackson, the American chargé in Paris.[14] Joseph was traveling incognito, and his passport was made out in the name of a "Monsieur Bouchard." Left behind in Paris were his wife and two daughters.

Commerce was no Baltimore Flyer. The next day, *Commerce* was overhauled by HMS *Bacchus*. After an interview with Captain Misservey, the British boarding officers left without noticing the passengers. The following day, HMS *Endymion* stopped *Commerce*. This time, the search by the boarding party was more thorough. Joseph, seasick, remained in his cabin while the British officers examined the passengers' papers. They found them to be in order and allowed the ship to proceed.

Carret reported fair weather on the 32-day passage, and Joseph, recovered from his case of seasickness, grew at ease and entertained his companions and the captain by reciting from memory passages of French and Italian poetry (Racine and Corneille were among his favorites).

As the ship neared New York, she was boarded by an American pilot to guide her in. At that very moment, a British war frigate gave chase:

> . . . we soon recognised . . . two frigates, bearing the English flag. We were mute with astonishment, especially when one of the frigates, descrying us, set sail, so as to bar our passage. . . . "Do you see," said he [the pilot] to the captain, "those damned English, hoping to stop our way. But let me alone: the breeze is in our favor, and I will hug the land so close that you will see them soon change their course." With all sail spread that could be, our brig, as if it felt the danger, ploughed the waters of the beautiful entrance with surprising rapidity. We were soon under cover of forts Richmond and La Fayette. . . . The frigate soon tacked about, and moved off from us. We then asked the pilot why the English cruised about, in these latitudes, in time of peace! he answered, that they had only been there the last ten days, to catch the Emperor Napoleon, who was to have embarked in France for the United States, and had resumed the right of search, which provoked all Americans. . . . If they had caught us, they would probably have taken us to Halifax, to Quebec, or perhaps to England, where King Joseph would soon have been recognised, and then they would have transported him to Russia, where the allied sovereigns had decided that he should be taken, as we afterwards learnt.[15]

The party disembarked safely at a pier on the East River. Joseph had accomplished what no other of the emperor's siblings would achieve. Lucien Bonaparte had fled to Italy and lived under the protection of the pope, all the while confident that he and his siblings would soon join Joseph in the United States. As late as 1817, he petitioned Wellington and Prime Minister Richelieu for passports to travel to America with his son Charles. He was refused because, as reported in *L'Abeille Américaine*, "it would be more dangerous that he not be in Europe where he can be more easily watched."[16] As a result, Lucien and all of Napoleon's siblings other than Joseph remained in Europe.

Once ashore in New York, Joseph wished to remain incognito. Captain Misservey had mistaken him to be Interior Minister Count Carnot and had spread a rumor to that effect as soon as he docked. The mayor of New York, thinking he was Carnot, called on him. Joseph explained that he was not Carnot but kept his identity secret. Joseph and his small entourage avoided the larger hotels and instead checked into an obscure boardinghouse, kept by a Mrs. Powell on Park Place where the son of a certain "Commodore Lewis"[17] happened to be staying. The commodore, calling on his son and discovering the king of Spain, whom he evidently had known in Paris, recognized him immediately. The secret was out, as Commodore Lewis might have made him generally known. Joseph therefore accepted the commodore's invitation to pass a few days at his residence in Perth Amboy, New Jersey, which was the first American hospitality he enjoyed. On his return to New York, a French officer accidentally met him while walking along Broadway. With loud and loyal exclamations of delight, he publicly addressed Joseph as prince and king, so that it would have been difficult to conceal his secret any longer.

In fact, Joseph was uncertain of his safety and position in the United States. Traveling in the company of Commodore Lewis and assuming it necessary, as in Europe, to have the protection afforded by a legitimate passport in order to reside legally in the country, Joseph left New York for Washington to call on the president and obtain a passport or whatever permission might be required to reside in the United States. He adopted the name Count de Survilliers, after a village near which he owned property in France. When he arrived at Philadelphia and checked into the Mansion House Hotel, he ran into Henry Clay, Speaker of the House of Representatives, who had just returned from Europe negotiating the Treaty of Ghent ending the War of 1812. Clay graciously offered him his own suite in which to stay, which he did.

However, Joseph got a colder official shoulder as he neared Washington. Word of his intention to call on the president had reached Attorney General Richard Rush via an informant. President Madison at the time was at his country residence Montpelier in Orange County, Virginia. Rush immediately shot off a letter to Commodore Lewis dated September 13, 1815, to try to abort the visit:

I have understood through an authentic channel that one of the brothers of the late Emperor of France is at present travelling [*sic*] to the city under an assumed name, with a view probably of proceeding on as far as Montpelier, the residence of the President in Virginia, and that he has the good fortune to be in your company.

It is evident that this conspicuous stranger comes to our shores as all others, upon the mere footing of the hospitality and protection which the laws hold out to all, without discrimination, which choice or misfortune may bring to us, and that beyond this the executive authority can impose none.

If the measure be intended as a mere mark of respect to the President I will take upon me the liberty of observing that I am sufficiently possessed of his wishes to be able explicitly to say that he would prefer declining at this time its personal offering; and I will take the further liberty to subjoin that in no way, or at no time, would it be acceptable to the President to become a party to the concealment under which the stranger in question may, for all other purposes, find it necessary or convenient to travel.[18]

Rush immediately dispatched the letter in the hands of a Mr. Duvall of the Justice Department to try to intercept Commodore Lewis and the king of Spain in Baltimore. He also wrote President Madison on the matter, and in the following days a flurry of anxious correspondence between the president, Secretary of State Monroe, and Rush ensued. Madison directed the attorney general to make sure that Joseph make no application to be presented to him, thus confirming the content of Rush's message to Commodore Lewis. "The anxiety," Madison wrote to Monroe, "of Joseph Bonaparte to be incog. for the present at least makes it the more extraordinary that he should undertake a journey that could not fail to excite curiosity and multiply the chances of discovery. Commodore Lewis has doubtless been misled into his inconsiderate agency by a benevolent sympathy; but he ought at least to have obtained a previous sanction to it from some quarter or other."[19]

For his part, Secretary of State Monroe was contemplating running for president and was concerned that welcoming the emperor's brother at Washington might hurt his chances of election. Attorney General Rush, who had already staked out his position, was even more implacably opposed. He did not trust any Bonapartes and was suspicious of ulterior motives behind Joseph's desire to proceed to Montpelier, much less meet with the president. He wrote to Madison, "To have come, at any time, to the seat of your public residence with the ulterior view of a personal visit, without a previous sanction through the usual channels, might have been thought not entirely respectful. . . . But so to invade the sanctity of your domestic retreat, really, sir, looks to me . . . as scarcely less than an outrage."[20] All three senior U.S. officials roundly condemned Commodore Lewis for his role in the affair.

Monroe recalled that, many years before, President Washington had declined to receive Talleyrand when he was in the United States waiting out the Reign of Terror. Madison explained his position thoughtfully and correctly in response: "Protection and hospitality do not depend on such a formality [as being officially received]; and whatever sympathy may be due to fallen fortunes, there is no claim of merit in that family on the American nation; nor any reason why its government should be embarrassed on their account. In fulfilling what we owe to our own rights we shall do all that any of them ought to expect."[21]

In the meantime, Rush's emissary Duvall found Commodore Lewis and the king of Spain stopped for the night at a tavern in Ellicott Mills (today's Ellicott City), just south of Baltimore. Armed with Rush's letter, he informed them that a visit to the capital or Montpelier was not only unnecessary but also unacceptable. The message was clear: neither the president nor his cabinet would receive Joseph. The emperor's older brother understood the message and turned back for New York.

It had not been an auspicious opening gambit.

The Aristocrat: Emmanuel Grouchy, Second Marquis Grouchy and Marshal of France (1766–1847)

Marshal Emmanuel Marquis Grouchy (illustration 4) was an anomalous figure: a high-cheek-boned, long-nosed aristocrat born into a noble Norman family who embraced the Revolution and served it and later Napoleon unstintingly. Grouchy was essentially born into the military calling and trained as an artillery officer starting in 1780. He later transferred to the cavalry. In a career that spanned decades and that took him to campaigns in Italy, Germany, the Netherlands, Spain, Russia, France, and Belgium, he fought in at least 37 battles and major engagements and, through merit, rose through the officers' ranks. In the Battle of Novi in Italy in 1799, he received 14 wounds and was taken prisoner for a year. At the Battle of Eylau in 1807, his horse was shot from under him, and he was again wounded. At the Battle of Borodino in the Russian campaign of 1812, he was wounded by grapeshot to the chest before taking command of the Sacred Battalion, a unit composed solely of officers that was charged with protecting the person of Napoleon. In 1814, he was wounded first at Troyes and then by a shot to his thigh at the Battle of Craonne. On Napoleon's return from Elba, Grouchy rallied to the emperor and defeated a royalist force sent to stop him, thereby earning Napoleon's gratitude (and the Bourbons' enmity). Napoleon rewarded him by making him a marshal of France, the last person to be so honored by the emperor. Napoleon gave him command of the Cavalry Reserve at Waterloo. Following the battle, he executed a masterful retreat, keeping his corps intact and capable of reuniting with Napoleon for further action.

Grouchy was among those sentenced to death by King Louis' proscription of July 24, 1815. This move focused Grouchy on the need to make his escape quickly, alone and without his wife or children. He hid out at an isolated country inn in the Calvados district of Normandy until Prussian troops occupied the area and began to harrow at his heels—a poetic *boulversement* for Grouchy given his assigned role at Waterloo. He then moved to the vicinity of Le Havre, where he tried unsuccessfully to arrange passage under the assumed name of "Monsieur Gauthier," a silk merchant from Lyons.[22] He eventually found passage under a false identity on a ship from Normandy to the island of Guernsey in the English Channel. He hid out there for several weeks until he found passage, again incognito, on a ship to the United States. He termed the 58-day passage "very hard."[23]

When his ship arrived at Baltimore in January 1816, he carried a personal letter of introduction for him dated September 8, 1815, from the Marquis de Lafayette to "My Dear Friend" Thomas Jefferson, by then the retired "Sage of Monticello."[24] That one of the principal authors of Napoleon's demise would have assisted Grouchy while he was under a death sentence was a sign of the respect in which Grouchy was held as much as of his wide-ranging political contacts across several spectrums. He was to play both to his advantage in the years that ensued. Grouchy, in the company of several other French émigrés, ultimately was received by Dolley Madison in her drawing room in Washington. Monroe, who was present, instantly left lest he become implicated in civilities toward them. "Despicable meanness," Grouchy complained to a friend.

Grouchy's two sons, Colonel Alphonse and Lieutenant Victor Grouchy, also traveling in disguise, joined him in the United States in late May 1817.

Grouchy's name is inscribed on the north pillar of the Arc de Triomphe.

THE ACTIVIST: LIEUTENANT GENERAL FRANCOIS-ANTOINE "CHARLES" BARON LALLEMAND (1774–1839)

Born the son of a Metz wig maker, Lallemand enlisted early in the French Revolution, initially in the artillery but, like Grouchy, subsequently was transferred to the cavalry. He served under Napoleon in putting down the royalist revolt in Paris on 13 Vendémaire 1795. Lallemand campaigned with Napoleon in Italy and then Egypt. He caught Napoleon's eye, for he was one of the fortunate few to accompany Napoleon when he left Egypt for France. Lallemand rose rapidly through the ranks based on merit. He fought in Saint-Domingue (Haiti) and visited the United States for what turned out to be the first of three times when he stopped at New York and elsewhere on the East Coast in 1804 on the way back to France. He even considered remaining and becoming a naturalized U.S. citizen.[25] He also fought at Austerlitz and Jena and as a dragoon commander in Spain. Napoleon elevated him to a baron in 1808 and then to general in 1811. Of Lallemand, Napoleon said, "He has the *feu sacré.*"[26]

At the time of Napoleon's escape from Elba, he joined with General Lefebvre-Desnouettes (see below) to try to seize an arsenal at La Fère as part of an ill-fated "Conspiracy of the North" to put the Duke of Orléans on the throne. They failed, and Lallemand was arrested. When Napoleon took power, he released him, appointed him lieutenant general, and placed him as deputy commander of the Chasseurs à Cheval of the Imperial Guard. Although wounded at Waterloo, he rejoined Napoleon in Paris after the battle, accompanied him to Rochefort, tried to arrange his escape on *Pike*, and, that failing, sought to accompany him into exile on St. Helena. The British disallowed his request, arrested him, and imprisoned him on Malta along with Savary. While imprisoned, he was tried in absentia and sentenced to death by the royalist government pursuant to the ordinance of July 24, 1815. Eventually released by the British in April 1816, he traveled to Smyrna, seemingly in the company of Savary,[27] to offer his services to the sultan of Turkey but instead was ordered to leave. He then apparently went to Persia or Egypt[28] before making his way to America under very murky circumstances, almost certainly traveling in disguise and on the lam. According to one account, Lallemand arrived in Boston aboard the ship *Triton*, from Liverpool, under the assumed name of General Cotting. According to the New York *Columbian* of April 29, 1817, quoting from the *Evening Post*, he was smuggled on board *Triton* at Liverpool (how he traveled to and entered England from the Middle East is unclear). "On leaving the river, as the Custom House boat passed from ship to ship to examine the rolls, the General was passed in a boat to and from several ships, so as to evade the boarding officer." The next day, April 30, 1817, the *Columbian* reported that "two more of Bonaparte's late officers have arrived at Boston, from Leghorn—Dufresne Cyprion and Liell Memon."

Charles Lallemand's name is inscribed on the west pillar of the Arc de Triomphe.

THE LITTLE BROTHER: BRIGADIER GENERAL HENRI-DOMINIQUE BARON LALLEMAND

Earlier, in 1816, Charles Lallemand was preceded to the United States by his younger brother Brigadier General Henri-Dominique Baron Lallemand (1777–1823), a veteran of the campaigns in Prussia, Spain, and Russia and who commanded the artillery of the Imperial Guard at Waterloo, where hc was wounded. He also was proscribed by the Bourbons. Henri Lallemand arrived at Philadelphia around April 4, 1816, as confirmed by a report in the May 23, 1816, issue of *L'Abeille Américaine*.[29]

Napoleon's Aide-de-Camp: General Charles Count Lefebvre-Desnouettes (1773–1822)

Like Lallemand, with whom he was closely associated, Lefebvre-Desnouettes (illustration 5) was of modest birth, the son of a Paris cloth merchant. He ran away from school three times to join the army; each time, his parents purchased his release from enlistment. The fourth time, they gave up. He served as a junior officer in the dragoons in many of the same campaigns as Lallemand, but his career break came when, as a captain in 1800, Napoleon appointed him his aide-de-camp. In this capacity he fought at the Battle of Marengo. He later commanded a division of reserve dragoons at Elchingen and Austerlitz. Service in Bavaria and Westphalia followed, as well as a stint as aide-de-camp to Napoleon's brother Jérôme. In 1808, he was elevated to count and appointed commander of the Chasseurs à Cheval of the Imperial Guard, whom he led in various campaigns in Spain. Captured there by the British, he was transported as a prisoner of war to England, where he lived until 1812 on parole at Cheltenham. He was joined there by his wife, who was a sister of Napoleon's banker Jacques Laffitte. Breaking his parole, he escaped back to France in time to join Napoleon's invasion of Russia, in which he commanded the Chasseurs à Cheval of the Imperial Guard. He was wounded but survived and returned with Napoleon to France. He was engaged in further heavy fighting in 1813–1814 in more than a dozen battles, during one of which he was bayoneted twice. At the time of Napoleon's return from Elba, he joined with Lallemand in the unsuccessful attempt on the arsenal at La Fère. He was once again placed in command of the Chasseurs à Cheval of the Imperial Guard, and he led a division of light cavalry of the Old Guard at Waterloo. Like Charles Lallemand and others, he was sentenced to death in absentia by the returning Bourbons. Although some historians have stated that Lefebvre-Desnouettes made his escape to the United States with Charles Lallemand, this was not the case. He arrived alone in April 1816, as discussed later in chapter 11. *L'Abeille Américaine* reported on September 12, 1816, "We received official notice of the presence in Philadelphia of Clausel, Grouchy, Lakanal, Hentz [Nicolas Hentz, compiler of the Code Napoleon], one Lallemand brother, Regnauld *père* and Joseph Bonaparte."[30] The one Lallemand brother was Henri Lallemand. Charles Lallemand did not depart Malta until April 1816 and does not appear in Philadelphia until sometime in 1817. Some writers have posited that Lefebvre-Desnouettes left via Bordeaux and was accompanied by the Corsican Pascal Luciani (see below) and a mysterious ginger-haired stranger traveling under an assumed name. Again, this was not the case. Lefebvre-Desnouettes was destined to play an important role in the Society of the Vine and Olive's settlement in Alabama (see chapter 6).

Lefebvre-Desnouettes's name is inscribed on the west pillar of the Arc de Triomphe.

THE PILLAGER: GENERAL DOMINIQUE JOSEPH RENÉ COUNT VANDAMME (1770–1830)

Napoleon reputedly remarked that if he had two Vandammes, he would have to order one to hang the other.[31]

Vandamme was born at Cassel in French Flanders, close by the Belgian border. He enlisted as a regular solider in the colonial service in 1788 and was stationed in Martinique in the Caribbean, rising to the rank of sergeant. He deserted, returned to France, joined the revolutionary army, and by 1792 was active as a captain in a cavalry unit he raised himself. He fought extensively in French campaigns in Germany and rose rapidly because of his success. He was elevated to general in 1793 at age 23, having gone from deserted sergeant to general in three years. However, he was accused of levying exactions on locals to line his own pockets and was placed on leave. Eventually recalled to service, he fought bravely at Austerlitz and elsewhere in the north, resulting in his ennoblement as a count. He continued fighting the Austrians and was wounded at Wagram. Following that battle, Napoleon declined to elevate him to the Marshalate, which infuriated him. The volatile Vandamme branded Napoleon a coward and a liar and declared that if it were not for Vandamme Napoleon would still be keeping pigs in Corsica. In fact, Vandamme's bad temper and the allegations of financial improprieties that still dogged him were the cause. The latter concern was borne out when in 1812 he was relieved of his command in Westphalia for looting and ordered to return to France.

He was without a command until 1813, when he was placed in charge of a corps fighting the Russians. He was captured and dragged before Tsar Alexander, who also accused him of looting. After being imprisoned in Moscow, he was eventually released and returned to France in 1814. During the first restoration of the Bourbons, he refused an audience with King Louis XVIII, who exiled him to his home in Cassel, where he remained until Napoleon's escape from Elba. Napoleon placed him in charge of the Third Corps of the Army of the North under Marshal Soult, whose orders he refused to obey. He fought under Marshal Grouchy at Waterloo. The newly restored Bourbons exiled him to Cassel once again, where he lived until January 1816, when he was exiled completely from France. He lived in Ghent four months until, expelled once again, he fled once again, arriving in Philadelphia in July 1817.

Vandamme's name is inscribed on the north pillar of the Arc de Triomphe.

THE COMMANDER OF BORDEAUX: GENERAL BERTRAND COUNT CLAUSEL (1772–1842)

Clausel (figure 4.1) was from a locally prosperous family of commoners in Mirepoix near the Pyrenees in southern France. He joined the local national guard at the start of the Revolution and then, when the Revolution opened the officers' ranks to commoners, obtained a commission in the regular army, first in the infantry and later the cavalry. He held a number of staff (as opposed to combat) positions and was involved in diplomatic missions, culminating in his appointment as chief of staff to Marshal Grouchy in the Army of England in 1798. He was promoted to general in 1799 and accompanied Napoleon on the Egyptian expedition and was briefly commander of Alexandria. On his return to France, he fought in Italy before being sent on the disastrous expedition to Saint-Domingue. Ordered back to France in 1803, he was shipwrecked off Spanish Florida but made his way to New York and thence back to France. The ensuing years saw active combat service in Holland and the Iberian Peninsula as well as Russia. Following Napoleon's first abdication, Clausel was rewarded by the Bourbons for his service and retained as a

Figure 4.1. General Bertrand Count (later Marshal) Clausel. Artist and date unknown. WIKIMEDIA COMMONS.

corps commander, but he quickly sped to Napoleon's side in 1815 and delivered Bordeaux to the emperor. Napoleon charged him with defending the Western Pyrenees. After Waterloo, he was in Bordeaux with a few thousand troops, acting in effect as military governor of the district. Because of Clausel's active support of Napoleon after Elba he was proscribed by the Bourbons under the July 24 ordinance. With the assistance of U.S. Consul William Lee,[32] he fled to Philadelphia from Bordeaux in early 1816 and was sentenced to death in absentia the following year. Like Lefebvre-Desnouettes, Clausel was to play a prominent role in the Society of the Vine and Olive's colony.

Clausel's name is inscribed on the west pillar of the Arc de Triomphe.

The Veteran: General Antoine Baron Rigau (1758–1820)

Somewhat older than the preceding generals, Rigau was a career soldier with service in the hussars and cavalry preceding the Revolution. With the advent of the Revolution, he served in the Army of the North and in Italy, very much a combat soldier who was wounded multiple times by saber cuts and musket balls (one to the jaw wounded him so badly that he could hardly speak). He fought at Marengo and, promoted to general, briefly commanded a brigade of heavy cavalry in Spain. He was then recalled to duty in France and more combat in Germany leading up to Napoleon's first abdication. The restored Bourbons rewarded him, but he assisted Lefebvre-Desnouettes in trying to evade capture after the La Fère incident. Once Napoleon's return gained traction, he threw his support to him and brought hussars with him to secure the Marne *département*. He did not fight at Waterloo but resisted the advancing Russians afterward. He was captured by the Russians and was proscribed and later sentenced to death by the Bourbons. He refused to obey their summons and fled to Ghent and from there to America.

Rigau's name is inscribed on the north pillar of the Arc de Triomphe.

The Engineer: Brigadier General
Simon Baron Bernard (1779–1839)

Not all the generals fled under dramatic circumstances. Brigadier General Simon Baron Bernard, the son of an uneducated laborer, rose, thanks to a scholarship education, the army, and Napoleon, to become a valued engineer and designer of fortifications. He served as aide-de-camp to Napoleon, followed him as far as Rochefort, and tried unsuccessfully to accompany him into exile. For his efforts, Bernard was ordered by the Bourbon government, which probably wished to avail itself of his talents, back to his hometown, but he was not slated for further retribution. Nonetheless, he left in 1818, bearing like so many others a letter of introduction from Lafayette. Two months later he was commissioned a brigadier general in the U.S. Army Corps of Engineers, where he went on to distinguish himself by designing and constructing, among other notable works, Fortress Monroe at the mouth of Chesapeake Bay, which was to play a key role in the Civil War. His wife joined him in America, and they had a son born there. Bernard eventually returned to France and was made minister of war by King Louis Philippe. Such was his standing that the U.S. Army observed 30 days of mourning on his death in 1839.

Many others were of lesser rank. An example would be Colonel Michel Combe (1787–1837), who fought with Napoleon in Austria, Prussia, and Russia. He returned from Moscow a colonel in the First Regiment of Grenadiers in the Imperial Guard. He accompanied Napoleon to Elba on his first exile, then participated in the Hundred Days and fought at Waterloo. He fled to the United States, where he married the daughter of Colonel Benjamin Walker, an aide to Baron von Steuben and General Washington.[33] Another is Colonel Louis-Jacques Galabert (1773–1841), whose checkered career included enlisting in an antirevolutionary regiment raised in England, participating in the disastrous Quiberon landing, traveling around the world (literally), serving as a spy under Napoleon, joining the army, and filling a variety of staff and intelligence roles in Spain before winding up as aide to Marshal Soult and rising to the rank of lieutenant colonel. He too joined Napoleon during the Hundred Days and fought at Waterloo. Under surveillance by the Bourbons, he fled to America via Bordeaux. Consul William Lee was later to claim that he saved Galabert's life at Bordeaux.

THE CIVILIANS

Of the civilians who fled to America in the wake of Waterloo, arguably the most prominent was Pierre-Francois Réal (1757–1834), a lawyer and close associate of Danton and coconspirator with Napoleon in the coup of 18 Brumaire 1799 that brought the first consul to power. Réal served on the Council of State, where his portfolio included oversight of the police in northern France, including Paris. He prosecuted royalist conspirators and was perceived by royalists to have had a hand in the execution of the Prince d'Enghien, one of Napoleon's most controversial and cynical gambits on his rise to absolute power. During the Hundred Days, Réal was one of Napoleon's top internal security advisers and head of the police (secret and otherwise) in Paris. Proscribed by the Bourbons, he fled from Antwerp to America with his wife and nephew.[34] A contemporary newspaper account places his arrival in August 1816.[35] Although initially in Philadelphia, by 1818–1819, he was living at Cape Vincent,

New York, near Joseph Bonaparte's landholdings in the vicinity of Chaumont.

Joseph Lakanal (1762–1845) (figure 4.2) was a regicide. He also was an ordained priest and member of a teaching order. He claimed never to have functioned as a priest and to have worked instead solely as an educator (his contemporaries found him to be "ultra-pedantic").[36] He was elected to the Convention in 1792 as a radical republican. Lakanal voted for the execution of King Louis XVI in 1793. He flourished in revolutionary France, becoming inspector general of the bureau charged with imposing the metric

Figure 4.2. Joseph Lakanal. H. Rousseau (graphic designer), E. Thomas (engraver), date unknown. WIKIMEDIA COMMONS.

system and ascending to membership in the prestigious Institut de France, established in 1795 by the Directory, as well as membership in the Legion of Honor. His regicidal action was enough to place him on the follow-on Bourbon proscription list dated January 12, 1816. Apparently, he was not in fact a practicing priest because his wife and two daughters joined him in fleeing to America in March 1816. They headed straight for Kentucky, where they settled on lands he may have purchased before leaving France.

Like so many revolutionaries, Jacques Garnier (de Saintes) (1755–1818) was a small-time lawyer. Like Lakanal, he also was a radical republican member of the Convention who voted for the execution of the king. He was an ardent supporter of the Reign of Terror and advocated even more bloodthirsty policies. Napoleon employed him in the criminal court system. Garnier (his real name; he added "de Saintes" later) was active during the Hundred Days as a member of the Chamber of Representatives, where he tried to push the appointment of political commissars to the army. Proscribed by the Bourbons, he fled to Belgium, where he published a radical journal until the Belgian authorities ordered him to leave. He returned to Bordeaux, where, possibly with the aid of William Lee, he secured passage for himself and his son, an Imperial Guard cavalry captain, aboard the American merchant ship *Magnet* and arrived under aliases in Philadelphia on May 4, 1816.[37] The manifest for *Magnet* shows a "P. Bouchey" and a "J. Bouchey" traveling together.[38]

Of a similar extreme leftist bent and also a regicide was Nicolas-Marie Quinette (1762–1821), a former small-town notary who went on to serve as minister of the interior under the Directory. He also fled to the United States and wound up in Philadelphia like so many others.

Another lawyer and Convention member, as well as a quasi regicide, was Jean-Augustin Penières-Delors (1766–1821). He was in fact more of a moderate and nuanced thinker than Lakanal, Garnier, or Quinette, as evidenced by his voting to find King Louis XVI guilty of treason but arguing to suspend the attendant death sentence. Penières opposed the deepening radicalism of the Convention, denounced Marat, and, at some risk to himself, spoke out against the terrorist elements within the Convention following the fall of Robespierre. Nonetheless, he was proscribed by the Bourbons in the follow-on ordinance of January 12, 1816, and he fled to Bordeaux, where U.S. Consul William Lee most likely helped him secure passage to America. He left Bordeaux in May 1816 aboard *Harriet*.[39] His trip was eventful in that his ship was wrecked off the coast of Africa, and he spent a week in a lifeboat before being rescued. He ultimately arrived in Philadelphia on July 16, 1816. His son later joined him there.[40]

Another prominent Bonapartist refugee was Michel Regnaud Count de Saint-Jean d'Angély (1760–1819), a lawyer and French politician who served Napoleon in various capacities. Like almost all the other noble refugees except Grouchy, he was raised to the nobility by Napoleon. He too fled to Philadelphia, where he lived for one year before being pardoned and returning to France. He died the night he arrived in Paris.

Not all the civilians who removed themselves to America were regicides or prominent radicals. Much more numerous were lesser players in the Napoleonic saga. These included Pasqual (Pascal) Luciani (?–1853), Napoleon's second cousin, who was born in the same house in Ajaccio, Corsica, as the emperor and who was Madame Mère's godson.[41] Luciani served as part of Napoleon's entourage on Elba and fought at Waterloo. He lived in Philadelphia from 1816 to 1843, was for a short time the

French consul in the city, and became a naturalized citizen in 1818. He married a wealthy American woman, Rosanna Wentling, in 1818, and together they had six daughters and two sons. Luciani was listed in the 1819 Philadelphia city directory as a "confectioner" located at the northeast corner of Chestnut and 5th streets.[42] By 1821, he styled himself a "confectioner and fruiterer" with premises at 136 Market Street. Together with his wealthy wife, he owned numerous valuable properties in Philadelphia. He also built and owned the first street railway system in Philadelphia, and his name appears frequently in city records from the period. He eventually suffered economic reverses and moved with his family to Wilmington, North Carolina, and from there to Montgomery, Alabama, where both he and his wife died of yellow fever in 1853. According to a signed affidavit by his last surviving daughter in 1926, he fled France in the company of Marshal Michel Ney and General Lefebvre-Desnouettes in late 1815 aboard the American ship *City of Philadelphia* out of Bordeaux.[43] Finally, Georges-Nicholas Jeannet-Oudin (?–?) was a nephew of Danton and a former cotton merchant in France before the Revolution who worked in the War Ministry under Napoleon. Even Napoleon's steward Rousseau and groom Archambault headed straight for Philadelphia when they were expelled from St. Helena by the British authorities. The list could go on and on.

Not all of the Napoleonic exiles went to America. Napoleon's brothers Lucien and Jérôme, together with Madame Mère, went to Italy. His sister Pauline, married to Count Bernadotte, went to Sweden. Savary fled to Smyrna. Napoleon's aide Lavalette went to Germany. Grand Marshal of the Palace General Henri Gatien Count Bertrand, sentenced to death by the Bourbons, accompanied Napoleon in his exile on St. Helena.

And some of the proscribed Bonapartists did not escape to safety. Napoleon's brother-in-law Marshal Joachim Murat, son of an innkeeper and later king of Naples, was shot by a firing squad.

And then there was Marshal Michel Ney, son of a cooper and later a prince, whom Napoleon famously called "the Bravest of the Brave." He stubbornly refused to flee France. History records that he too was shot by a firing squad. Or did he survive to become a schoolteacher in rural North Carolina? That mystery is the subject of the final chapters of this book.

CHAPTER 5

The Philadelphia Story

Joseph will found a great establishment over there. . . . If I were in his place, I'd weld all the Spanish Americas into a great empire. But Joseph—you'll see—will make himself into an American burgher and spend his fortune on laying out gardens.

—NAPOLEON ON ST. HELENA

JOSEPH HAD INDEED ESCAPED WITH A FORTUNE, ESTIMATED BY Napoleon at 20 million francs[1] and including royal jewelry and other valuables. Now styling himself the Count de Survilliers, Joseph remained a short time in New York City before settling in Philadelphia. In 1815, he moved to a rented town house at 260 South 9th Street in the fashionable Washington Square neighborhood of Philadelphia. The house still stands (figure 5.1).

While he took care to maintain a low political profile, Joseph's home became a center and a beacon for the French émigré community. That community took on added luster with the arrival in late 1815 of Marshal Grouchy and subsequently General Henri Lallemand, soon to be followed by others.[2]

The Count de Survilliers had a common touch that pleased Americans. Although his English skills were rudimentary at best, he stopped to talk with his neighbors when out for walks, and he tipped local tradesmen with gold coins. *Niles' Weekly Register* of September 28, 1815, reported, "Joseph Bonaparte seems determined to conform to the manners of our country. When assisting personally to unload the furniture brought to his

Figure 5.1.   260 South 9th Street, Philadelphia.
PHOTOGRAPH BY THE AUTHOR.

house, to a person who said something about sending for other hands, he said 'No, everybody worked here.'"

The Count de Survilliers quickly became known to the neighborhood children as "the good Mr. Bonaparte." He even attended a Quaker meeting at least once.

By the end of 1815, Joseph reported favorably on his life in the United States:

The place where I live is very beautiful and has a good climate. There are perfect peace and quiet, no sign of judges or policemen or criminals. Everyone works and enjoys such general respect that we detect no bothersome gesture, no wounding discrimination, no revolting injustice, no offense painful to ourselves or others. Liberty is complete. Domestic morals are perfect, practical skills very advanced, the arts still in their infancy. Essential goods are fairly cheap, luxury items overpriced. In Switzerland they hide their wealth, here they display it. Here they live on work and credit, in Switzerland on work and savings. . . . Americans are cold but hospitable and kind, not ceremonious like Spaniards or polite like Frenchmen, but more cordial and obliging to foreigners. Generally speaking, I like the country and its inhabitants.[3]

Joseph spent the winter in Philadelphia. The French consul in Philadelphia wrote in February 1816 that Napoleon's brother "receives invitations to dinners, teas and private social gatherings. Up to now he has turned down public balls, including the one given yesterday to celebrate Washington's birthday. He entertains local businessmen and other wealthy people. Generally speaking, he leads a quiet life and does not make himself conspicuous. He shows great respect for local customs and manners, saying quite often that he prefers his residence here to the flattering and distinguished places offered him in Europe."[4]

Joseph's circle of new friends prominently included Stephen Girard (figure 5.2), one of the wealthiest men in the United States.[5] Girard, originally from Bordeaux, was a one-eyed, self-made banker who had financed the U.S. war effort during the War of 1812. Among other things, Girard acted as American agent for Napoleon's banker Jacques Laffitte, and it is likely that the funds Napoleon directed Laffitte to send to America ahead of him were destined for Girard to hold and invest. His wife having been committed to the Pennsylvania Hospital for insanity, Girard lived simply, almost miserly, with his serial mistresses on Water Street near the docks in Philadelphia. He was a tough and shrewd man, at once tight with money and a civic philanthropist. In one famous anecdote, Joseph tried to buy a property at Chestnut and Market streets from Girard when the latter was at his house for dinner. Joseph said he would offer a fair price. Girard asked, "Well, now, what will you give? What do you consider a fair price?" Joseph responded, "I will cover the block from Eleventh to Twelfth, and from Chestnut to Market Streets, with silver half dollars." Girard, who was sipping soup at the time, stopped and suspended his spoon in midair and, with a calculating look out of his one good eye, replied very slowly, "Yes, Monsieur le Comte—if you will stand them up edgeways." The deal never was struck, but Girard and Joseph remained close friends and often dined together.[6]

Figure 5.2.   Stephen Girard. "NATIONAL PORTRAIT GALLERY OF EMINENT AMERICANS FROM ORIGINAL FULL LENGTH PORTRAITS BY ALONZO CHAPPEL," VOL. I, NEW YORK: JOHNSON, FRY & CO. 1862. WIKIMEDIA COMMONS.

Girard introduced Joseph to many leaders of Philadelphia society, and he became close friends with General Thomas Cadwalader, politician and historian Charles Jared Ingersoll, Senator Richard Stockton, Judge Joseph Hopkinson, and others, some of whom he left bequests to in his will. Joseph was accorded the high honor of being elected a member of the prestigious American Philosophical Society in Philadelphia.[7] It would be fair to say that Joseph's eventual circle of American friends was notable for its selection rather than its size and that the friendships were genuine rather than political.

A glimpse into Joseph's life at the time is provided by the following passage from the same April 23, 1816, letter from the French-speaking William Short to Thomas Jefferson quoted earlier. Writing from Philadelphia, Short observed,

> The late revolution in France as you probably know brought some of its actors amongst us—The ex-king of Spain, & Marshal Grouchy . . . are the most remarkable—The former passed the last winter at N. York—but there declined altogether going into society. He has lately come here, says he prefers the appearances of things in this quarter, & gives a proof of it by renting a house in the neighborhood where he intends to take up his residence— He appears disposed also here to partake of society—I have dined once in company with him, & am to meet him again in the same way to-morrow. As he does not speak English I of course I have a great deal of his conversational company. He converses sensibly & with a great deal of philosophy—affects to be much pleased with the manners, ou plutot la maniere d'etre, of this country—He has written for his wife to join him & hopes she will come—. . . . I do not believe she will come or that he will stay amongst us finally.[8]

Fear of royalist assassins remained an ever-present concern for Joseph and other members of the Bonapartist French community in Philadelphia. Trials, banishments, and executions continued to play out in France. Both Joseph Bonaparte and Lakanal were expelled from the Académie des Inscriptions et Belles Lettres in Paris, and Regnault de Saint-Jean d'Angély suffered the same humiliation at the Académie Française.[9] Moreover, in June 1816, Joseph's wife, Queen Julie, was banished from Paris under a law that barred from France in perpetuity all members of the Bonaparte family.[10] Although his fear of assassination appears to have ameliorated the more accustomed Joseph became to life in his new country, he consciously cultivated an apolitical profile.

Joseph's aversion to political involvement was so intense that he several times declined the throne of Mexico when it was offered him. On one such occasion, in 1817, he responded that a republican form of government is a "gift from heaven" and admonished his interlocutors that Mexico was better off without a king: "Seek among your fellow citizens a man more capable than I am of acting the great part of Washington."[11]

Clearly, Joseph had played his cards wisely and had recovered from his initial faux pas in trying to call on the president. By mid-1817, there was even a thaw in the official attitude toward Joseph. The newly inaugurated President James Monroe embarked on a multistate tour of the country, and June 7–9 found him in New Jersey. "The party made a call on Joseph Bonaparte [in Bordentown] en route to lunch. Joseph seemed an unpretending common sense gentleman. . . . The President and Joseph were old acquaintances."[12]

In August 1817, Joseph sent his secretary Louis Maillard to Switzerland on a secret mission. Following a shipwreck off the Irish coast, he arrived in Germany and proceeded to Switzerland disguised as an English tourist wearing a red wig and sporting a fake British accent. His mission was to dig up a box of jewels and important papers that he and Joseph had buried on Joseph's Swiss property before going to join Napoleon in Paris in the Hundred Days. After two days of digging, Maillard located the box and returned with its contents to America. It supposedly contained diamonds from the crown of Spain that were so valuable that Napoleon commented enviously on them from St. Helena. The box also contained documents and letters between the two Bonaparte brothers.[13]

At the same time, Joseph began to shop about for a country seat. He rented Lansdowne in bucolic Fairmont Park, Philadelphia. Here he threw a lawn fête during the summer of 1817 that was attended by the cream of Philadelphia society. Joseph himself was the center of attention as he stood on the open greensward before the house. Those who saw him that day noted his resemblance to "an English gentleman farmer."[14]

But Lansdowne was only a temporary diversion. On August 27, 1816, his American assistant James Carret, acting as his agent, took title to an estate called Point Breeze in Bordentown, New Jersey, just up the Delaware River from Philadelphia. Carret took title because Joseph, as a foreigner, was not allowed to own property. This was remedied by a special act of the New Jersey legislature, and in late 1817, Joseph was able to title the property in his own name and move in. He was 48 years old. Point Breeze was effectively to remain his home in the United States for the remainder of his life, although he also kept for occasional use a town house at 11th and Markets streets in Philadelphia and in the summers visited his lands in upstate New York.

By all accounts, Point Breeze was a spectacular holding (illustration 6). Originally 211 acres, Joseph expanded it to more than 1,200 acres. In a sharp departure from formal French and indeed European and American garden design at the time, he developed the grounds as a carefully planned, naturalized wilderness or "picturesque landscaping." He based the concept on his château at Mortefontaine in the Picardie region of northern France. The result was little short of revolutionary in terms of garden design in America. The park-like estate was traversed by 12 miles of drives and bridle paths that wound through the forested landscape decorated at strategic spots with statuary. The landscaping also included rustic cots or rain shelters, bowers and seats, sheltered springs, and solitary retreats. Joseph dammed a small stream to create a lake 200 yards wide and half a mile long. It was dotted with small islands, and swans graced the waters. The grounds at Point Breeze later influenced Frederick Law Olmsted's designs for Central Park in New York City as well as the development of Fairmount Park in Philadelphia.

The house itself also was a wonder. Built on a 100-foot-high bluff at the confluence of the Delaware River and Crosswicks Creek and boasting sweeping views up and downriver, Joseph turned the mansion into an enclave of regal old Europe in New Jersey, just across the river from Philadelphia. Joseph's private apartments on the second floor consisted of a bedroom with mahogany empire furniture, bath, living room, library, and study. A visitor allowed into his private apartments described them thus:

> The curtains, canopy and furniture were of light blue satin, trimmed with silver. Every room contained a mirror, reaching from the ceiling to the floor. Over the bed hung a splendid mirror and also one over the table. The walls were covered with oil paintings, principally of young females, with less clothing about them than they or you would have found comfortable in our cold climate. . . . In every room of the house there were statues of Napoleon in different positions. To the statue of [his sister] Pauline [by Canova], in particular, the Count called our attention and asked us to admire it. He stood some time perfectly enraptured before it, pointing out to us what a beautiful head Pauline had, what hair, what eyes, nose, mouth, chin.[15]

In a secret cabinet in his study Joseph kept a collection of jewels, including the crown and rings he wore as king of Spain. The public rooms contained an art gallery with a notable collection of paintings by masters, reportedly including works by Rembrandt, Titian, Raphael, Rubens, and da Vinci. The collection also included paintings by Velasquez, Murillo, Teniers, Bassano, Bidault, and Vernet.[16] On one wall hung a full-scale copy of David's dramatic *Passage of the Alps* showing Napoleon on rearing horse and with cape flowing. Following Joseph's death, an auction catalog for the collection dated 1845 (believed to be the first-ever American auction catalog) lists, among other items, two Rembrandts (both *Head of a Turk*) and two Rubenses (*Two Lions and a Fawn* and *Judgment of Paris*).[17]

Point Breeze became a salon for the exiled Bonapartists, much as Mortefontaine had been a salon for visiting intellectuals and dignitaries hosted by Joseph.[18] Joseph was far from a recluse; people came to him. Visitors arrived at Point Breeze by a 16-oar barge that Stephen Girard gave him. Visitors included Marshal Grouchy, the Lallemand brothers, Clausel, Bernard, Lefebvre-Desnouettes, and other exiled officers.[19]

There, they indulged their memories of the past, and they plotted while Joseph listened.

The Count's routine was at once simple and sociable. Frenchman that he was, he spent much time dining, often in the company of his visitors. He typically arose early and had coffee and toast served in his room at 7:00 a.m. He then read and wrote in his library until 11:00. Guests, who occupied the third floor, then joined him for a full breakfast in the dining room at a table that accommodated 24 people and that was set with large candelabras. Two fine consoles brought from Egypt stood against the walls. Lunch was served at 2:00 p.m., dinner at 8:00, and supper at 10:00. Between meals, there was no shortage of entertainment. There was conversation on historical and political topics, reading in the library, horseback and carriage riding about the grounds, and even hunting and fishing (Joseph imported from Europe rabbits, pheasants, and doves to stock the estate). Strolling about the gardens was also a favorite pastime for Joseph and his visitors. In good weather they would row about the lake and take lunch at a summer house on one of the artificial islands surrounded by tulip beds. The evenings often wound up in the billiard room, one of the most handsome in the house, with its green-bordered muslin curtains, mahogany furniture, and fine paintings.[20]

On Sundays, Joseph held an open house for Philadelphians, who ascended the Delaware by steamboat to his private dock. After admiring the marble statuary and furniture of the entrance hall, they were shown to the drawing room with its pier mirrors, Gobelin tapestries, bronzes, and candelabras. It contained two large marble fireplaces sent to Joseph by his uncle Cardinal Fesch. The walls were adorned with seascapes by Vernet, Neapolitan street scenes by Denis, and a series of family portraits—a life-size portrait of Napoleon in court robes, Joseph in the regalia he wore as king of Spain, and his wife, Queen Julie, and their two daughters. Beyond the drawing room was the *salon de bustes*, a gallery in which were displayed busts of various members of the Bonaparte family.[21]

Despite the grandeur of his lifestyle, Joseph was a good neighbor. He employed many of the local people in landscape maintenance and wood chopping, even to the point of "make-work" to help them financially. He was deservedly popular.[22]

In January 1820, his mansion burned because of a fire left unattended by a guest. The citizens of nearby Bordentown rallied and came to Joseph's aid, saving most of the valuables. Joseph was deeply touched that they returned everything they saved; not a jewel, not a franc was missing. Joseph rebuilt the mansion. Unfortunately, the house no longer stands, but the two pillars of its front entrance and the gatehouse remain, as do some of the trees and plantings from his time.[23]

Although his wife, Queen Julie, remained in Europe, Joseph's younger daughter, Charlotte, arrived for a visit on December 21, 1821, following the death earlier that year of Napoleon. She was a gifted landscapist and exhibited her paintings at the Academy of Fine Arts of Philadelphia. Joseph's elder daughter, Zénaïde, and her husband (and first cousin) Charles-Lucien Bonaparte also came to join him in September 1823, and they stayed for several years. Charles-Lucien was a noted ornithologist and collaborator of the Franco-American artist John James Audubon. He and Zénaïde bore Joseph a grandson while in Philadelphia. Joseph built them a house, called "Maison du Lac," close by Point Breeze. He connected the two houses with an underground brick tunnel, which for 200 years has been the subject of speculation about quick exits from royalist assassins and buried treasure but which in fact was probably designed for domestic convenience. Portions of the tunnel still exist.[24]

Although Joseph entertained Napoleon's restless, plotting generals as houseguests, he largely refrained from allowing himself to be drawn into their schemes. The most salient exceptions were recurrent schemes to liberate Napoleon from St. Helena. These perennial plots, some farcical, some serious, never failed to catch the attention of the Count de Survilliers. Many involved lightning-fast raids on St. Helena by privateers out of Argentina, Uruguay, or Brazil. One involved a Jamaican submarine. Of course, at the end of the day, all came to naught, but Joseph and Napoleon managed to maintain sporadic contact with one another through encoded smuggled letters. One letter from Joseph received by Napoleon on November 11, 1817, undeciphered to this day, reads as follows: "She's from July. He asks for news. High hopes. Written in Δ."[25]

In addition to more or less factual reports on Napoleon's health on St. Helena, wild reports occasionally circulated. On September 19,

1816, *L'Abeille Américaine* reported, "The corvette Reommee tells us that Bonaparte fled St. Helena and disembarked at the Cape of Good Hope where he enlisted 500,000 Hottentots and 20,000 dinghies. Nothing has yet transpired as to the point of these immense preparations."[26]

Not all was plotting, however. Romance blossomed quickly. The November 8, 1817, issue of the *National Intelligencer* reported the following marriage:

> Mrd: at Phil, on October 28, by Rev Mr. Carr, at the residence of Stephen Girard, Gen. Henry Lallemand, to Miss Harriet Girard, niece of Stephen Girard. There were present, Messrs. Cte de Survilliers, Mrshl de Grouchy & Son, Genrls Vandamme & Chas Lallemand, sen, & family & friends.

And there were lighthearted moments as well. The Philadelphia-based coterie of Napoleonic exiles found themselves in New York for the wedding of another one of their number. Present were the Count de Survilliers, Marshal Grouchy, Generals Renaud St. Jean d'Angély, Vandamme, Lefebvre-Desnouettes, Lallemand, and others. As reported by the sole American present, Fitz-Greene Hallock, Joseph conversed freely and easily, referring to his former position as "Quand j'étais roi d'Espagne" ("When I was king of Spain"). As the evening went on, the celebration became raucous. The former king of Spain fashioned a trumpet out of a newspaper and blew on it. Marshal Grouchy sang songs, with all present joining in the chorus. The former cavalry general Lallemand hopped about on all fours with a four-year-old boy on his back. Another veteran general of Waterloo offered an impersonation of a stuttering French soldier.[27]

The September 5, 1816, edition of *L'Abeille Américaine* summed up its editor's contented view of the United States after recounting all the manifold unhappinesses plaguing the European powers: "The United States—Continuation of abundance;—of peace and of justice;—of tolerance;—of liberty;—of equality."[28]

Throughout his time in America, Joseph devoted considerable attention to the administration of his fortune and to the support of his far-flung family. To judge from his extant letters, his principal banker was William

Bayard Jr. of LeRoy, Bayard & Cie. of New York, to whom he wrote regularly in French with instructions. Bayard was of French Huguenot descent and a close friend of Alexander Hamilton, who died in his house after his fateful duel. Onward instructions were conveyed to Hope & Co. in Amsterdam, which handled his European affairs. Hope & Co. was a Scots-owned Dutch firm that financed Quaker emigration to Pennsylvania as well as the slave trade. Occasionally, he had dealings with Jacques Laffitte in Paris and with Stephen Girard in Philadelphia, with the latter seeming to handle his local finances. As has already been seen, he used Carret as his purchasing agent early on to provide anonymity. However, Carret was still in his employment as late as 1825, when he sent him to London to sell some of his diamonds and one of his Rubens paintings.[29] Joseph offered to use his diamonds as collateral for a loan on at least one occasion.[30] He instructed LeRoy, Bayard to pay Madame Mère at Rome $4,000 (also described as "quatre milles piastres fortes") each year toward her upkeep.[31]

Lafayette visited and dined with Joseph at Point Breeze in September 1824 on his triumphal tour of the United States. Before dinner, the two men met privately in Joseph's study. According to Charles Jared Ingersoll, who was well placed to know, Lafayette expressed regret over his role in restoring the Bourbons and tried to interest Joseph in a scheme to place Napoleon's son, the king of Rome, on the throne of France if Joseph would bankroll it with 2 million francs. Although Joseph was a dedicated advocate of his nephew's claim to the throne, he was less than convinced of the prospects for a Liberal–Bonapartist alliance and declined.

Like all the Bonaparte brothers, Joseph took a mistress: a young, French-speaking Quaker girl named Annette Savage. She was a dark-eyed beauty. She and her mother conducted a small dry-goods shop in Philadelphia, where Joseph reputedly met her while she sold him suspenders over the counter. She was born in 1800, and her family roots were in New Kent County, Virginia. She supposedly was a descendant of Pocahontas. In taking Annette as his mistress, Joseph was following a long-established pattern of behavior, especially of the two eldest Bonaparte brothers. Napoleon's first love was Desirée Clary, the sister of Joseph's wife, Julie; she rejected Napoleon and married Count Bernadotte. In the ensuing years, Napoleon had at least 21 mistresses while married to Josephine and Marie Louise of Austria.[32] Joseph also had a fondness for pretty women. Before leaving Europe, he counted among his mistresses in 1814 the Marquesa de Montehermoso and the Comtesse Saint-Jean d'Angély, the wife of a Bonaparte intimate who was soon to be exiled in Philadelphia. Joseph's personal life became even more complicated the same year when he turned his attentions to Napoleon's wife, the empress Marie Louise, while his brother was on campaign desperately fighting to save his throne from invading Prussians and Russians. Napoleon got wind of his brother's amorous advances and admonished his wife to hold Joseph at a distance and not receive him when alone.[33] Life was complicated indeed.

For a time, Joseph visited Annette in the city of Philadelphia, but he later installed her at Point Breeze. Philadelphia society (of which Joseph was fond) disapproved, and so Joseph looked around for another solution. He rented her an estate called Bow Hill near Trenton, New Jersey, and not far from Point Breeze. The house still stands.

Annette's room at Bow Hill contained a secret door through which Joseph allegedly used to enter (why he or she needed a secret door when everyone knew of the relationship is a bit puzzling). On one of her windowpanes facing the Delaware River, the statement "God is love" stands to this day scratched with a diamond. The tradition is that it was her work. Annette, with the help of Joseph's Hungarian bodyguard, planted the field of daffodils that still graces the sweep from Bow Hill to the Delaware River.

At the time, Bow Hill was somewhat isolated, which was no doubt Joseph's intention, and Annette was not invited to his salon at Point Breeze. Trenton society followed the lead of Philadelphia, and very few if any of the ladies of the city called on her. Stung by the ostracism, she made several pitiful attempts to enter the charmed circle, but the only attentions paid her were from the wives of the followers of the Bonaparte fortunes.

Annette in time bore Joseph two daughters, Pauline Anne and Catharine Charlotte. There is a lovely extant portrait of her with their two daughters (illustration 7). Pauline tragically was killed as a small child by a falling flowerpot, but Catharine Charlotte survived, grew to womanhood, and married an American named Zebulon Howell Benton. They had children. Later in life, she went to France and successfully prevailed on Napoleon III to legalize her mother's union with his uncle and present her to the French court as his cousin.

For her part, Annette Savage lived at Bow Hill until 1822, when she moved to Joseph's estate in upstate New York, where she was always addressed as "Madame Bonaparte."[34] Following Joseph's return to Europe in 1832 and with no evident prospect of his return, she married a Frenchman, Joseph de la Foille, whom she had met earlier at Joseph's estate in New York. Her later years were attended by straitened circumstances, and in the early 1840s, when Joseph was back in Europe, she, aging and "grown vicious,"[35] threatened to publish her memoirs if Joseph did not pay her $20,000. "That is one devil of a woman!!!" Maillard wrote in his diary. In the end, Joseph settled with her.[36] She once again kept a dry-goods store before dying in 1865 in Watertown, New York, forgotten by the world.

About the time that Annette Savage moved to upstate New York Joseph also had an affair with Emilie Lacoste, the young wife of a French Caribbean planter named Félix Lacoste. Earlier, following a visit to Point Breeze, Lacoste returned to the Caribbean, allowing his wife to tarry as a companion for Charlotte and Zénaïde. In 1823, Charlotte painted a portrait of Emilie Lacoste that is now in the possession of the Philadelphia Atheneum. Joseph was likely the father of Emilie's twin sons, born on March 22, 1825. One son, Félix-Joseph, survived.

Joseph remained at Point Breeze, with summer visits to his lands in upstate New York, until 1832, when he learned of the serious illness of his nephew the king of Rome. He sailed for England to try to join him. There, he learned of his tragic death at age 21. Joseph remained in England for five years, until 1837, when he returned to Point Breeze. He remained there two more years until he received permission to take up residence in Genoa. He stayed briefly in Genoa but then at long last rejoined his wife and daughters in Florence. His daughter Charlotte died in 1839, and he suffered a severe stroke in 1840. Joseph died in Florence in the company of his family, including his wife and his brothers Louis and Jérôme, on July 28, 1844, at the age of 76. In his will Joseph stated accurately, "I possess in America Real Estate, Personal Property and Invested Capital." He then proceeded to provide generous legacies of all three types of property to his servants, friends, and family members, including, in the case of several people to whom he was close, his shareholdings in American companies.

A final vignette from the life of Joseph Bonaparte in the United States epitomizes the man. In 1819 he traveled as a private citizen to Washington. While there, he made a detour to visit Mount Vernon, some 16 miles away, to pay homage to the home and tomb of George Washington. Along the way he recounted to his companions the solemn ceremonies Napoleon had ordered in mourning the death of America's first president. At Washington's tomb the former king of Spain, now a republican, plucked a flower and carefully folded it into his wallet.[37] Joseph's acquired admiration for Washington was profound.

Marshal Grouchy's American sojourn differed from Joseph Bona-parte's for at least three reasons. First, he did not expect to stay long, and he constantly considered moving on to the Low Countries. However, neither of those plans succeeded. Second, and perhaps most important, he hoped to obtain a royal pardon and for that reason tried to maintain a low profile while in the United States. He was said to be irritated when American newspapers reported his presence at the wedding of Henri Lallemand and Stephen Girard's niece because it linked him with prominent anti-Bourbon exiles. As time wore on with no reprieve in sight, he sent for his two sons Colonel Alphonse Grouchy and Lieutenant Victor Grouchy, who joined him in May 1817. His intent was that they stay with him for up to a year while he awaited his pardon. Third, while in the United States, Marshal Grouchy devoted considerable time to penning apologias for his conduct at Waterloo, which came under increasing criticism not only by other generals but also by Napoleon himself in exile. In effect, Grouchy spent countless hours refighting the Battle of Waterloo over and over again—on paper. Notably, Joseph Bonaparte did not join in this criticism of Grouchy, and the two remained on close personal terms.

The May 16, 1816, edition of *L'Abeille Américaine* contains a report titled "Homage to Persecuted Merit," which provides a unique glimpse into the life of Grouchy and his fellow exiles in Philadelphia at this time:

> A well attended reunion of Frenchmen, citizens of Philadelphia, would give to the Illustrious Leaders that the political revolutions of their country forced to find an asylum among us, a witness of the respect and of the esteem that they feel for these distinguished persons, and that they share with all their co-citizens, were given a fete, Tuesday, the 2nd of this month in the new hall of the French Masons, for Messieurs the Marshal Count de Grouchy, Clausel and Lefebvre-Desnouettes. The Count Regnaud de Saint-Jean d'Angély, his son and other principal American citizens of this town attended by invitation. At five o'clock, when everyone sat down at the table, there were around 80 people. They were served with as much delicacy and fuss as sumptuousness. Mr. Du Ponceau [Étienne Duponceau, president of the prestigious American Philosophical Society in Philadelphia] officiated as President and Mr. Dubarry [Jean-Marie Dubarry, a Domingan merchant] as Vice President.
>
> At dessert they drank the following toasts:
>
> 1. The United States of America.
>
> 2. France, our former country, happy on the inside, powerful on the outside.
>
> 3. The perpetual union between America and France.
>
> 4. The independence of nations, and their defenders, in the two worlds.
>
> 5. To the memory of Washington, the model citizen warrior.
>
> 6. The brave who obeyed the first obligation of a citizen, in defending all the land of their country. Their imperishable glory will go down through the centuries.
>
> 7. The American Army and Navy. Their attempted blows are blows of masters.
>
> 8. Liberal ideas. May they be the rule of conduct for all governments! . . .

12. The Country [France]. Sometimes ungrateful but always dear.

13. The consoling sex [women]. . . .

Among the other toasts that were drunk, one recalls with enthusiasm that of Mr. Charles J. Ingersoll, Attorney General of Pennsylvania. We will give it in English, for fear it will lose in translation, "The French Citizens of Philadelphia, excellent members of an exemplary community." It is sweet to receive the kiss of a respectable citizen. . . . We would wish that the limits of this journal would permit us to give the other toasts . . . such as that of Mr. Regnaud de Saint-Jean d'Angély: "To liberty, to prosperity, to the glory of American hospitality. May all the French refugees of all epochs, keep forever the memory of the generous asylum they have received here!"

. . . The French love to sing . . . during the intervals between toasts there were sung couplets in one or the other language. One volunteer from the Dupont camp, animated by the republican spirit, . . . sang the famous hymn The Marseillaise, which often accompanied the French to victory. This song will always be in honor among us [in fact, Napoleon discouraged it], where it recalls nothing other than the noble sentiment of independence. We are strangers to the parties who have divided France, and we desire northing more than to see her happy under the government that best suits her. . . . It is only fitting that a republican song be sung in a republican country.[38]

Grouchy spent the bulk of his time in Philadelphia, where he purchased a house,[39] but he also led a somewhat peripatetic existence. Armed with the letter of introduction from Lafayette, in 1816 he set out with one of his sons for Monticello to call on Jefferson. Unlike the case of Madison and Joseph Bonaparte, Jefferson was willing to receive him at Monticello: "Your name has been too well-known in the history of the times, and your merit too much acknowledged by all, not to promise me great pleasure in making your acquaintance."[40] However, the illness of one of Grouchy's sons forced him to abort the trip but not before meeting with Jefferson's granddaughter Ellen W. Randolph in Washington, D.C.

Grouchy spent Christmas 1816 with Joseph Bonaparte at Point Breeze, from which he wrote Mrs. William Lee, who was then visiting Trenton, New Jersey, that she should stop by Bordentown en route back to Philadelphia so that he might accompany her and so she could meet the king of Spain, who would be "satisfied and happy to meet and get to know one of the Americans [meaning Mrs. Lee] whose heart is most French."[41]

Grouchy also visited property he purchased in upstate New York near that of Joseph Bonaparte, and he frequently visited his friend Eleuthère Du Pont de Nemours in Wilmington, Delaware. While there in 1818, a horrific explosion wracked the Hagley gunpowder works, killing 30 people. Grouchy and his son Victor were on the scene at the time and immediately threw themselves into the emergency response. In all, Grouchy traveled, made American friends, and enjoyed the pleasures of life in the New World, including hunting.[42]

Grouchy was surprised to find that he was not the first Grouchy in America. While in Philadelphia, he and his son Alphonse met a John de Grouchy from Northumberland, Pennsylvania, who had earlier emigrated from England. After comparing family stories and crests, which were identical, the two families concluded that they were indeed distantly related in that the English de Grouchy's ancestors also hailed from Normandy and had accompanied William the Conqueror in his invasion of England while Marshal Grouchy's ancestors had stayed home. On June 10, 1817, Alphonse wrote from Northumberland to this mother in amazement at this "rather extraordinary" encounter.[43]

Although joined by his two sons, Grouchy, like Joseph, had fled, leaving his wife behind. This separation did not prevent "Le Maréchal" from engaging in a frequent and warm correspondence with his wife, "La Maréchale." The letters show a man missing Europe (he often thought of seeking refuge in the Low Countries) and clearly set on his rehabilitation and restitution. Writing to his wife from Philadelphia on September 10, 1817, Grouchy complained of the unhappiness of his son Victor in exile: "Victor not having at all hidden how bored he is in Philadelphia, lacking the facility and real will to learn English and having few of the attractions for society in general and that of this city in particular which is lacking in charm, when ones does not speak the language fluently."[44]

Three weeks later, on October 4, he wrote his wife, "Assuredly, I was well served not to leave for Holland, if that which is announced in the papers is true, that the French who sought and found asylum there up to now have been exposed to new persecutions and obliged to leave."[45]

Following this spell of ennui and uncertainty, Grouchy devised a plan to send his son Alphonse, who had been in America for one year, back to Europe to advocate for his rehabilitation with the Bourbons. He left in the spring of 1817 and arrived in France in early May. Grouchy wrote to his wife almost a year later on April 18, 1818, "My friend, in sending my children to Europe, my principal object is to utilize the perfect good will and the clear devotion of Alphonse for me to reopen, if it is possible, the doors of France: this is the important matter."[46]

Alphonse did as he was bidden, and Grouchy began a correspondence with his son. On November 10, 1818, he wrote Alphonse from Philadelphia thanking him for his efforts on his behalf and acknowledging the hope that he might be able to return to France the following spring. He continued, "I also am happy that the set of your overtures were satisfactory (which I pray that you continue), [with] the magnanimous sentiments of the Duke d'Angoulême [nephew of King Louis XVIII] and with the thought that my separation from all the persons who are dear to me in Europe will not be forever." In the same letter, he reported, "General Clausel is here, as well as General Desnouettes. The one and the other have come to buy some Negroes in Virginia. The first does not sing the praises of the country he inhabits, the second speaks completely differently. Clausel is staying at my house, he is always a loyal friend; I would be content if I kept him here all winter, but he does not have the means."[47]

Grouchy's hopes of an early return were not rewarded, and he continued to languish in Philadelphia. On December 3, 1819, he wrote to Alphonse,

One does not find me in Belgium because I would be under a more active and immediate surveillance than is exercised against me in the United States . . . . I have thus decided to stay in the United States awhile longer. . . . In waiting, I prefer to vegetate in Philadelphia, where I am established and where I have a part of the *comforts* of life [emphasis in the original]. . . . Moreover I would like to leave now but could not, M. [Hyde] de Neuville not having received to date any order as to expediting the passports about which you do not cease speaking to me about. Finally, Stephen Girard sends no ships directly from Philadelphia to Amsterdam or to Anvers; he sends them from here to Charleston, where they take on cargoes of cotton and from which they are sent to one or the other of these two ports. Currently there is no chance for Holland and there will not be until the spring.[48]

Finally, on November 24, 1819, Grouchy's long-suffering patience and the three-year-long indefatigable efforts of Alphonse (and the Duke d'Angoulême) paid off. The king issued an ordinance opening the doors of France to Marshal Grouchy and restoring to him all the "rights, titles, grades and honors" he held as of March 19, 1815. Grouchy learned of his amnesty in January 1820 in a letter from Alphonse. He departed Philadelphia for France in May 1820. However, another 10 years were to pass before King Louis Philippe was to restore his Marshal's baton and his seat in the Chamber of Peers. Like his friend Lafayette, he occupied an ambiguous position in French society: at once distrusted by the royalists as a perceived class traitor who joined the Revolution and the Bonapartes and criticized by the veterans of the Grande Armée as absent and missing at Waterloo (notwithstanding his vigorous efforts to defend his reputation). However, Grouchy retained an abiding affection for his friends in America and Philadelphia in particular. He continued to exchange letters with Charles Jared Ingersoll, writing from Paris on September 4, 1821, to thank him for "the memory of all the regards and proofs of friendship with which you surrounded me during my stay in the United States" and asking to be remembered to "all the social, political and literary circles of that city [Philadelphia]."[49]

Grouchy died in France in 1847.

Not all of the émigrés settled permanently in the Philadelphia area. A good example would be Pierre-Francois Réal, the former police chief. Although he sojourned briefly in Philadelphia and was received by Joseph Bonaparte at Point Breeze, he decided to settle permanently in upstate New York near the St. Lawrence River and lands owned by Joseph Bonaparte. Although the French government pardoned him in 1818 and allowed him to return to France, he instead chose to stay in America. On his property at Cape Vincent near the Canadian border, he built a most singular dwelling known as the "cup and saucer" house because its octagonal shape and construction resembled an inverted teacup. The home, in its luxury and expression of the utopian tastes of its individual owner, echoed Point Breeze. Belowground, it contained a well-stocked wine cellar, and on the ground level, a spacious veranda ran along all sides. The first floor, on which Réal entertained, contained oil portraits of Napoleon and his marshals, richly sculpted mantelpieces, silver candelabras, a first-class library, and even a Stradivarius violin. The second floor boasted numerous smaller rooms separated by wheeled panels that could be moved at will to create spaces of varying size. The "cup" part of the house contained a laboratory where Réal tinkered and a sort of sanctuary stocked with Napoleonic relics. Réal collected about him a Professor Pigeon, who was an astronomer with a world-class set of French-made instruments, and an entourage of wandering Bonapartists. It was perhaps only fitting that Réal refused to wear a hat as long as Napoleon remained in exile.[50]

Two other arrivals from France caught the attention of *L'Abeille Américaine* in the first year of the émigré colony in Philadelphia.

The first was Jean-Guillaume Baron Hyde de Neuville, who arrived in New York on June 17, 1816. The June 20 issue of the paper reported that on "Saturday afternoon the French frigate Euridice, commanded by Captain Menard, arrived from Brest" and that Hyde de Neuville was aboard as "[e]nvoy extraordinary and minister plenipotentiary of France to the United States of America." The article noted that on its arrival, the ship was given a 17-gun salute, which was returned in kind. In the ensuing years, Hyde de Neuville was to prove to be a veritable Inspector Javert to the errant Jean Valjeans of the empire in America.

The second, dramatically reported on August 8, 1816, was the August 2 arrival in New York of William Lee from Bordeaux:

> If his family and friends rejoice on his return, the regrets of the good Frenchmen who accompany him and follow him in the New World [*sic*]. If some noble descendants of the Goths and the Vandals excite against him a riot of bipeds ... it is by his courage to beat back the seditious in their endeavors. He will render justice to this immense majority of citizens, who labor under the chains forged in the English Ministry and riveted together by a million jailers under the orders of Wellington.[51]

Both were to be intimately bound up in the next part of the story of the French in America.

How did Americans, Philadelphians in particular, react to the French refugees in their midst? The answer is nuanced. At a certain level, it depended on the Americans' domestic politics. Federalists remained skeptical of both France and anyone associated with the imperial trappings of Napoleon. In contrast, the Democrat-Republicans tended to be fascinated by them. The royalist French minister in Washington, Hyde de Neuville, wrote Paris of the Bonapartists' reception in the United States: "Democrats look on our rebel refuges as martyrs. Bonaparte, in spite of his despotism, remains in their eyes a man of the Revolution." He then quoted a U.S. newspaper that called Napoleon "a man who asserted himself among the sons of democracy, who marched against the status quo of Europe and did not leave a single monarch by divine right on the throne."[52]

That was at the partisan level. The official U.S. position aimed at a more principled reaction and in fact was probably shared by the majority of Americans and even generally Francophile Philadelphians. Setting aside their fascination with the novelty of faux nobility,[53] as evidenced by the weekly levees Philadelphians attended at Point Breeze, they tended to adopt a live-and-let-live attitude. Consistent with President Madison's treatment of Joseph Bonaparte, they treated them as they would treat any other new arrival to American shores: welcoming, cordial, and hopeful of their integration into the American fabric as framed by the rights and duties of citizenship broadly construed.

The only problem was that some of them found themselves incapable of integration.

CHAPTER 6

The Altruistic Adventurers

MANY OF THE BONAPARTIST ÉMIGRÉS WERE MILITARY MEN WHO HAD known no life other than fighting. Often of humble origins and elevated through a combination of their own merit, luck, and the favor of the emperor, many had fought all over Europe for more than two decades. It was therefore hardly surprising that many of the French refugees did not envisage the United States as a place to which to emigrate permanently[1] or otherwise realize that "they were aware of the America myth but not acquainted with American reality."[2]

Talleyrand, who had sojourned in the United States in the 1790s, put it another way: "The American's ways make him an Englishman, attached to England with bonds that no declaration or recognition of independence can sever."[3]

As a result, many of the Bonapartist refugees failed to integrate into American life and instead embarked on a series of adventures, one benign, two less than benign, that tested their welcome.

The first venture, put simply, was to establish a francophone colony for the cultivation of vineyards and olive trees on the Tombigbee River in the wilds of the Territory of Alabama. Needless to say, it did not work out.

This was not the first attempt at a French-speaking utopian community in the United States. Several other previous attempts dating to the 1790s had come to naught. One, called Azilum, was a farming town planted on the far northern reaches of the Susquehanna River in what was then Pennsylvania wilderness. Despite great pretensions, it failed.[4] Another, the 500-person Gallipolis (or "French Town") Colony located on the western bank of the Ohio River adjacent to what is now West

Virginia, was led by an Alsatian nobleman who was a member of the National Assembly. It failed largely because of faulty land titles and the inability of its venturers, many of whom were French aristocrats fleeing the Revolution, to farm. Most of its settlers eventually dispersed to other Anglo settlements.[5]

The exact impetus for what became known as the Society for the Cultivation of the Vine and Olive[6] is shrouded in mystery. However, it started in Philadelphia. As early as August 22, 1816, *L'Abeille Américaine* ran an unsigned letter exhorting the émigrés to band together to form their own community far from the corruptions of urban life. After dutifully thanking the United States for its hospitality, the article warned that the exiles would lapse into traditional French habits of "inconstancy" and "turbulence" if they did not establish their own "homeland to cherish." In a rhapsody of Rousseauian and Jeffersonian themes on the virtues of a return to nature and of the agricultural life, the letter then suggested that the exiles go "hand in hand, into a mild region to found a new Thebaide" (an area of Egypt famed for its Christian monastic retreats) in order to "prove themselves excellent citizens of a happy republic." The author of the entreaty recommended the vast, thinly populated area between the Ohio, Mississippi, and Natchez rivers as being fertile, temperate, and healthy.[7]

It is difficult to conjecture who planted this seed and at the same time sought anonymity. Jean-Simon Chaudron, the publisher of *L'Abeille Américaine*, subsequently expanded on the theme and allowed his publication to be used as a propaganda tool for the colony by fully disclosed authors. Chaudron or another thought leader among the exile community possibly might have been the author. There is no evidence that Joseph Bonaparte was involved with formulating its conception or even would have been temperamentally inclined to do so. Marshal Grouchy, with his other preoccupations, would have been a most unlikely source. But there is one other distinct possibility. Although there is no conclusive evidence of its authorship by William Lee, it was published three weeks after his arrival in the United States. Moreover, Lee spent approximately one week in Philadelphia in August 1816, the month the letter was published.[8] He would have had a long transatlantic voyage on which to compose it. He wrote polemic pieces in fluent French, as demonstrated by his earlier book *Les États Unis et L'Angleterre.* He was actively involved in promoting French émigrés in the United States. He had knowledge of U.S. geography. His Jeffersonian politics were consistent with the themes the proposal embodied. In the past, he had objectively examined and noted in his writings—and was to do so later—French national characteristics akin to "turbulence." He had the motive to maintain anonymity because he was still employed by the Department of State and because of the adverse reaction to his recent book. And within months, he was vice president of the society advocating the colony.

In any event, the idea spread quickly, and by later summer to early autumn 1816 concrete steps were afoot to translate the dream into reality. The January 9, 1817, edition of *L'Abeille Américaine* reported, albeit belatedly, the minutes of an October meeting in Philadelphia of the "Colonial Society of French Emigrants," one of the predecessor names of the society. The meeting, whose exact date was not recorded in the report, was presided over by Garnier de Saintes and with Lee as vice president and Nicholas-Simon Parmentier as secretary. The secretary of the society noted a letter received from Joseph Lakanal, who was already ensconced on the banks of the Ohio in Kentucky. Lakanal wrote, "I pray you, my honorable friend, to inscribe me on the list of future citizens of Demopolis"—a reference to the planned colony and a name that in fact would be given to its first town. Warmed by the endorsement from such a notable figure "in literature and the sciences," the meeting directed its officers to respond to him with thanks. The minutes then recorded that Penières-Delors announced his imminent departure for the "South west" of the United States to scout out appropriate lands on which to settle the colony. The meeting endorsed his trip, pledged it support, and asked him to maintain a correspondence as much as possible with the society's bureau in Philadelphia, Lee in "Washington City," Lakanal, and Generals Lefebvre-Desnouettes and Henri Lallemand, "who are going to visit the same country." Importantly, the meeting then charged Lee as vice president of the society with approaching the federal land office in Washington to find appropriate lands for which it could "solicit a concession." It then resolved to set up a "permanent bureau" to draft any necessary documents. The bureau consisted of Garnier de Saintes, Lee, and three others.[9]

The organizers approached Joseph Bonaparte in October 1816 about participating, but he declined. A letter from the French consul in Philadelphia dated October 10 stated, "Monsieur Joseph Bonaparte was asked to take part, but he refused in order to stave off any suspicion of political ambitions."[10]

Plans nonetheless moved with alacrity from there. While Chaudron beat the drum of publicity with glowing and encouraging reports,[11] the society's permanent bureau organized itself, sorted through various territorial options for colonization, and launched a sophisticated lobbying campaign in Washington. The initial suggestion for a settlement on lands recently conquered from the Creek Indians near the Tombigbee River appears to have come from a Francophile resident of Louisville, Kentucky, and it was debated by the society at its January 2, 1817, meeting under the chairmanship of Vice President Lee (who by this time, having left the State Department, was an employee of the War Department). Advocates for the Tombigbee described it as a "healthy country, enjoying a temperate climate," accessible by land or sea and proximitous to the "great establishments of the Tennessee and New Orleans." They also noted that the Tombigbee was a navigable river that had already attracted the attention of the U.S. government.[12] The meeting concluded by resolving that Lee, acting in concert with other society officers, was to petition Congress for a grant of the Tombigbee lands and that "the Sage of Monticello shall be written requesting him to draw up the foundations of a social pact for the local regulation of our association."[13]

Thus, what had started as a vague private sector scheme to colonize the Ohio River valley quickly changed into stimulating a quasi-governmental plan to populate a remote and recently seized region. Drawing on his various connections, Lee immediately launched a multipronged lobbying effort in concert with other officers of the society aimed at the U.S. Congress to obtain a concession on the Tombigbee lands. In the waning days of the Madison administration, Lee personally approached not only the president but also Secretary of State James Monroe, the Francophile Speaker of the House Henry Clay, and even General Andrew Jackson, who had seized the land from the Creek Indians in 1814. He also drew on his relationship with Thomas Jefferson by facilitating a letter signed by two other officers of the society asking the Sage to draw up a constitution for the colony. Jefferson responded directly and solely to Lee and wisely declined the project on the grounds that peoples' laws should flow from themselves and not be imposed by a stranger and that the proposed colony was not to be a separate state. Still, Lee had piqued Jefferson's interest in the colony and opened the door for journalists to observe that the former president had been consulted, thereby linking the prestige of his name with the project.[14]

What ensued was remarkable by any measure. On February 10, 1817, the Senate Committee on Public Lands marked up and approved a bill to grant the Tombigbee lands to the society. The full Senate passed the bill by a large majority on February 21 and sent it to the House, which opened debate on it six days later. Despite opposition by Federalists, Speaker Clay shepherded the bill to passage on a largely party-line vote and sent it to the president for signature. On his last day in office, March 3, 1817, President Madison signed into law the resulting "[a]ct to set apart and dispose of certain public lands, for the encouragement of the cultivation of the vine and olive."

The grant was tantamount to a giveaway. Technically, the act allowed the society to choose four contiguous townships totaling 92,000 acres in the so-called Creek Cession, thus giving the society first choice of the best lands in the Cession before the holding of any public auction while at the same time exempting those chosen lands from laws applicable to public lands. Certain conditions applied, including attaining a minimum of 288 members in the society, limiting single holdings to no more than 640 acres, and cultivating a minimum percentage of the acreage in vines and olives pursuant to a contract to be negotiated with the secretary of the treasury (who coincidentally happened to be former U.S. minister to France William H. Crawford). Assuming these conditions were met, at the end of 14 years the society was to pay the government $2.00 per acre, or a total of $184,000, which was a bargain given land speculation in Alabama at the time. In addition, the society had the free use of the tracts for 14 years without having to pay anything.

Why did Congress do this? Setting aside motives of hospitality, compassion, and gratitude for French assistance during the Revolution, there undoubtedly were unspoken geopolitical reasons for making the concession. These included the desirability of solidifying the U.S. hold on Alabama and on westward expansion more generally, providing a bulwark on the ground against Spanish claims in a still-disputed border region, providing additional leverage for U.S. efforts to acquire Spanish West Florida, and bolstering U.S. control over and communications with nearby Mobile and New Orleans. The geopolitical factors were in fact intricate and complex.[15]

Still, one is left to wonder why normal westward expansion by Anglos during this period of "Alabama Fever" would not have sufficed to meet the above concerns and why Congress felt compelled to take special measures to favor a francophone colony that was not even thinking of following U.S. laws or being an integral part of the United States.

Indeed, the congressional act, rammed through in quick time in the dying days of an administration and with relatively little deliberation, wasted no time in attracting critical fire and not just from Federalists. The themes of the criticism were generally twofold: the French refugees were not cut out for taming the wilderness and why should the French get favored treatment from Congress over Americans? Thus, Boston's *Columbian Centinal* predicted that "something very different from fiddling, dancing and book reading" would be necessary to "subdue a wilderness." And *Niles' Weekly Register*, which initially supported the venture, changed its tune and archly observed, "Among the splendid fooleries which have at times amused a portion of the American people, as well as their representatives in congress, was that of granting, on most favorable terms, to certain emigrants from France, a large tract of land in the Alabama territory, to encourage the cultivation of the vine and olive."[16]

This criticism failed to deter the society. Potential settlers, many of them Domingan exiles, subscribed to its shares. Among the shareholders were Marshal Grouchy and his sons, the Lallemand brothers, Clausel and Lefebvre-Desnouettes, and a host of lesser-ranked military men and civilians like Lakanal. Although not shareholders, Réal and Vandamme were closely supportive.

None of this activity escaped the attention of the French minister in Washington, Jean-Guillaume Baron Hyde de Neuville. Although generally suspicious of the Napoleonic émigrés, he took a more restrained view of the society, seeing in it the potential for the implantation in the heart of America of French culture and values as well as a potential incubator for U.S.–French trade and an outlet for French exports. It may also have helped that it would have occupied the restless Bonapartists far, far away, where they could do little obvious harm.

In the wake of passage of the March 3 act and with Lee back in Washington working full-time for the War Department, Lefebvre-Desnouettes and Clausel effectively took charge of the society (Garnier de Saintes had left for Indiana). The vanguard of the settlement, headed by Parmentier, left Philadelphia for the Tombigbee in April 1818 aboard the chartered schooner *McDonough*. Their mission was to make a preliminary survey of the site of the settlement and prepare for the bulk of the settlers. The ship ran aground in Mobile Bay and had to be rescued. The passengers and cargo were saved, and, after being feted by the leaders of Mobile, they ascended the Tombigbee River with the help of a borrowed government barge.

By July they were at a place called White Bluffs, where they determined to lay out their township, to be called Demopolis—a name chosen earlier by Réal back in Philadelphia. They unpacked, laid out streets, and constructed log cabins. Government surveyors then arrived, who informed them that their new City of the People was not even within the lands granted by Congress. So they pulled up their stakes and moved inland, where they laid out a new town called Aigleville or Eagle Town.

It is perhaps notable that the society's first instinct was to lay out a town. Unlike the English and Scots-Irish who settled the frontier and whose first priority was to clear land and support families on often isolated farms, the French settlers wanted to found a metropolis about which they could gravitate.

In any event, by midsummer the advance party was able to report back to Philadelphia that the site had "fertility, healthfulness, and navigation." They were right on two points at least: the soil was rich and it was near a river. Its healthfulness was to prove quite another matter. The reports back were enough to convince Lefebvre-Desnouettes and Clausel that they could safely transport the main body of colonists to the Tombigbee.

They therefore contracted with various captains to transport the settlers to Mobile and thence upriver to the concession lands. They carried with them the plant stock of vines and olive trees imported from France to start the mandated cultivations. Lefebvre-Desnouettes and Clausel sailed on August 27, 1817, accompanied by Marshal Grouchy's younger son Victor, a handful of other former military officers, and some 30 German indentured servants whose labor the society had purchased. A correspondent reported their departure thus to *L'Abeille Américaine*: "I saw yesterday more than thirty French engineers, among whom were the Generals Clausel and Lefebvre-Desnouettes, preparing to leave the fortunate shores of the Delaware, to be transported on far and uninhabited rivers of Tombigbee, where a virgin land, and liberty awaits them." The correspondent went on to extol the "Fertility, Healthiness and Navigability" of the new lands.[17]

L'Abeille Américaine ran a series of lengthy discourses on the settlement by Charles Lallemand, who had newly arrived in Philadelphia and had involved himself in the society but had never seen (and was never to see) the Tombigbee. They were puff pieces designed to encourage subscriptions.[18]

The reality on the ground was far different than what was presented in the pages of the newspaper back in Philadelphia. Lefebvre-Desnouettes took up residence on the grant, but Clausel decided that he preferred to reside near Mobile, where he lived with a mulatto mistress, ran a store, and raised staple crops to sustain the colony upriver. It appears that Clausel at least at one point returned temporarily to Philadelphia, as evidenced by a November 11, 1818, letter he wrote from there.[19]

The settlers laboriously cleared the forests and planted the vines and olive trees, which withered and died in the Alabama climate. Flooding and sickness ravaged the colony. The lack of infrastructure, high cost of imported necessities, and lack of a large labor pool all took their toll on the colony. The shortage of workers was particularly acute, with what white labor they had commanding wages so high that the situation threatened the economic viability of the colony. The planters turned to slaves to try to ameliorate the situation, but they represented a significant capital investment and were hard to come by in the booming Alabama economy of the time.

The sense of isolation is hard to imagine. Prior to the advent of steamships, barges were dragged upriver from Mobile, a tedious process taking up to 25 days. The alternative was to travel overland through thick forests (there were no roads worthy of the name) and across unbridged streams that had to be forded—a dangerous and unpleasant journey.

The more important members of the society began to realize the hopelessness of making a living on small tracts of land in the wilderness. Only Lefebvre-Desnouettes made any significant permanent settlement there. He was by far the largest single landholder, with about 500 acres. In addition to his main dwelling, he built a log cabin "sanctuary" in which he reportedly kept a large bronze statue of Napoleon and swords and pistols he had taken in battle and with the walls draped in the tricolor.

Perhaps more typical of the domestic situation is the picture presented by Garnier de Saintes, who, though at one time president of the society, settled at New Albany, Indiana, opposite Louisville on the Ohio River:

A log cabin, in rather poor condition, was the dwelling of the former representative of the people. We knocked at the door of a sort of shop, for he sells whisky, rum, and cigars for a living. A little boy opened and led us into the kitchen—that is, the bedroom, livingroom, and in short the only room of the house. Monsieur Garnier came to greet us with a spoon in one hand and a notebook in the other. He does his own cooking and, at the same time, he is writing a book. He received us with a cordiality that hardly exists nowadays outside a novel, and which, in view of his situation, we especially appreciated. . . . Without any formal invitation to dinner, he killed and plucked two chickens and made them into a stew, doubled the beans, already on the stove, made a salad, and then asked us to sit down at his table. We ate with a good appetite, and I can assure you that our conversation was gayer than could have been hoped under the humble roof of an exile's log cabin. After dinner, I asked Monsieur Garnier to read a few pages from his book. The title is Emerides, or Evenings with Socrates.[20]

Others who made the journey included the regicide Penières-Delors, who maintained a small place just outside the concessional lands. Jean-Simon Chaudron, the publisher of *L'Abeille Américaine*, eventually shut down his printing press and made the move with his family, though they stayed only a short while before moving to Mobile, where he died in 1846. Henri Lallemand and Clausel made settlements only through lessees. The Grouchys, Charles Lallemand, Galabert, and others, though shareholders, never settled, and their claims lapsed. For all his initial enthusiasm, the same applied to Lakanal. By 1822, only about 70 of the original grantees (out of 347) had made permanent establishments on the concession.[21] Of these, more than 20 percent had died by 1825.[22]

In addition to the utter impossibility of cultivating vines and olive trees in the heat and humidity of Alabama, the surveys of the concessional lands were so imperfect that no one could be certain of his title. Although some continued to eke out a meager existence, most of the settlers gave up and repaired to Mobile, where they formed a small French community. By 1830 all the Bonapartists were gone.

The fates of the principal Napoleonic refugees who migrated to the colony were mixed. Clausel received a pardon from the Bourbons in 1820 and, leaving his mulatto mistress, promptly returned to France. He was restored to the general officers' active list, elected as a legislative deputy, and, with the accession of Louis Philippe in 1830, was appointed general in chief of the Army of Africa, in which capacity he directed the French conquest of Algeria, resulting in his being bestowed the baton of a marshal of France. He died, much honored, in 1842.

In contrast, Garnier de Saintes drowned with his son in an 1818 steamboat accident on the Mississippi River. Similarly, Penières-Delors fell to yellow fever in 1821.

Perhaps most poignant was the fate of Lefebvre-Desnouettes. He addressed regular pleas for clemency to Hyde de Neuville and even met with him on a trip to Washington to beg for a pardon. In September 1818 Lefebvre-Desnouettes and Clausel went to Washington to try to renegotiate their contracts. The most prominent citizens of the capital welcomed them, and they even received an audience with President Monroe and dined with Secretary of War John C. Calhoun. Lefebvre-Desnouettes called on the French minister, Hyde de Neuville, to seek a pardon and reentry to France. Although reportedly charmed by Lefebvre-Desnouettes personally, Hyde de Neuville demurred on the grounds of the seriousness of his actions during the Hundred Days. He nonetheless quietly advocated for his pardon in the ensuing years. *L'Abeille Américaine*, in reporting their warm reception in Washington, took up the cause: "We cannot believe the French government will prolong the exile of men who are a credit not only to France but to the times in which we live. Until there is a general amnesty for men of their caliber, the Bourbon dynasty will appear to be a tool of the British Cabinet."[23]

Although the French minister was sympathetic and made representations on his behalf, Paris was dilatory. Lefebvre-Desnouettes's wife, the sister of the French banker Jacques Laffitte, worked the issue tirelessly from France. Meanwhile, Lefebvre-Desnouettes waited in an increasing state of melancholia on his concession lands, apart from his wife and a young daughter whom he had never seen. In 1822, it appeared that the efforts of Hyde de Neuville and his wife were about to bear fruit and that he could soon return to France. He grew a beard and using a false name boarded the ironically named *Albion* bound for Belgium via Liverpool. The ship wrecked in a storm off Kinsale, Ireland, and he drowned at age 47. His widow erected an odd sugarloaf-shaped monument to him at Le Havre (figure 6.1), and there he is buried.

Most of the Tombigbee lands eventually were sold to Anglo planters who converted them to slave-based cotton production. Long before the Vine and Olive colony issued its last whimpering breath, Philadelphia had resumed its status as the hub of activity of the exiled Bonapartists, with Joseph Bonaparte the center of attention and the font of largesse.

But the story was not so simple. Largely lost in the sweep of events was the fact that certain prominent Bonapartists in Philadelphia had pledged their claims to bankers in that city for significant ready cash loans and had no intention of settling in Alabama. Chief among these was Charles Lallemand, who at the time wrote to his brother Henri, "I have more ambition than can be gratified by the colony upon the Tombigbee."[24]

Thus begins the second and less benign chapter of French adventures in America. Simultaneous with the moves to launch the Society of the

Vine and Olive in the second half of 1817, two other initiatives were afoot that would have profound effects on the community of Bonapartist émigrés in America. The first was a plot to place Joseph Bonaparte on the throne of Mexico. The second was an armed incursion into Texas. Needless to say, neither of these moves turned out well either.

Figure 6.1.   Lefebvre-Desnouettes Monument, Le Havre, France. WIKIMEDIA COMMONS.

CHAPTER 7

The Alarming Adventurers

JOHN QUINCY ADAMS WAS SWORN IN AS SECRETARY OF STATE UNDER
President James Monroe on September 22, 1817. Adams was one of the
most qualified persons ever to hold the office of secretary of state. The
oldest son of President John Adams, as a young man he accompanied
his father on official missions to France and the Netherlands, attended
Leiden University, and graduated from Harvard. He spoke French,
Dutch, German, Latin, and Greek. He went on to become, in succession,
the U.S. minister to the Netherlands, Portugal, Prussia, and Russia. He
also negotiated the Treaty of Ghent ending the War of 1812 and served
as the U.S. minister to Great Britain.

At the time he took office, the Department of State consisted of five
whitewashed rooms on the second floor and four rooms in the attic of
the recently rebuilt Public Buildings just to the west of the White House.
The British had burned them in 1814 for good measure after torching
the President's Mansion. Together, they housed the dozen personnel—
clerks, assistants, and messengers—who made up the entire staff of the
Department of State, which shared the building with the War and Navy
departments.

On his first day in office the intelligent Adams, with his high forehead
and sharp Roman nose, immediately found himself inundated by paperwork and callers ("There was a multitude of Letters and despatches which
have been laying for me some time on the table of the Office," Adams
wrote in his diary later that day).[1] His first day in office saw him receive,
among others, none other than William Lee, who called on him for an
unrecorded purpose and who returned the following day to ask him to hire

the son of a colleague from Bordeaux. On the afternoon of his first day in office Adams also received courtesy calls from the resident diplomatic corps, including the French minister to Washington, Hyde de Neuville.[2]

The following day, September 23, as Adams began to tackle the backlog of correspondence piled on his table, he read with alarm a letter from Hyde de Neuville. He recorded in his diary for that day, "Began the morning by making a draft of a Letter to Hyde de Neuville, in answer to a communication from him to the Department of State, concerning a project for invading Mexico from the United States, and declaring Joseph Buonaparte king of Spain and the Indies." Evidently he found the drafting difficult, for he recorded that later in the day he "had much conversation with Mr. Rush [former attorney general and acting secretary of state Richard Rush] on the answers to be returned to the French and Spanish Ministers, and with him visited Mr. Hyde de Neuville."[3] The fact that the new secretary of state, accompanied by his predecessor, would on his first full day in office break protocol and leave the department to meet with the French minister at his legation attests to the seriousness with which he viewed the message. Rush in fact was familiar with the content of Hyde de Neuville's *démarche* because the French minister had presented it to him some days previously, but he had held it pending the arrival of Adams, to whom he was only too glad to hand it off.

The set of documents that the three men had before them had been intercepted by Hyde de Neuville's network of spies. The French minister had long had Joseph Bonaparte under surveillance, as well as many of the principal Bonapartist refugees, such as Lefebvre-Desnouettes, Clausel, and the Lallemand brothers. Hyde de Neuville's primary concern was any effort to free Napoleon from his exile on St. Helena. Both the foreign ministry in Paris and the new French minister in Washington viewed the United States as a potential breeding ground for plots to liberate the former emperor. A provision in his instructions from Paris ordered Hyde de Neuville to "seek to learn if any enterprise or intrigue is afoot . . . to spirit Bonaparte away from [St. Helena]."[4] There is no question that the committed royalist Hyde de Neuville was assiduous in following this instruction. Blaufarb describes the sophistication of the French minister's intelligence operation:

"The increasing activity of the refugees during the past six months," Hyde wrote to the French consul in New York . . . "should make you more vigilant than ever and increase the diligence with which you send me all the information you can gather. We must investigate everything that is possible and even what is unlikely." The consuls collected even seemingly insignificant bits of information about the Bonapartist exiles and shared it both horizontally with their colleagues in other cities and vertically with the consul-general and legation. Guillemin, the consul at New Orleans, even began . . . to keep records of all French citizens entering the United States through that port . . . they all regularly forwarded to the Ministry of General Police in Paris lists of all French citizens in their jurisdiction leaving the United States for Europe. Collated by Hyde and sent on to [Prime Minister] Richelieu, their reports on the activities of local Bonapartists also found their way to this ministry. In turn, it periodically shared with the Ministry of Foreign Affairs the intelligence it had gathered in Europe about Bonapartist activities in America. The Ministry of War also cooperated frequently with Foreign Affairs, both sharing information on the Napoleonic officers in America and asking for intelligence on them procured by the diplomatic agents in the United States. The impressive coordination that characterized French interministerial relations sometimes even extended to relations with other governments. For example, Hyde worked out a system with the British ambassador in Washington for keeping tabs on French citizens and naturalized Frenchmen in America who sought to sneak into Europe on English passports.[5]

Hyde de Neuville's efforts were aided as time went on by Bonapartist refugees seeking pardons. The French minister effectively turned them into informants in exchange for his assistance. Moreover, France was not the only country interested in and keeping tabs on the Bonapartists in America. The British and, to a lesser degree, Spanish legations had active programs in place. In contrast, it appears that the naive and woefully understaffed U.S. federal government had nothing.

Thus, Hyde de Neuville's *démarche* was an eye-opener for the new secretary of state. As Adams, Rush, and Hyde de Neuville met on the afternoon of September 23, they pored over the documents produced by the French minister.

And a remarkable set of documents they were.

They consisted of six papers contained in a packet addressed to "Monsieur le Comte de Survilliers, pour lui seul" ("The Count of Survilliers, for himself only"). It was sealed with the insignia of the Revolutionary National Convention that had voted the death of Louis XVI, a liberty head on a pike, and surrounding the seal were the words "Lakanal, Deputy of the National Convention." Each of the six handwritten documents within was signed by Lakanal. The indispensable William Lee had earlier confirmed to Adams both the handwriting and the signatures to be those of Lakanal, presumably based on, if nothing else, his familiarity with the letter of support that Lakanal had previously submitted to the Society of the Vine and Olive. Hyde de Neuville was convinced of their authenticity; Adams reserved judgment.

The first document was a four-page letter styled "ULTIMATUM" at the top. Addressed to Joseph Bonaparte, it was a sort of cover letter asking him to review and respond to the enclosed documents ("I await Your Majesty's answer with extreme impatience," he announced). A personal "PETITION" from Lakanal followed in which he laid out a proposal for a "Napoleonean Confederacy." It started,

> Sire:
> Deign to cast your eyes on this petition, which is of a personal nature, although closely connected with the great enterprise [ostensibly a reference to the Society of the Vine and Olive].

What followed read like the ravings of a madman. After making several non sequiturs involving Hugh Capet and Louis V in the tenth century, it addressed the present:

> Our villagers, our very children, now-a-days, know that men are born free; that populous nations are the sovereigns, and that the only legitimate Kings are the Kings of their free choice.

Two ages of darkness, the diplomatic quackery of the cabinets of Europe, the juggling of the priesthood, will never prevail against these immutable truths.

Sire, Your Majesty alone reigns lawfully over the Spains [*sic*] and the Indies.

It then got down to what seemingly was really on Lakanal's mind:

In the position in which I am placed by the momentous interests of Your Majesty, I respectfully request of you to confer upon me a Spanish distinction, which may affiliate me in some sort with that nation. . . .

This new mark of your gracious favor will give me a degree of political importance in the eyes of your Mexican subjects, which, I venture to assure you, will promote Your Majesty's best interests.

Lakanal was careful to note, however, that "[m]y irrevocable resolution is to make known that Your Majesty has taken no part in this great affair." In other words, he wanted to keep Joseph's involvement secret and deniable should something go wrong.

The enclosed "REPORT" spelled out how Lakanal proposed to bring the "Napoleonean Confederation" to fruition:

Article 1. The Napoleonean Confederation shall be extended to the effective number of nine hundred members, armed and equipped as flankers of the Independent Troops of Mexico.

Article 2. With a view to combine secrecy with celerity in this operation, there shall be named immediately one hundred and fifty members, as Commissioners, who shall repair without delay to the different points of the states, of the Missouri Territory, of the Illinois Territory, of the District of Columbia [sic!], of the Michigan Territory, of Tennessee, Kentucky and Ohio. . . .

Article 4. Each Commissioner shall repair to the places, where are his relations, friends, acquaintances and connections and shall associate with him as many as five individuals, known by their principles to be favorable to the nature of the undertaking . . . ;

he shall not unfold himself as to the ultimate object of the enterprise, and on all occasions, he shall employ economy and circumspection.

The "REPORT" then went on to discuss the economics of the plan and had the audacity to ask Joseph Bonaparte for 65,000 francs to help finance it.

The remaining documents in the packet consisted of a vocabulary of the "wandering Indians" in the vicinity of Mexico "towards Santa Fe," a list of the Indian tribes inhabiting northern Louisiana, and an enigmatic vocabulary of 42 columns or alphabets with a Latin word corresponding with each letter, seemingly some kind of a code in which to communicate.[6]

Adams did not know what to make of these documents. Were they simply the ravings of a lunatic? Surely, the more comical aspects of their presentation were not lost on the astute Adams. Were they in fact authentic, or were they forgeries? Hyde de Neuville was convinced of their authenticity and compared the plot to the earlier one of Aaron Burr to carve out a new country in the West. He requested Adams to take legal action against those involved. If the documents were authentic, had Joseph Bonaparte involved himself in the conspiracy? If so, did the conspiracy have any credibility? These were all questions that must have run through Adams's mind.

He might have been inclined to dismiss them if the geopolitical situation of the Spanish Empire in the Western Hemisphere had not been so tenuous. The fact that in 1809 Napoleon deposed the Bourbon king of Spain Ferdinand VII and made the throne a spoil to be disposed of as he wished had given additional impetus to the growth of revolutionary fervor in Latin America. In part because of the weakened throne during the period of French occupation of Spain many Spanish colonies saw the emergence of juntas that governed, at least in theory, in the name of the deposed Ferdinand VII. The colonies both sensed the weakness of the throne in Madrid and got a taste of self-government. Thus, their loyalty to the deposed monarch ironically fostered a growing sense of independence during the period of the Bonapartes' rule in Spain. Although Mexico had been more stable than some other Spanish dominions in the hemisphere, it was increasingly viewed as a land of opportunity, and the United States was full of freebooters willing to act on their own without regard to the wishes of the U.S. government. While the prospect of successfully redeclaring Joseph king of Spain and the Spanish colonies and actually installing him in Mexico to replace the existing, legitimate, and relatively stable government there may have seemed remote at best, it would have been a move that would have upset the delicate relations between the United States and Spain and would have had profound reverberations in England and France as well. The ramifications would have been multiple and all bad for the United States: the possibility of a civil war in Mexico over which was the legitimate government; further destabilization of an already contested border; a safe haven for plots to liberate Napoleon from exile; the eventual growth of an expansionist, Bonaparte-led power geographically near the United States; and further acceleration of independence movements in the other Spanish colonies, where there was little or no enthusiasm for King Joseph stemming from his days as king of Spain and the Indies. In short, the move was potentially destabilizing to U.S. interests. The fact that there was a precedent in the removal of the Portuguese royal court from Lisbon to Brazil in 1809 in the face of Napoleon's invasion of Iberia—and where it still remained—may have added some credibility to the scheme if it were real.

Faced with these dilemmas, Adams finished his letter and sent it to Hyde de Neuville on September 24. In it, he took a more reserved position than that sought by the French minister, who had called for Lakanal's arrest. He assured Hyde de Neuville that while the president would take "every measure within the competency of the government and compatible with the rights of individuals," taking a page from Queen Elizabeth I, he declined to prosecute on the grounds that such projects "however exceptionable in their character, have not been matured at least into an attempt or commencement of action." In short, the U.S. government could take no legal action notwithstanding "the friendliness of its disposition toward France." In lieu of taking legal action, Adams proposed that the documents be published so as to make them public and subject them to ridicule.[7] And he promptly engaged William Lee to find out what was really going on. Clearly feeling a bit overwhelmed on his first few days on the job, he wrote, "At the office from ten to four O' Clock; but the Papers to read, and the visitors absorb the Office hours so that I find there scarcely a moment for writing."[8]

The next day, September 25, Adams noted in his diary, "Lee came to make some disclosures about the project for invading Mexico; but they amounted to little. He hoped to have more to say tomorrow." Adams also noted that he "received from the French Minister a reply to my letter of yesterday."

The following day, September 26, while Lee investigated further, the diplomatic pace intensified. Hyde de Neuville sent Secretary Adams a note saying he was to leave Washington on a planned trip earlier than anticipated and requesting an interview, which Adams immediately granted. What ensued was enigmatic, as described by Adams:

> We had a long Conversation of which as well as of all others it is henceforth utterly impossible for me to keep any record. It gave me some insight however into his character. . . . Mr. De Neuville's views changed so much in the course of our Conference from what they had been by his Letter of last Evening, as made it necessary for me to consult with Mr. Rush; and to write to the President.

That evening, he started the letter to the president but gave up because of the strain on his eyes: "But even in less than one week since I entered upon my Office, I find my eyes already so much affected that before ten I was obliged to desist from writing and retire to repose."[9]

The next morning, Adams arose at dawn and finished drafting his two-page letter to President Monroe. In it, he recounted his meeting with Hyde de Neuville, who advocated "seizing upon the person and papers of the writer of the papers" or, if that were not feasible, then their immediate publication "with an introductory commentary . . . upon the wickedness and the absurdity of the conspiracy." On the conspiracy, Adams reported that the French minister "said that he had the most perfect certainty of it—that they were recruiting the men; that they were marching—*that he had men of his own among them* [emphasis in the original] and was perfectly informed of their movements; that he knew individual American citizens who were engaged in the plot, but could not make known who they were . . . the existence of the conspiracy and of its real motives could be no subject of question."

Adams told the president that he had responded that Hyde de Neuville's allegations of the levy and its motives were not a "positive fact" because the documents had not been authenticated by a handwriting analysis (notwithstanding Lee's confirmation that they were in Lakanal's hand), which, he noted, would not be admissible in a court of law. However, Adams agreed they could be published "with an introductory note." Hyde de Neuville concurred that he would be satisfied with this, at which point Adams said he would refer the matter to President Monroe for a decision. The French minister said there was time for this because "he had by his *frigates* [emphasis in the original] and by other measures that he had taken given them the . . . check upon their progress." Adams then warned the president darkly, "In the mean time I think it is necessary to suggest to you, that indications are coming in from various quarters, that projects are in agitation among some of the emigrants from Europe, to which it will be necessary for the government to put a stop as soon as possible."[10]

The emphasized words in Adams's letter to the president suggest he was surprised that Hyde de Neuville's spies had penetrated the organization and that the French government had already taken naval action against it. The exact nature of that naval action was unspecified but probably consisted of interdiction of supplies.

Later that morning at the office, Adams visited Secretary of the Treasury William Henry Crawford at the Department of the Treasury. There, he found in Crawford's company the ubiquitous William Lee (who by this time was working at Treasury) and a "General Van Darmine," by which he presumably meant General Dominique Joseph-René Count Vandamme, who had fled to America two months earlier. One can only speculate on the purpose of the meeting, but it may have been a courtesy call, as Crawford probably knew Vandamme from his earlier service as U.S. minister to Paris, although, as will be seen, the meeting also likely dealt with the Society of the Vine and Olive. In any event, Adams raised the alleged plot with Crawford, "but he had heard nothing of the project for conquering Mexico, or for making Joseph Buonaparte king of Spain and the Indies till I told him."[11]

The following day, September 28, was a Sunday, but that did not prevent William Lee from calling on Adams at his lodgings to report. He "read me an account drawn up by him of all the information obtained by him from the french [*sic*] exiles and projectors here. He is to make out another copy to be sent to the President to-morrow."[12]

What did Lee's report find? It seemed that Henri Lallemand, the younger of the two Lallemand brothers, had recently returned from New Orleans and that while there he had sent a French officer to Mexico on a clandestine mission to sound out rebels on the prospect of sending French exiles to their assistance. On his return to Philadelphia, the French officer reported the rebels eager for aid and that two of the "most opulent and influential men" in Mexico "are ready with all their means, being proprietors of the largest mines and having at their disposal ten thousand raw troops, who only wait for French officers to discipline them." Moreover, Lee was convinced that there was American involvement in the form of a mercantile house in Charleston that has offered "money and two brigs well armed" and that additional merchants in Philadelphia (one Curcier), New York, and Boston (Stackpole and Adams) were involved. The two Lallemand brothers and Colonel Galabert were the ringleaders in the plot, and Lee concluded that they had already engaged "eighty French officers and one thousand men."

So the plot was indeed real. But Lee's report got worse, as it drew a connection with the Society of the Vine and Olive and why so few of its allotments made to French military officers were occupied:

> They represent that though they have ample funds in Mexico for all their purposes, they are in want here of the means of putting their plans in execution. For the purpose of obtaining the means, they have been endeavoring to force upon the company . . . about an hundred officers as subscribers. . . . These shares, when obtained, to be placed in the hands of certain merchants in Philadelphia, who are to advance them 50 or 60,000 dollars

thereon, which, they calculate, will be sufficient to begin their expedition with.

However, Lee noted, in this they are bound to be disappointed, for the president of the society heard about their plan and communicated it to Generals Clausel, Lefebvre-Desnouettes, Vandamme, Grouchy, and Count Réal, "who have taken measures to prevent the mass of these officers from becoming subscribers to their company" and to block those who already subscribed from taking title to their allotments. Lee went on:

All the French officers of distinction except the Lallemands disapprove of this project. Gen. Vandamme censured yesterday Genl. Lallemand and Colo. Galaber [*sic*] in so pointed a manner, before Mr. Villar and Colo. Taillorde (who were sent here by the Tombeeby [*sic*] Company to confer with Mr. Crawford) [thus partially explaining why Vandamme and Lee might have been at the meeting the day before in Crawford's office] that a serious quarrel like to have ensued.

Lee's report then made a crucial point: "It appears certain that Joseph B. has pointedly refused all aid and assistance to this and the like schemes;— that he has been solicited in every way and all means used, to induce him to patronize these adventurers without success, on which account they are liberal in their epithets against him." Indeed, no evidence was ever produced that Joseph Bonaparte was involved. He himself subsequently denied any involvement, having refused to accept the package sent by Lakanal before it was intercepted.

Lee added that he had denounced the scheme in person to the elder Lallemand, who must have been in Washington at the time. "I laid upon him in as strong terms as I am master of, a picture of the mischiefs his projects were calculated to heap upon his countrymen and their friends in the U. States;—the pain it would cause to the administration, to find him sacrificing his reputation by violating our laws and that hospitality and protection they afforded him."

Lallemand responded rather lamely to Lee that he would hold off on attacking Mexico until the next winter, when he expected to have support from Congress, and that he had been operating under the impression and belief that the U.S. government "wished well to the revolution in Spanish America." Lee remained skeptical of Lallemand's assurance and therefore interviewed Vandamme and the officers of the Society of the Vine and Olive who were visiting Washington. All disavowed the scheme in no uncertain terms. Lee concluded, "Genl. Vandamme in taking leave of me this morning said he would on his return to Philadelphia probe this affair to the bottom, that he would himself denounce it to the Government before he would suffer the last asylum offered to himself and his countrymen to be endangered by the conduct of a set of boys, fools and madmen."[13]

Lee's report, along with Adams's letter, went to President Monroe, who initially approved Adams's plan to publish the documents. Adams drafted an introduction to the publication that was at once mocking and concerned:

> That foreigners scarcely landed upon our shores should imagine the possibility of enlisting large numbers of the hardy republicans of our western states and territories in the ultra-quixotism of invading a territory bordering upon their country for the purpose of proclaiming a phantom king of Spain and the Indies is a perversity of delirium, the turpitude of which is almost lost in its absurdity.[14]

Adams's introduction also contained a warning: "nor may it be unreasonable to remind the foreigners who are now enjoying the hospitality which our country ever delights to extend to the unfortunate, that the least return which that country has a right to expect from them, is an inviolable respect for her laws."[15]

President Monroe then reconsidered publication and ordered Adams to hold off while he consulted further within his administration. His hesitancies were manifold: U.S.–Spanish relations at too sensitive a juncture to allow publication, uncertainty as to how Lakanal would react, and the risk of public criticism of the government for allowing the French to concoct and start to implement the scheme. For his part, Adams continued to have doubts about the authenticity of the documents and wondered if they might have been an elaborate ruse to ensnare Joseph Bonaparte by parties unknown for reasons unknown.

In the meantime, Adams shared Lee's concerns about the intentions of the Lallemand brothers and in effect sent Lee to warn them off any unwise schemes. On October 6 Lee reported to Adams with a letter from the two Lallemands "disclaiming all intention of engaging in an enterprize contrary to the Laws of the United States."[16] Then, on October 20 he called on Adams to advise him "that the project of the French emigrant Officers for an invasion of Mexico, were all broken up and abandoned."[17]

This intelligence proved crucial as a prelude to a cabinet meeting that ensued on October 30 at which the whole matter was discussed in the context of larger U.S.–Spanish relations and the activities of American freebooters at Amelia Island, Florida and Galveston, Texas. The decision was taken not to publish the documents—for all of the reasons noted above but also because the matter of Bonapartist émigré schemes now appeared moot.

On November 2 Adams and his wife paid a formal visit on Lee. This was unusual because Lee was a workplace colleague with whom the Adamses did not normally socialize, such as they did with Mrs. Adams's sister, the Portuguese minister in Washington, Abbé José Corrêa da Serra,[18] and even potential political rivals, such as Speaker of the House Henry Clay and Secretary of the Treasury and former U.S. minister in Paris William Henry Crawford, as well as a handful of other regular friends. During this period, during business hours Lee continued to have easy access to Adams and was in and out of his office often.

The following week Lee asked Adams's permission to introduce to him General Charles Lallemand, who was visiting Washington on behalf of the Society of the Vine and Olive. Adams declined. Not one to be deterred, Lallemand showed up at the Department of State the next day (November 8) anyway, introduced himself, and asked to see Adams the following day. This time, Adams consented, perhaps out of admiration for his persistence.

The meeting that ensued on November 9 was lengthy and occupied most of Adams's diary entry for that day. Coming just over two years after the refusal of the secretary of state and president to receive the king of Spain, it was the first meeting of the secretary of state with any of the ranking exiled Napoleonic brass. It was much more than a mere courtesy call, and the description provided by Adams is worth quoting in full:

General Lallemand called again this morning and entered into a long explanation of his views and intentions, with a strong denial of his having ever contemplated engaging in any project contrary to the Laws of the United States. He said he had been invited to join in M'Gregor's expedition to Amelia Island, but had declined.—That he had refused to engage in some other projects of a similar nature; though he had an ardent love of Liberty, and a warm sympathy with the South-Americans whom he considers as struggling for that cause. He had never been the partizan [*sic*] of a man; but that of his Country. He had followed the Emperor (Napoleon) in his misfortunes, and of all his Counsellors, had alone advised him not to trust himself to the English [Lallemand spoke truthfully on this point]—He added that if after these explanations he was still an object of uneasiness and suspicion to this Government, he would quit the Country and seek a refuge elsewhere, as he was determined to all Events to preserve his personal independence [again, he spoke truthfully]—I told him he was in no wise an object of uneasiness to this Government—That they had received from various quarters information of a project of levying men, in the United states for an expedition to join the Mexican insurgents; that Joseph Buonaparte was to be placed at the head of this movement, and that his Lallemand's name had been implicated in it—That as this project was contrary to the Laws of the United States, which the Government were bound to see executed, its existence had given them uneasiness, particularly as its tendency was to force them to take a decisive part against the exiles from France who had sought and were enjoying an asylum in this Country—That the Government had now reason to believe that this project was abandoned; that there was no suspicion entertained against him and so long as he should conform his conduct to the Laws, the Government would neither have the power nor the inclination to molest him.

Lallemand then responded to Adams:

He said he knew the French and Spanish Ministers were both much alarmed at the new project of French settlement on the Tombigbee, and the French Minister had sent to him Lallemand, a Garde du Corps of the king, to offer to enlist himself to go to Mexico [in what appears to have been an entrapment scheme by Hyde de Neuville]—He said he had laughed in the Garde du Corps's face; for it was really too absurd—I told him that his name had not been mentioned in any Communication from the French Minister to this Government—He said he had heard of some pretended Letters from Lakanal to the Count de Survillier (Joseph Buonaparte) but he lived in perfect retirement and had refused to receive those Letters, which had been the only cause of their being intercepted. He, Lallemand did not know Lakanal; had never seen him; knew nothing whether he had written the Letters, whether they were forgeries, or what they were. But it would be hard if the Comte de Survillier should be held responsible for Letters written to him, which he had refused to receive.[19]

As usual with diplomatic engagements, the interchange was a mix of fact and dissembling on both sides. But the matter did not end there. Despite having received an ostensibly satisfactory response from Secretary of State Adams, the assiduous Lallemand sought an audience with President Monroe. Adams wrote with evident surprise and annoyance in his diary the following day:

When I came to the President's I found Mr. Crawford with him ... now Lallemand, who is outlawed and under sentence of Death in France, has applied to be presented to the President. This led to some discussion of the subject, and to the question how the intercourse between the President and the foreign ministers should in future be regulated—It was interrupted by a visit of Wyandot, Delaware, and Seneka [*sic*] Indians, whom the President received in form but without the ceremony of smoking the Calumet.[20]

Whether smoking the peace pipe or not, Lallemand did not get his audience with the president.

From there, the matter quieted down, and on November 21, Lee, whose day job at this time was decorating the rebuilt White House, took Adams on a tour of the president's personal apartments: "W. Lee took me into the Apartments of the President's house now furnishing, and shewed me the furniture lately imported from France."[21]

A wave of frigid weather gripped Washington starting in late November that rattled even the Boston-bred Adams, who complained that it was too cold to write diplomatic dispatches when he arose at his customary 5:00 a.m. to attend to correspondence. On December 3, Hyde de Neuville stoked one last flicker in the flame by calling on Adams and to urge "again for something to be done about Lakanal, and his papers." When Adams pushed back, the French minister "admitted that all the projects which had alarmed him were at an end."[22]

Or so it appeared.

The new year of 1818 brought fresh revelations, as Adams commissioned Lee to investigate further to find out what was really going on. On January 20, Lee reported to the secretary of state. The news was far more unsettling and pervasive than even Adams had suspected. Lee explained,

> It appears the Generals L'Allemand are seriously engaged in an expedition destined for some part of Spanish America.
>
> They are purchasing arms and ammunition in New York.
>
> They have agents in Louisiana and the Mississippi enlisting frenchmen and others. . . .

They have it is said engaged in the U States about three hundred men. . . .

They calculated on about 1500 men besides officers—with this force they are to leave St. Thomas for some port in the Gulf of Darien to cross the Isthmus for Panama there embark for Guayaquil & throw themselves into the mountains of Quito in the Province of Peru where there are no troops to oppose them and where they mean to make a stand. They expect to conquer that province and intend to organize it in such a manner as to afford protection to all who chuse to join their standard.

Another expedition is talked of at the head of which is to be placed the Count of Galvez son of the count of Galvez who was proclaimed King of Mexico in the insurrection of 1787.[23]

Only the first four paragraphs of Lee's report were true, as later events were to prove.

Adams met with Lee again the next day. The secretary of state may have been privy to intelligence generated by Hyde de Neuville's network of spies and shared by the French minister. Alternatively, Adams may have gathered pertinent intelligence himself when earlier that day he sat with the Spanish minister to Washington, Don Luis de Onis, at a memorial mass for the executed French king Louis XVI. Either way, the secretary of state noted that Lee "came to say something further about Galabert and the L'Allemand's, and who was amazed at my asking him to ascertain from Galabert, whether he was not holding communications with Onis."[24]

Lee reported back the following day, January 22, that "to his utter amazement he last Evening saw Galabert go into Onis's house—That he had not seen him since, but would see and ask an explanation of him."[25]

True to form, Lee dutifully reported to Adams one day later. Adams noted in his diary,

At the office W. Lee came and told me that he had demanded of Galabert an explanation of his going in to Onis's, and received a very imperfect one. He had written from Philadelphia to Onis telling him that if he could be furnished with the means of coming here, he could make communications which would be useful to him.—Upon which he sent him a hundred dollar bill—He had therefore come; and made his Communication, but would not tell Lee what it was—He said he had asked of Onis a Passport to go to Mexico which Onis had not given him; but took it into consideration and told him to call again—But Galabert had received a Letter from Joseph Bonaparte, urging him not to enter into the wild and extravagant projects of these french fugitives, and offering him the means of settling himself in Pennsylvania. This Letter affected him so that Lee said he cried like a child, and inclined to return and settle in Pennsylvania—Lee says that he saved Galabert's life at Bordeaux; but that the intriguing ways of a Frenchman are past all finding out.[26]

January gave way to February with conspiracy theories swirling all about the top levels of the U.S. government against a backdrop of a deepening crisis over complex territorial claims between the United States and Spain that at times teetered on the brink of hostilities. There was concern throughout the highest levels of the U.S. government that the machinations of the French exiles could unwittingly upset the delicate balance and spark conflict. President Monroe remained skeptical of the intentions of the Lallemands. In January, he had asked his personal friend Nicholas Biddle of Philadelphia, who was the visiting Washington, to watch and report on the movements of the Lallemands when he returned home. Biddle wrote to Monroe on February 7 that he did not believe the Lallemands were in the employ of the Spanish minister Onis even though Onis was aware of their plans. An ensuing letter from Biddle to Monroe provided more detail:

You recollect our conversation about the Lallemands and the speculations as to their designs. From what I can learn, the two brothers sailed from New York with two or three officers, forming a staff, for Mobile or New Orleans. About the same time a vessel left Philadelphia with nearly one hundred and fifty persons, chiefly Frenchmen, who had been disciplined and prepared by the Lallemands and were to join them. It is said that other vessels from other ports would unite with them at some point. . . . The funds for the expedition were raised almost entirely by the sale of the lands given to the officers and men in Alibama [*sic*]. . . . This fact is very decisive as to their not going to cultivate vines, and it is equally certain that they are destined against some of the possessions of Spain in South America.[27]

While Biddle's figure of 150 Frenchmen was reminiscent of Lakanal's 150 "Commissioners," Monroe was concerned lest the expedition might be one fomented by Onis and directed against the United States.

What in fact was occurring was even more bizarre.

On December 17, 1817, General Antoine Rigau and a party of associates left Philadelphia aboard the chartered schooner *Huntress* with a cargo that included six field pieces, 600 muskets, 400 sabers, and 12,000 pounds of gunpowder—hardly the utensils needed to help plant vines and olive trees. The ship was ostensibly bound for Mobile but was in fact secretly headed for Galveston, Texas. It sailed past the Tortugas to near New Orleans, where it was stopped by an "independent corsair" flying the Spanish flag that turned out to be part of the pirate fleet operated by Jean Lafitte based in Galveston. After mutually concluding that neither was a threat, the two ships sailed for the coast of Texas.

Arriving at Galveston, Rigau and his associates found themselves warmly welcomed by Lafitte and his pirates, who helped them set up a temporary encampment. Little did Rigau know (or maybe he did) that Lafitte, who had allied with the Americans during the Battle of New Orleans, was in fact a Spanish double agent.[28] In any event, the Frenchmen and the pirates made good neighbors. As described by one of the French venturers, Lafitte's men at Galveston were "freebooters gathered from among all the nations of the earth and determined to put into practice the traditions of the buccaneers of old. They gave themselves up to the most shameless debauchery and disgusting immorality and only their chief, by his extraordinary strength and indomitable resolution, had the slightest control over their wild and savage natures. Thanks to him the pirates became harmless neighbors to the exiles, with whom they often exchanged marks of political sympathy, crying amicably, 'Long live liberty.'"[29]

While the advance party waited at Galveston, General Charles Lallemand tarried in New York trying to arrange additional support. Finally, on December 31, Lallemand, his brother Henri,[30] and a few associates sailed from New York with a smaller complement of venturers and arrived at New Orleans to purchase additional supplies. By early March, Lallemand and his group (minus Henri, who remained at New Orleans working on logistical arrangements) reached Galveston and reunited with Rigau and his followers, who had wearied of waiting on the sandy island on the coast of Texas. The reunion was a happy one. "Songs of glory were sung. We drank to our fatherland, to our friends who remained there, to our own good-fortune, to the success of our enterprise."[31] They were soon to depart for the interior of Texas to found the Champ d'Asile (Field of Asylum) (illustration 8).

But what was their enterprise?

The French and British ministers in Washington thought they knew, and they did not like it one bit. The same was true of Adams, who, like them, was convinced it was a Spanish plot aimed at the United States. On March 18, Hyde de Neuville called on Adams to express his concerns about the Lallemand expedition that he said "arrived at New Orleans and of their associates who have landed at Galveston. He says Onis has protested to him upon his honor that he knows nothing of them or their project. I [Adams] told him he might rely upon it that Onis did know something of them. He said that as they were Frenchmen and most of them might return to France if they chose, it would be equally displeasing to his Government whether their projects were against Spain or the United States."[32]

In the case of Adams, the plot and the overall U.S.–Spanish relationship had assumed a personal political dimension as well. Earlier the same day, the ubiquitous William Lee called on Adams to inform him of a "very ridiculous affair" in which candidates jockeying to succeed Monroe as president—namely, Secretary of the Treasury Crawford, Speaker of the House Clay, and Governor DeWitt Clinton of New York—were making a point "to deny me as much as possible in the public opinion"—and this just a year into Monroe's first term. Lee cited Clay in particular, who thought he, not Adams, should have been made secretary of state and who had been "running me down" by saying Adams was being too soft and accommodating to the Spanish—which no doubt fanned Adams's suspicions about Onis's possible involvement in the expedition.[33]

The British minister to Washington, Sir Charles Bagot, also shared his unease over the expedition with Adams because he feared (wrongly) that a Bonaparte was involved with it, in which case "of course his Government would consider it as deserving high attention."[34]

As political and diplomatic pressure built, following a cabinet meeting on May 13, 1818, Adams dispatched a troubleshooter, Chief Clerk of the War Office Captain George Graham, a versatile man who at one point had served as acting secretary of war, to go to Champ d'Asile, ascertain its "precise and real object," and tell the Frenchmen to leave.[35] Graham did not arrive at Galveston until August 27, at which point he learned that the Champ d'Asile was no more.

What had happened?

Whatever the leaders in Washington saw in the Rorschach test posed by the expedition, the reality on the ground was far different.

Two weeks after the arrival of Lallemand at Galveston, the consolidated expedition departed on March 10, 1818, for a spot on the Trinity River in Texas that Lallemand had selected for the military colony to be known as the Champ d'Asile. The entourage was a polyglot assemblage. In addition to the French exiles and soldiers of fortune recruited at Philadelphia, it contained Americans, Poles, Spaniards, Mexicans, and pirates from the Gulf Coast. Lafitte indeed had actively supported the expedition by lending Lallemand 24 boats to head upriver.

No sooner had the small armada departed than disaster struck in the form of a raging storm that scattered the boats in the bay at Galveston. Some turned back. One capsized, drowning six colonists. Perhaps it was an omen.

The colonists battled storms and tide for three days before Lallemand gave up and decided to split the party. The first group, with the bulk of the colonists, was to proceed overland to their destination some 30 miles upriver. The remainder were to go by water under Colonel Charrassin, bringing up the food, arms, and ammunition.

The overland route soon came to naught as the colonists quickly became lost in the wilderness. Inadequately supplied with food, they soon grew hungry and began to graze on what they thought were edible plants growing wild in the forests. One plant, which resembled a lettuce, attracted particular attention, and many partook of it. Within half an hour, they lay sprawled on the forest floor writhing in agony from the poisonous plant. Although both Lallemand and the colony's surgeon had been prudent enough not to eat the noxious weed, there was nothing they could do to alleviate the suffering, as all the medicines had been left behind with the boats. The prospects for the land route leading to the putative colony appeared grim indeed until, as so often happened in American settlement narratives, a wandering Indian appeared. When shown the plant that poisoned the Europeans, he allegedly raised his eyes and hands skyward, gave a sorrowful cry, disappeared as suddenly as he came, and then reappeared with hands full of antidotal herbs, which he administered with efficacy before continuing on his way.[36]

Six days into their trek, the colonists reached the chosen site of their settlement. As described by the pseudonymous Just Girard, it lay on the banks of the Trinity River at the edge of "an immense uninhabited plain, several leagues in extent and surrounded by a belt of woods down to the river. A fruitful soil, an abundance of tropical plants and flowers, a river as wide as the Seine, but full of alligators, a sky as pure and a climate as temperate as that of Naples—such were the advantages of the place we had chosen and which is now christened Champ d'Asile."[37]

To their relief, the exhausted and starving colonists found the regrouped boats with the supplies, arms, and ammunition already on-site awaiting their arrival. So it was down to business in establishing the colony. The generals worked with the rest of the company on the manual labor required. Because of the heat, they labored in the early morning between 4:00 and 7:00 and similar hours in the late afternoon each day to erect a series of four fortifications complete with ramparts and blockhouses based on designs by the renowned French military engineer Sebastien Vauban. The hours in between were devoted to fishing, hunting, constructing homes, and planting crops.

The roster of known names in the colony amounts to 149, although the total was probably much higher (some estimates run between 400 and 600).[38] In addition there were four women, four children, three enlisted orderlies, several servants and laborers, and a handful of others. The colony was run as a military camp with General Charles Lallemand as commander and General Antoine Rigau as his deputy. It turned out to be less than an ideal chain of command, as the two generals increasingly quarreled and the colonists took up sides.

From the start, the camp was run under strict military discipline. The approximately 100 officers were organized into three companies or cohorts of infantry, foot cavalry, and artillery. After completion of the fortifications, regular military drills occupied several hours each day on an improvised parade ground. An oversized tricolor hung from a large tree at the center of the encampment (they evidently did not possess a flagpole). Each night, a watch was mounted around the camp, and the old soldiers would sit by the central bonfire (grandly called the *palais royal*) and discuss their old campaigns. Again according to Just Girard, "Sometimes General Lallemand would join the circle and entertain the veterans gathered under his sway with some scraps of his last conversations with the Emperor."[39] Less happily, desertions and duels began to proliferate, and Lallemand resorted to placing sentries around the perimeter of the camp with orders to shoot any deserters.

But the ultimate purpose of the colony remained vague. The attempts at agriculture were perfunctory: a few melons and a dream of cultivating tobacco. Lallemand apparently offered his services to Spain (thus confirming Adams's suspicions), but the viceroy declined his offer (thereby refuting them).[40] There was—inconsistently—talk of aiding Mexican insurgents in throwing off the Spanish government in exchange for a fast ship to liberate Napoleon from St. Helena.

Lallemand authored a manifesto that articulated the philosophical underpinnings of the Champ d'Asile. Parts of it read not unlike Lakanal's "Ultimatum." Printed in the May 11, 1818, edition of *L'Abeille Américaine*, the manifesto started with a coda of self-pity:

Gathered together by a series of similar misfortunes which at first drove us from our homes and then scattered us abroad in various lands, we have now resolved to seek an asylum where we can remember our misfortunes in order to profit by them. We see before us a vast extent of territory, at present uninhabited by civilized mankind and the extreme limits of which are in the possession of Indian tribes, who, caring for nothing but the chase, leaves these broad areas uncultivated. Strong in adversity, we claim the first right given by God to man, that of settling in this country, clearing it and using the produce which nature never refuses to the patient laborer.

The document went on to promise peaceful coexistence:

We attack no one and harbor no warlike intentions. We ask peace and friendship from all those who surround us and we shall be grateful for the slightest token of their goodwill. We shall respect the laws, religion and customs of our civilized neighbors. We shall equally respect the independence and customs of the Indian tribes.... We shall do our utmost to make ourselves useful and to render good for good.

Then came the big "but":

But if it shall appear that our settlement is not respected and if persecution follows us even in the wilds in which we have taken refuge, no reasonable man will then find fault with us for resisting. We shall be ready to devote ourselves to the defense of our settlement. We are armed . . . as men in similar situations have always been. The land we have come to reclaim will either witness our success or our death. We wish to live here honorably and in freedom, or to find a grave which the justice of man will hereafter decree to be that of heroes.

In fact, neither happened. Lallemand then turned to the social contract and the goal of moral development, drawing a distinction between the Americans the Frenchmen "meet" and the colonists, making the point that it was to be an organized agricultural society and not live by hunting and fishing. This in turn would lead to the perfection of moral qualities. But the military structure of the colony was paramount:

> We shall call the new settlement "Champ d'Asile." This name, while it will remind us of our misfortunes, will also express the necessity which we have of providing for the future, of establishing new homes, in a word, of creating a new Fatherland. The colony, which will be purely agricultural and commercial in principle, will be military solely for its own protection. It will be divided into three companies each under a chief, who will keep the names of those forming his company.[41]

After Lallemand sent the grandly worded document east, it was picked up and published in English in *Niles' Weekly Register*. It received even greater press play in Paris, where the plight of the exiled soldiers-laborers mourning the loss of their country struck a nostalgic chord. A subscription was opened up to support the colony, and it gathered close to 100,000 francs by July 1819 (none of which apparently ever reached the Champ d'Asile). A song was composed in the colony's honor that became popular in the Parisian cafés, and various artists churned out sentimental and idealized paintings and lithographs of the little corner of France in the wilds of Texas. One of the more preposterous presentations of the colony that appeared in Paris papers conflated the Alabama grant with the Champ d'Asile and stated,

> The Congress of the United States has not only encouraged the formation of the new colony, but has given it an unequivocal proof of its good-will so as to bear witness to the entirely honorable motives which led the French officers to dispose to the lands

granted them on the Mobile. It has hastened to make a formal declaration in their favor. By this act the republic . . . has by deed of gift made over in perpetuity to the French refugees the entire territory of Texas. The integrity and inviolability of the territory will be under the protection of the military forces of the United States, which will recognize and adopt the colonists as allies and give them assistance in case of attack.[42]

The only problem was that as the Champ d'Asile seized the imagination of the French populace, the colony had already collapsed.

Within months of arriving, the colonists learned that the Spanish garrison at San Antonio was sending soldiers, together with some Indian allies, to oust them from the Champ d'Asile and from Texas altogether (thus in the process exploding Adams's theory that the colony was a Spanish plot). Although the colonists initially determined to resist the Spanish consistent with Lallemand's manifesto ("to die like Frenchmen," as Lallemand put it), provisions were running low, and relatively few men were able to bear arms because of the high numbers of sick and disabled. Rumors spread that the Spanish force included 1,200 cavalry and artillery.

The Spanish force, whatever its true size, surrounded the Champ d'Asile at a distance and simply waited. As described by Just Girard,

> The Spanish general . . . merely encamped his troops within three days march of our camp and waited until disease and discouragement should undermine our not very formidable body. This maneuver could not but be successful in the long run and the Spanish general soon reaped its consequences. Meanwhile no help came from Europe or the United States [surely they did not expect any] and we could not fight an enemy that seemed determined not to attack. We were obliged to beat a retreat, which we accomplished in good order.[43]

The colonists returned to Galveston, where at least food was available. That is where Graham encountered them. At first, Graham found them diffident and offering only platitudes about their peaceful intentions. But as he and Lallemand gained a level of mutual confidence, Lallemand let slip that he had engaged in a secret agreement to aid Mexican insurgents in an uprising against Spain but that he had held off initiating hostilities until he could learn from Graham the position of the United States. Notwithstanding Graham's instructions to demand their departure from Texas, for unknown reasons, he in fact proposed that they remain at Galveston and promised great rewards should they do so. Naturally, they agreed. Lallemand then turned command over to Rigau and returned with Graham to New Orleans. When Adams learned of Graham's actions, he immediately disavowed them.[44]

Meanwhile, the viceroy of Mexico, who equally distrusted the French incursion and the Spanish minister in Washington, determined to oust the intruders. He arranged a small naval and land force that eventually caught up with them at hurricane-ravaged Galveston in October. They met with Rigau at his headquarters, which was a beached, dismasted ship. Amid the usual protestations of peaceful intent and lamentations about Lallemand's abandonment of the colony, Rigau negotiated passage for himself and most of the colonists to New Orleans on a Spanish prize.[45] Thus ended the Champ d'Asile.

General Antoine Rigau continued to disparage Lallemand following his return to New Orleans. He died in 1820 at the home of his daughter, a teacher in Opelousas, Louisiana.

General Henri Lallemand never ventured to the Champ d'Asile. He returned to Philadelphia, where he authored a well-received book titled *Treatise on Artillery*. In 1819, he sought an audience with President Monroe through the good offices of Nicholas Biddle. He was turned down. He died on September 16, 1823, at Point Breeze, the home of Joseph Bonaparte at Bordentown, New Jersey, at the age of 46. He is buried at Holy Trinity Catholic Church in Philadelphia. His widow Henrietta Girard Lallemand remarried in 1829. She and her husband, a doctor, lived in Joseph Bonaparte's former home at 12th and Market streets in Philadelphia.

General Charles Lallemand remained in New Orleans, became a U.S. citizen, and purchased various properties and slaves on credit, on which he defaulted. In late 1821, he was back in Philadelphia. From there, he proceeded first to England and then to Spain and Portugal, where he was involved in a series of misadventures involving a "Legion of French Refugees" gathered to fight a royalist French army invading Spain. When that effort collapsed, he wound up in London, where in 1825 he became an agent for the insurgent Greek government, which wanted to purchase warships to fight against Ottoman rule. He returned to the United States and negotiated the construction of two frigates with two New York shipbuilders. There were cost overruns and allegations that Lallemand absconded with thousands of dollars. He then turned to running a school in New York. Documentary evidence suggests that at this stage Joseph Bonaparte was financially supporting Lallemand.[46] However, with the 1830 July Revolution in France that ousted Charles X and replaced him with Louis Philippe, Lallemand's fortunes turned. He could now safely return to France. Before he left America, Joseph Bonaparte entrusted Lallemand with a letter he had written making the case for Napoleon's son to succeed to the throne of France. His intent was for Lallemand to take the letter to France and have it published for the Chamber of Deputies. Instead, Lallemand turned it over to Louis Philippe, who told him to burn it because he could do nothing to help the Bonapartes. In the process, thousands of dollars Joseph had entrusted to Lallemand for the project allegedly disappeared.[47]

The remainder of Lallemand's career proved felicitous. Louis Philippe restored the old Napoleonic military grades, and Lallemand once again became a lieutenant general. He saw service as military governor of Corsica, inspector general of the cavalry, and finally inspector general of the military academy at Saint-Cyr. He died a peer of France in 1839.

From an American perspective, the verdict on Lallemand remains unresolved. Certainly, Napoleon's judgment that he possessed the "sacred fire" was not wide of the mark. He was an energetic, capable, creative officer who pushed the boundaries and who probably would have saved Napoleon from St. Helena if he had only listened to him. But in his actions in America one cannot help but suspect there was a bit of the con man in him. He hijacked the Society of the Vine and Olive to help pay for the Champ d'Asile, he operated in great secrecy, he (to put it charitably) repeatedly failed to account for funds entrusted to him, and he cynically manipulated both U.S. and French media to inflate the strength and success of the Champ d'Asile, probably in order to increase its attractiveness to the highest bidder, be that the United States, imperial Spain, or the Mexican insurgents. That he was a world-class adventurer few would deny.

The priest *manqué*, regicide, and former enforcer of the metric system Lakanal dwelled on a different, lower plane. After leaving Kentucky, he resided in New Orleans, where in 1822 he accepted the presidency of the Collège d'Orléans, a prestigious institution chartered in 1811 so that Creole boys would not have to travel to Paris for higher education. However, he held the position for only 14 months. The fact that Lakanal was an ex-priest and an atheist did not sit well with the pious Creole mothers of New Orleans. They held a meeting and declared that they "would have no anti-Christ teach their boys; that the trustees of an institution who could appoint such a man were unfit to be entrusted with the education of youth."[48] A mass meeting of citizens ensued, demanding that the trustees rescind their action. They refused, at which point the mothers withdrew almost all their sons, causing the college to collapse. Having wrecked the Collège d'Orléans, Lakanal next moved to Mobile, where he lived for 11 years as a slaveholding plantation owner. With the accession of Louis Philippe in 1830, Lakanal was free to return to France, which he did in 1834, disembarking from his ship wearing the uniform of the Institut de France, in which he was active in his final years. A widower, he remarried at the age of 77 and had a son. He died in 1845 and is buried at the Père Lachaise Cemetery in Paris, much honored among Frenchmen.

In assessing the Society of the Vine and Olive and the Champ d'Asile, one cannot help but judge both to be utopian experiments gone wrong. Elements of them were high-minded. In their published propaganda, their progenitors held them up as an exercise in the civic virtues of antiquity. The examples of Cincinnatus returning to the plow and of George Washington, as well as Spartans and Thebans, figured in their philosophical underpinnings. So also did elements of Rousseau's social contract. Both sets of colonists consciously chose not to live as noble savages by hunting and fishing. In this, they contrasted sharply with their French

Canadian brethren the *couriers de bois*, who attained a highly adaptive and, one might argue, more successful lifestyle by doing precisely that.

However, in both cases, the utopias "represented an image of America seen by European and, more particularly, French eyes," as Inès Murat put it.[49] And in the case of the Champ d'Asile, that image became blurred and haunted by the Napoleonic epic. In their military routines and camp-fire reminiscences, the asylees were no longer following Cincinnatus as a model but were little more than homesick *demi-soldes* trying to recapture their past glory.[50]

Both utopias encapsulated a static ideal of small landholders happily tilling their plots within a supportive localized community, a concept as Jeffersonian as it was Jacobin. The static ideal was breathtaking in its impracticality and lack of knowledge of the context in which it was being attempted. What the ideal failed—and failed utterly—to take account of was nature in America—nature in the form of geography, distances, climate, weather, and crops. It also failed to take account of human nature—greed, boredom, loneliness, and despair. The combination proved fatal.

At the end of the day, both utopias collapsed and left no tangible mark on America because they failed to take account of and integrate with America. One cannot help but note with irony that one of the few ways some—but not all—of the emigrants (such as Clausel, Lefebvre-Desnouettes, and Lakanal) accommodated American norms was by holding slaves. Looking at it from the luxury of the present, this was a drop in standards by these warriors of the Enlightenment, who had fought in a revolution to free humanity and whose Army of the Alps was at one time commanded by a black general.

Ironically, at approximately the same time in Europe, the foundations were being laid for a cosmopolitan pan-European culture that would thrive throughout the 19th century. Spearheaded by operatic composers like Gioachino Rossini, writers like Alexandre Dumas, and painters like Eugène Delacroix and encouraged by the development of railroads, which quickly moved people and ideas, a truly "European" culture was beginning to develop from Paris to Vienna to St. Petersburg.[51] Why did the influx of sophisticated French émigrés not stimulate a similar movement in the United States? The answers are complex. Although Joseph Bonaparte was both sophisticated and a consumer of European culture, he did not create it. The other errant generals and marshals had the wrong skill sets. Rather than create art or beauty that fired humanity's imagination and inspired its soul, they were warriors who had served an enlightened despot. Although they traveled to a remarkable degree, their presence here largely preceded the advent of railroads in America. Even if they had coincided with the railroads, their intellectual contribution, if such it can be called, would have misfired: they brought principles of enlightenment and meritocracy to an America already enlightened and thriving by merit and, moreover, deeply antipathetic to despots.

The next chapters of this book examine the intriguing mystery of Marshal Michel Ney and Peter Stewart Ney, a most unusual story that exemplifies the exact opposite: a cunning and remarkably successful effort by one man (whatever one may conclude about his bona fides) to efface himself in the hinterlands of America precisely by adapting to it and integrating with it so as to become almost—but not quite—invisible. Therein was launched one of the great mysteries of the past 200 years.

CHAPTER 8

The Strange Case of Michel Ney, the "Bravest of the Brave," Duke of Elchingen, Prince of Moscow, and Marshal of France

THE QUESTION IS SIMPLE: WAS MARSHAL NEY EXECUTED BY A FIRING squad on December 7, 1815, and buried in Père Lachaise Cemetery in Paris, or was the execution staged and did Ney in fact escape France to live as an obscure schoolteacher named Peter Stewart Ney[1] in the rural South of the United States? The arguments on either side of the question are intriguing and have been at the heart of a mystery that has persisted for 200 years.

First, a word about historicity. Questions about the execution of Marshal Ney surfaced the day the execution took place and immediately thereafter, including among purported eyewitnesses, but the public connection with Peter Stewart Ney (hereinafter P. S. Ney) did not appear in print in the United States or elsewhere until the 1850s. As early as 1867, this connection was the subject of newspaper articles in North Carolina.[2] By 1876, these articles appeared nationally and indeed internationally. In 1895, Dr. James Augustus Weston, an Episcopal clergyman who was rector of the Church of the Ascension in Hickory, North Carolina, and also a former Confederate army officer and trained lawyer, wrote a book following 13 years of research, *Historical Doubts as to the Execution of Marshal Ney*.[3] The book was based on and contained many scores of eyewitness recollections of P. S. Ney in the United States. Most of them, despite a few variants, paint a remarkably consistent picture of the American Ney.

Unfortunately, because Weston's book as well as several subsequent ones supportive of the theory, especially James Edward Smoot's 1929 study *Marshal Ney before and after Execution*,[4] were written by Southern Americans broadly from the area in which P. S. Ney lived and who were not academic historians, they have tended to be dismissed by academics. For example, Dorothy Mackay Quynn begins her scholarly article "Destination: America: Marshal Ney's Attempt to Escape," *French Historical Studies* 2, no. 2 (1961) with the sentence "Much has been said and written about the legend of Marshal Ney's life and death in America, although it is a tale completely unsupported by documentary evidence."[5]

Is that so? Why are the primary source letters and affidavits of P. S. Ney's many contemporaries who knew him personally not "documentary evidence"? True, many were written after the fact, but is that not true of any eyewitness account?

Worse still, because the literature on the subject was written and published largely in the post–Civil War period, some twentieth- and twenty-first-century academics have dismissed it as being a mere manifestation of the "Lost Cause." Thus, the topic has become more of a reflection of the American Civil War than an impartial inquiry into lives lived in the first half of the nineteenth century. An example is John Mitchell's *Southern Mythology and Marshal Michel Ney*, written in 2003, which flatly states that "Southern Culture created the legend of Peter Stuart [*sic*] Ney."[6] Conclusory statements like the foregoing do not prove or disprove the validity of the evidence.

For that, one must look to the massive research compiled by William Henry Hoyt (1884–1957), a mid-twentieth-century Wall Street lawyer in New York (but with family roots in North Carolina) who spent the final 14 years of his life relentlessly and scrupulously researching the evidence surrounding Marshal Ney and P. S. Ney. Virtually nothing escaped Hoyt's sharp eye and keen mind. At great personal expense, he cast his net not only in the United States but also in France and elsewhere in Europe. The result is an astounding collection of primary source documents housed today in the Southern History Collection at the University of North Carolina, Chapel Hill (the Hoyt Collection).[7] Unfortunately, Hoyt died in 1957 before he was able to write up his findings, although some notes and rough sketches of chapters of his contemplated book reside in the collection. Those materials were sufficient to enable George V. Taylor to write a monograph, "Scholarship and Legend, William Henry Hoyt's Research on the Ney Controversy," published in the *South Atlantic Quarterly* in 1960. Taylor's monograph is faithful to the materials in the Hoyt Collection and to Hoyt's argument that the P. S. Ney story collapses if it can be proven that (1) Marshal Ney in fact was executed on December 7, 1815; (2) because of differences between Marshal Ney and P. S. Ney, they could not have been identical; or (3) there is evidence that P. S. Ney had an identity other than that of Marshal Ney before coming to America in 1816.[8] Taylor then adduces strong evidence from the Hoyt Collection, including Hoyt's incomplete notes, to try to prove each of these points.

Thus, the issue is teed up. Weston and his followers produced first-hand testimony that P. S. Ney was the marshal. Hoyt produced seemingly compelling evidence that he was not. In both cases, that evidence can be dispositive unless refuted by evidence to the contrary. The purpose of the next chapters in this book is to provide a summary of—and fresh look at—both sides of the argument as a lawyer might examine them while drawing on new material not available to either Weston or Hoyt.

First, this book will review in capsule form Marshal Ney's career and character. Ney's career spanned multiple scores (if not hundreds) of military engagements in at least 12 major campaigns over 28 years and would easily be the stuff of a separate multivolume study in and of itself.[9] Second, it will discuss in detail Ney's trial and execution. Third, it will draw on Weston's collected testimonials to provide the hypothetical case that the two men were one and the same. Fourth, it will examine those testimonials in a systematic, lawyerly, and open way against the evidence of the materials in the Hoyt Collection with a fresh look and other more recently available materials to determine if the documents in the Hoyt Collection successfully refute the Weston hypothesis in light of what we can know now.

Michel Ney (illustration 9) was an ethnic German born in France. His hometown was Saarlouis in Lorraine, about 26 miles from Metz and near the border with Germany and Luxembourg. Today, Saarlouis is in Germany. Historically, it was an often-contested border town. Ney was born on January 10, 1769, the same year as Napoleon and the Duke of Wellington. He grew up speaking German; French was a second language to him, learned at school or on the streets. As attested by Grouchy, Lallemand, and others,[10] by the time he was an adult he also spoke some English; where or how he acquired it is unknown, but it was likely self-taught. According to most sources, his father Peter Ney, of German descent but living in what was then France, was a skilled artisan, a master cooper. He would have been of modest means, neither poor nor wealthy but almost certainly respected. Peter fought in the Seven Years' War at the Battle of Rosbach. Likewise, according to most sources, Michel's mother was Margaret Groevelinger, also of German descent.[11] Ney reportedly was especially close to his mother. He was the second of six children. Michel had the advantage of an education in Saarlouis at the Collège des Augustins, an academically demanding school administered by Augustinian monks. Destined by his father for a career as either a notary or a lawyer, he almost certainly would have studied at least some Latin and the classics. At the age of 13, he began to apprentice with the town notary, a M. Vallette. But he tired of it after a year and applied for and obtained an appointment as clerk to the Procureur de Roi, the local royal prosecutor. Performing similar legal duties for the prosecutor proved equally restricting for him, so at the age of 15[12] he reinvented himself by becoming overseer of the Apenwerler or Oppenweiler mines near Stuttgart. Two years later, he moved to become superintendent of the Saleck Iron Works, where he remained three years. Both were much more hands-on management positions than those offered by entry-level legal jobs. He excelled at his work by displaying strong common sense, general intelligence, and faithfulness to his duties. His prospects for advancement looked good. However, from an early age, he had longed for a military career, perhaps under the unwitting influence of his father and his stories of the Seven Years' War or from having grown up in a fortified border town. So, on December 6, 1788, at the age of 19 and against the advice of his parents, he sought to remake himself for the second time by enlisting as a private in a regiment of hussars at Metz. His talent, drive, and ambition quickly showed through:

His good conduct, his application, and the rapidity with which he made himself master of his duty attracted the attention of his officers, while his patient submission to discipline and his orderly conduct elicited their good will; and, as he wrote a beautiful hand he was soon employed in the Quartermaster's office. Whatever leisure time he could command he devoted to hard study, laboring day and night to qualify himself for his new duties.[13]

Like Napoleon, he was an autodidact. He also quickly distinguished himself as an expert swordsman and accomplished equestrian who broke the most dangerous horses in the regiment previously considered unmanageable. His was an unusual combination of attributes: clerical skills learned from his legal background and management expertise gleaned from his years superintending the ironworks, both of which advanced him to a local quartermaster's role—and, at the same time, the ability to outfence and outride his peers.

Physically, Ney probably stood about 5 feet 10 to 11 inches, which was tall for the time, and was exceptionally athletic, fit, and broad-chested.[14] He had penetrating blue-gray eyes. As stated in the Ney *Memoirs*, "A soul of fire seemed contained in a frame of iron. His rather pale complexion, large forehead, under lip and chin rather prominent, and his strongly marked, though not harsh features, gave a manly and severe character to a countenance strongly depicting the workings of his mind, and the rapid impressions it received. The play of his features strongly expressed the feelings by which he was excited." As also noted in the *Memoirs*, by middle age the fatigues of his profession had made him almost bald. His hair, of a ginger or auburn color, had caused the soldiers to give him the nicknames "Peter the Red" and "the Red Lion" as well as "Le Rougeaud" (the "Redhead").[15]

A vignette from his early career illustrates two recurring characteristics of Ney's personality that were to repeat themselves throughout his life: his fierce professional expertise and his unusual compassion. In this story, Ney took on a bullying fencing master from another regiment stationed at Metz in an illegal duel for the honor of his own regiment. He wounded and defeated his antagonist, which subsequently led to the discharge of the bullying fencing master from the service. This man was afterward reduced to poverty, and Ney, "who had become rich, sought him out and settled a pension upon him."[16]

Ney rose with breathtaking rapidity in the Revolutionary army, where advancement to the officer corps was for the first time open to non-nobles. He was promoted five times in 1792 alone: to *maréchal des logis*, February 1; *maréchal des logis chef*, April 1; adjutant, June 14; sublieutenant, October 29; and lieutenant, November 5. On March 29, 1793, he was appointed aide-de-camp to General François Lamarche, one of the best soldiers of the Revolutionary period.

"Thus Ney, almost at the outset of his career, found himself in a situation to study the art of war without being subjected to the painful drudgery of the lower grades. Being placed upon an eminence whence his eye could embrace the whole field of military tactics, he was thus initiated into the secret of grand movements, which he was in a situation not only to study and comprehend, but at times to dissect in person; and he soon proved that the lessons he received were not thrown away."[17] Ney, from the very outset of his career, was a soldier who used his brain. Despite aspersions cast by Napoleon on Ney from St. Helena many years later after his own disastrous fall, Ney's career demonstrated at every turn a man of immense talent and deeply perceptive intellect. Ney spent these formative years fighting the Habsburg Austrians in Germany and along the Rhine. He was not part of Napoleon's early campaigns in Italy or Egypt and was not yet in the Bonapartist orbit.

General Lamarche was killed in action, and Ney next served for a short time on the staff of General Claude Colaud. He was made a captain in his old regiment on April 25, 1794. After the Battle of Fleurus, in which Ney distinguished himself, General Jean-Baptiste Kléber appointed him adjutant general of his division. An adjutant is a military appointment given to an officer who assists the commanding officer with unit administration. Therefore, the promotion was a logical extension of his service as quartermaster. Like most of his prior service, it was essentially a desk job. But shortly afterward, Kléber opened another door of opportunity for Ney that allowed him to reinvent himself a third time in his young career. This move had profound implications for his future.

He placed him at the head of a select body of 500 men, called Partisans, whose duty it was to act as the vanguard of the army, execute missions of extraordinary peril, cross the enemy's lines, reconnoiter his positions and strength, cut off his convoys, and destroy or make prisoners of detachments they might encounter and generally be ready for any enterprise.[18] This was most decidedly not a desk job but a frontline combat position of responsibility requiring courage, energy, judgment, and skill.

Ney not only met Kléber's expectations in this command but also exceeded them. "I can't do without him," Kléber said. "In every operation entrusted to him he displays the most consummate skill and bravery." In fact, General in Chief Jean-Baptiste Jourdan and Kléber allegedly had a quarrel about Ney. "I must have him," said Jourdan. "I must have him," said Kléber. The dispute could be settled only by an appeal to higher authority. Ney's men had high confidence in him. They were willing to go anywhere and attempt anything at his bidding.[19]

During the siege of Mayence or Mainz on the Rhine in January 1795, Ney received a severe bullet wound in the arm that did much damage to his limb and became infected. Although he was invalided while his wound slowly healed, Ney was informed that he had been promoted to general of brigade. In a move that was to be repeated several times in his career, he declined the promotion because he thought he did not deserve it. His superiors implored him to accept it, but his modesty caused him to resist. Although his wound continued to fester, Ney could not sit still. "The spring was advancing, active operations were about to be resumed, and Ney's wound was not yet healed. With anxiety, though resigned, he watched the slow progress of his convalescence. His hopes were still buoyant, and he trusted that his youth and the approaching season would speedily restore him to health."[20] The campaign soon opened, and Ney could not sit still. He set out for headquarters despite the condition of his wound and against the express commands of his surgeon. He still persisted in declining the office of brigadier general. Kléber and others again entreated him to accept, but he continued to demur.

His men warmly welcomed his return to active duty. Although his wounds had not altogether healed, he at once addressed his tasks with his customary energy. At Wurtzburg with 100 cavalry, he took 2,000 of the

Austrian enemy and seized the town. At Forcheim, he led two columns straight into the river against a cannon-defended opposite bank. Before his troops crossed the river, the opposing Austrian army fled, and Ney quietly rode up to the gates and summoned the garrison to surrender. The commander hesitated, and Ney swore that he would bombard the place unless his demands were instantly met. The commandant wished to parley in order to gain time. "Bursting into a violent rage at such useless obstinacy, [Ney] . . . swore that he would put the whole garrison to the sword if the surrender were delayed another instant. This menace had the desired effect, and the alarmed commandant capitulated, and delivered up the town and fortress of Forcheim to the French, together with its arms, ammunition, and a considerable store of provisions."[21]

Kléber was delighted at Ney's success. He complimented him before the other officers in the highest terms. "But," he continued, turning to Ney, "I shall not compliment you upon your modesty, because, when carried too far, it ceases to be a good quality. In sum, you may receive my declaration as you please; but my mind is made up, and I insist upon your being general of brigade."[22]

The chasseurs clapped in applause, and the officers expressed their satisfaction at the general's determination. However, Ney remained thoughtful. He seemed still in doubt whether he should accept a promotion that he had already declined, and he stood in silence. "Well," Kléber said, "you appear very much grieved and confused, but the Austrians are there waiting for you; go and vent your ill humor upon them. As for me, I shall acquaint the Directory with your promotion."

Which he did. These were his words to the Directory:

Adjutant-General Ney in this and the preceding campaigns has given numerous proofs of talent, zeal, and intrepidity; but he surpassed even himself in the battle which took place yesterday, and he had two horses killed under him. I have thought myself justified in promoting him upon the field of battle to the rank of general of brigade. A commission of this grade was forwarded to him eighteen months ago, but his modesty would not allow him then to accept it. By confirming this promotion, Citizens Directors, you will perform a striking act of your justice.[23]

The Directory forced the promotion on Ney, and on August 1, 1796, he received his commission as general of brigade[24] with the following complimentary letter from Jourdan, the general in chief : "I inclose you, general, your commission of general of brigade, which I have just received from the War Minister. Government has thus discharged the debt which it owed to one of its worthiest and most zealous servants; and it has only done justice to the talents and courage of which you daily give fresh proofs. Accept my sincere congratulation."

Ney determined to prove himself worthy of the honor, and in the next engagement (near Sulzbach), he defeated the Austrians, although they occupied almost impregnable positions.

Jourdan resigned his command of the army in September 1796, and General Pierre Bournonville replaced Jourdan as general in chief in September 1796. He soon recommended Ney for promotion to general of division. He wrote,

> To the Minister of War:
>
> I recommend your proposing to the Directory that Brigadier-General Ney be appointed general of division, to command the vanguard in the place of General Lefebvre. This officer, intrepid in action, has, during the campaign, covered himself with glory. He has always commanded corps in the vanguard, and is the only one I know who could efficiently command that of the army of Sambre-et-Meuse.[25]

The requested promotion did not come through immediately, and during the intervening years Ney continued to distinguish himself. A company of Austrian dragoons captured him at Giessen north of Frankfurt when his horse slipped and tumbled with him into a ravine. While in captivity, Ney saw an Austrian riding his former mount. The animal balked. The Austrian officers began to laugh at Ney about the worthlessness of his horse. "Let me show you how to manage him," Ney said. Permission was granted. Ney leaped into the saddle, and the animal, conscious of bearing his master, stepped smartly away. Ney made directly for the French lines and nearly escaped. The Austrians sounded the alarm to capture him. Soon, every avenue was closed. Ney wheeled and with equal speed rode back to the Austrian camp. However, there was no more jesting about his horse.[26] Ney's superb horsemanship was admired and commented on by many people over the course of his career.

Ney was eventually exchanged and put at the head of part of the forces destined for the invasion of England. But the project came to naught. By February 1798, Ney's command was integrated into the Army of Observation under General Jean-Baptiste (and later Marshal and King of Sweden) Bernadotte on the Rhine. Bernadotte was anxious to capture the city of Mannheim. It was an important objective, separated from the French army by the Rhine. It was defended by a powerful Austrian garrison. It seemed to be almost impossible to take by force. The resourceful Ney therefore proposed to take it by stratagem. He was convinced that a few chosen men might cross the river a short distance from the city, march around the enemy's pickets, and attack the rear before a force sufficient to repel them could be assembled. Before engaging in this enterprise, Ney personally crossed the river in disguise to reconnoiter the enemy's position. The story is worth reciting in detail:

> He resolved . . . to ascertain in person the extent of the difficulties he had to encounter, and accordingly crossed the Rhine under the disguise of a peasant. Having entered Mannheim, with a basket on his arm, he proceeded through the streets, made his observations, and obtained precise information concerning the force which defended it and the provisions it contained. The garrison were ill disposed to defend the place, and the duty was carried on in a slovenly and unequal manner. He was about to leave the fortress full of hope, when he perceived a soldier of the garrison supporting a female in the last stage of pregnancy. Having accosted the woman, he expressed an interest in her situation, and her fear that her illness might begin before the night was over.

"No matter if it does," the soldier replied; "should this be the case, the commandant will allow the drawbridge to be let down at any hour of the night, so that the instant she is taken ill she can have assistance."

This was all Ney wanted to know; and he soon recrossed the Rhine to make his preparations.

Having selected a hundred and fifty of his bravest soldiers, he crossed the river with them in skiffs, marched rapidly forward, and concealed them under the walls of Mannheim, in the hope that the woman's labour-pains would soon come on. She did not disappoint him: her sufferings began, the bridge was lowered, and an instant after Ney and his men took possession of it. They then pushed forward with their general at their head, and the weakness of their force was masked by the darkness of the night. Ney threatened and alarmed the garrison, and succeeded in obtaining a surrender of the place.[27]

The above incident is worth noting because it demonstrates a resourcefulness in Ney, an ability to think "out of the box." It also demonstrates his willingness to assume another identity in disguise and pull it off to such a point of confidence that he could even banter with the locals in German. It also was a very "hands-on" approach. It is hard to picture many other brigadier generals pulling off such a stunt.

It was not the only use by Ney of costume and deception to achieve his ends. Slightly earlier in his career, his unit captured two French priests, "half dead with fright, hunger, and fatigue." They were royalist fugitives who refused the constitutional oath. They would have been sent to the guillotine if he had not taken steps to save them. In the presence of their captors, he spoke sternly to them, reminding them of the penalty they had incurred; then he sent away the soldiers on the pretext that he wished to interrogate the prisoners privately. As soon as he was alone with them, he reassured them, provided them with food and money, put them in the charge of an officer he could trust, gave them directions on how to get away from the towns that would be traversed by the French advance, and arranged that they should have a disguise and escape during the night.

The following day, he pretended to be angry at the prisoners having been so badly guarded. There were some awkward rumors of his having connived at their escape, but Commissary Gillet turned a deaf ear to them and said to Kléber, "Your friend Ney knows how to spare the blood of his countrymen."[28] This incident also illustrated another lifelong trait of Ney: a reluctance to shed French blood gratuitously.

On March 28, 1799, Ney received his long-delayed appointment as general of division. Once again, his overly developed sense of modesty and self-effacement ruled, and he received his commission only to send it back. He felt that he might be competent to command a brigade but not a division. He therefore wrote to the minister of war,

> I have received your letter of the 8th of Germinal (March 28), in which was inclosed the decree appointing me general of division. The Directory, in conferring this promotion upon me, probably yielded to advantageous reports of my conduct; but it is my duty to be more severe on my own merits. If my talents were truly such as the Directory have conceived, I should not hesitate to accept the promotion; unfortunately such is not the case, and I am forced to decline the honor the Government would confer upon me. I trust that this refusal will be considered nothing more than a proof of the sincere patriotism by which I am actuated, and of the disinterestedness with which I perform my professional duties. May I beg you will assure the Directory that I shall never have any other aim than that of deserving its esteem.[29]

It was an extraordinary display of humility in a profession renowned for competition and ego in the pursuit of advancement.

This time, the Directory paid no attention to Ney's refusal. The minister who forwarded Ney's letter was instructed to tell him that the government persisted in its decree. Ney still hesitated. He had already performed the duties of the new office to which he was appointed, but he was loath to accept the title.

At this point, General Bernadotte wrote to him not to displease the Directory by refusing the promotion:

Look around you, my dear Ney, and say candidly whether your conscience does not call upon you to lay aside a modesty which becomes out of place and even dangerous when carried to excess. We must have ardent souls and hearts as inaccessible to fear as to seduction to be able to lead the armies of France. Who more than yourself is gifted with these qualities? It would be an act of weakness, then, to shrink from the career that is open to you.[30]

Ney yielded to Bernadotte's entreaty and assumed the rank of general of division. In May 1799, he was transferred to the Army of Switzerland, commanded by General André Masséna.[31] Soon thereafter, in an engagement at Winterthur, he was "struck with a musket-ball, which, after passing through his thigh, spent itself in the shoulder of his horse and he remained on the field, after allowing some of the men to bind up his wound and stanch the blood with their pocket-handkerchiefs." Afterward, at the head of a small body of cavalry, Ney "charged a whole squadron of Hungarians, . . . being attacked by a foot soldier just as he had struck down a hussar, he had not time to turn aside the bayonet, which pierced through the sole of his foot . . . he cut down his rash assailant, who, however, in falling, fired his piece and shattered Ney's wrist."[32]

The severity of Ney's wounds forced him to retire temporarily from active command, but his wounds healed within two months, and he rejoined Masséna. However, on August 14, 1799, the Directory ordered him to the Army of the Rhine over the objections of Masséna, who viewed him as too valuable to lose.

In September 1799, the Directory promoted Ney to provisional commander in chief of the Army of the Rhine. True to form, he at first declined the appointment. His innate modesty, the difficult situation in which that army was placed by his bumbling predecessor, and his own wounds being not yet fully healed pushed him to decline the honor. But the Directory had forwarded his commission, and the other generals and officers unanimously entreated him to accept. He therefore acceded reluctantly to their wishes.

His reluctance and modesty were illustrated by a letter he wrote his colleagues on assuming the command:

The Executive Directory has called upon me to assume the provisional command of the army in the room of General Muller. You are aware of the inefficiency of my military talents for this important station, particularly in our present critical situation. I shall perhaps become the victim of my obedience, but under the circumstances in which we are placed I am bound to accept the appointment. I therefore claim your kind solicitude for the safety of the troops under your command, as also your individual kindness toward myself. I must, moreover, inform you that I have signified to the Directory my intention of not retaining the command beyond ten days.[33]

Ney did not disappoint. He acted with decision and vigor to reorganize the army. He weeded out incompetent officers. He made sure his soldiers were comparatively well fed, well clothed, and well armed. He enforced the strictest discipline. The frontiers were carefully fortified and guarded. The Austrian enemy was closely watched. Confidence, even enthusiasm, began to take hold and grow. However, his appointment being only provisional, the Directory eventually replaced him with another commander, General Claude Lecourbe, under whom Ney remained to serve. However, morale and effectiveness suffered, and Lecourbe had to call on Ney to restore what he had earlier achieved. He asked him to "employ his influence in rekindling the courage of the men, in rousing the energy they were capable of displaying, and again exciting that confidence in themselves which had so often led them to victory."[34]

Once again, Ney succeeded not only in reinvigorating the army but also in translating that esprit into battlefield victories in which he led from the front with daring and imagination.

And so it went until Ney gained the reputation as one of the ablest generals in the French army.

A treaty of peace between Austria and France ensued on February 9, 1801, and Ney returned with his army to France, where he held a less-than-taxing assignment as an inspector of cavalry. He retreated to his small country place Petite Malgrange at Meurthe-et-Moselle in northeastern France, not far from his birthplace at Saarlouis, where he enjoyed a measure of anonymity. He had never before visited Paris. He was a soldier's soldier, a man of the field, not a political general of the Tuileries. However, First Consul Bonaparte soon summoned him to Paris because of his nascent reputation and warmly received him. It was the first encounter between the two. Ney of course had taken no part in Napoleon's earlier campaigns or the 18th of Brumaire coup, but subsequent events had seemed to him to justify the change that had taken place, and he supported the new government.

Bonaparte in turn was lavish in his praise. He maneuvered to attach Ney to his person and fortunes. He even enlisted the aid of Josephine, who introduced the young hero to the woman who would become his wife, the dark-haired beauty Aglaé Louise Auguié[35] (illustration 10), who was a close friend and former classmate of Josephine's daughter Hortense de Beauharnais at Madame Campan's famous school in Saint Germain. Aglaé's father was a senior civil servant, and her mother had been a lady-in-waiting to Queen Marie-Antoinette. Aglaé's mother was a Genêt, and her maternal aunt was Madame Campan, whose school she attended. Her maternal uncle was Edmond-Charles "Citizen" Genêt, the infamous French minister to the United States during the 1790s.[36] Because of her closeness to the queen and fearing her own demise, Aglaé's mother committed suicide during the Terror. Aglaé herself eventually became a lady-in-waiting to the empress Josephine.

It was not love at first sight. Aglaé reportedly found Ney awkward. However, they warmed to each other, and Ney and Aglaé married in 1802. Ney was a battle-hardened 32, and his courtly bride was barely 20. Ney's wife was known variously through her life as Aglaé, Madame Ney, La Maréchale, and La Moskowa. Ney probably privately called her Louise.[37]

Ney had prospered modestly on his salary but was not yet wealthy. He had multiple opportunities for amassing wealth, but he was not a plunderer like Masséna, Vandamme, or many other Revolutionary and empire generals. In fact, he strictly forbade plundering by his troops and enforced the prohibition vigorously. "Everything for France and her soldiers," he once said, "nothing for myself." His wife's fortune was commensurately modest. But both of them were young, happy, and hopeful. It is perhaps an insight into Ney's character that when he and Aglaé wed—not in Paris but in the countryside, which Ney clearly preferred—there was in the village an old couple who had been married half a century. Ney clothed them in fine apparel and arranged for them to receive their second nuptial benediction on the same day and at the same altar with himself and his young bride, thus marking his own marriage by an act of benevolence. Madame Campan described the scene in her reminiscences:

> The marriage took place at the Chateau de Grignon. Only a few were invited: Hortense, then married to Louis Bonaparte, was the only lady present outside of the family. . . . The band of one of the regiments of the general was placed for a week at the Chateau de Grignon; the park was illuminated; all the inhabitants of the neighboring hamlets were admitted to enjoy the fete, which continued for two days. The general adored his pretty companion, and joy gave him a radiant air, but how much we were touched when, upon the day the nuptial benediction was given in the chapel of the chateau, we saw him leading an old shepherd and his wife whom he had discovered on the farm of the chateau, and who at that time, according to Catholic usage, had to celebrate by a second marriage the fiftieth year of their union! He had had each completely dressed in the fashion of the province.[38]

"These old people," Ney observed, "will recall to my mind the lowliness of my own origin; and this renewal of their long union will prove of happy augury for my own." Alas, the prediction behind the noble gesture proved wrong.

While in Paris and engaged to Aglaé, Ney first met a courtesan who styled herself "Ida Saint-Elme" (figure 8.1). She was a blond amazon, née Tolstoy, of Hungarian, Russian, and Dutch extraction (or so she claimed; more circumspect thinkers peg her as Maria Versfelt of humble origin from Brabant). She frequently donned men's clothes and fought in the French army as a man, including in at least one cavalry charge. She had been the mistress of General Jean-Victor Moreau (who helped Napoleon to power but later became a rival and was banished to the United States)[39]

Figure 8.1.   Ida Saint-Elme, "La Contemporaine."
WIKIMEDIA COMMONS.

as well as a close friend and lover of Marshal Grouchy. Early on, she was attracted to Ney and had started a long-distance correspondence with him after his exploits at Mannheim. It appears to have been a largely one-sided and indeed probably an unconsummated love affair, to judge from her sometimes embroidered memoirs. She was, what might have been called in another twentieth-century context, a "groupie." In any event, she first met Ney in person, alone, during his stay in Paris shortly before he married Aglaé. At that meeting, Ney told Ida of his engagement to Aglaé and of his unavailability. "Good-bye, dear one, whom I have met too late," she recalled him rather gallantly telling her.[40] Nonetheless, she made sure their paths crossed over the ensuing years, even going so far as to collect his letters to other people[41] and to follow him on the invasion of Russia and partake in the harrowing winter retreat during which she shot marauding Cossacks. On more than one occasion Ney was annoyed to find her in the junior officer ranks on campaign and tried to have her sent back. But she was persistent, and Ney did occasionally meet her for private breakfasts. But on those occasions he always made clear his devotion and loyalty to his wife, the wife whom "he cherished and respected," as Saint-Elme put it in her memoirs.[42] Part of their attraction, according to Saint-Elme, who also went by the sobriquet of "La Contemporaine," was their shared Bonapartism, and following Ney's role in the first abdication in 1814 her ardor for the Prince of Moscow cooled. Still, she stayed in touch and met him, including privately but not intimately, from time to time. She claimed to have witnessed the Battle of Waterloo on horseback from behind the French lines and to have seen Ney on the battlefield (providing an eyewitness account cited later in this study), to have been an active participant in a plot to free him after his arrest, and to have witnessed the start of his execution, all as discussed below. These elements of her book appear to be accurate in their details and in accord with other eyewitness accounts.

In the fall of 1802, Napoleon appointed Ney minister plenipotentiary to the Republic of Switzerland. It was an unusual appointment in that Ney also came as a general at the command of some 30,000 French troops. The country at the time was riven by feuds between its francophone and German-speaking cantons. Ney's mission was to support and restore the dominance of the French-speaking (and French-leaning) Helvetian Republic with the implied threat of invasion and annexation. Despite seemingly insurmountable difficulties, Ney conducted negotiations with the various factions, showing patience, prudence, and tact, qualities he is not generally credited with possessing. In a little more than 12 months he had accomplished his mission to the satisfaction of the demanding first consul and, in addition, to the satisfaction of the Swiss people (at least the French-speaking portion of them on whose behalf he had intervened). He established "peace and concord" in Switzerland. Francophone Swiss leaders honored him with gifts and letters of gratitude on his departure.

Back in Paris, Talleyrand wrote to Ney, "The Government relies upon your talents and zeal. You are equally distinguished, General, both as a soldier and a politician."

This was an important episode in Ney's life in that it showcased Ney's diplomatic skills and political savoir faire. He was not merely a soldier. Ney's diplomatic mission in Switzerland was a precursor for other, non-military roles he was later to play. For example, in 1813, following the disastrous invasion of Russia, Napoleon convened a series of meetings to devise an order of succession should he die and to set up a regency for his son. In the council of a dozen or so prominent civilians and government ministers assembled to handle this sensitive and important issue, Ney was the sole military man.[43] Surely, this was proof enough of the esteem in which Napoleon held him. Likewise, Ney was later instrumental in convincing Napoleon to abdicate in 1814, and he was one of two marshals dispatched to sell the abdication to Tsar Alexander I. The tsar was then in Paris at the head of an occupying army, but he personally respected Ney, against whom he had just fought in 1812.

Following his service as an armed diplomat in Switzerland at the end of 1803, Ney returned to Paris and sat for a bust by the noted sculptor Jean Antoine Houdon.[44] Subsequently, Ney commanded forces at Montreuil near Boulogne on the northeast coast of France opposite Dover, England, preparing, yet again, to invade across the English Channel. Applying his customary energy and organizational skills, he made his units the envy of the army in terms of preparation, appearance, and readiness. During this period, he also took time to write a treatise on the art of war titled *Military Studies*. The book was well received and even translated into English. The treatise is lucidly written, well organized, and based on practical experience. It refutes any notion, harbored by some of his contemporaries, historians, and popular opinion, that Ney was an ill-educated bumpkin.

On May 18, 1804, Napoleon proclaimed himself emperor. Ney was supportive. The next day, he was one of 18 generals made marshals of France, the first draft of officers so honored. Ney was 35 years old. The Gérard portrait of Ney probably dates from about this time.

Beginning with his elevation to the Marshalate, Ney, who in earlier years had been approachable and companionable with his fellow officers, deliberately chose to distance himself and become aloof. According to one account, his confidence had been betrayed by an officer who served with him in the Boulogne camp, and henceforth he protected himself by trusting no one. According to another theory, he felt that his rapid rise in rank made it prudent for him to continually assert his position in order to prevent others from presuming on their earlier associations with him. However this may be, his staff officers were taught that they must not speak to him unless he addressed them or unless they had some communication to make to him in the routine of duty. On the line of march, he rode alone. In camp or quarters, he dined in solitary state. But this lonely reticence was habitual to him also in matters that affected the practical working of his corps. The orders received from the imperial headquarters were usually not communicated to the staff generally. They heard only fragments of them when they were asked to carry an executive order to a divisional general or a brigadier. Thus, they had only a vague idea of what was happening. Ney rarely if ever convened councils of war to seek advice from his colleagues. He increasingly became a loner, a state of existence imposed by his own will for whatever reason.[45]

It was often noted that Ney was susceptible to bursts of anger as well as occasional bouts of depression, especially as he grew older. As stated in the *Memoirs*, "Ney was severe, but just. Being of an irritable temper, he sometimes gave way to anger, but as readily offered reparation to those he had offended."[46] Another observer put it this way: "He was kindly humoured though liable to sudden fits of temper."[47] Nonetheless, his soldiers adored him and regularly followed him into the situations of most forlorn hope.

Bonaparte's planned invasion of England again came to naught, and the French army wheeled and marched to the Austrian border. Ney commanded the Sixth Corps of the Grande Armée. He left Montreuil on August 28 and arrived at Lauterburg on September 24. In this short interval, Ney's division had executed a march of more than 300 leagues, which was upward of an impressive 10 leagues a day. At Elchingen on the Danube in Bavaria, Ney won a major victory on October 14, 1805:

> Marshal Ney, on horseback, early in the morning of the 14th, in full uniform and wearing his decorations, laid hold of Murat's

arm, and shaking him violently before the whole staff and before the Emperor himself, said haughtily, "Come, prince, come along with me and make your plans in face of the enemy." Then, galloping to the Danube, he went, amid a shower of balls and grape, having the water up to his horse's belly, to direct the perilous operation assigned to him. This operation consisted in repairing the bridge, of which nothing was left but the piles, without flooring; passing it; crossing a small meadow that lay between the Danube and the foot of the eminence, then making himself master of the village, with the convent of Elchingen, which rose amphitheatrically, and was guarded by twenty thousand men and a formidable artillery. It was, indeed, an extraordinary, difficult, and perilous task. . . .

Undaunted by all the obstacles which presented themselves, he ordered an aide-de-camp of General Loison and a sapper to lay hold of the first plank and to carry it to the piles of the bridge for the purpose of re-establishing the passage under the fire of the Austrians. The brave sapper had a leg carried away by a grape-shot, but his place was immediately supplied. One plank was first thrown in the form of flooring, then a second, and a third. Having finished one length, they proceeded to the next, till they had covered the last piles under a murderous fire of small arms, poured upon the laborers by skilful marksmen on the opposite bank.

Ney crossed the bridge only to encounter fresh difficulties; but these, instead of dampening, served but to increase the ardor and determination of himself and his men. He marched on from victory to victory until he "gloriously reconquered the left bank," shut up [Austrian general] Mack and his army in Ulm, and virtually forced them to one of the most ignominious surrenders to be found in the history of war. The Emperor freely acknowledged the value of Ney's services by according to his corps the place of honor in the final surrender of the Austrian army and in the bulletin announcing the victory.[48]

For his contribution to this victory, Napoleon rewarded Ney with the title "Duke of Elchingen" almost three years later on June 6, 1808, when he created the Bonapartist peerage.

Although Ney was not at Austerlitz, he fought boldly and with distinction against the Prussians at Jena on October 14, 1806. He was attacked by the whole Prussian cavalry, justly celebrated as the finest in Europe, but after repeated and desperate charges, Ney's two weak squares, though suffering severely, remained unbroken. As soon as reinforcements arrived, Ney coolly formed his men again into column, marched straight on the center of the enemy's position at Vierzehn-Heiligen, and, after an obstinate conflict, captured it. On November 8, the great fortress of Magdeburg, an important Prussian fortress containing a garrison of 22,000 men, 800 cannon, and significant stores, surrendered to Ney, who had a greatly inferior force, almost without resistance.

The examples go on and on: Soldau, Eylau, and others. At the Battle of Deppen against the Russians and Prussians on June 5 and 6, 1807, Ney first displayed a new skill that was to recur at critical junctures and shape his legacy during the latter part of his career: the art of the strategic withdrawal. The contemporary Prussian historian Carl von Plotho describes it:

> The French, consummate masters in the art of war, resolved on that day this very difficult problem to execute a retreat that is become indispensable, in the face of an enemy who is much stronger and urgently pressing, and to render it as little prejudicial as possible. They extricated themselves from the situation with the utmost skill. The calmness and order and, at the same time, the rapidity shown by Ney's corps in assembling at the signal of three cannon shot; the coolness and attentive circumspection with which it executed its retreat, during which it opposed a resistance renewed at every step, and knew how to avail itself in a masterly manner of every position all this proved the talent of the captain who commanded the French and the habit of war carried by them to perfection as strongly as the finest dispositions and the most scientific execution of an offensive operation could have done.[49]

After the Battle of Friedland in June 1807, Ney was able to enjoy a few months of home leave. He sold la Petite Malgrange to his brother-in-law in 1808 and bought a new country house, the estate of Coudreaux near Châteaudun in the Loire Valley. He divided his time between this retreat and his town house at 74–76 rue de Bourbon (current rue de Lille) parallel to the Seine on the left bank in Paris, which he maintained primarily for his wife, who was active in Josephine's court, and his children. The house, which still stands, was located several doors down from the far grander town house of Napoleon's stepson Eugène de Beauharnais.[50] Ney could afford to spend money, but compared to many other marshals, he still had only a modest fortune. In any event, neither Ney nor Beauharnais spent much time in Paris, as they were almost constantly on campaigns.

At some point—it is not clear when—Ney became a Freemason. According to the records of the Masonic temple in Paris, "Field Marshal Ney Prince of Moskwa 33 G.O.F." is listed among the Masons who were under Napoleon's command. This was the highest rank in the order.[51]

On September 7, 1808, Ney was sent to Spain as commander of the Sixth Corps of the Army of Spain, but the Iberian war did not suit him. He opposed it from the beginning. Had Napoleon listened to him, he would have avoided one of the greatest errors of his life.

As it was, Ney served in Iberia initially under Marshal Nicolas Jean de Dieu Soult, who was jealous of his subordinate and refused to cooperate with him. Nonetheless, during Ney's occupation of Galicia and Asturias, he defeated the organized forces, put down most of the insurgent bands, and governed the country with a firm yet even hand. The British navy constantly threatened the northern coast (Ney had an extensive coastline to guard), and guerrilla partisans waged pervasive asymmetrical *petite guerre*, which was a new form of warfare to which Ney was unaccustomed. Nonetheless, he finally reduced the country to something approaching orderly submission and, in addition, succeeded by his "kindness and humanity"[52] in gaining some level of the confidence of the people whom he governed. Ney's command was largely cut off from the other French troops, and he was compelled to exercise his best judgment as to his military operations or else fail in the accomplishment of his purpose.

In 1810, Ney served under Marshal André Masséna in the invasion of Portugal. In addition to engaging in many successful offensive actions, once again Ney commanded a strategic retreat after the Battle of Bussaco, covering Masséna's withdrawal. Ney commanded the rear guard and effectively saved the French army from complete destruction. In the beginning of the retreat, Ney adroitly deceived Wellington and thus gained time for the army to get a running start. Ney's movements were so bold and mysterious that Wellington thought, as Ney wished him to think, that he was planning to advance to Torres Vedras near Lisbon. This uncertainty as to Ney's movements caused Wellington to suspend offensive operations for several hours. Meanwhile, the French army was marching rapidly to the rear. At Pombal, Wellington overtook Ney, and a considerable battle ensued. Ney drove back the English to the Arunca River, set fire to the town of Pombal, and continued his retreat leisurely on the right bank of the Arunca in defiance of the British, who were strongly posted on the opposite bank. This well-executed movement retarded the march of the English army for several more hours. After leaving Pombal, Ney disputed every inch of ground with the pursuing enemy. The English general Sir Thomas Picton, who was there, said that every movement that Ney made was a "perfect lesson in the art of war. Moving at all times on his flank, I had an opportunity of seeing everything he did, and I must be dull in the extreme if I had not derived some practically useful knowledge from such an example." The subsequent Battle of Redinha, when taken in connection with the operations leading up to it, was a tour de force by Ney. His positions were well chosen, his "handful of men" skillfully arranged, and his maneuvers well conceived and executed. He kept Wellington's whole army at bay for six consecutive hours. Wellington thought that Masséna's whole army was before him. The Iron Duke was deeply chagrined when he discovered that he had been deceived. Ney had saved Masséna's army.[53]

Subsequently, Ney let his temper get the better of him, and he quarreled with Masséna, whom he little respected. He refused to obey his orders and was relieved of his command. He returned to France on April 8, 1811. Ney's absence was immediately noted by the English, who pushed ever harder against Masséna. At the end of the campaign, Masséna withdrew in ignominy.

Atteridge described Ney's legacy before and during the Peninsular campaign thus:

To some extent what was best in Ney's character had retarded his advancement. He was no fortune hunter. He had none of the spirit of intrigue that led others to push their way to the front at the expense of their comrades, and he was quite free from brigand touch that made so many of the soldiers of the Empire enrich themselves with almost open peculation and plunder. From the days when, as a Republican officer, he had more than once refused a well-earned promotion he had done his duty as a soldier without troubling himself much about tangible rewards.

And he had not always been lucky. In the famous years after Boulogne, when the Grande Armée was marching about Central Europe making swift conquests and tumbling down thrones, he had missed some of the greatest battles. In Spain he had failed at the outset to carry out the Emperor's orders. He had been given no high command, and as a subordinate he had drifted into a dispute with his Commander-in-Chief, which had temporarily severed him from the armies in the field. But his great opportunity was to come. The terrible campaign in Russia revealed him as "the Bravest of the Brave."[54]

The next—and, arguably, most important—chapter in Ney's career was indeed Napoleon's 1812 invasion of Russia, where Ney commanded the Third Corps of the Grande Armée. Here too he exhibited his unique combination of offensive and defensive skills and executed a strategic retreat that went down in the annals of military history. Ney commanded the 37,400-strong Third Corps, to which three divisions of the First Corps were subsequently added. Like many of Napoleon's best officers, Ney opposed the invasion. Nonetheless, he was the right arm of Napoleon from the beginning to the end of the campaign.[55]

Before the Grande Armée reached Moscow, Ney was constantly in the vanguard, pursuing the Russians with his usual vigilance and vigor. At Krasnoi, Ney had a serious brush with the enemy, but his dispositions were sound, and the Russians were quickly defeated and retired in considerable confusion. At Smolensk, a ball struck him on the neck and tore away a portion of his coat collar. As the French advanced, the Russians conducted a strategic withdrawal, leaving behind a scorched earth that deprived the Grande Armée of food and fodder.

Ney made an unsuccessful effort to convince Napoleon to suspend his operations, to winter at Smolensk, and to be ready for a general advance in the spring.[56] He believed that to penetrate into the heart of Russia so late in the year, especially when the Grande Armée had already suffered significant attrition and supply interruptions, was foolhardy. Napoleon pushed on.

At the massive Battle of Borodino on September 7, 1812, the Russians finally turned and fought. It was possibly the bloodiest battle of modern times to date. For a considerable time after the battle began, Napoleon kept Ney close by his side and would not allow him to engage in the fight. Napoleon wished to save him for a critical moment. It was well for Napoleon that Ney was with him, for Ney saved him from a crushing defeat and emerged the hero of the day.

Napoleon's aide-de-camp General Philippe-Paul Count de Ségur, an eyewitness to the battle, described Ney's action:

Ney with his three divisions, now reduced to six thousand men, galloped out on the plain to support [Marshal] Davout. The Russians turned half their fire on him, without slowing him up. Compan's 57th Regiment, finding themselves reinforced, rallied to make a final dash against the enemy's entrenchments, scaled them, swarmed over the Russians, and routed them with their bayonets. Those who were not killed or wounded fled, leaving the 57th in full command. At the same time Ney was charging the other two redoubts, and with such violence that he snatched them from the enemy.

Napoleon awarded Ney the title "Prince of Moscow" for his taking of the Great Raevsky Redoubt.

The French occupation of Moscow, however, was short lived—only 35 days. The retreating Russians set the city afire, and Tsar Alexander I would not come to terms. Napoleon ordered a retreat to begin on October 19. As in Egypt, Napoleon hastened back to Paris ahead of his army, leaving the bulk of his troops to retreat on their own. In this case, the main body of the army was protected by a rear guard of fluctuating size under Ney's command that took the brunt of attacks by pursuing Russians and Cossacks.

As soon as the Russian commander Mikhail Kutuzov realized Napoleon was retreating, he wheeled his army about and pursued a parallel march to harass and attack French weak points but not give full battle. The temperature plunged to –4°C in late October. The French retreat passed the battlefield at Borodino, strewn with bodies, and villages they had marched through earlier, grisly with atrocities they themselves had committed.

The first heavy snow came on November 4. Ney took command of the rear guard on November 5 as snow obliterated roadbeds and landmarks. Rumors spread among the French of what the Cossacks would do to them if captured, including skinning them alive.

The temperature dropped to –30°C on November 7 as blizzard conditions continued. The retreat became a crawl. More than 5,000 horses died within days. Ségur described the harrowing scene:

> Russian winter in this new guise attacked them on all sides; it cut through their thin uniforms and worn shoes, their wet clothing froze on them, and this icy shroud molded their bodies and stiffened their limbs. The sharp wind made them gasp for breath, and froze the moisture from their mouths and nostrils into icicles on their beards . . . [when fallen] their moans for help went unheeded. The snow soon covered them up and only low white mounds showed where they lay. Our road was strewn with these hummocks, like a cemetery.

All the while, the Russians attacked Ney's rear guard, whose numb fingers could not work their muskets. Ney stepped into the breach. Again, as described by Ségur, "Ney rushed into their midst, snatched a musket from one of them, and led them back into action by firing the first shot, exposing his life like a soldier, as he had done before he became rich, powerful and esteemed. He fought as if he still had everything to gain, whereas he had everything to lose. While he became a soldier again, he remained the general—availing himself of the terrain, backing up against a hill and concealing himself behind a stockaded house." Ney fought like this for 10 days and infused his energy and courage into those around him. With the main French army well ahead of him with Napoleon in its van hastening back to Paris, Ney suspected and probably knew his commander had forsaken him. He nonetheless kept the pursuing Russian army at bay. The famous Minard map/chart (figure 8.2) graphically illustrates the shrinking manpower of the Grande Armée as it retreated back across Russia.

Ney abandoned what was left of his baggage and cannon when there were no more horses left to pull them. At a bend in the Borysthenes River, he stationed his cannon to cover the crossing of his troops and then sacrificed them by dumping them into the icy river, faced about, and made the hostile river, which crossed his route, the barrier for his defense.

Just before Ney reached Smolensk, he turned about to give battle to the Russians when he suddenly saw on his left a large body of disbanded men rushing wildly on his own troops as if they intended to attack them. They were Prince Eugène de Beauharnais's soldiers, closely followed by the Cossacks. Ney was at first astonished, but quickly taking in the situation, he made his dispositions to meet the threefold danger of the enemy attacking him in the rear, Eugène's crazed corps, and the Cossacks in hot

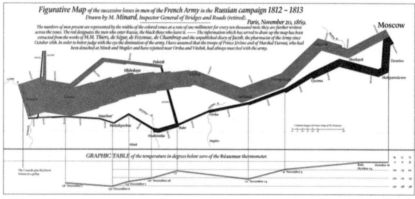

Figure 8.2.   English translation version of Minard Map of 1812 Russian campaign. WIKIMEDIA COMMONS.

pursuit of them. He finally succeeded in arresting the progress of these swirling armies and then, taking Eugène under his wing, marched away.

Ney's difficulties grew still greater after he reached Smolensk. The stores that Napoleon promised to leave him there were nonexistent, the town sacked and looted. His resources were rapidly disappearing, and there was no way to replenish them. His little army was thinning out at every step while his enemies were multiplying. He had no choice but to push on. He departed Smolensk on November 17 with 6,000 armed men, 12 cannon, 300 horses, and 7,000 unarmed stragglers. "As they proceeded from the city, the Marshal time and again demonstrated great care for the wounded and the women and children, showing how the bravest was also the most humane," Ségur recalled. As they left Smolensk, Ségur recorded, a French mother abandoned her little son, only five years old. In spite of his cries and tears, she drove him away from her sledge, which was too heavily laden. Ney twice replaced the child in the arms of its mother, and twice she cast him from her on the frozen snow. The child was entrusted to another mother and remained as an orphan in the ranks. The child was afterward seen at the Berezina, then at Wilna, and again at Kowno and finally escaped all the horrors of the retreat.[57] According to later tradition, Ney subsequently adopted the child.

The scene on the line of retreat was devastating. The way forward was almost blocked by the deepening snow, fallen trees, and treacherous ravines into which the soldiers were continually plunging; by dead and dying men, women, and horses, even children; and by abandoned baggage, cannon, caissons, carts, wagons, and carriages laden with the spoils of Moscow: every form of danger, suffering, and death seemed to confront the deserted leader (illustration 11).

As Ney approached the banks of the Losmina near Krasnoi in a mist on November 18, he was astonished to find the Russian commander Kutusov, with 80,000 men, directly in his front. Kutusov had captured Napoleon's papers near Krasnoi, and from these, he had learned the exact situation of Ney's rear guard and the deplorable condition to which it had been reduced. Kutusov now concluded, not unreasonably, that he had Ney trapped. He sent a Russian officer to offer surrender terms to Ney. The demand was polite, respectful, and even flattering. "Kutusov," the officer said, "would not have presumed to make so cruel a proposal to so great a general, to a warrior so renowned, if there had remained a single chance of saving yourself. But eighty thousand Russians are in front of you and around you. If you doubt it, Kutusov will permit you to send a person to pass through his ranks and count his forces."

The officer had not finished his speech "when," according to Ségur, "suddenly forty discharges of grape-shot, coming from the right of his army, and cutting our files to pieces, struck him with amazement, and effectually put a stop to what he had further intended to say." At the same moment, a French officer darted forward, seized, and would have at once killed him as a traitor, but Ney checked his fury, angrily saying to the Russian, "A Marshal of France never surrenders. And we do not parley under fire. You are my prisoner." The officer was accordingly disarmed and detained as a prisoner (he was not released until after 26 days of captivity, during which he shared all the miseries of the retreating Grande Armée).

The Russian batteries now opened up in earnest on Ney's troops. All day, the French withstood the persistent onslaught and repeated charges by the enemy. Ney lost many of his troops so that as the afternoon wore on, his 4,000 remaining armed French with six cannon faced 80,0000 Russians with 200 cannon. Ney held out until the dark winter night descended. He then ordered his men to build campfires and begin to march back toward Smolensk. Incredulous at first at being ordered to march back into Russia and away from their line of retreat, the men soon realized that Ney had a plan. They obeyed and marched back into the scene of their prior misery in the pitch-dark night. After about an hour, Ney, with his unerring sense of geography and warrior's instinct (both of which his enemies commented on), stopped at a stream flowing through a ravine. He ordered the snow cleared and the ice broken. Gazing at the current under the ice, he realized the stream flowed westward and was a tributary of the Dnieper River, which, if he could cross, would deliver his force to relative safety on the opposite side.

At about 8:00 p.m., Ney and his scouts discovered the banks of the Dnieper. The immediate question was whether the ice was thick enough to support the crossing. Blocks of ice carried by the current had jammed together at a bend in the river. The cold had fused them together but only at that one point. Elsewhere, the current continued to flow. Ney perceived that he would have to move quickly because the ice was beginning to give way. Ney's escort suggested that he cross with the armed men to ensure his safety and wait on the other side for the stragglers, who were strung out at a considerable distance during the nocturnal march. Ney decided to allow three hours to gather as many stragglers as possible. Ney gathered his cloak about him and slept for those three hours on the riverbank.

The crossing of the Dnieper began at midnight. Most of the stragglers made it, but several carts carrying the wounded fell victim to cracking ice when they were partway across the river. "The men on the opposite bank listened to the long drawn-out agonized shrieks that dwindled to intermittent moans, then fell into silence. All had disappeared!" Ségur wrote. He added, "Ney, staring down into this gulf, thought he saw something still moving among the shadows. It was one of the victims of the catastrophe, an officer named Briqueville, who was prevented from rising to his feet by a deep wound in his groin. A sheet of ice had lifted him to the surface. Soon he could be clearly seen crawling on his hands and knees from one floating ice cake to another, slowly approaching. Ney himself drew him to safety."

At dawn, the Russians found only spiked cannon at the former French encampment. But the rear guard was not yet out of trouble. In the preceding days, some 3,000 armed men and 4,000 stragglers had died or strayed from the ranks. Now came the Cossacks.

For the next two days, during which the depleted rear guard marched some 50 miles, the Cossacks attacked it almost continuously, forcing it at any moment to stop and form squares to fend off attacks.

Finally, on November 21, Ney and his ragged band, now numbering 900, arrived at the town of Orsha and found momentary respite. When Napoleon, who thought Ney's rear guard had been annihilated after Krasnoi, heard the good news, he literally leaped for joy and cried, "So I have saved my Eagles! I have three hundred millions in my coffers at the Tuileries. I would willingly have given them all to save Marshal Ney!" (in fact, he had nothing of the sort in his coffers). After the emperor heard the details of Ney's harrowing but heroic ordeal, he declared him on the spot "the Bravest of the Brave." And the name stuck.

Ney's arrival electrified the French army. According to General Armand Marquis de Caulaincourt (who was on the Russian campaign and accompanied Napoleon on his trek back to Paris), "Never has a victory in the field caused such a sensation. The joy was general, everyone was drunk with delight, and went running to and fro to spread the news. . . . It was a national triumph, and you shared it even with your grooms."

But the Grande Armée was not yet safely home. Both the army and tens of thousands of stragglers had to cross the Berezina River. Unfortunately, though frigid and clogged with ice floes, it was not sufficiently frozen to allow passage on its surface. The army's wagon train still was encumbered by significant artillery and captured loot. Working heroically and braving hypothermia, the army's Dutch engineers and others stood in the water, in some cases on each other's shoulders, to construct two bridges to facilitate the crossing—all while under fire from surrounding Russian and Cossack forces. Napoleon ordered Ney to sally out and relieve the pressure from the Russians, which he did, defeating Admiral Tchitichakov's 27,000 Russians with only 8,000 men.

The crossing took place in the waning days of November. The hastily constructed artillery bridge broke down under fire from Russian artillery. The other bridge was burned by the engineers as soon as the last of Marshal Victor's Ninth Corps, which had protected the crossing, had crossed. Many others, mostly stragglers, lost their lives in a desperate effort to force their way across the flaming bridge. Many more were drowned in an attempt to pass on the shifting ice. Still more were massacred by the Cossacks on the left bank. In the spring, the Russians collected and burned in great heaps nearly 30,000 corpses.[58]

It is perhaps not surprising that the miseries of the retreat had hardened Ney into something approaching insensibility. Captain De Noailles of the general staff had been killed on November 28 on the Beresina. He was a friend of Ney's aide-de-camp, De Fezensac,[59] and the young colonel spoke to Ney of his loss. The Marshal's comment was, "Well, it is better that we should be regretting him, than that he should be regretting us." In another instance, a soldier fell wounded beside Ney and begged to be carried off and saved from the pursuing Cossacks. "What do you want me to do? You are one more victim of the war," Ney replied coldly and walked away.[60]

In the ensuing days after crossing the Berezina, Ney continued to command the rear-guard and protect the retreating main army despite temperatures of −10°C and constant harassment by the advancing Russian armies.

Still the master of the retreat, Ney reached and took Vilna on December 8 with the remnants of his force. His method was the same each day. He would halt his force at 5:00 p.m. and hold the Russians at bay while his men ate and rested. Then they would march at night. Ney drove the laggards with both threats and supplications. At daybreak, about 7:00 a.m., he would halt again and rest under guard until 10:00 a.m., at which point the Russians generally reappeared and the straggling column would resume its flight, trying to make as much ground as possible while being attacked and harassed. The number of the rear guard grew depleted by the day, as it dropped to 2,000, to 1,000, to 500, and finally to 60. At one point during the evening rest stop, Ney realized that he and the Bavarian general Prince Karl Wrede[61] were alone, abandoned by what was left of their soldiers who had left their muskets stacked by the fireside. Ney and Wrede immediately corralled their errant troops and restored the rear guard.

Never was there a more apt exemplar of Churchill's reputed axiom "If you are going through hell, keep going."

On December 13, the army reached Kovno, a town on the Russian western frontier. Ney found himself alone in command of some 700 foreign, mainly German, recruits. At dawn the next morning, the Russians attacked. Only 300 of Ney's Germans were armed. Early on, a Russian cannonball killed their commander, and the German recruits threw down their arms and fled. Not Ney. After a futile attempt to stop the fleeing Germans, Ney gathered their loaded muskets and faced the Russians alone. The boldness of his stand momentarily halted the Russians. Seeing what had happened, some of the fleeing Germans were shamed into rearming themselves and rejoining the marshal. So with a band of about 30 soldiers Ney personally held the Vilna road open for the retreating French army until nightfall.

Then, still fighting in a strategic withdrawal, he led his men across the Nieman River, which marked the frontier of the Russian Empire with

Poland. The band of 30 crossed before him. Ney was the last French soldier to leave Russia.

A story, perhaps apocryphal, perhaps not, is told that the next day in Gumbinnen, Poland, the French general Mathieu Dumas was about to sit down for breakfast when (in his words) "a man in a brown coat entered, his beard long, his face was blackened and looking as though it had been burnt, his eyes were red and glaring. 'At length I am here,' he exclaimed. 'Don't you know me?'

"'No,' said the General, 'Who are you?'

"'I am the rear-guard of the Grande Armée. I have fired the last musket shot on the bridge of Kovno. I have thrown the last of our arms into the Nieman and have come hither through the woods. I am Marshal Ney.'"[62]

The legacy and importance of Ney's performance on the retreat from Russia are summarized by Atteridge:

> Ney had not received even the slightest wound during the continual fighting of the retreat, and though he looked worn and haggard when he reached Konigsberg, he was in perfect health. He had evidently an exceptional physique. It was men of this stamp that survived the horrors of the Russian campaign. The weaker had all been swept away.
>
> His service with the rear-guard of the Grande Armée was undoubtedly the most brilliant episode in his military career. Never was there a more conspicuous illustration of the fact that in war the man counts for more than the men. It was to Ney's iron will, calm courage, ready resource and initiative, and his influence as a leader that Napoleon owed it that even the debris of his army reached the Niemen, and that he himself escaped from captivity or death.[63]

Following Ney's bravura performance on the retreat through Russia[64] his stock with Napoleon rose commensurately, and the emperor relied on him ever more closely as he fought multiple engagements to try to save his throne during 1813–1814 as the net cast by advancing Prussians and Russians grew ever tighter.

Following the disaster in Russia, the Grande Armée was no more, and Napoleon sought to reconstitute it with new levies of raw recruits. Ney led such troops at the Battle of Lutzen on May 2, 1813, where he commanded the Fourth and the Seventh Corps, composed chiefly of conscripts. Ney molded them into a proficient fighting force in the months leading up to the battle and claimed they were better than the old soldiers. Napoleon was surprised at Lutzen, but Ney, by his promptness, energy, and perseverance, saved him from a major defeat. He similarly rendered signal service at the Battle of Bautzen. Ney, with 60,000 men, crossed the River Spree and early the next morning fell on the flank of the allied army as Napoleon attacked it in front. It was a difficult and perilous operation, but Ney exhibited great prudence and skill and routed the enemy. He had practically an independent command, was entirely separated from Napoleon, and was compelled to rely on his own judgment on a "vast, complicated, and unknown field."

Napoleon was also surprised at Dresden. While he was pursuing Blücher, who eluded him constantly, purposely drawing Napoleon away from his base, the main body of the allied army suddenly advanced on Dresden. This city, held by the French, was defended by Marshal Laurent St. Cyr with about 20,000 men. The allies numbered about 150,000. In a few hours, they had swept everything before them, and St. Cyr was about to surrender when the surprised Napoleon quickly marched to his relief. Napoleon in turn assumed the offensive and gained a decisive victory. Ney and Murat were the chief actors in this struggle. They fought with courage and skill under the most disadvantageous circumstances. It was here that General Moreau, returned from the United States, was killed.

Notwithstanding the victories at Lutzen, Bautzen, and Dresden, a series of defeats ensued, culminating in Napoleon's loss at Dennewitz. Ney acquitted himself credibly in most of these engagements, but a variety of factors conspired against the emperor. During the defense of Schonfeld that year, Ney was badly wounded by a ball to his shoulder and was invalided to recover as the French army retreated to the Rhine.[65]

Ney hit his stride again in the frenetic campaign of 1814, when a badly outnumbered Napoleon adroitly fought—and mostly won—12 battles within a matter of months. Ney, in command of young and barely trained conscripts, played an integral role in this campaign and performed peerlessly at Brienne, Montmirail, Craonne, Laon, Etouvelles, Arcis, and other engagements at arcane venues. But his efforts were for naught, as France was exhausted. Paris surrendered on March 31. As noted previously, Ney made the case to Napoleon at Fountainbleu to negotiate a conditional abdication. Indeed, he was instrumental in forcing Napoleon into this option, an action that Napoleon held against him ever afterward. Ney then went with Marshal Étienne MacDonald to negotiate the terms of the abdication with Tsar Alexander I. For a variety of complex reasons having nothing to do with Ney, the mission failed, and Napoleon was obliged to sign an unconditional abdication on April 6.

It was perhaps a tribute both to his role in forcing Napoleon's abdication and to his standing as a soldier that Ney fared well with the accession of Louis XVIII. He retained his rank and titles and remained a peer of France. Although he had pledged his loyalty, Ney was patently uncomfortable with the airs of the new regime. The dynamic is worth examining in more detail because it provides an insight into Ney's character and reactions:

> He [Ney] was too old to acquire new habits. Plain in his manners, and still plainer in his words, he neither knew nor wished to know the art of pleasing courtiers. The habit of braving death and of commanding vast bodies of men had impressed his character with a species of moral grandeur which raised him far above the puerile observances of the fashionable world. Of good nature, indeed, he had a considerable fund, but he showed it not so much by the endless little attentions of a gentleman, as by scattered acts of princely beneficence. The sobriety of his manners was extreme, even to austerity. His wife had been reared in the court of Louis XVI, and had adorned that of the Emperor. Cultivated in her mind, accomplished in her manners, and elegant in all she said or did, her society was courted on all sides. Her habits were expensive; luxury reigned throughout her apartments and presided at her board; and to all this display of elegance and pomp of show, the military simplicity of the marshal furnished a striking contrast. . . . While

she was presiding at a numerous and brilliant party of guests, he preferred to remain alone in a distant apartment, where the festive sounds could not reach him. On such occasions he almost always dined alone. Ney seldom appeared at court. He could neither bow nor flatter, nor could he stoop to kiss even his sovereign's hand without something like self-humiliation. . . . [F]rom the monotony of his Parisian existence, he retired to his country-seat in January, 1815. . . . There he led an unfettered life; he gave his mornings to field sports, and the guests he entertained in the evening were such as, from their humble condition, rendered formality useless, and placed him completely at his ease.[66]

Thus, as demonstrated before in his life, Ney's instinct was to avoid Paris and retreat in solitary fashion to the anonymity of his country place.

By now, the couple had four sons: Napoleon Joseph, born on May 8, 1803; Michel Louis Félix, born on August 24, 1804; Eugène, born on September 12, 1806; and Edgar, born on March 12, 1812. The third son, Eugène, was destined to play a hitherto unknown but potentially important role in the mystery of P. S. Ney.

Ney was therefore at his rural estate when, on March 6, 1815, he received a summons from Minister of War Marshal Jean de Dieu Soult to join the Sixth Division at Besançon and await further orders. Ney later claimed that he had no idea why. En route to Besançon, he stopped in Paris to pick up his military uniforms. There, at the home of his notary, Henri Batardy, Ney was later to testify at his trial for high treason that he first learned that Napoleon had landed near Cannes on the south coast and he was being mobilized to oppose him (not surprisingly, the crown prosecutor took a different view and argued that Ney was in on the plot to free Napoleon from Elba from the start). Ney's initial reaction, as expressed to and testified by Batardy, was that Napoleon was mad and had to be stopped. Ney then sought an audience with the king, at the conclusion of which he promised to "bring Napoleon to Paris in an iron cage." (At his trial Ney remembered his words a little differently as "If he was taken he deserved to be brought to Paris in an iron cage.") Either way, these were words he would live to regret because instead of capturing

Napoleon Ney joined him with his entire army and thus destroyed the last hope of Bourbon resistance.

Ney by all appearances remained loyal to the king until March 14, 1815, a critical date as events were later to prove. During the night of March 13, he received letters from General Henri Bertrand, who had accompanied Napoleon from Elba, stating, among other things, that Napoleon's success was ensured, that everything had been arranged beforehand, that England and Austria concurred in Napoleon's return (!), and that the emperor had received the secret submission of every regiment in the service. Bertrand also made the point that if Ney opposed him, he would be responsible for a civil war. Ney had already observed that his own troops showed no will to fight Napoleon. "I cannot," he said, "keep back the ocean with my hand."[67]

Accordingly, on March 14, Ney read a proclamation under his name to his troops in support of Bonaparte that Bertrand had prepared and sent to him. Dated March 13, it announced that the "cause of the Bourbons was forever lost" and that the emperor Napoleon was the legitimate sovereign of France. "Soldiers," Ney said in the proclamation, "I have often led you to victory; I am now going to conduct you to that immortal phalanx which the Emperor Napoleon is conducting to Paris, where it will be in a few days, and then our hope and happiness will be forever realized." No doubt concerned at the prospect of a civil war, Ney concluded that it would be better to direct the torrent than to be swept away by it.

Ney met with Napoleon at Auxerre. Napoleon received him graciously and embraced him, calling him once again "the Bravest of the Brave," but there was a certain mutual distance, at best a transactional nature, to their new relationship. As stated by Ney in his eventual trial, Napoleon addressed him in the more formal "*vous*" rather than the familiar "*tu.*" Bonaparte sent him to Lille to inspect fortifications. That mission accomplished, Ney went back to his château at Condreaux, and for six weeks he lived there with Aglaé and their children, learning only from the newspapers and a few letters from friends what was happening in Paris. The emperor was handing out new promotions to the rank of general of division, and Grouchy had been given a marshal's baton. But there was no command for the hero of Moscow and the retreat from Russia. The emperor apparently did not trust him.

In the last week of May, Ney received a dispatch from the War Ministry. He opened it, hoping to find in it an appointment to a command. It was a mere invitation to a ceremonial display on the Champ de Mars, a great gathering at which the emperor was to take the oath of fealty to the new constitution and distribute the eagles to the regiments assembled in Paris. Ney accepted. For the last time, Madame Ney accompanied him to the court to share his honors. On June 1, a day of brilliant spring sunshine, 45,000 soldiers formed in glittering lines around the altar erected on the Champ de Mars, and 200,000 spectators looked on at the last great ceremony of the empire. Napoleon drove to the parade ground in a carriage drawn by eight horses with four marshals riding beside it—Ney, Soult, Jourdan, and Grouchy.

But Ney was a mere prop in the great display. To have left him out of it would have confirmed the current rumors that he was in disgrace and in danger of arrest. Although he had found no active employment for him, Napoleon could not afford to omit so famous a figure from the ceremonial display at a time when a number of marshals had abandoned him. This, too, was the reason why the next day Ney was informed that he had been named a member of the Chamber of Peers, the new Senate of the reorganized empire. So far, he had not had an audience in Paris with Napoleon, even though he had ridden beside his carriage as one of his state escorts. On June 6, Ney finally met Napoleon at the Elysée Palace, where he had gone to collect an arrearage in pay. When Napoleon saw him, he stated acerbically, "I thought you had emigrated."

"I ought to have done so," replied Ney, "but it is now too late."[68]

Ney's involvement in Napoleon's last battle was rushed and almost had the appearance of an afterthought. On the eve of his departure to engage Wellington, Napoleon sent a message to Ney via his minister of war to "join the army at once if he wished to see the first battle."

Why Napoleon waited so long to summon him is unknown, but it probably stemmed from distrust over Ney's prominent role in forcing his earlier abdication. It was not the only mistake Napoleon made at Waterloo. Ney perceived it at the time as a slight. As it was, Ney was given no time for preparation. It was only by the exercise of great diligence that he reached the front when he did, and that was at 5:00 in the afternoon of June 15, after the French had crossed the Sambre and the preliminary moves in the battle to come were already occurring. Napoleon assigned Nye the command of the First and Second Corps, headed by Lieutenant-Generals Jean-Baptiste Drouet Count D'Erlon and Honoré Charles Count Reille, respectively, as well as a few other units, but he was ignorant of their organization. Ney himself said,

On June 11th I received an order from the Minister of War to repair to the imperial presence. I had no command and no information upon the composition and strength of the army. Neither the Emperor nor his minister had given me any previous hint, from which I could anticipate that I should be employed in the present campaign. I was consequently taken by surprise, without horses, without accoutrements, and without money, and I was obliged to borrow the necessary expenses of my journey. Having arrived on the 12th at Laon, on the 13th at Avesnes, and on the 14th at Beaumont, I purchased in this last town two horses from the Due de Trevise, with which I repaired on the 15th to Charleroy, accompanied by my first aide-de-camp, the only officer who attended me. I arrived at the moment when the enemy, attacked by our troops, was retreating upon Fleurus and Gosselies. The Emperor ordered me immediately to put myself at the head of the First and Second corps of infantry, commanded by Lieutenant-Generals D'Erlon and Reille . . . , of the division of light cavalry of the guard under the command of Lieutenant-General Lefebvre-Desnouettes and Colbert, and of two divisions of cavalry of Count de Valmy, forming in all eight divisions of infantry and four of cavalry. With these troops, a part of which only I had as yet under my immediate command, I pursued the enemy, and forced him to evacuate Gosselies, Frasnes, Millet, Hepignies. There they took up a position for the night, with the exception of the First Corps, which was still at Marchiennes, and which did not join me till the following day.[69]

Historians have long argued whether Napoleon ordered Ney to seize Quatre Bras on June 15 or simply to "push the enemy," the former of which he did not do, to Napoleon's chagrin, but the latter of which he did do. At the end of the day, it matters little for purposes of this summary.

On June 16, two days before the actual Battle of Waterloo, Ney did attack Wellington at Quatre Bras. After wasting most of the valuable morning hours doing nothing (and thus inviting some historians' comment that Ney was not the general he previously had been), Ney launched the attack. It was a fierce and bloody struggle. Notwithstanding Wellington's dogged resistance, he would likely have been defeated if Napoleon had not at the critical moment taken away Ney's reserve of 20,000 men. At this stage, the British were fighting with their Dutch allies and yet to be reinforced by Marshal Blücher's long-awaited Prussians. At the end of the engagement, Wellington prevailed but repositioned his troops away from Quatre Bras and toward Waterloo, 10 miles south of Brussels, to avoid being outflanked by developments elsewhere on the battlefield.

The next important engagement for Ney came two days later. At about 11:30 a.m. on Sunday, June 18, 1815, as the climactic Battle of Waterloo got under way, Napoleon directed his chief of staff, Marshal Soult, to order Reille's corps to move against the British right at Château d'Hougoumont, apparently as a feint to mislead Wellington. However, the movement became a persistent and fiercely pressed attack. A cannonade that began on the left gradually extended along the French front. Napoleon ordered Ney to attack in the center with D'Erlon's corps. He massed some 90 guns in front of La Belle Alliance to cover his advance. At 1:30 p.m., this "Great Battery" opened fire. At 2:00 p.m., Ney gave the order to attack and himself led the advance with D'Erlon beside him. The four divisions of the First Corps, more than 20,000 strong and with bayonets bristling, had been drawn up in four massive columns, each fronted by a battalion. This deployment had gained usage during the latter Napoleonic wars as a better way to control the inexperienced recruits who increasingly manned the army. However, it diminished the firing front and also made an easy target for enemy artillery. Ney's order was that the advance should be in echelons of four columns moving out in sequence from the left with an interval of about 400 yards separating them so that they presented an attacking front about a mile wide. As the columns descended into the wide hollow in their front, the French artillery fired over their heads, ceasing only as they went up the ridge held by the British. One of the columns cleared the orchard and garden of La Haye Sainte but could not take the buildings. Another column, flanked by a mass of cuirassiers, went up the slope and broke an Allied division. The four columns reached the crest of the English position, and it looked as if Ney was on the verge of prevailing when the British general Sir Thomas Picton counterattacked with redcoats and Highlanders. Sir William Ponsonby's cavalry charged into the French columns about the ridge. The British cavalry crashed into the cuirassiers. Ney, while trying to steady his flank above La Haye Sainte and apparently at the center of the action, had his horse shot from under him. He caught another and rode back amid the confused retreat of the broken columns, which were charged again and again by the British cavalry.[70] As the British cavalry approached the main French position, French cavalry in turn charged them and drove them back. The defeated French infantry disengaged and re-formed, and the artillery duel began again. It was now nearly 4:00 p.m.

At the very time Ney was leading D'Erlon's corps to the attack, Napoleon grew concerned about the sudden emergence of troops on his right front, which proved to be Blücher's late-arriving vanguard. Fear that Wellington would shortly be reinforced caused Ney to force the British position at all hazards. While D'Erlon was re-forming behind the guns, Ney rolled the dice and ordered General Édouard Count Milhaud's division of cuirassiers to charge the British center. Thus, after 4:00 p.m. began a series of heavy cavalry onslaughts that lasted for two hours. Division after division was thrown into action until there were no more. Ney, who had begun his military career as a cavalryman, on his last battlefield led charge after charge against the British squares. In the last great onset, no fewer than 77 squadrons of French cavalry were engaged.

On several occasions, Ney rode right up to the British bayonets forming squares. Two more horses were killed under him, and his clothes were torn with bullets, but he reportedly remained unwounded. At times, his ardor was like that of a madman. One of the officers who rode in the last cavalry attack described how he saw Ney dismounted, standing beside one of the guns of a British battery, through which the charge had penetrated to attack the squares beyond. The marshal stood sword in hand beside the cannon, angrily beating the metal of the gun with the flat of his blade.

As the survivors of the final charge came back toward La Belle Alliance, Ney still hoped for victory. La Haye Sainte had been taken at last. Along the ridge, numbers of guns overturned by the cavalry in their charges lay silent and abandoned. The British infantry were unseen behind the crest where they had been withdrawn from the fire of the French batteries, and Ney suspected a retreat was in progress. He sent an aide to ask Napoleon for fresh infantry to try to break the British center. "Where does he think I can find it? Does he suppose I can make it?" replied the emperor. He still had 14 battalions of the Guard in reserve, but these were his last stake in the game, and he could not bring himself to commit them.

After 7:00 p.m. the Prussians were rapidly filling the battlefield, and Napoleon concluded he must either abandon the field or try one more effort. He therefore moved the Guard forward, formed in three great columns, and ordered Ney to lead it to the attack. Ney personally led the final attack of the Guard, first on horseback, then on foot with sword in hand. When the onward march was stopped by the British fire, he did "all that despairing courage could attempt to steady the wavering ranks. As the columns were swept back before the counterattack of the British, he fought among the bayonets, and his sword was broken in his hand. D'Erlon, riding toward La Belle Alliance amid the rout, saw the marshal standing by the road calling out to the beaten troops to rally again. Ney was hardly recognizable, his face black with powder, his sword broken in two, his uniform riddled with bullets, one epaulette hanging down, torn by a saber cut to his upper body.[71] When he saw D'Erlon, he waved his broken sword and called out to him, "D'Erlon, if you and I escape from this we shall be hanged!"[72]

Amid the confused crowd toward the rear of which the British cavalry were charging, Ney saw a French brigade retiring with formed ranks, though reduced to half its strength. He forced his way toward them, halted, and faced them about. "Come and see how a Marshal of France can die," he said as he led them against the enemy. But they broke, and he found himself again without followers.

Near La Belle Alliance, three squares of the Guard still stood like islands in the flood of fugitives. In one of these, Ney found refuge for a while. He remained with the square while it slowly retired, beating off hostile charges. When it at last broke up, he began to tramp in the darkness along the Genappe road, a solitary figure in a disorganized mob in the rout of Napoleon's last army. Ney had been among the last to leave the battlefield.[73]

Perhaps the truest assessment of Ney's character is to be found not among French sources but rather among those of his enemies, the English. The *Times* of London published the following précis on Ney on September 6, 1815, following his arrest and while he awaited trial for high treason:

> . . . his name rendered illustrious by 25 years of eminent services and brilliant exploits, was dear to the country, and even the enemies of France admired in him the character of the Great Captain. All allowed him to possess as much generosity of sentiment as bravery and skill at the head of armies. No trait of weakness, adulation or rapacity, had ever cast shade over his loyalty and military virtues. His sole defect seemed to be a certain vehemence of character and expression, which rendered him little suited to public affairs.[74]

That was his public persona. However, there is little question that there was a dichotomy between Ney the soldier and Ney the private man that rendered him enigmatic at the end of the day. He was a very private person. His wife's aunt Madame Campan summarized it aptly when she wrote, "All that relates to the military life of the brave Ney belongs to history, but all that relates to his private life and to his truly patriotic services is the particular property of his family."[75]

Nonetheless, it is possible to conclude that Marshal Ney was the following:

- A self-made man with an early scholarly bent who likely had some rudiments of a classical education. Although his years at school were limited, he likely was better educated than many people have assumed.
- A motivated autodidact who mastered disparate disciplines, including law, industrial management, organizational specialties in the form of quartermaster and adjutant duties, combat, leadership, diplomacy, and strategic retreats. In doing so, he literally reinvented himself for each calling.
- A man of compelling willpower who could make himself accomplish whatever goal he set for himself, however unreasonable it might be.
- A man of an iron constitution and strapping physique.
- An expert swordsman and equestrian.
- A man of inordinate, almost unseemly modesty and self-effacement in a profession of competitive egos.
- At the same time a man of inordinate bravery who nonetheless had a common touch and showed compassion on occasion to those less fortunate.
- A general who never pillaged and to whom money meant little.
- A general who eschewed pomp and pretense and preferred the company of common men.
- A man of generally good humor whose temper occasionally flared.
- The possessor of virulently anti-English sentiments.
- A loner whose first instinct, when not in command of troops, was to retreat into isolation in the country and avoid large cities.
- A Freemason.
- A man who drank (though not to excess) and who used tobacco in the form of cigars and snuff.[76]

These characteristics defined the man and are also central to the mystery of P. S. Ney.

CHAPTER 9

The Flight, Trial, and Execution
of Marshal Ney

THE AMERICAN CHARGÉ IN PARIS, HENRY JACKSON, TOOK PEN TO PAPER on July 12, 1815, just 12 days before the July 24 ordinance of proscription, and wrote Secretary of State James Monroe a confidential dispatch. He stated, "The only instance of individual prosecution I have yet heard of is that of Marshal Ney of whom they are now in search, whose horses and carriages they have seized and whose picture has been removed from the Hall of Marshalls [*sic*] at the Thuilleries [*sic*]. He appears to be altogether without friends and will therefore in all probability be sacrificed."[1]

Jackson was prescient. The jarring world into which Ney emerged from the battlefield at Waterloo was one of revenge, desperation, and an ever-tightening dragnet focused on him, second only to Napoleon, as the most wanted man in France. And it was clear that from the very start, Ney had America on his mind.

On June 26, Ney sent a message to Fouché, as head of the provisional government, complaining that Napoleon was unjustly blaming him for the stalemate at Quatre Bras and the loss at Waterloo. Three days later, on June 29, Ney publicly denounced Napoleon before the legislature, warning that the enemy would be in Paris within days and that further resistance would be useless, explicitly ruing his decision to back Bonaparte over the Bourbons.[2] Napoleon had in fact left Paris four days earlier, although Grouchy's corps remained intact and available to fight.

The same day, just 11 days after Waterloo, Ney wrote Fouché requesting a passport to the United States.[3] "I would repose my head on the soil

201

of liberty, in America, waiting while my country might obtain a Government of its choice," he explained to the former police chief and head of the provisional government. Fouché obliged him by issuing him two passports, one in his correct name and the other in the pseudonym of Michel Theodore Neubourg.[4] Both were valid for Switzerland, not the United States. They were dated June 20, possibly because they came from a predated stock of passports Fouché maintained. At the very time Fouché issued the passports to Ney, he was starting to draw up the list of names for the ordinance of proscription on which Ney would be number one.

It is evident that Ney was considering several possible alternative destinations in the United States. Ida Saint-Elme, who was in touch with him at the time, said,

> Ney intended to leave France altogether, utterly disheartened by the turn of events after Waterloo. He proposed to go to the United States, there to live with an uncle of Mme. Ney. This was M. Genêt, a Girondist, who had once been a member of the National Convention, but was now an American citizen. He was a brother of Mme. Auguié (Mme. Ney's mother), and had married the daughter of Judge Clinton at New York. M. Genêt was fond of the marshal, with whom he had long been in correspondence, and whom he had invited to Albany, his place of residence.[5]

On July 5, Ney obtained a leave of absence from the army, and he departed the following day, ostensibly for Switzerland, which he of course knew well from his service there. His third son, Eugène, was later to recall the moment: "Although I was about eight years old at the time, I remember distinctly how my father, of whom I stood in great dread, came in disguise to my home, kissed his wife and sons goodbye and mounting the horse that stood waiting at the door, rode away into the night."[6]

Based on press reports at the time that he was headed for Switzerland and on his own testimony at his trial to that effect, it appears that he in fact started for Switzerland. Interestingly, at his trial Ney testified that the minister of war "authorized me to repair to that country for the re-establishment of my health,"[7] which is possibly indicative of wounds he received at Waterloo, as he was not known to be in ill health prior to the battle. In any event, apparently traveling with his secretary and servants, he got as far as Lyon, where the police advised him not to cross the frontier in that vicinity. He then repaired to a spa town on the upper reaches of the Loire called Saint-Alban, some 60 miles northwest of Lyon. He arrived there July 12, the day Chargé Jackson reported on his fall from grace. It seems to have been a prearranged rendezvous spot for Ney to receive instructions from his wife on alternative plans for escape. The intent of those plans was to revert to "Plan A," namely, an escape to America by ship from Bordeaux.

Ney waited at Saint-Alban under an assumed name until around July 23. With the publication of the ordinance of proscription and the police closing in ever closer on him (they narrowly missed him at the inn where he was staying in Saint-Alban), Ney struck out alone with a fraudulent military pass, circling in the vicinity and still waiting for the arrival of the messenger from his wife confirming the escape plan. The messenger finally arrived toward the end of July bearing instructions to travel from Bordeaux to New Orleans as well as a false passport that he carried made out in the name of "Falize," a merchant traveling from Bordeaux to New Orleans. Falize was the name of Ney's footman, who was complicit in arranging the passport.[8] Falize was later rewarded for his troubles by being arrested the day after Ney's execution.[9] Ney's New Orleans connection came through the family of his former aide-de-camp in the Iberian campaign, Joseph Delfau de Pontalba, of whom Ney was fond and whose career in the French army Ney had assisted. Joseph's father, Baron Delfau de Pontalba, wrote Ney on July 12, 1815, inviting him to New Orleans, where he had family, should Ney decide to depart France. The letter reads like a travelogue for visiting New Orleans, expanding on how a Frenchman would be at home there, even explaining away the unhealthy months of September and October. The letter included two other letters dated the previous day and addressed to Pontalba's cousin and nephew in New Orleans asking them to receive Ney in their homes until he found permanent quarters.[10] More to the point, Pontalba directed the shipping firm of Charles-Oliver Durand in

Bordeaux to book and pay for an anonymous friend's passage to America and instructed them on how to connect with Ney at a certain hotel and room number in Bordeaux.

Then Ney did the most extraordinary thing: rather than head straight for Bordeaux, he wandered around in circles in the Auvergne region in the company of two of his wife's relatives. Perhaps he thought this was necessary to elude the police dragnet that was closing in on him; Saint-Elme believed he thought the idea of flight to America beneath his dignity once the ordinance was published.[11] Either way, he miscalculated badly. Ney next sought refuge at a remote iron works in the dense forest of Azay owned by the Michel brothers, who were army contractors he knew. They declined to shelter him.

Having almost caught him at Saint-Alban, the police again narrowly missed him when he spent the night of July 31 at Aurillac. His next stop was a château belonging to one of his wife's relations near Bessonies, a remote and mountainous spot some 20 miles from Aurillac. The police learned that he dined there on August 1. According to legend, which may or may not be true, he was given away by an ornate Egyptian saber, a gift from Napoleon to Ney on his wedding day that he had carelessly left on a sofa. The saber had been taken at the Battle of Aboukir. An unnamed house guest spoke of the saber in the town, and one of the villagers who heard it reported it to the prefect of police, suspecting that either Ney or Murat might be in residence (what is certain is that the informant later applied for a pension for his services from the royalist French government). Two days later the police swooped down on Ney at Bessonies and arrested him. Ney did not resist. Altogether, Ney had traveled some 675 miles, while the direct route to Bessonies is only 335 miles, and he had come no closer than 150 miles to Bordeaux.

When the police arrested him they seized his passports and documents, which confirmed his plan to escape to America. They also documented his belongings, which included numerous changes of clothes, both summer and winter, but evidently no military uniforms or equipment (what became of the legendary saber is unclear).

The local authorities in Aurillac, where he was taken, were nervous about attempts to free him. They put up posters announcing his arrest and calling on all loyal subjects of the king to cooperate and prevent any attempts to rescue him. On hearing of his arrest, Louis XVIII, aware of the popular sympathies Ney commanded, is said to have commented, "This arrest is more disastrous than his defection."[12] The Ministry of Police sent officers and gendarmes who, supplemented by a troop of dragoons, escorted him to Paris, where he arrived August 19. He was taken directly to the Prefecture of Police and was then incarcerated in the fortress-like Conciergerie on the banks of the Seine to await trial.

It is important to understand the tense and chaotic atmosphere that gripped Paris when Ney arrived. Paris was an occupied capital, with British, Prussian, Dutch, and Russian troops everywhere. Frictions between these nationalities and between them and the French abounded. Soldiers were coming and going, being redeployed and disbanded. The Duke of Wellington was the primus inter pares among the chief occupying powers. Louis XVIII had returned to his throne but sat on it uneasily. In Paris, as throughout the country, Bourbon reprisals, or the "White Terror" as it was called, were rampant. In some areas Catholic gangs were murdering Protestants by the dozens whom they accused (perhaps correctly) of being Jacobins or Bonapartists.[13] It was an ugly, swirling, uncertain scene in a city and country laid waste by over 25 years of revolution and war and awash in the dross of ignominy, defeat, resentments, and, worse, fear of the future.

Immediately following his arrest and incarceration at La Conciergerie, Ney was interrogated by the authorities, at first alone and without counsel present. His interrogation was led by the suave new minister of police, Élie Decazes, who was easing out Fouché in the king's favor and was soon to replace him (apparently, Louis XVIII could not stomach the thought of the regicide Fouché remaining in power). In fact, Decazes had taken the lead in running Ney to ground and capturing him. During this period, Ney produced two sets of interrogatories that were introduced at his initial trial before a military tribunal. In certain parts of his first interrogatory, he evinced despondency and suicidal thoughts, for example, "I have frequently been tempted to blow my brains out, but the desire to justify myself prevented me" and "I truly deserved death and I did all that lay in me to find it at Waterloo."[14] In his second interrogatory, he acknowledged having wanting to escape to the United States: "I could have gone to the United States; I remained to save the honor of my children."[15]

The above two statements are of some significance in understanding Ney's thinking and state of mind. The first statement evidences a suicidal impulsiveness as a character trait, a point that will receive further comment in the final chapter. The second statement goes to why he would or would not have gone to America. In contemporary English-language accounts, it was also translated as "I would have gone to the United States, where I wished to remain for the honor of my children,"[16] which raises a very different interpretation of its meaning. The translation in the paragraph above seems to be the more correct one, although the original French is ambiguous because of its apparent dropping of a punctuation mark or word at a key point. It reads in full as follows (the context of its referral to his alleged treason against the king in March 1815, not flight in July 1815, being of potential significance):

> *Ce que j'ai fait est un grand malheur, j'ai pendu la tête, je n'ai jamais formé le complot de trahir le Roi. J'aurai pû passer aux États-Unis je ne suis resté que pour sauver l'honneur de mes enfants; j'avais annoncé, en portent de Paris, que j'étais prêt à me mettre à la disposition du Roi. Je ne tiens pas à la vie, je me tiens qu'à l'honneur de mes enfants.*[17]
> [That which I did is a great unhappiness, I lost my head, I never had the intention of betraying the King. I could have gone to the United States nothing remained for me but to save the honor of my children; I announced on reaching Paris that I was ready to put myself at the disposition of the King. I do not hold on to life, I hold on to nothing but the honor of my children.]

The implications of this response, properly translated, are that (1) Ney actively considered leaving for America as early as March 1815 but that (2) he did not do so then or later because he wanted to justify his actions for the sake of his children's "honor."

As September and October wore on, Ney began to prepare for his trial. His lead lawyer was Pierre-Nicolas Berryer, one of the senior lights of the Paris bar, who took on the representation after another prominent lawyer declined (that lawyer became Ney's prosecutor). A royalist, Berryer was the elder of a prominent father–son team (Berryer *fils* provided some additional political cover as a particularly well-known royalist, although he did not participate in the case). Berryer's courtroom style could be described as verbose, even by the standards of the time. Ney's secondary counsel was the much younger 32-year-old André Dupin. He worked closely with Berryer and actively contributed to Ney's defense. According to Dupin's *Memoires*, the core legal team consisted of the marshal, Madame Ney, Ney's brother-in-law Charles-Guillaume Gamot, and the two attorneys.

While imprisoned at La Conciergerie, Ney passed the time by playing the flute (see figure 9.1), as attested by his fellow prisoner Antoine Marie Chamans Count de Lavalette and by the inclusion of his flute and several sheaves of music in an undated inventory of his possessions prepared in Ney's own handwriting while at La Conciergerie. "He played tolerably well on the flute," Laval-lette observed. Lavallette, who had served as Napoleon's one-time aide-de-camp and as postmaster general of France, was also being tried for high treason in a separate but parallel case. He escaped imminent execution by fleeing in his wife's clothes on December 23, 1815, and was aided in his escape from France by three Englishmen resident in Paris—Sir Robert Wilson, Captain John Hely-Hutcheson, and Michael Bruce—the last of whom possibly was Madame Ney's lover at the time.[18] In January 1816, while Sir Robert Wilson was being examined by the police in connection with Lavallette's escape, "he admitted that he had attempted to

Figure 9.1. Ney Imprisoned in the Conciergerie, from a drawing made in December 1815. Note his flute. PWB IMAGES / ALAMY STOCK PHOTO.

save the Marshal [Ney] from his fate, and he spoke of such attempts in the plural."[19]

Ney's fellow prisoner Lavallette observed, "Even before his trial came on, the number of his guards had been considerably augmented. Day and night three sentries were stationed under his window, which was also mine: one gendarme, one national guard on horseback, and one Grenadier of the old guard, or rather a disguised life-guard, for they could not place confidence enough in the soldiers of the old army."[20] Lavallette's observation that the government was so nervous that it placed regime loyalists in disguise on Ney's guard detail is borne out by other contemporary sources that indicate the guards in question came from the *Compagnie de Sous-Officiers Vétérans*.[21]

Plots to free Ney began to hatch almost immediately. Ida Saint-Elme wrote of one such plot, of which there were a number,

> It came to my ears that a plot was brewing in Paris to bring about Ney's escape, should he be condemned to death. I was heart and soul with the scheme to rescue the bravest soldier of the French army and the idol of my admiration, and did my utmost to further it. Gamot, Ney's brother-in-law . . . was one of us. But Gamot had slight hopes. He was afraid of the consequences of Ney's bluntness, and of the pride he was sure to exhibit under cross-examination.[22]

The British ambassador to Paris, Sir Charles Stuart, reported, perhaps with a whiff of optimism, to Foreign Secretary Viscount Castlereagh on November 6, "It is generally believed that attempts to rescue him [Ney] have been discovered and frustrated."[23]

Ney's trial, as it unfolded, was a political drama that elicited high public interest. It was attended by journalists and was from the start a media event of its time. It spawned a spate of verbatim accounts, some based on shorthand notes taken by observers, in both French and English. The haste with which these transcripts appeared in December 1815 just days after the trial concluded led to inaccuracies and ambiguities in the reporting, but they do not lack for either immediacy or drama.

Ney's trial before a military tribunal commenced on November 9. Meeting in the great Hall of Assize in the Palace of Justice, the panel consisted of four marshals and three lieutenant generals. General Louis Count Grundler acted as advocate general or prosecutor for the crown. Marshal Bon-Adrien Moncey, the most senior of the marshals, had earlier refused to preside, a stance that resulted in his subsequent imprisonment by the king. Following an initial procedural hiccup in which Marshal Masséna volunteered to recuse himself because of his past feuds with Ney but was told that would not be necessary, the court-martial settled down—somewhat reluctantly—to business. Ney made his appearance the next day, November 10. The *Times* of London describes the scene:

> Marshal Ney was introduced by Captain Hendelin. His countenance was firm and assured. No emotion was depicted on his physiognomy. It would appear as if the habit of strong impression which he must have contracted in his military career, prohibited him from exhibiting their effect. He was in a plain military blue frock [coat], without embroidery, with the epaulets of his rank, the ribband of St. Louis, and the plate of the Legion of Honour; he wore a crape around his arm in consequence of a recent loss [his father-in-law had recently died]; and he sat down on an arm-chair in the centre of the semicircular space in front of his judges.[24]

From the start, Ney and Berryer objected to the court-martial as incompetent to try a marshal because of the peculiar nonmilitary status of marshals under the French constitution (they were treated as "cousins of the king") and because, as a peer of France, Ney was entitled to be tried criminally only by the Chamber of Peers. The Chamber, located in the Luxembourg Palace on the Left Bank, was the upper house of Parliament, analogous to the House of Lords. It had recently been reestablished during the 1814 Bourbon Restoration. In its current composition, following the post-Waterloo return of the Bourbons, it was loaded with royalists, many of whom were adamant in their convictions. It is unclear why the defense team argued for this change of venue from what likely would have been a more sympathetic military tribunal. It was not a wise strategy.

The court-martial immediately considered the argument and agreed in a vote of five to two that it was indeed incompetent to hear the case and that it should be referred to the Chamber of Peers (one can almost hear the sighs of relief among the marshals and lieutenant generals as they folded up their papers and left).

The Chamber of Peers met the very next day (November 11) and the following Monday and Wednesday (November 13 and 15) to organize itself to try Ney. The Monday session was unusually well attended, except by the ecclesiastical peers who as a matter of principle would not sit in a trial for life. Although the trial was to be public, ladies were barred from attending. Marshal Pierre Augereau, who had participated in the abortive court-martial, declined to sit as a judge. The Chamber debated whether a simple majority or two-thirds vote was required for a conviction and decided on the former.

The Chamber of Peers continued to occupy itself with largely procedural issues on November 16 with 101 peers present and 51 absent, a marked decline from the attendance on Monday. Others involved in the prosecution, such as Prime Minister Armand Emmanuel, the Duke de Richelieu, and Foreign Minister Talleyrand, declined to sit as judges. The proceedings commenced with the calling of 16 witnesses and inconclusive debate on whether Ney was involved in Napoleon's escape from Elba prior to March 14. The Chamber determined to confirm Ney's arrest, seemingly a rather technical point given his incarceration the last three months. Richelieu emotionally called for Ney's condemnation "in the name of Europe." Ney's lawyers sought from the outset to argue that Article 12 of the July 3, 1815, Convention on the Capitulation of Paris protected Ney from prosecution. The peers disallowed the argument on the grounds that the convention was a treaty to which the king had not been a party.[25]

This decision had two immediate consequences. The first was an effort by both Marshal and Madame Ney to pull political levers to nullify the decision if not the trial itself. The second was, separately, more plots by Ney's friends to free the marshal by ruse or force.

Ney took the first step by writing a letter to the Duke of Wellington, general in chief of the British army, on November 13. He opened by explaining "the critical circumstances" to which he was "reduced" and the "just alarm" excited in his mind by his prosecution. The gist of his appeal was the factually correct statement that in the immediate aftermath of Waterloo a French army corps still opposed the British and Prussians and that the warring parties negotiated a Convention on the Capitulation of Paris dated July 3 to cease hostilities. Ney explained that Article 12 of the convention provided a safe haven for residents of Paris no matter which side they had previously taken:

> Shall be likewise respected private persons and private property. The inhabitants, and, in general, all the individuals in the capital, shall continue in the enjoyment of their rights and of their liberty; nor shall it be lawful to disturb or call them to account in consequence of any matter having reference to the employment which they either hold or have held, or to their conduct or public opinion.

After noting that the British and Prussians had ratified the convention and the French king relied on it in entering Paris and citing it positively "more than once,"[26] Ney argued that it should protect him and put an end to any criminal proceeding against his conduct and political opinions. In closing, he advised that if he had not "implicitly confided" in Article 12 and the promises the sovereigns made therein, he would "by this time be in some unknown land, and should be no more thought of."[27]

On the same day Ney sent similar letters to the ambassadors in Paris of the four occupying powers: Britain, Prussia, Austria, and Russia. Madame Ney hand delivered the letters and met with the British ambassador Sir Charles Stuart as well as some or all of the other ambassadors. Her reception by them was reported by the *Times* of London as "cool."[28] She also sent under separate cover copies of her husband's letter to the Earl of Liverpool and to the prince regent (the future King George IV) in London.[29] Finally, she met on November 13 with Wellington in a private audience to present her husband's appeal. Wellington told her right away and to her face that he would not personally intervene in her husband's trial because the king of France had not ratified the convention and because, in any event, the undertakings of Article 12 were given only by the occupying powers and "it was not their duty to interfere in any way with the acts of the King's government." Thus, the Neys' appeals were stillborn.

Madame Ney (or more likely Ney's lawyer Berryer) immediately wrote an "additional note," intended for the prince regent, trying to refute Wellington's Pilate-like recusal, stating that she "cannot believe" that Wellington's position on Article 12 "can be definitively maintained in the conference of the Plenipotentiaries" to whom Marshal Ney had sent his November 13 appeal.[30] It may be recalled that Napoleon also appealed to the prince regent five months earlier. Madame Ney's hopes were equally misplaced.

Stuart wrote Foreign Secretary Viscount Castlereagh, also on November 13, "An allusion to the desire of the Allies to terminate this Trial, has induced the Council [*sic*] of Marshal Ney to seek protection under the Convention for the evacuation of Paris by the French Army." He went on to report to his superior, "The proceedings in the Chambers during the last week, acquired a character which I consider to be highly prejudicial to the true interests of the Crown," and he cited in particular the rescission of the king's ordinances prior to the assembly of the Chambers and the extension of amnesty to all except regicides.[31] It therefore was apparent that behind the scenes the British government—or at least its representative in Paris—wanted not only to not interfere with the Ney trial on technical legal grounds but also to proceed so as to perfect retribution against those who took action in support of the Hundred Days.

In any event, Wellington did not wait for the meeting of the allied ambassadors to seek their guidance. He drafted a curt response to Marshal Ney dated November 15 that he held until the meeting of the allied ambassadors. In the note, he restated his position conveyed orally to Madame Ney:

The Capitulation of Paris of the 3rd July was made between the Commanders in Chief of the allied British, & Prussian Armies, on the one part, and the Prince D'Eckmuhl Commander in Chief of the French Army on the other; and related exclusively to the military occupation of Paris.

The object of the 12th Article was to prevent any measures of severity under the military Authority of those who made it, towards any Persons in Paris on account of the offices which they filled, or their conduct or their Political opinions; but it was never intended to prevent either the existing French Govt. under whose authority the French Commander in Chief must have acted, or any French Govt. which should succeed to it, from acting in this respect as it might deem fit.[32]

The allied ambassadors met in conference the following day, November 16, and endorsed Wellington's proposed response to Ney, which was then delivered.[33] Stuart reported to Castlereagh a second approach by Madame Ney on November 16 to present argumentation, reading like a legal brief prepared by Berryer, about the Convention. Stuart dutifully forwarded the correspondence to Castlereagh but made clear he was at one with Wellington's decision.[34]

Wellington's last word on the matter was a memorandum he wrote, presumably for the file, on November 19. In it he stated, "It is obvious from this letter [his November 15 letter to Ney] that the Duke of Wellington, one of the parties to the capitulation of Paris, considers that the instant contains nothing which can prevent the King from bringing Marshal Ney to trial on such [wording illegible] as His Majesty may think proper." The memorandum went on to state that Article 12 applied only to "Allied Generals and their troops" and not to "other parties to whom the Convention did not relate in any manner." It then asked, "Would the Duc d'Otrante have given a passport under a feigned name to Marshal Ney if he had understood the 12th article as giving Marshal Ney any protection, excepting against measures of severity by the two Commanders in Chief?"[35] Evidently by November 19 Wellington felt the need to justify his action in light of concern about possible criticism of his decision in Parliament—which did in fact come. And he tried to justify his decision by hanging it on the sophistry of an allusion to one of many instances of Fouché's double-dealing. It was not the Iron Duke's finest hour.

The dispatches from Stuart and Wellington thenceforward turn to other issues, such as negotiation of the evacuation of the Allied armies from Paris.

Meanwhile, as the trial by the Chamber of Peers proceeded, the plots to free Ney gained momentum. Saint-Elme sheds some oblique light on that murky world:

> Being unable to witness the trial, I made arrangements to be informed of every step in its progress. There were several meeting places agreed upon among the prisoner's friends. All my energies were bent towards the completion of the plan by which he might be rescued if condemned to death. Thirty resolute men had promised to act, and fifty more were ready to help them.
>
> While the trial went on, my efforts continued, and I must avow that I met with many weak souls. I will mention no names. On the other hand, one of those who received me most favorably was Marshal Davout.[36]

The likelihood of a plot to free Ney was even reported by the *Times* of London while the trial was under way. On November 21, 1815, that paper observed, "Great numbers of strangers have crowded into Paris, since the first sittings of the Court Martial. There is strong reason to believe, that they are drawn thither by a conspiracy intended to break out during Marshal Ney's trial, or at the time fixed for his execution. The police, one would think, might easily stop the greater part of these persons before they reached the capital; but, with the usual weakness displayed by the Ministry, they content themselves with increasing the number of patrols in the city itself."[37]

In fact the police were more active than the *Times* imagined. On November 23, Stuart wrote Castlereagh,

> The reports of the Police having ascertained that the conversations of several General officers who frequent the House of

Illustration 1.   Captain Charles Baudin. *PORTRAIT OF ADMIRAL CHARLES BAUDIN AFTER 1838* BY LECOMPTE-VERNET HIPPOLYTE CHARLES (1828–1900) AND HORACE VERNET (1789–1863). MUSÉE DE LA MARINE, PARIS, FRANCE. WIKIMEDIA COMMONS.

Illustration 2.   Lieutenant General Charles Baron Lallemand. YOGI BLACK / ALAMY STOCK PHOTO.

Illustration 3.   Joseph Bonaparte, the King of Spain. JOSEPH BONAPARTE, KING OF SPAIN, BY FRANÇOIS GÉRARD (1770–1837), 1808. MUSÉE FESCH, AJACCIO, CORSICA. WIKIMEDIA COMMONS.

Illustration 4.   Marshal Emmanuel Marquis Grouchy. *MARQUIS DE GROUCHY BY JEAN SEBASTIEN ROUILLARD, C. 1835.* WIKIMEDIA COMMONS.

Illustration 5.   General Charles Count Lefebvre-Desnouettes. ARTIST AND DATE UNKNOWN.

Illustration 6.   Point Breeze, home of Joseph Bonaparte. CHARLES B. LAWRENCE, DATE UNKNOWN. ART INSTITUTE OF CHICAGO, CHICAGO, IL. WIKIMEDIA COMMONS.

Illustration 7.   Annette Savage, Pauline Anne and Catharine Charlotte Bonaparte. PAINTING BY BASS OTIS, 1823. PHILADELPHIA MUSEUM OF ART, PURCHASED WITH THE EDGAR VIGUERS SEELERS FUND, 1965.

Illustration 8. A contemporary fanciful French view of the Champ D'Asile. PAINTING BY AMBROISE LOUIS GARNERAY, 1819. THE MUSEUM OF FINE ARTS, HOUSTON.

Illustration 9. Michel Ney, "the Bravest of the Brave," Duke of Elchingen, Prince of Moscow, and Marshal of France. FRANÇOIS GÉRARD (1770–1837), C. 1805. WIKIMEDIA COMMONS.

Illustration 10.   Aglaé Louise Auguié Ney. FRANÇOIS GÉRARD. WIKIMEDIA COMMONS.

Illustration 11.   *Marshal Ney Supporting the Rear Guard during the Retreat from Moscow* by Adolphe Yvon, 1856. WIKIMEDIA COMMONS.

Illustration 12.   *The Execution of Marshal Ney* by Jean-Léon Gérôme, 1868.
GRAVES ART GALLERY, SHEFFIELD, UK. WIKIMEDIA COMMONS.

Illustration 13.   The Execution of the Sentence on Marshal Ney, in the Garden of the Luxembourg Palace at Paris, December 8th, 1815 [*sic*]. Aquatint, 1816.
HERITAGE IMAGE PARTNERSHIP LTD / ALAMY STOCK PHOTO.

Illustration 14. *The Sons of Marshal Ney* by Marie-Eléonore Godefroid (1778–1849). Three of Marshal Ney's four sons. Eugène is in the middle.

Marshal Augereau, encouraged the formation of a Plan to secure Marshal Ney an order was issued on Monday Evening for the Arrest of Generals Belliard, Colbert, Ornano, Campi, Bacheleux and Boyer, the latter was apprized of the intention in sufficient time to escape. The five former are now in confinement where they will remain until the conviction of the persons under trial [Ney and Lavallette]. After that period they will be directed to repair to the Departments the Government may point at a distance from the Capital.[38]

The above dispatch makes clear that (1) Ney's conviction was a foregone conclusion by both the French and British governments[39] and that (2) there was an active, high-level plot within the military to free Ney that was partially or wholly foiled by the arrests. This plot was in addition to the shadowy "British" plots involving Hely-Hutchinson, Bruce, and Wilson and other schemes that Ney's family and civilian friends were concocting.

While the plots bubbled the trial began in earnest on November 21. Ney appeared at 11:00 a.m. "He was escorted by four Royal Grenadiers, dressed in a plain military habit without embroidery, wearing a Marshal's epaulettes, the cross of the Legion of Honor and the simple ribband of the Cross of St. Louis, after having respectfully saluted the Assembly, he shook hands with M. Dupin, one of his advocates, and seated himself between his two defenders."[40]

When asked to state his name and date of birth, Ney responded with a different birth date than he gave when asked the same question by the military tribunal. This time, he said February 17 rather than the commonly acknowledged January 10, which he had used earlier.[41] Why he did this is unclear.

The trial then adjourned to November 23, during which session Berryer argued on Ney's behalf and requested an adjournment until December 4 in order to summon more witnesses. The Chamber granted the request.

The nervousness with which the government viewed the possibility of an effort to free Ney was attested to by the extraordinary security measures it instituted as to his person. A most unusual unsigned and undated document titled *"Journal de Service extraordinaire ordonné pour la guarde du Maréchal Ney"* (Journal of the Extraordinary Service Ordered for the Guarding of Marshal Ney) provides a day-by-day account of the security measures instituted by the government and of Ney's visitors and routine.[42] It evidently was written in French by one or more persons posted immediately outside Ney's prison cell, first in the Conciergerie and later in the Luxembourg Palace to which he was transferred, who were in a position to observe him closely and even eavesdrop on the conversations within his room. As early as November 18 the Journal explains,

> The sums of money promised or even already paid to facilitate the escape of Marshal Ney, currently detained in Paris in the prisons of La Conciergerie; the defiance that inspires in general agents not yet purged from the police and the lack of security that is afforded by the Luxembourg Palace to which he is to be transferred the 22nd of this month, have made felt the necessity of resorting to means of surveillance less equivocal, in placing around the prisoner of state, during the course of the proceeding, some men of honor, with proven courage and [who have] . . . a limitless devotion to the cause of the King.

The document goes on to describe the measures taken as a consequence of these concerns. First, four officers from the royal bodyguard are disguised "under the name and uniform of the royal Grenadiers of La roche-Jacquelin [*sic*]" to keep the prisoner in view at all times. Second, a detachment of 50 are charged with guarding the immediately nearby avenues and the entrance to the prison. This detachment is divided into two equal companies wearing blue uniforms, one company of 25 young officers of the royal guard and the other of 25 officers of any grade having served in different armies during the Revolution under the flags of princes or in royal units.

The four "Grenadiers" in disguise then visited Ney's cell to inspect its security along with the governor of the Luxembourg Palace, M. de Semonville, and the commandant of the palace, M. de Montigny, who was under his orders. They observed and reported on the weakness of barriers to escape spaced too far apart on the exterior of the building and the feebleness of the wicket gates on the interior, which would allow "the least adroit man to escape without much trouble." Security had to be tightened before Ney could be transferred.

On November 21, the two companies of guards inspected the room prepared for Ney, which had hitherto been the office of the chief palace archivist. They found the room to be well lit and furnished "decently" with a bed with blue taffeta curtains and armchairs upholstered in blue velvet. But the decor was ancillary, as the Journal noted that "the most exact discipline" prevailed among the guards. They were to be isolated in their communications, not only with the outside but also with other parts of the palace. Each company was to alternate twice a day in taking meals downstairs and returning to guard duty "without taking the tiniest excursion in the courtyard or garden."

Ney was transferred to the Luxembourg Palace in the dead of night—at 2:25 a.m. on November 22 and with the four disguised Grenadiers riding in the coach with him. Such was the fear of an escape attempt. Once there, security was tightened even further, according to the Journal. One hundred and twenty veteran soldiers occupied the vestibule of the palace and furnished 10 details to guard the corridors and staircases leading to the Chamber of Peers. Another contingent of 50 soldiers guarded the area of the palace housing Ney and were placed at various strategic points in the building. One of the Grenadiers was posted between two wicket gates from which he could observe through a barred dormer window all that was going on in the prisoner's room, while another Grenadier was locked in the room with the marshal. With the exception of the turnkey, no one else entered the room except when in the presence of M. de Montigny or one of the heads of the archives. The Journal notes on November 22, "The individuals admitted up to now" are Ney's two lawyers and his wife, whom he was allowed to see alone on the express order of M. de Montigny. A barber was sent in to shave Ney whenever he requested it because his handlers were afraid to leave him alone with a razor for fear he would slash his throat, a precaution that prompted some literal gallows humor from the marshal.

The Journal kept track of who visited and for how long. For example, on November 22, it recorded that his lawyers visited toward 6:00 p.m. and left after 10 to 12 minutes, during which time they "discussed a little about the trial." That night, M. de Semonville met with the prefect of police and the commander of one of the two guards contingents, Colonel Roger. The latter argued for allowing Ney to walk in the gardens under the watch of his troops, in whom he had complete confidence. The other two turned it down as too risky.

They were right. A test of the security measures occurred later that night. According to the Journal, around 11:00 p.m., a man wearing the uniform of a captain of the National Guard presented himself as an inspector of prisons saying that he had orders to remove Ney back to La Conciergerie, but he was not able to "justify his mission" and did not know the correct password. Colonel Roger ordered him back onto the street, where he was accompanied by a man who said he also was employed as an inspector of prisons but who was not allowed admittance even though he showed an identity card. This individual, the Journal noted, resembled Marshal Ney and was dressed the same as him in a blue greatcoat. The self-proclaimed inspector then went to plead with Montigny that he was not able to carry out his orders. Montigny returned to the entrance and announced with some embarrassment that Ney was indeed to be returned to his former prison (why is unclear, but security was likely the motive). However, he did not hand the marshal over to the captain, and it is possible (if not probable) that his visit was an attempt to free Ney, especially given his accompaniment by a Ney look-alike.

The Journal also noted the increased presence of "many Brigands" on the streets of Paris and expressed concern that the marshal, "a very vigorous man" with strong organizational skills, could orchestrate a sudden attack in numbers while he was being conveyed between locations that would overwhelm his guards and permit him to escape.

Again in the dead of night, at midnight on November 23, Ney was transferred back to La Conciergerie accompanied by his ever-vigilant disguised Grenadiers. Later that day, he received his lawyers, wife, and children. He even asked his jailer what the news was on the outside.

"But Mr. Marshal, the judgment of Mr. Lavallette," he replied.

"And well?" Ney asked.

"He is condemned to death."

"Today his turn, tomorrow mine," Ney replied rubbing his brow.

At 6:30 a.m., while it was still dark, Ney was returned to the Luxembourg Palace the following day under a heavy escort of cavalry and with the fake Grenadiers riding in the carriage with him. Ney joked with the Grenadiers that they had returned already.

"We never left," they responded.

Ney attended his trial on November 24 and spent the night at the Luxembourg Palace. However, at 6:30 the next morning, he was once again shuttled under cover of darkness to La Conciergerie, this time to remain there until the trial resumed on December 4.

Shortly after the granting of the delay in the trial, Richelieu wrote in a letter to the minister of police, Élie Duke of Decazes, who had succeeded Fouché in that post two months earlier, "It seems to me that the delay demanded by the lawyers of Marshal Ney can have no other motive than the hope of evading [the trial] or of saving him in whatever manner. It would be therefore, I believe, necessary to redouble the surveillance to avoid any attempt in this regard, you have already thought of all possibilities, but I did not want to neglect in any case to remind you."[43]

During the suspension in the trial, Ney remained at La Conciergerie planning his defense with his lawyers. On November 27, the Foreign Office in London dispatched a response to Madame Ney's appeal to the prince regent. Its operative provision stated that the prince regent had read her letter "with every sentiment of compassion which her unhappy situation cannot fail of exciting" but that he could only refer her to the Duke of Wellington's previous reply.[44]

Meanwhile, plots to free Ney continued to come to the attention of the government, including one notified by the subprefect of Soissons northeast of Paris to the minister of war on December 2.[45] Further, the government learned of a certain Colonel La Motte suspected of being part of a plot to free Ney if he were convicted, but he was later deemed innocent.[46]

Ney's lawyers continued to work to advance their arguments about Article 12 of the Capitulation of Paris, sending a letter summarizing their position on it on December 3 to British ambassador Stuart.

The trial resumed on Monday, December 4. The Journal noted Ney's heightened impatience and somberness, as "each day carried away with it a portion of hope." Ney observed the curiosity that his appearance stimulated among the National Guardsmen on duty and snapped angrily, "Do these people take me for an ape?" The Journal also noted that the disguised Grenadiers "redoubled" their vigilance as the judgment approached. A move was made to prohibit Ney from meeting alone with his wife and lawyers. But Montigny nixed it on orders from the king, who recalled how his own brother had been denied this consolation and did not want to deprive Marshal Ney of it. Nonetheless, the strain was beginning to show on Ney. His lawyers shifted legal tactics and tried to argue that Ney was protected by another treaty by which his birthplace, Sarrelouis, was ceded to Prussia and that he could not commit treason against France because he was not French. Ney would have none of it and blurted out in the Chamber, "I am French and I will die French!"[47]

Following the session on December 5, which was largely devoted to presentations by the prosecution, Ney conversed with his guards, describing his military campaigns and stating that he had no regrets. "I could have fled, if I had not counted on the capitulation," he averred. "I said to Grouchy 'what are we to do?' 'I will stay,' he told me, 'Paris is an abyss where one can easily lose oneself from the eyes of the police.' He stayed eight to ten days, after which he embarked [for America]." The Journal noted that that evening, based on diverse intelligence arriving to Montigny and communicated by him to the commandant at the prison, the guards redoubled their vigilance and were issued new cartridges. In addition, two Grenadiers rather than one were placed in the room with Ney. The night passed without incident.

December 6 was the final day of the trial. The marshal was visited in his cell before 9:00 a.m. by his wife, who left visibly troubled. The Chamber of Peers met at 10:30 a.m., and after the first pleadings by the lawyers, Ney was taken back to his cell, where he ate and chatted with his guards. He returned to the Chamber for the trial from 4:00 to 6:00 p.m.

During this final day, the pressure on Ney became intense, and he did a most extraordinary thing at that afternoon session: he ordered his lawyers publicly in the Chamber to cease defending him and to stand down. In an obvious reference to Richelieu's accusation, Ney looked to a higher order, appealing his case "to Europe and posterity."[48]

The trial was over except for the judgment and sentencing. Those were in the hands of the peers, who met late into the night. Back in his cell, Ney met with his lawyers, thanked them, and told them he no longer had need of them and would meet them again in "the other world."

As they left down the staircase at the Luxembourg Palace, Berryer said to Dupin of Ney, "He threw it into the fire." The guards on the staircase heard only the word "fire" and reported it. Minister of Police Descazes immediately summoned the two lawyers to explain whether they intended to set fire to the palace in order to free the marshal. Such was the level of paranoia that infested the government.

Back in Ney's quarters, Montigny wrestled with questions from his underlings about how the marshal should be guarded, clearly fearful of a breakout. He told the commanders of the guards, "Don't believe all the noise of alarms that come from the salons, everything is thought out, the King's order is in the hands of M. de Semonville who is solely responsible for his execution, this no longer concerns the Ministry of Police."

The peers met until 15 minutes past midnight in the early morning of December 7. According to the Journal, their arrival at a judgment was announced by the continual noise of their carriages as they departed. Ney had eaten calmly earlier, smoked a cigar, and fallen asleep.

The Chamber of Peers was composed of 161 members. Of these, 139 voted for the marshal's death, 17 voted for exile, and five abstained from voting. At the time, there reportedly was widespread sentiment among the peers for the king to grant clemency notwithstanding the verdict. Indeed, the sentence of death was scarcely pronounced when Prime Minister Richelieu was allegedly surrounded by a great number of the voters who declared that they did not desire the marshal's death and that they had voted for it in obedience to the royal wish but under the tacit condition of a commutation of the penalty by the government. They therefore "conjured the prime-minister to solicit from the king exile to America for the condemned instead of the scaffold." Richelieu, although he had demanded Ney's condemnation in the name of Europe, was receptive, no doubt influenced at least in part by the nervous police reports brought in every 15 minutes to the peers. A cabinet council was hastily summoned, unanimously resolving to petition the king for a commutation of the penalty. Richelieu hastened to the royal apartments and, boldly "infringing the regulations of the palace," entered the king's chamber between 1:00 and 2:00 a.m., where he anxiously pleaded for mercy. The prime minister frankly told the king that the situation was critical; that a large number of the peers, although they had condemned the marshal, were strongly opposed to his death; that public sentiment was against it; that a general uprising of the people was imminent; and that it was necessary to commute the sentence. The king retorted, "I pity Ney. I have no hatred against him. I would gladly preserve a father to his children, a hero to France," but he refused to change the sentence of the peers. Others also came to plead for Ney's life, but when they "arrived at the palace, his gracious majesty was going to bed, and would not receive them. Waving his hand as he was wheeled away, he exclaimed: 'Let me hear when I awake that the traitor has paid the forfeit of his crime!'"[49]

Indeed, it had been a long night for the king. It has been widely believed that earlier in the evening, the Duke of Wellington also attempted a plea for clemency. Lady Anne Crosbie Hutchinson was the Irish wife of a British parliamentarian, the Honorable Christopher Hely-Hutchinson (one of the three British plotters), then resident in Paris. She was known as "Madame Hutchinson" and many years earlier had been a flame of the Duke of Wellington when he was young, unknown, and still Arthur Wellesley. Her home was a salon frequented by liberal-minded British officers. She had importuned Wellington, in emotional terms, to ask the king for clemency. The Iron Duke had rebuffed her. "The Duke replied that his hands were tied by imperative considerations, and that whatever might be his personal sentiments of interest and commiseration for an unfortunate adversary, his duty was to be silent."[50]

Nonetheless, Wellington privately may have believed that enough blood had already been shed, a point he apparently made on several occasions with the king. On the evening of December 6 Wellington was invited to a reception at the royal palace. He attended, with the object, as he afterward said to a few intimate friends, of asking the king to spare Ney's life. The king saw Wellington coming and suspected his objective. Just before he reached the king, the king's younger brother, Count d'Artois, darted between Wellington and His Majesty. The king at the same moment deliberately turned his back on Wellington in the presence of the whole court in the most obvious manner. The Iron Duke felt this insult keenly. He turned to the king's courtiers and said, "You forget that I commanded the armies which put your king on his throne. I will never again enter the royal presence." And he walked out, his mission unaccomplished.[51]

As 3:00 a.m. sounded, the guard was unexpectedly changed by orders from Lieutenant General Hyacinthe Despinois,[52] the military commander of Paris, who had recently received fresh intelligence on efforts to free Ney. At Despinois' direction, General Louis Count Rochechouart, a 27-year-old army officer directly under Despinois' command and with impeccable royalist credentials, took charge of the marshal.[53] Rochechouart was a family relation of Richelieu. The Duke had married his cousin, and both Rochechouart and his brother served as Richelieu's aide-de-camp (Louis' term was from 1805 to 1813, when Richelieu was governor of Odessa in the service of Russia).[54] Rochechouart was effectively Richelieu's "man," both then and in the Ney affair. As noted above, just one to two hours earlier, the king had rejected Richelieu's personal plea for a commutation.

What transpired next depends on whether one believes the official account, conspiracy theories, or the handful of eyewitness accounts. Rochechouart's voice, as recounted in his autobiography, now enters the picture in addition to that of the anonymous Journal: an official recounting, to be sure, but also one of a credible eyewitness to what he termed a "great and terrible event."

Despinois' orders issued at 3:00 a.m. and delivered in a sealed envelope to the sleeping Rochechouart were explicit:

Four sergeants, four corporals and four fusiliers, the longest serving, in the company of veteran sub-officers (*sous-officiers vétérans*) currently are proposed to guard the condemned. These twelve soldiers will be placed in two ranks; these are those who will be charged with shooting the guilty party when the signal is given them by the adjutant. . . . [You] will give orders to this effect and will choose from your command the firmest and most capable adjutant and with him go over in advance the terrain and inspect the arms.

The orders noted in a postscript, "There will be, for more security, a detachment of twelve other men, who will be placed in a second line and in reserve."

These orders, supplemented by at least four others during the night from Despinois, were also specific about the guard:

The condemned will be taken from the Palace of Luxembourg by an escort composed of gendarmes and Grenadiers of la Roche-jaquelin [sic], who will surround his person; at his sides will be the two gendarme lieutenants, on foot if he is on foot or in the vehicle beside him if he asks for one; in this latter case, the gendarmes and Grenadiers will surround the vehicle at its two doors, before and behind the wheels. . . . After the escort the company of veteran sub-officers, a picket of National Guard on foot; the mounted National Guard will close the march. It will traverse in this disposition the garden [of the Palace of Luxembourg] and will come to exit by the iron gate of the Observatory, directing itself toward this last point. At its exit, three hundred gendarmes on foot, who have the order to assemble on the Place de l'Odeon . . . will march on the right and left flanks of the escort in such a manner as to close all the entrances of the indicated terrain. Arriving on the site, the gendarme officers will accompany with the gendarmes and the Grenadiers the condemned to the place of execution, and the troops being in battle array by squares, will put him on his knees, facing the detachment of shooters, blindfold him, immediately retire, and the adjutant will give the agreed signal [to fire]. . . . The body will be exposed some time and guarded by the pickets of infantry and cavalry. If the relatives want to claim the body and remove it, it will be given to them. . . . If it is not claimed, it will be relegated to the diligence of the civil police and deposited in the hospital of the Maternity.[55]

The choice of Grenadiers from the regiment commanded by Auguste de la Rochejaquelein is curious. Colonel de la Rochejaquelein (1784–1868) (figure 9.2) was an aristocrat with a checkered military career. He fled France with the Revolution and served with a French monarchist unit based in England. However, he later enlisted as a sublieutenant in Napoleon's army and served with the carabiniers (mounted riflemen) in the invasion of Russia in 1812. His unit saw heavy fighting as part of the Fourth Cuirassier Division of General Nansouty's First Cavalry Corps in charging the Shevardino redoubt at the Battle of Borodino. He was wounded three times at Borodino, earning him the nickname of "Le Balafré" (The Scar). In these engagements, he fought closely with Ney, who commanded the Third Army Corps, if not directly under him. Ney almost certainly saved his life on the retreat from Moscow, as he

Figure 9.2.   Colonel Auguste de la Roche-jaquelein. WIKIMEDIA COMMONS.

effectively did that for all those in the Grande Armée who made it out of Russia alive.[56]

Rochechouart picks up the narrative: "I mounted my horse and . . . went to the Palais du Luxembourg; in accordance with General Despinois's instructions I went first to M. de Seminville, who told me he was awaiting me with great impatience, being in haste to rid himself of responsibility for his prisoner. . . . The delivery took place without the Marechal taking any notice; he remained in conversation with M. de Canchy [sic], the Secretary Archivist of the Chamber of Peers."

It is perhaps telling that the aristocrat Rochechouart bungled the name of the commoner Louis-François Cauchy (1760–1848), archivist and keeper of the Seal of the Chamber of Peers. Cauchy was a mere functionary and scarcely worthy of note by Rochechouart. If he had noted him, he might have learned that, quite unlike the peers he served, Cauchy was an ardent Bonapartist who owed his job to the emperor and who had "supported the new regime" after the 18 Brumaire coup "enthusiastically and praised its virtues in several writings." He also might have learned that Cauchy started his career as principal clerk to the lieutenant general of police of Paris and was no stranger to the world of the all-seeing secret police. Finally, he might have learned that Cauchy was a devout Catholic and parishioner at the nearby church of Saint-Sulpice. (Cauchy was also the father of the renowned mathematician Augustin-Louis Cauchy and was himself elevated to the peerage later in life).[57]

According to the Journal, shortly after 3:00 a.m. Cauchy had appeared at the prison accompanied by two hussars, Montigny, Roger, and a National Guard officer. They entered Ney's room, awakened him, and asked him to sit.

"What is the news?" Ney asked.

"I come, Mr. Marshal, to give you a reading of the judgment of the Peers of France."

The archivist and keeper of the Seal then began to read a long preamble. Ney interrupted him. "Get to the point. Omit the formulas!"

He continued to read. "Come to the conclusion!" the marshal snapped.

When he read the words "penalty of death," Ney stated, "It would have been better to say 'bite the dust,' that would have been more military."

On learning that the execution was to take place within 24 hours, he said, "When it will be desired. I am quite ready."[58]

The Journal described "a silence that reigned around the Marshal," who no longer sat but walked about with great agitation and then cried out, "This is just like the reign of Caligula! One takes a man, he wants to defend himself, he is muzzled and then sent to his death!"

A few moments after taking charge of the prisoner, Despinois sent Rochechouart word that the king would allow Ney to receive his wife, his notary, and his confessor. When he relayed the message, Ney said, "I will first see my notary; he is probably in the Palais waiting for permission to see me; then I will see my wife and my children; as for my confessor, let them leave me alone, I do not want any priests."

Rochechouart described what happened next:

At these last words one of the old Grenadiers rose and said: "You are wrong, Marechal," and, showing him the stripes on his uniform, went on: "I am not as distinguished as you, but I am as old. Well then! I never went so bravely under fire as when I had first commended my soul to God." These few words, spoken with much feeling and solemnity by this colossus, seemed to make a strong impression on the Marechal. He went up to the Grenadier, and, laying his hand on his shoulder, said gently "Perhaps you are right, my brave man; it is good advice you are giving me." Then, turning to Colonel de Montigny: "What priest can I send for?"

"The Abbe de Pierre, Cure de Saint-Sulpice, he is a distinguished priest in every way."

"Ask him to come, I will see him after I have seen my wife."[59]

That was Rochechouart's version of the exchange. Some versions of the story have Cauchy suggesting the name of the curate of Saint-Sulpice to Ney.[60] In the Journal's version of the above exchange, Ney himself first mentioned the curate of Saint-Sulpice when the old Grenadier suggested he meet with a priest, although Ney asked the Grenadier if the curate were a spiritual man, suggesting that its reporting of the conversation missed the Grenadier or someone else having originally raised his name. Colonel de Montigny is not mentioned. In the United States, *Niles' Weekly Register*, which was noted for the quality of its reporting, stated at the time that Ney himself suggested Curate de Pierre by name.[61]

Saint-Sulpice is the second-largest church in Paris, only slightly smaller than Nôtre Dame. It is located midway between Ney's home on what used to be the rue de Bourbon and the Luxembourg Palace. It is not far from either the Faubourg Saint Germain neighborhood of Ney and his friends or the Luxembourg Palace. The curate's name was Father Charles de Pierre (1762–1836). De Pierre was born into a poor but noble family; he was related to Cardinal François-Joachim de Pierre de Bernis (1715–1794), a famous French cardinal and diplomat. He had a strong, chiseled face surmounted by a prominent nose. De Pierre was appointed curate of Saint-Sulpice in 1802 as a result of Napoleon's Concordat with the Catholic Church earlier that year, and he had spearheaded a major costly renovation of the Revolution-ravaged church financed by wealthy donors during the empire period. He also was a tough and devoted priest who survived the Reign of Terror in a semiclandestine fashion while never ceasing to administer to his flock.[62] According to the inscription on his tomb behind the high altar at Saint-Sulpice, he turned down a bishopric in order to remain with his parishioners.

Ney's notary, Henri Batardy, arrived first, and the two men met briefly alone.

After his departure, Ney wrote a short farewell note to his brother-in-law Claude Monnier. His hastily drafted and unpunctuated note to Monnier, dated "The 7. de.ber 1815 4 o'clock in the morning," is particularly probative of a man expecting to die. It reads,

> My dear Monnier. My trial is ended, the gentleman-usher of the chamber of peers has just read to me the sentence that condemns me to the penalty of death. Spare this news from my good father, who is on the verge of the grave, within twenty-four hours I should appear before God, with bitter regrets at not being able any longer to be useful to my country, but he will know just as I have said before men, that I feel free from remorse. Embrace my sister, say a thousand things for me to your children, they will love

I hope, notwithstanding the terrible catastrophe that strikes me, their good little cousins. Good-bye for ever I embrace you with all the feelings of a good brother [signed] The Mal. pce. De la Moskowa, Ney.[63]

At about 4:00 a.m., Madame Ney and the four children arrived, having been summoned for a last meeting. The children were accompanied by Madame Gamot, their aunt. The youngest child, too young to understand what was happening, was carried up the stairs to his father by Rochechouart's aide-de-camp and amused himself by playing with the soldier's moustache.[64] The Journal noted a "cry of grief" emanating from within as Madame Ney threw herself toward her husband and collapsed on the floor unconscious. The tearful children threw themselves into his arms as they said their final good-byes in a heart-wrenching scene. "The Marechal being unable any longer to struggle against his emotion, put an end to it himself," observed Rochechouart.[65] He did so by promising his wife that he would see her later in the morning, knowing full well he would not. The meeting lasted about three quarters of an hour to one hour.

After the family's departure, relative quiet prevailed. Soon thereafter, Curate de Pierre was shown in. According to Rochechouart, he "remained with the Marechal a full hour." They met alone, according to both Rochechouart and the Journal. On leaving, the Journal noted that he expressed satisfaction at the "sentiments expressed by the Marshal" in their private session. He promised to return to accompany Ney to his execution.

While Ney was meeting with the curate, Rochechouart received in succession three further orders from Despinois specifying details for the execution. They confirmed the location stated in the previous orders rather than the Plaine de Grenelle, the usual venue for military executions. For security reasons, Rochechouart was to receive the final order as to the location only half an hour before it was carried out. Rochechouart noted that the authorities had "learned that there would be an attempt at a rescue near Grenelle."[66] Ida Saint-Elme confirmed this in her memoirs, where she stated, "I afterwards learnt that the police had been warned the day before of an attempt to be made to set the marshal free. It was true that a body of our friends were to have assembled, all armed, at Grenelle. . . . But the government had selected another spot near the Luxembourg."[67]

After the curate departed, Ney threw himself on his bed, fully clothed and wrapped in his coat as if he were catching a nap on campaign. He slept quietly until 8:15 a.m.

Toward 8:00, an armed escort came to fetch Ney for his execution. According to contemporary military records, the escort consisted of a detachment of Royal Grenadiers de la Rochejaquelein, a picket of gendarmerie, and another picket of mounted National Guard "*sous-officiers vétérans de service au Luxembourg.*"[68]

The curate returned at 8:20. Rochechouart observed that "the good priest, though prepared for his sad duty, was seized with a nervous trembling, which lasted until the execution was over."[69] One might well ask why a sophisticated prelate charged with the second-largest church in Paris and well used to dealing with the wealthy and powerful in political Paris was "nervous" and "trembling." Certainly, the enormity and sadness of the event could have affected him. Anything beyond that is speculative in the absence of additional evidence, but the visible nervousness of the priest, who was one of the only persons to have met alone with Ney, raises an interesting question as to whether he might have been a messenger or even privy to one of the plots to free Ney that so clearly existed.

Curate de Pierre, according to Rochechouart, was greeted by Ney, who said, "Ah! M. Le Curé, I understand. I am ready." He then knelt and received absolution from the priest. The Journal observed that no one heard a "single word" between them.

At 8:45, Ney asked the head jailer if he owed anything to the prison, according to the Journal.

"A mere trifle," the head jailer responded. (In fact, the government was to charge Ney's family the entire expenses of his imprisonment, trial, and execution, about which it kept meticulous records. Such is the banality of evil.)

"Here, take this to remember me," Ney replied as he handed the jailer a 20-franc gold piece.

The four disguised Grenadiers who had been his constant and close guard then debated whether they should accompany the condemned to the execution ground. Interestingly, they elected not to.

At 9:10, Colonel Roger, followed by another officer, opened the door to Ney's cell and announced that the marshal should descend. He exited surrounded by the Grenadiers and the curate, who followed him. Ney wore his customary blue riding coat, a round hat, and no military decorations (as part of their judgment, the Chamber of Peers had stripped him of his Legion of Honor). Rochechouart noted in his *Memoirs* that he was relieved that Ney wore civilian clothes; otherwise, he would have had to "degrade" him by stripping him of his military insignia. According to the Journal, on exiting, Ney exhibited a "calm air" but a "light pallor that was consistent with a courageous and resigned man."

Thursday, December 7, was an ugly day: cold, foggy, and drizzling. "La Contemporaine" Ida Saint-Elme, who was present at the execution, described the day: "It was a gloomy winter's morning. The sky was black and low, the weather chill and foggy. A fine, piercing, gelid rain was falling with merciless persistence, changing the earth to mud, and soaking to the bone the national guardsmen who formed the line. It was a mournful picture."[70]

Ney took note of the weather as he exited the building. "What a wretched day," he said with a smile.

Rochechouart had ordered a fiacre, a small carriage commonly used for hire as a taxi. The curate stepped aside to let Ney enter the vehicle. "Go first, M. le Curé," Ney said, "presently I shall go first." The two men then entered the carriage accompanied by two officers of the Gendarmerie (but no Grenadiers) who took their seats in the front.

According to Rochechouart's *Memoirs*, the procession stopped in the Avenue de l'Observatoire a few hundred yards from the gate of the Luxembourg gardens. The carriage door was opened. "What! There already?" Ney stated, surprised at the location, having expected Grenelle (and, according to Rochechouart, "probably . . . aware that a manifestation would have been made there in his favour").[71] Alighting from the coach, Ney gave Curate de Pierre a gold snuffbox to give to his wife and handed the priest a few gold coins he had in his pocket "for the poor of Saint-Sulpice."

Ney was conducted to the execution spot, near where the aptly named rue d'Enfer ("Hell Street") intercepted the east side of the place de l'Observatoire. A wall under construction lined one side of the street.

There the firing squad stood ready, as ordered by Despinois. The firing squad stood at the center of a square formed by the troops, facing the wall.[72] Figure 9.3 shows a circa 1880s photograph of the execution wall.

Consistent with Despinois' orders, the firing squad consisted of four sergeants, four corporals, and four fusiliers from the *Compagnie des Sous-Officiers Vétérans*. The commanding officer of the firing squad, handpicked by Rochechouart, was an adjutant on his staff named Frederic Beltratti Comte de St. Bias, also known as Beltrut de St. Bias. He was a Piemontese royalist whose mother had served in the royal court of Sardinia.

Figure 9.3. Circa 1880s photograph of original placement of Ney statue showing execution wall. WIKIMEDIA COMMONS.

Rochechouart admitted having selected him with relief because a Frenchman would likely have found the mission difficult. St. Bias was born on March 31, 1768,[73] and was thus some 10 months older than Ney.

Rochechouart picks up the narrative:

> He [Ney], of course, refused to kneel down and be blind-folded; he merely asked the Commandant Saint-Bias to show him where he should stand. He stood facing the platoon, who held their guns ready to fire. Then, in an attitude I shall never forget, it was so noble, calm and dignified, without bravado, he took off his hat, and availing himself of the moment when the Adjutant stepped aside and gave the signal to fire, he said these words, which I distinctly heard: 'Frenchmen, I protest against my sentence; my honour. . . ." As he said these words he placed his hand on his heart; the volley was fired, and he fell. A rolling of drums, and the shout of "Vive le Roi" from the surrounding troops closed the mournful ceremony.
>
> Such a death made a deep impression on me, and turning to Auguste de la Rochejaquelein, Colonel of the Grenadiers, who was beside me, and who, like me, deplored the death of the *bravest of the brave*, I said: "There, my dear friend, is a lesson how to die."
>
> The words spoken by the Marechal in face of death have been incorrectly reported, both by journalists and by so-called spectators; it was even said that the Marechal had given the order to "fire." The events happened as I have stated. I have no interest in disguising the truth.[74]

Others saw it differently, as discussed in the final chapter. Even another official but probable eyewitness report, made by M. Laisne, inspector general of prisons, recorded the execution differently: "He [Ney] took some steps, removed his hat, and in a loud and clear voice: 'I protest,' he said 'before heaven and mankind, that the judgment that condemns me is iniquitous; I appeal from it to Europe and to posterity.' . . . Before these words there was presented to him a handkerchief to bandage his eyes: he answered with exultation, 'do you not know that a soldier does not fear death.' He advanced again four paces, laying his hand on his heart and said to the soldiers: 'do your duty, it is there that you must hit, do not miss me.' Instantly he fell dead."[75] *Niles' Weekly Register* contained a similar report at the time, with Ney himself giving the order to fire: "the marshal turned and fronted the *Vétérans* who were to fire upon him; he took off his hat with his left hand, put his right on his heart, and said to the soldiers— '*My comrades, fire at me.*' At that moment the officer gave the signal with his sword, and the marshal fell under their fire without moving [emphasis in the original]."[76]

"La Contemporaine" Ida Saint-Elme even made it to the execution. Accompanied by a friend named Belloc, she evidently had followed the fiacre as it left the Luxembourg Palace. She wrote,

> Ney got out of the carriage. He was wearing civilian clothes: a long dark coat, a white necktie, black breeches and stockings, a tall beaver hat with curved brim. He uncovered. His slightly raised head showed that his face wore a tranquil expression. He looked first to the right and then to the left. He caught sight of me. Then, as though fearing to compromise his faithful friends by the least sign of recognition, he bent his brow downward a trifle. He walked on with firm step. At that instant I discerned through the mist, in the centre of the square of troops, and standing out from the dark background of the wall, the firing squad. I tried to rush forward. Belloc pulled me back, and forced me into the cab. Then I dropped weakly upon the seat. A few minutes elapsed, each a whole century long. Then I heard a sharp report. I went into a dead faint.[77]

No one delivered the customary coup de grâce, nor did a doctor confirm the death, both usual procedures at executions. The body lay sprawled forward with its stomach on the ground for at most 15 minutes.[78] No family member claimed it (Madame Ney was in fact ignorant of the execution and was at that very moment unsuccessfully appealing for a reprieve at the Tuileries). While the body lay exposed and guarded by pickets of infantry and cavalry, Secretary-Archivist of the Chamber of Peers Cauchy penned the following report,[79] which was addressed to no one specifically:

> To-day, the seventh of December, eighteen hundred and fifteen, at twenty minutes past nine in the morning, We, Louis-Francois Cauchy, secretary-archivist of the Chamber of Peers, performing in accordance with the terms of the ordonnance of the king, of the twelfth of November last, the function of the clerk of the court of the said Chamber, were transported onto the place de l'Observatoire, designated for the execution of the sentence rendered yesterday by the Chamber of Peers, against Michel Ney, marshal of France, ex-Peer of France, more fully styled by the said sentence by which he was condemned to the penalty of death, applicable in the form prescribed by the decree of the 12th of May, 1793.... The execution has taken place, in our presence, and in the form prescribed.[80]

According to an official report, approximately 200 persons witnessed the execution. Presumably, most of these were soldiers involved in the process, as the site of the execution was a closely held secret until the last minutes and the cold, misty December morning was hardly conducive to strollers. The people kept a mournful silence. Some broke out into murmurs. One man stepped forward and dipped his handkerchief into the blood of the marshal. Curate de Pierre, still on his knees at some distance, continued to pray.

Probably not included in the authorities' count of 200 witnesses was a 13-year-old student at the École Polytechnique named Étienne Arago, who later claimed to have witnessed the execution by peering over the wall of the Observatoire Gardens toward the Closerie des Lilas dancing garden. Arago's oldest brother, the astronomer François Arago, resided at the Observatoire. The younger Arago went on to achieve fame as a playwright, radical Republican politician, cofounder of *Le Figaro*, and, briefly, mayor of Paris. When Jean-Léon Gérôme painted his *The Execution of Marshal Ney* (illustration 12) in 1868, he consulted with Arago on the accuracy of the painting. If Arago in fact witnessed Ney's execution, the result is what is probably the most accurate of the several visual renditions of the execution. Unfortunately, Arago left no written account of what he witnessed; he spoke only through Gérôme's painting.[81]

After 15 minutes, the unclaimed body was placed on a stretcher, covered with a blanket, and carried to the nearby Maternity Hospital, all as stipulated by Despinois. Curate de Pierre led the procession. Once there, it was in the care of the nuns. An official police report states that hundreds of dignitaries—military officers, ambassadors, and government officials—came to view the body. Interestingly, not one of them appears to have written of the experience, and the only two extant accounts of the body inside the hospital were written by Ida Saint-Elme and a neighborhood interloper who should not have been there. Those accounts are discussed in the final chapter.

Also present with the body in the hospital that night was Ney's brother-in-law Charles-Guillaume Gamot. He "himself washed the bloody wounds, and rendered Ney those last duties that France in tears should have bestowed upon a hero who had so gloriously served her."[82] He was a politically active Bonapartist who, as prefect of l'Yonne near Auxerre, was the first prefect in all of France to officially welcome Napoleon on his return from Elba. He was a known conspirator plotting to free Ney. Also present was Ney's steward or administrative officer Louis-Frédéric Rayot. He had worked for Ney since 1805, accompanied him on his campaigns, and handled the accounts and receipts of those campaigns. He was no doubt a man adept at organizing matters. He also had been the subject of police surveillance for having "relations" with Ney and had been arrested in November but released because the authorities could find no basis for accusing him.[83] He was therefore undoubtedly as motivated as he was adept.

The body was buried in a remote location in Père Lachaise Cemetery at 6:30 the next morning while it was still dark. Madame Ney never claimed the body and did not attend the burial even though by that point she had learned of his death. The body was sealed in a lead coffin within an oak one.[84]

The Parisian newspapers, beginning with the December 8 edition, reported the execution largely along the lines outlined above.[85]

The conspiracy version of the execution, based mainly on statements by P. S. Ney and a few others,[86] is broadly as follows. Ney was widely admired by his soldiers and even his British adversaries. None of them wanted him killed. A last-minute plot was hatched by unnamed persons with the knowledge and cooperation of Ney. Wellington or fellow Masons may have been in on the scheme. On arriving at the place of execution, Ney recognized many of his old soldiers among the veterans who made up the firing squad. Beneath his coat and shirt, he concealed a bladder containing a blood-like fluid placed over the area of his heart. When he addressed the firing squad, he told the soldiers to aim for his heart but to "shoot high," which they would have recognized as a variant on his customary admonition in battle to "shoot low." He then simultaneously gave the order to fire, struck the bladder hard with his hand holding his hat, and threw himself hard on the ground face forward. The bullets narrowly passed over him and struck the wall behind. He lay there motionless until removed on the stretcher. Once inside the Maternity Hospital, either he or a look-alike was made up to appear to have bullet wounds for purposes of the viewing of the body, while the real Ney escaped during the following night in a desperate horseback ride to Orléans and thence to Bordeaux, accompanied (in some versions though not those of P. S. Ney) by General Lefebvre-Desnouettes, who was also proscribed and likely to face trial if caught, and Pascal Luciani, Napoleon's second cousin. The next morning, either a substitute cadaver or no cadaver at all was buried in the double casket at Père Lachaise Cemetery.[87]

Either way, the network of police informers nervously monitored the public reaction in the 24 hours following the execution. Their reports, which still exist, came in *arrondisement* by *arrondisement*. To read them is like being a fly on the wall of the cafés of Paris in 1815. Their unanimous verdict: all was quiet.

CHAPTER 10

The Eyewitnesses

P. S. NEY WAS A MAN OF GREAT MYSTERY WHO APPEARED OUT OF NOWHERE but left a profound impression on many people he encountered. According to Weston, he could find no trace of P. S. Ney in the United States prior to 1819, nor has anyone since then with any certainty. Weston records that Chapman Levy, a South Carolina lawyer, stated that he was told by some French refugees that they saw P. S. Ney in Georgetown, South Carolina, in the early part of the fall of 1819 and recognized him as Marshal Ney, whom they had frequently seen in France, and that when P. S. Ney heard of this recognition, he left Georgetown, and no one knew where he went. In September or October 1819, Colonel Benjamin Rogers of Brownsville, South Carolina, met P. S. Ney at a hotel in Cheraw, South Carolina, and engaged him to teach the village school. He taught in Brownsville for about three years. The only obvious extant evidence from this period in his life is an 1821 tentative application for citizenship (discussed in chapter 11) and an 1821 lawsuit in a South Carolina state court to collect $43.83 in bad debts from Ney.[1] He then went to Mocksville, North Carolina. He taught in Mocksville and in other portions of what was then western North Carolina until 1828. In that year, he went to Mecklenburg County, Virginia, where he taught for about two years. He returned to North Carolina around January 1, 1830. From that time, he was engaged in teaching in various parts of North Carolina, chiefly in Lincoln, Iredell, Davie, Cabarrus, and Rowan counties, until August 1844. During the fall and winter of 1844–1845, he taught in Darlington District, South Carolina. He then returned to North Carolina and taught in Lincoln and Rowan counties until his death in 1846. He appears to have eluded census takers in the three federal censuses conducted between 1820 and 1840. Rarely if ever was he more than two years at any one teaching position. P. S. Ney's itinerant existence is well illustrated by an entry he made around 1834 in the guestbook of an unidentified North Carolina inn where he stayed: after signing his name, instead of stating his hometown like the other guests, he entered, "An atom floating on the atmosphere of chance."[2]

In each case, Ney's pupils were drawn from local gentry families, and he associated with and was highly respected by the finest families in the areas where he taught. An advertisement he placed in the November 30, 1841, *Mecklenburg Jeffersonian*, published in Charlotte, North Carolina, captures the spirit of his professionalism:

ENGLISH
And Classical School
P. S. NEY

Will open a School in the immediate vicinity of the Catawba Springs, Lincoln County, on Monday the 20th instant. The Studies will embrace all the branches requisite to qualify students for entering College. . . .

The reputation of Mr. NEY as an instructor of youth, is so well known in Western North Carolina, as to require no commendation. As to his capacity and unwearied attention to the advancement of his pupils, reference may be made to most of the leading men of the adjoining counties.[3]

The advertisement was completely truthful.

If P. S. Ney were Marshal Ney, how did he escape from France, and where was he from the time of his landing in the United States until the fall of 1819? The consensus narrative based on testimony from eyewitnesses who knew P. S. Ney and spoke to him about it was that Marshal Ney's execution was faked through the collusion of certain unnamed persons and that he escaped to Bordeaux and from there took a ship to America, landing in Charleston, South Carolina, on January 29, 1816. He then secluded himself for three years studying and preparing himself for a reinvented role as a schoolmaster in rural America.

There follows a redacted summary of 49 eyewitness testimonies collected and published by Weston in his book, from which all of them are taken verbatim.[4] The many scores of testimonials that Weston included were made by highly credible witnesses: doctors, lawyers, judges, college presidents, army officers, clergymen, and others who were pillars of their communities and who either knew or were students of P. S. Ney. Not all believed he was Marshal Ney, but most did. Others did not opine on that point. Setting aside a few technical inconsistencies in the memories given by witnesses of events that occurred many decades earlier, the testimonies are nonetheless remarkable for the consistent and vivid portrait they paint of P. S. Ney. It is abundantly clear that he was a man who made an impression.

COLONEL JOHN A. ROGERS, FLORENCE, SOUTH CAROLINA (SEPTEMBER 1888)

"I first saw Peter S. Ney . . . in the fall of 1819. My father, Colonel Benjamin Rogers, met him at a hotel in Cheraw in September or October (1819), and engaged him as a teacher. He taught with great success about three years, and then went to North Carolina. . . . I saw him often afterward, for he made occasional visits to his friends in South Carolina, and taught again in the State about 1844. He told my father that he was a French refugee; that he had left France for political reasons, but would give no further account of his life. He was a man of remarkably fine presence, and would arrest attention anywhere. No stranger could meet him without asking the first individual that he saw, Who is that man? He was tall I suppose about six feet high, large, not corpulent, but muscular; a little round-shouldered, though otherwise erect, with fine military form and carriage. He looked every inch the soldier, even when he was quite an old man. His head was slightly bald on top. His hair was not a decided auburn, but was what might be called a reddish-blonde. His complexion was fair and ruddy; chin round; mouth tolerably large; lips compressed; nose high and large; eyebrows heavy and full; forehead broad, high, and massive. His eyes are hard to describe. They were a dark blue, verging on gray, with remarkably large pupils. When quiet, they had the mildest expression, but when excited, they were terrible, an eagle would dart from them in sheer envy. He spoke English well, though with a slightly foreign accent. He appeared to be more of a Scotchman than a Frenchman. He was very neat in his person and dress. He always wore a long blue coat, cut in a semi-military style. He was very reserved in his manners, and would allow no one to take the slightest liberty with him. I was in the schoolroom in 1821 when a newspaper was brought to him by one of the boys containing the announcement of Napoleon's death at St. Helena. He read it, turned deathly pale, fainted, and fell to the floor, exactly as if he had been shot. Some of the older scholars threw water on his face, which soon revived him. He dismissed his school, went to his room, and shut himself up for the balance of the day. He burnt a large quantity of his papers perhaps everything that he thought might lead to his identity. Among other things burnt was a very exact likeness of the Emperor Napoleon. The next morning Mr. Ney did not make his appearance as usual, and my father went to look after him. He found him with his throat cut.* . . .

(*When my father reproved Mr. Ney for this extraordinary account, he gently took hold of his arm, and said with deep emotion, 'Oh, colonel, colonel, with the death of Napoleon my last hope is gone.').

"Some time afterward he went with two of my brothers to Columbia [South Carolina]. While there a general military review took place. Mr. Ney made his appearance on the field mounted. So splendid was his horsemanship, and so magnificent his bearing every way, that he attracted universal attention. There were several foreigners in Columbia at the time, and they declared in the most positive manner that this man was Marshal Ney. They said they had seen Marshal Ney many a time in Europe, and that they could not be mistaken. When Mr. Ney heard this he rode immediately off the field, went to his hotel, and stayed in his room during the remainder of the day. That night he told the boys that they must start home very early the next morning. The boys were astonished, as they expected to remain two or three days longer, and begged Mr. Ney earnestly to change his mind. 'No, no,' said he, without offering any explanation, 'we must go.' They left at daybreak the next morning.

"Mr. Ney was a perfect master of fence. No one in this country could equal him. . . . One day he entered my room, and picking up my sword, which was lying on the table, surveyed it a moment and said, 'Why, John, this is only a baby to the sword which I carried in battle. I could cut off a man's head at a single blow, and my horse was trained to ride to the cannon's mouth.' He had a long and deep scar on the left side of his head, which he told me, I think, he received in battle. He complained greatly at times of a wound in the thigh. . . .

"He drank wine, and sometimes, though not often, to excess. That was his only fault. He was very methodical in his habits, and retiring in his disposition. He avoided company for the most part, but was kind and obliging to his friends. My father was very hospitable, and entertained a great deal of company. On one occasion, when he had as his guests some of the most distinguished men of the State, the conversation turned in the course of the evening upon military subjects. The discussion waxed warm, every one held to his opinion, and finally my father appealed to Mr. Ney, who had been an attentive listener, to give his opinion upon the subject. Mr. Ney gave his views in the simplest, clearest, and most forcible manner, entering fully into the details of the question, and explaining them to the satisfaction of every one present. When he concluded there was a profound silence. Every one looked at Mr. Ney in astonishment. In a little while Mr. Ney rose and went to his room. One of the gentlemen turned to my father and said, 'Colonel Rogers, your friend, Mr. Ney, must be Marshal Ney. True, Marshal Ney was shot, but he must have risen from the dead. No one but Marshal Ney could have talked like that. . . .'

"He was a man of the highest character, and though a little rough and blunt in his manners and ways, was very tenderhearted and charitable, and entirely above everything that was dishonest, mean, or little. As a teacher he was surpassed by none and equalled by few. There was something about the man that drew all hearts to him. My father was devotedly attached to him, and his students fairly idolized him. He was certainly one of the most extraordinary men that I have ever known."

CHARLES A. POELLNITZ, REMBERT, MARENGO COUNTY, ALABAMA (1887)

"I knew P. S. Ney well. I was a pupil of his when he taught at Brownsville, S. C., from the fall of 1819 to 1821 or 1822. He was, without doubt, one of the best teachers that ever lived. I laid the foundation under him for all

I know. He taught Latin and Greek in addition to the ordinary English branches. He sometimes delivered lectures. If not an eloquent orator, he was at all times a forcible and impressive speaker. He had a very distinct Scotch-Irish brogue. He was a very large, well-built, fine-looking man. His head was large and round and bald, complexion fair, eyes gray, teeth good. At the time of Napoleon's death, in 1821, he burned up valuable papers, relics of royalty and high military position, badges of honor, etc. The general belief then was that he was Marshal Ney. I remember it well. It was said that the guns of the soldiers detailed to shoot him were loaded with blank cartridges. He tried to cut his throat when Napoleon died. My father sent for Dr. Nicholson, who dressed the wounds. Mr. Ney sometimes drank to excess, but he never became intemperate until after Napoleon's death. He was a good marksman; taught me how to shoot a rifle. In the school-room he paid much attention to the derivation of words from Latin and Greek. He was rough, sometimes severe, but his heart was good, and he was beloved and honored by everyone."

BURGESS GAITHER, FARMINGTON, DAVIE COUNTY, NORTH CAROLINA (1883)

"Peter S. Ney taught school on one of my father's plantations in 1832. I was his pupil at that time, and became very much attached to him. I was his pupil again in 1834–35, when he taught south of Mocksville. I will answer your questions in regular order:

"1. I do not know when Peter S. Ney came to Mocksville. I suppose, from what I have heard, somewhere about 1820. A gentleman in whose word I can place the fullest confidence relates the following incident: One day in 1820 (it may have been later), during a heated political campaign, a party of men met in Mocksville (then consisting of but a few houses) to drink whiskey and to talk politics. One of the men was Dr. Schools, an educated gentleman, who had some years before come from Ireland, and settled in Mocksville. Words ran high, and at length one of the crowd used language which Dr. Schools deemed personally insulting. He demanded an apology. His opponent refused to make any. Thereupon the doctor drew his dagger, seized his adversary by the collar, and swore he must retract or he would thrust him through. No one would interfere, as most of the crowd were the doctor's friends. Just at that moment a stranger stepped up, and taking hold of the doctor's arm, remarked, 'What! kill a man unarmed, with no chance to defend himself?' Dr. Schools turned quickly around, and looked the stranger full in the face. He immediately dropped his arm, and put his dagger in his pocket. The stranger was at once the hero of the hour. Dr. Schools shook him warmly by the hand, and to the day of his death Peter S. Ney (for he was the stranger) had no warmer, truer friend than this gallant, open-hearted Irishman. Mr. Ney needed no formal introduction to that crowd. He told them his name, and that he was a French refugee looking for a school. That was just what the people wanted. They gathered around him, and begged him to remain with them and teach their children. He did so. He taught in this county and in the adjoining counties for several years, acquiring a reputation as a teacher which, I think, has never been equalled, certainly never surpassed in the entire State.

"2. He was a fine scholar. Those who were capable of judging say he could speak with ease and fluency the French, Latin, Greek, and Hebrew languages.[5] He was a splendid mathematician. He seemed never to grow weary of solving hard and intricate problems. His mind was strong and vigorous, and seemed to be capable of grasping any subject.

"3. Mr. Ney was a large, heavy-built man, but not corpulent, with a round body and an erect figure. He would weigh, I suppose, over two hundred pounds. He had powerful muscles, and was remarkably quick and active for a man of his age. His person appeared to be uniformly straight from his hips up. He had a robust constitution, and could stand any amount of exposure. He was little affected either by heat or cold. It was a rare thing to see him near the fire, even in the coldest weather. He was about five feet ten and one half or eleven inches high, and very graceful, though simple and unaffected in all his movements. His head was large, round, and well shaped. It was nearly bald. There was a little hair on the back and sides of his head. His forehead was broad and full; his eyes were of a light blue color, keen and full of intelligence, and at times very fiery and piercing; his nose was prominent, broad at the base, and a little tipped at the point; mouth of medium size, with thin lips; chin round, prominent, and on the thin order; complexion fair, and face dotted from small-pox. He walked rather rapidly, except when in deep thought, and was quick and sprightly in all his actions. . . .

"4. He spoke English as well as any Englishman. I suppose he was familiar with the language when he came to this country, for he spoke it when he first came to Mocksville. He spoke French as if it were his mother tongue. I have heard him speak of his family. He told me that he had a wife and children in France, but did not say how many children. He said that his mother had Irish blood in her veins, and from her he inherited his impetuous temper.

"5. I do not know his exact age. I heard him say, in 1832, that he was over sixty years old, but that the people in France looked upon him as a dead man.

"6. He had the highest opinion of Napoleon Bonaparte. He thought him the greatest man that ever lived. If you wished to rouse up the old man, you had but to watch your chance and ask him of Napoleon or his battles. I have listened to him with inexpressible delight when I could draw him out on these subjects, but I was too young to remember or to comprehend all that he said. He told me about the Russian campaign, giving the names of persons and places, the details of battles fought, etc. I remember that he spoke with much feeling about the French soldiers attempting to cross a river on the ice, but too many crowding on it at once, the ice gave way, and a great many of the poor fellows were drowned in his sight, and he was unable to help them. I have heard him speak of the Junior Reserves when called out (I suppose), in the campaign of 1813, how they would dread to go into the heat of the action, how sorry he would be for them, how after a few rounds he would send them to the rear, and how after a few trials they would become sturdy and fight like veterans. He often alluded to Waterloo, and sometimes to Elba and St. Helena, but the mention of these places always appeared sadly to trouble him. He sometimes spoke of Wellington. He said that at Waterloo Wellington was so hard pressed that he looked at his watch, and murmured, 'Oh, that night or Blücher would come!' To show how great events oftentimes spring from small causes, he said that Blücher's horse was killed at the battle of Ligny, that Blücher was so badly hurt by the fall he could not get up, and that the French troops marched over him and then back again without discovering who it was; but had they discovered him, the Prussians would not have reached Waterloo and that before night Napoleon would have annihilated Wellington's army, and perhaps have changed the fate of Europe. It always pained him deeply to say anything about the reverses of Napoleon. He seldom referred to Louis XVIII. When he did, it was with the utmost contempt. Mr. Ney was a splendid swordsman. I have heard him speak of fencing contests between him and Murat. He said they never could decide which was the better fencer. Sometimes in presence of Napoleon they would be trying their skill, and, both being high-tempered and impetuous, they would get their mettle up and become too much excited, when Napoleon would say, 'Come, come, that will do,' and put a stop to the fun. That he was firmly attached to Napoleon you may judge from the fact that he wore the same style of coat that Napoleon used to wear. It was long, almost touching his ankles, generally of bluish-black broadcloath, and without lapels.

"7. He had a notable wound on the left side of his head. It was a sabre cut directly above the left eye, three or four inches long and about two and one half inches broad. It appeared to have been produced by a glancing stroke which cut up the scalp, but did not entirely separate it from the bone. The skin was sewed back, but rather unevenly, as every stitch was distinctly visible. He had another wound in the calf of his leg, produced by a musket ball. The ball, I think, was still in his leg, and pained him at times, especially when he walked. These are the only wounds that I have any personal knowledge of. He told me in what battle he received the sabre cut, but I have forgotten the name. He said he was on horseback at the time, in a hand-to-hand encounter; that he cut down a man from his horse just in front of him, but before he could recover, another man struck him from his horse; that his head would have been split open but for one of his friends on the right, who saw the danger, and threw up his sword to defend him, but was too far off entirely to avert the blow. He turned the sabre, however, and caused only a glancing stroke. He said it was like a flash of lightning, and that he knew nothing for some time afterward.

"8. He was anxious to get back to France to his family and home and country. That seemed to be the absorbing object of his life. One Monday morning in the year 1832 Mr. Ney came to school feeling somewhat unwell from the effects of a little spree on the Saturday previous. He told his pupils there would be no school that day, but to come back the next day, Tuesday. 'If, however,' said he, 'any of you choose to remain, I will instruct you, but there will be no regular school.' I stayed and went on with my studies, as usual. Some time in the day Mr. Ney told me that he was suffering a good deal, and asked me to get him some brandy from my father's house, which was not far off. I did so. He drank it off, and said it gave him great relief. He then remarked that I had always been very kind to him, and he would be glad to reward me when in a position to do so. 'People here,' said he, 'call me old Ney, but they do not know who I am. Young Napoleon will soon be of age, and then the French people will put him on the throne, and I shall go back to France, and have rank and position and influence. I am not what I seem to be. I am Marshal Ney, of France.' He then told me how he escaped. He said he was tried and condemned to be shot, and was apparently shot, and that his countrymen thought he was a dead man. 'Louis XVIII,' said he, 'was full of revenge. He ordered that some of my old soldiers, whom I had often led into battle, should be my executioners. The thing was so revolting to Frenchmen that a plan was formed for my escape. The officer appointed to superintend my execution told one of my friends to apply to the king for my body for interment. He did so, and the necessary permission was granted. I was told to give the command fire, and to fall as I gave it. I did so. The soldiers, who had previously been instructed, fired almost instantly, the balls passing over my head and striking the planks or wall behind. I was pronounced dead, hastily taken up, put into a carriage, and driven off to a neighboring hospital. That night I was disguised and left for America.' If he gave the names of any persons concerned in the plot, I do not recollect them, but I think he gave no names. In October, 1832, while sitting calmly at his desk in the schoolroom, one of the pupils brought him his papers. In a few minutes he threw down the paper which he had been reading, and began walking the floor in great excitement. As soon as I got to the door I saw that he was greatly troubled, and I felt very sorry for him. He turned to me, his eyes wildly glaring, the deepest agony depicted in his looks, his powerful frame convulsed with emotion. He pointed to a pair of andirons in the fireplace, and said to me, 'Little fellow, can you eat those dogirons?' I said that I could not. 'Well, then,' he replied, 'I have a harder task than that. Young Napoleon is dead, and with him dies all hope of ever going back to France, of again seeing wife and children and home and friends.' He then walked the floor, and in the most pathetic terms bewailed his unhappy lot. I never saw such grief. All of his scholars were deeply affected, for they almost worshipped the man. In a few minutes he dismissed his school, and went to Mr. Thomas Foster's, where he was boarding. The next morning, being anxious to hear from him, I went up to Mr. Foster's and saw Wiley Ellis, a student who boarded with Mr. Foster, and he told me that Mr. Ney took a large roll of manuscript from his trunk and burnt it, and that he had been so wild and restless that Mr. Foster had had him watched all night, fearing he might commit suicide. I had seen the manuscript to which Wiley Ellis alluded. Mr. Ney showed it to me one day, and said that it contained an account of his life, and that if he should die before he got back to France, his full history would be known. There was quite a large quantity of the manuscript, and Mr. Ney always kept it locked up in his trunk. It was several days before Mr. Ney's friends could induce him to resume his school. From that time on he was a changed man. He never spoke again, so far as I know, of going back to France.

"9. Mr. Ney was entirely free from hobbies or idiosyncrasies of any kind. His mind was clear on all subjects, and he was thoroughly practical in every thing that he did. He was plain in his ways, outspoken on all subjects, sometimes rough and apparently severe, but always just and generous and merciful. If he wounded or hurt anybody by word or deed, he was quick to apologize, and to repair, to the fullest extent, any wrong which he may have committed. As a teacher he seemed to know exactly what each pupil could accomplish; that much he required, and nothing more. If a pupil was obedient and studious, he was gentle and indulgent; but if disobedient and idle, he was very strict and rigid. I have seen grown-up young men, who had been spoilt at home, and who openly declared they intended to do as they pleased in school, cower before him in perfect submission to his will.

"10. Mr. Ney's character as a man and citizen was above all reproach. He was quiet, orderly, industrious, public-spirited, and honorable in all the relations of life. Nothing could be said against the man except his habit of drinking too much at certain times; but even then he was guilty of no disorder, or rude and improper conduct of any kind. You never saw him in a grog-shop or drinking-saloon, or mixing in with a drinking crowd. He was talkative and communicative when drinking, but careful to say nothing offensive or to give trouble to any one about the house. He was not only kind-hearted, but benevolent. He gave a great many poor orphan children their tuition free. He was polite and gentlemanly in his manners, but quick to resent an insult.... I never saw him drunk enough to stagger, though I have heard that he was occasionally in that condition. It has been said that he used profane language when he heard of the death of young Napoleon. I do not think he did. He was too refined and well-bred to use profane language in presence of his pupils. I certainly never heard him do so, though in this case he may have been carried away by his feelings. The only expression like an oath that I ever heard him use was 'By Jove!' He was remarkably modest and unobtrusive in his general deportment. There was no bluster or brag or affectation about him. He lived entirely in the country, always boarding with the best people, and seldom went to town. He avoided large crowds and public places, and spent much of his time in reading and writing. He wrote for several newspapers. As a rule, he would not talk about himself, even to his intimate friends. If you interrogated him about his history, you would be almost sure to get a rebuff. I think he left no likeness of himself. If he had pictures of Napoleon and Josephine, I never saw them. I do not think he ever wrote letters to France. I used to take letters for him to the post office, but I do not remember that he ever sent any to or received any from France or any other portion of Europe. He died beloved and lamented by all who knew him."

COLONEL THOMAS F. HOUSTON, HOUSTONIA, MISSOURI, FORMERLY OF IREDELL COUNTY, NORTH CAROLINA (1877)

"About 1826 (fifty-one years ago) my uncle, Colonel Francis Young, of Iredell County, N. C., engaged P. S. Ney to teach the languages to his sons at Oak Hill Academy. I was too young at that time to attend school, but in January, 1830, I became his pupil, and continued so most of the time until 1838. Mr. Ney was about five feet eleven inches high, of fine physique and muscular power, and would weigh about two hundred pounds. His head was large so large, in fact, that it was necessary to send away to have his hats made. His head was bald, save at the sides and back, and there was but a slight fringe of hair there, though it grew long and was combed over the top of his head partially to hide his baldness. On one side of his head the left, I think there was a scar about two and one half inches in length, which he told me was a sabre cut received in battle. It was healed, but there was an indenture in which a quill could have been placed. He told me, I think, that he had been 'trepanned.' On one occasion he opened his shirt-bosom and showed me scars upon his body, inflicted at the same time that he received the wound described above, by the shoes of the cavalry horses charging over him. While I was his pupil he boarded a great part of the time with my father (Placebo Houston), and a strong attachment was formed between us, at least on my part. During the life of Napoleon's son the Duke of Reichstadt he frequently told me of his intention to return to France, and asked me to go with him. Many times he reverted to the subject, always asking me if I would accompany him. Assuring him that I would, he said, 'I'll make a man of you.' I was not a student of his at the time of the death of Napoleon's son (1832), but never after that event, to my knowledge, though his pupil for several years after, did he speak of returning to France. Young Napoleon's death seemed to have blasted all his hopes. When he heard this sad news he trembled, turned very pale, dismissed his school for several days, destroyed many of his private papers, and his grief was so great that fears were entertained that his reason might be dethroned, and that he might commit suicide.

"Mr. Ney was a good Latin and Greek scholar, and a splendid mathematician. He was the best of teachers, and gave universal satisfaction. He had a rare faculty for imparting instruction. He would at once seize the vital points of a question, and make it plain to the dullest understanding. He taught more for the pleasure and employment which it afforded him than for the profit, as he asked only his board and $200 per annum. He preserved the strictest order and discipline in his school. His scholars feared him, but loved him. Indeed, no one could help loving him. Mr. Ney was a man of martial appearance, the finest specimen of manhood I ever saw. He showed his military training in his step and bearing. His countenance was open and noble. His eyes were of a bluish-gray color, and in repose they had an exceedingly gentle and even tender expression; but when he was thoroughly aroused upon any subject, they were indescribably keen and piercing. He seemed to look down into the inmost depths of your soul. He ruled men all classes of people as Marshal Ney is known to have ruled his soldiers. I do not hesitate to avow my belief that he was Marshal Ney. He was always reticent when with strangers, and rarely spoke of himself and his connection with the French Army, even to his intimate friends, unless the hinges of his tongue were loosened by an extra glass of wine or brandy, and his characteristic reserve thrown off. Then he never manifested any boastful disposition, but sometimes spoke of his connection with the army and the part he had borne in its campaigns.

"On one occasion Ney, while intoxicated, lay down in the snow near my father's house. . . . Father sent several negro men with a horse to bring Ney to the house. I accompanied the negroes, and found him asleep. Repeated efforts to arouse him proving ineffectual, I concluded to have him placed on the horse and taken to the house. One of the negroes mounted the horse, when the others lifted Ney and placed him across the horse's shoulders. In that act the old man was awakened, and his first words were, 'What! put the Duke of Elchingen on a horse like a sack! Let me down.' He struck one of the negroes, and they let him down. He walked with military tread a few steps to the fence, and placing his elbows thereon, wept at the indignity which had been offered him. One of the negroes, addressing him, said, 'Mr. Ney, can you ride?' 'Yes, I could ride into battle.' He mounted the horse and rode to the house without reeling, sitting erect and dignified in the saddle. I told father what Ney had said, and he told me that Marshal Ney was Duke of Elchingen, which was my first information upon the subject, as I did not understand Ney's meaning. This affair was never mentioned to or by Ney afterward. Mr. Ney liked his glass, but he rarely drank to excess. He said that trouble made him drink. He once related to me, when we were alone in his room, the circumstances of his escape. 'Much of history,' said he, 'is false. History says that Marshal Ney was executed, but it is not true. I was sentenced to be executed, and was marched out for that purpose, but the soldiers detailed to do the work were veterans,' and I think he said 'belonged to my old command. As I walked by the file of soldiers I whispered, 'Aim high!' My old command in war had always been, 'Aim low at the heart!' As I took my position in front of the file, refusing to have my eyes bandaged, I raised my hand and gave the command, Fire! They fired. I was pronounced dead, and my body was delivered to my friends for interment. I was secretly conveyed to Bordeaux, from which place I sailed to America, landing in Charleston, S. C.' I think he said 'January 29th, 1816.'

"Mr. Ney also gave me an account of his famous retreat from Moscow, amid the snows and across the rivers upon ice; how the ice bridge gave way under his army and drowned many of them; how they perished from hunger and cold; how the Cossacks hung upon his rear and flanks, cutting off his men, and slaughtering those who from cold and exhaustion straggled, and lay down in the snow to die; how he marched on foot with his men, and finally brought up the rear-guard of a few hundred soldiers; and how Napoleon embraced him and called him the 'bravest of the brave.' In the fall of 1874 (if not mistaken as to the date) I read in the Dayton (O.) Journal the account of an interview between the Journal reporter and an old French soldier named Philip Petrie, who once belonged to Marshal Ney's command. He stated to the reporter that after the fall of Napoleon and capture of Ney he deserted from the French Army, and in December, 1815, shipped as a seaman on board a vessel bound from Bordeaux, France, to Charleston, S. C., landing in Charleston, January 29th, 1816. He noticed after sailing a man whose appearance struck him very forcibly as some one whom he ought to know. He tried for several days to remember who it could be. At last it flashed across his mind that it was his old commander, Marshal Ney.

"He sought the first opportunity to satisfy himself, and the next time the mysterious personage appeared on deck Petrie approached him, and told him he thought he knew him. He replied, 'Who do you think I am?' Petrie answered, 'My old commander, Marshal Ney.' In a gruff tone he responded, 'Marshal Ney was executed two weeks ago in Paris!' and turning round walked directly to the cabin, and was not seen on deck again during the voyage, though they were thirty five days in reaching Charleston. Petrie said he knew Marshal Ney was not executed, but escaped to America. This corroborative statement was made by Petrie prior to the discussion of the question as to the identity of P. S. Ney with Marshal Ney, which has been so extensively commented upon by the public press, and almost surely without any knowledge of the whereabouts and occupation of P. S. Ney in the Carolinas and Virginia. . . . Ney was a splendid swordsman, and taught me how to fence, at first using wooden swords. At length we had an encounter with two real swords. One of these swords was my father's, and the other belonged to my uncle, Samuel Houston, who carried it in the War of 1812. I was, of course, no match for Ney, and he could easily have cut me down had he so desired. I have his old Latin grammar, published in 1818, in which are inserted a large number of Latin and Greek exercises in his handwriting, such exercises as he used in instructing his pupils. . . .

"In speaking of his family, P. S. Ney, according to my recollection, told me that his father was a Frenchman named Peter, and his mother was a Scotchwoman of the Stewart family. In the prominence of his cheeks and the general expression of his face, as well as in his general appearance, he resembled the Scotch more than the French. He spent his leisure hours chiefly in reading and writing. He read the newspapers attentively, and occasionally wrote for the National Intelligencer Washington City, and for the Carolina Watchman, published at Salisbury, N. C.

"It was his custom to sit up very late at night, only sleeping from four to six hours in the twenty-four. He said that was a habit contracted in camp while in the army. He was a great admirer of Napoleon Bonaparte, and always spoke of him in terms of the highest admiration. It was evident to every one who knew Mr. Ney that he was a man of genius, and must have been a soldier of the highest rank. It was generally believed by those who knew him best that he was Marshal Ney. I have studied the subject in all its bearings for upward of forty years, and I repeat my conviction, long since entertained, that he was the great marshal of France."

MRS. MARY C. DALTON, HOUSTONVILLE, IREDELL COUNTY, NORTH CAROLINA (1885)

"I was a pupil of P. S. Ney for several years. He taught near the residence of my father, Colonel Placebo Houston, with whom he boarded. I knew him well. He told me twice, when perfectly sober, how he escaped, and how he spent the first few years of his life in the United States. He said: 'My name is not Peter Stewart Ney. I am Marshal Ney. History states that I was executed, but I escaped death through the aid of my friends and others. On the day appointed for the execution I was told that my life was to be spared. I was instructed to give the command to fire, and to fall while giving it, so that the balls might pass over me. I carried out my instructions. In battle I never knew what fear was, but when I took my position in front of the soldiers, and gave the command to fire, *bedoust*,'[6] that was the very word he used, 'I was almost frightened to death. I was taken up by the soldiers' I think he said they belonged to his old command 'and carried to the hospital. That night I was disguised, and went to Bordeaux. From that place I sailed to the United States, landing in Charleston the latter part of January, 1816. The next few years I spent in seclusion, and prepared myself for teaching by studying the classics and the higher mathematics.' He said he thought everyone ought to have a visible means of support, and that he chose the profession of teaching, because it was in many respects like the military profession, to which he had been accustomed all his life. He could not bear the thought of engaging in any occupation where he would be commanded or controlled by others whom he might regard as his inferiors. In the school-room he would be supreme; hence he remained in seclusion three or four years.

"...Most of the facts related in the testimony of my brother, Colonel Houston, are well known to me, and I need not repeat them. His description of the person, character, habits, etc., of P. S. Ney is very accurate. Perhaps I knew Mr. Ney as well as any person in this country. I had every opportunity to learn his real worth, and I assure you that I never knew any person who was governed by higher principles, who possessed more sterling merit in every relation of life. There was nothing dishonest, low, little, or vulgar about him. He sometimes offended people by his abrupt manner and his plainness of speech on all subjects, but he never failed to apologize and make full reparation for any wrong that he may have done. He was a giant intellectually; could master any subject that was brought to his attention. On one occasion Judge Pearson said to me: 'Nature has done much for Mr. Ney; he possesses a very clear and vigorous mind, but I do not believe he is Marshal Ney.' Some years afterward, when Judge

Pearson had become better acquainted with Mr. Ney, he said to me in substance: 'I have made a special study of your friend, Peter S. Ney. He is one of the strongest-minded men I have ever met, he has all the qualities ascribed to the great marshal, and the resemblance is so striking in other respects that in spite of history I cannot doubt that he is Marshal Ney himself.' I have often heard Mr. Ney speak of his mother seldom alluded to his father; he seemed to think that his mother was perfect. He said that he was not a native Frenchman; pointed out in Cummings' atlas the place (Lorraine) where he was born; said he had to change his name after coming over here, but he could not give up the name of Ney. One day, about dark, a stranger rode up to our gate and asked father if he could stop with him that night. We had a good deal of company at the time, and every room was occupied. My father told him that he was sorry he could not accommodate him, but the young man insisted, and said he was willing to sleep on the floor, and that his horse being tired and completely worn out, he could go no farther. My father then told him that if he could suit himself to circumstances he would be glad to have him remain. The stranger, a fine-looking man, thanked him and went in. When he was conducted into supper he took a seat at the table opposite Mr. Ney, who was occupying his usual seat on the left hand of my father. They glanced at each other, and though not a word was spoken, it was evident to all present that it was a glance of recognition. My mother said a sign passed between them. Immediately after tea Mr. Ney and the stranger, taking their hats, left the house together, and were not seen by the family any more that night. An old negro man (Frederick) reported that he saw them near midnight sitting behind a straw stack in the field, in close conversation, and, although unobserved by them, could hear them distinctly, but could not understand a word they said. The stranger ordered his horse very early the next morning, and left. He gave no information about himself, except in a general way. After the man had gone Mr. Ney went to his room and remained in it all that day, reading and writing. He never made any allusion to the matter, and we had too much respect for him to question him about it. The stranger had black hair, black eyes, and a dark complexion.

This incident happened, I think, in 1834 or 1835. Mr. Ney said he had been recognized as Marshal Ney in South Carolina, and that he came to

North Carolina to escape further recognition. . . . He avoided strangers. His fear of an assassin never left him, though he was as brave and intrepid as any one possibly could be. He said he must protect his friends in France who had aided in his escape. . . . When he was in trouble on account of any bad news which he had received, he would drink more freely than at other times. When intoxicated he would tell any one freely. . . . He did a great deal of good in the neighborhood; gave many poor children their tuition free, and encouraged them to persevere in their studies after they had left school . . . he was greatly beloved, not only by his pupils (who venerated him), but by all persons who came within the circle of his influence. I have heard him speak of his wife and children; said his wife was a beautiful woman, and had dark eyes and long black hair so long that she could sit on it; said he had four children; used to tell the girls about his boys never heard him say that he had any daughters; gave the names of his boys, but I don't recollect them. One day father asked him why he did not bring his wife to America. He said he had several reasons: one was it would be found out where he was, and it would be dangerous for his wife to come over here. Besides he lived in constant expectation of going back to France. After the death of Napoleon's son, however, he seldom spoke of going back, and in 1836 he seemed to have lost all hope of ever returning to his native country. . . . He told me that he helped to bring Napoleon back from Elba; was in the plot before Napoleon left Elba. He did not regret it. The people wanted Napoleon, and the people ought to rule. Father had a fearful time with him for a week when Louis Philippe was placed on the throne of France; sat up with him; was sick and delirious a great part of the time; drew plans of battles; showed father the scars on his person received in battle. Some of the scars he said were made by his own cavalry. When he fell they ran over him. Have heard him speak of the fine horse he rode on the night of his escape. I think he said he rode eighty miles before sunrise the next morning. Did not like Lafayette; said he was a base ingrate, a traitor to Napoleon and France. Spoke often of Josephine and Hortense. His wife and Queen Hortense were great friends. . . . Told my mother, in 1830, that he saw his son in Virginia in 1828 or 1829. Taught school in Mecklenburg County, Va., in 1828–29. The newspapers stated that one of Ney's sons was in this part of the country in 1828.

"... He said no letters from abroad were sent directly to him, but were sent through a man in this country. I don't think he mentioned his name. Blamed Grouchy severely for not coming to Waterloo. Mr. Ney had a strong, guttural voice. He pronounced Grouchy's name in a very peculiar manner Ge-rw-shy.... Mr. Ney told father he was sorry he burnt his papers when young Napoleon died; was at a loss for dates in re-writing his history. Blamed Napoleon for his Russian expedition. His description of the horrors of the retreat was awful. Had money in the United States Bank. I once saw a letter which he wrote to Nicholas Biddle. He asked father what he should do with his money when the bank failed. I think he had $10,000 in the bank. Said he had no use for it intended to send it back to France. He would reprove his pupils sharply for wasting bread, fruit, etc. He said, 'You may come to want, and it is wrong in principle. In the army I was oftentimes thankful for a crust of bread.' I well remember the incident to which my brother refers (the intoxication of Ney by the roadside, etc.). It made a deep impression on my mind. Mr. Ney combed his hair so as to hide the scar on the left side of his head. He was careful to keep it covered. His head was very large and roundish oval; did not run up to a point. He said he was five feet eleven inches high when he was a young man, but that old age had settled him down half an inch. He never slept more than five hours out of the twenty-four.... Some persons said Mr. Ney was an infidel, but he was not. He detested hypocrisy in all its forms, but no man ever had a higher respect for the Christian religion and the pure worship of Almighty God."

COLONEL JUNIUS B. WHEELER, U.S. ARMY (1884)

"I knew Peter S. Ney. He was thick set, and had a massive head. His speech was guttural. He had a large scar on the left side of his head. He drank whiskey, and was a great tobacco-chewer. He told me once that he was Marshal Ney, and how he escaped. He said the officer in charge of the troops had served under him in the Napoleonic wars I think he said he was his aide-de-camp. This officer told him that he would not be hurt; that he must fall and simulate death. He did so, was disguised, and finally escaped to America. I did not believe that he was Marshal Ney; but if the officer of the day was really one of his old staff officers, the story is probably true. He was a man of decided ability, and everybody respected him."

CAPTAIN F. M. ROGERS, FLORENCE, SOUTH CAROLINA (1887)

"I was a pupil of Peter S. Ney when he taught at my father's house in Darlington County in 1844 or 1845. I was quite small, but I have a very clear recollection of him. He was then quite an old man, and stooped considerably; but his eye was still bright, his faculties unimpaired, and he appeared to be unusually strong and vigorous for one of his age. My father had a very high opinion of Mr. Ney, and was probably acquainted with his history. When asked about the matter, he would invariably give an indirect answer, and would change the subject as quickly as possible. He corresponded regularly with Mr. Ney until the time of his death in 1846. Some time after Mr. Ney's death a man named Pliny Miles wrote to my father, making certain inquiries about Mr. Ney in the interest of some historical society in New York. My father sent Mr. Ney's letters to Mr. Miles, and they were never returned. One day when my father was absent my mother said she intended to find out who Mr. Ney was. So at the dinner-table she asked Mr. Ney one or two questions, with this object in view. Mr. Ney smiled and said, 'Mrs. Rogers, your dinner is good, very good'; but he did not answer her questions satisfactorily . . . I have always heard that Mr. Ney landed at Charleston in the early part of 1816, and that he afterward went to Georgetown, where, in the early fall of 1819, he was recognized as Marshal Ney by a party of French refugees. These refugees (according to the statement of Chapman Levy, a prominent lawyer of Camden) asserted in the most positive terms that this man was Marshal Ney, as they had frequently seen the marshal in Paris and other places in France. When Mr. Ney heard of these declarations he left Georgetown and went to Cheraw, where my grandfather, Colonel Benjamin Rogers, saw him in the fall of 1819, and employed him to teach school. He taught about three years, and then went to North Carolina."

WALLACE M. REINHARDT, LINCOLNTON, NORTH CAROLINA (1890)

"I went to school to Peter S. Ney in 1838. He taught at Houstonville, Iredell County. All of his pupils, from the greatest to the least, were afraid of him, and yet there wasn't one who wouldn't have shed his blood for him. He was very strict with his scholars. Two things he especially required absolute obedience and good lessons. Woe to the boy who dared to disobey him, or who came to him with a bad lesson! He didn't have many rules and regulations. He said he wanted the boys to govern themselves. He liked to put them on their honor. If a boy told an untruth, or imposed upon a smaller boy, or did any kind of dishonest or unmanly thing, Mr. Ney would be certain to punish him for it; and sometimes, if it were a bad case, the punishment would be quite severe. His school was of a military cast. Even his very small boys were required to take a military posture. A lounging, stooping boy would be straightened up quickly. The sharp, commanding voice of our teacher brought all shoulders square to the front. He required neatness in person and dress, and perfect order at all recitations. When he got excited, his eyes would go clear through you. I couldn't look at him. He was a perfect Bengal tiger. He admired Washington, but said he ought to have pardoned Major Andre. He ought to have shown his greatness by riding over public clamor and the crazy desire for retaliation. He had no use for General Lafayette. One of his pupils was named after Lafayette. One day Mr. Ney said to him, 'Lafayette, I am sorry for you; you ought to have another name. Lafayette was not a true man. He treated Napoleon shamefully.' In walking, he used a very long stick or staff, holding it about five or six inches from the end. In the school-room he sometimes walked about with his hands crossed behind him. He seemed to be fond of me, and often asked me to cut his hair, though there was not a great deal to cut. He had a long scar on the left side of his head, and he told me one day, while I was cutting his hair, how he received it. He said that during the battle of Waterloo he happened to come in contact with an English officer named Ponsonby I think he said General Ponsonby and that in the melee Ponsonby gave him this wound; but that he cut Ponsonby down, and broke his sword in doing so. This is my recollection of the matter, and I do not see how I can be mistaken. Mr. Ney had other wounds. One was in his thigh, caused, he said, by a bayonet; another in his foot or ankle. On one occasion, when we were fencing with cornstalks, my stalk broke and a piece of it flew off and hit Mr. Ney on the scar on his head. It brought the blood, but Mr. Ney did not get angry. He asked me afterward if I knew whose head I had wounded. I said I did not. He then told me that I had wounded an old marshal of France. Mr. Ney sometimes attended the militia drills. They amused him in a quiet way. He said he had a Damascus blade which he could bend double; that a sword was worthless unless you could bend it double.... Mr. Ney would sometimes drink too much whiskey, and then he would tell a great deal about himself; but you couldn't get him in the presence of ladies when he was drunk.... Mr. Ney often spoke of his mother, and always with the utmost affection. Never heard him speak of his father. On horseback Mr. Ney had an easy and commanding appearance. Even the horse seemed to feel that he had a master. He would at once prick up his ears and move off quickly. Mr. Ney was in many ways a public benefactor. His influence for good is felt to this day. His old pupils have moulded public opinion in the counties where they lived. They have almost uniformly been sober, honest, industrious, and useful citizens. There is scarcely an exception to this rule."

WITHERSPOON ERVIN, MORGANTON, NORTH CAROLINA (1890)

"Some years before my day Peter S. Ney taught school in the Brownsville neighborhood of Marlborough County, S. C. My older brothers attended this school. One day his mail was brought in and delivered to him. He read one of the papers and fell to the floor as if struck by a thunderbolt. He was greatly depressed, and attempted to commit suicide by cutting his throat; but a surgeon was promptly summoned, sewed up the gaping wound, and Ney recovered from the injury. It was during this period of convalescence that he employed himself in painting in water-colors, from memory alone, a life-size, half-length portrait of Napoleon that for many years occupied a prominent place in our parlor at home. Comparing it with fine steel engravings of Napoleon, I know that it was a wonderfully correct likeness. It could only have been produced by an artist of uncommon skill. It was lifelike, and full of character and expression. The man who painted it must have been born with all the natural gifts that are essential to the artist, and must have had them developed and trained by careful cultivation. The portrait had a fascination for me as if it were a living thing. I remember, when a mere child, lying alone upon the floor in the parlor for hours looking up into that wonderful face. I have often heard the inquiry made of my father as to whether P. S. Ney was indeed the French marshal. His opinion was very promptly given that he was not; and I think his mere opinion, as a leading lawyer of the State, is entitled to great weight. When the inquiry was made of him, he stated that Ney never claimed to be the marshal except when under the hallucination produced by drinking, and was seriously offended, when sober, if any one pregained to address him by that title. Another reason assigned for his opinion was that Peter S. Ney was a scholar of fine literary attainments, while Michael Ney was a rude and uncultivated soldier, only knowing how to set 'legions in the field.' Another objection was that Peter S. Ney was a somewhat younger man than the marshal was supposed to be. His opinion, founded on what reason I do not know, was that Peter Ney was a nephew of the marshal."

HON. H. G. BUNN, CAMDEN, ARKANSAS (SEPTEMBER 15, 1892)

"A year ago I was travelling on the cars and made the passing acquaintance of a foreigner of reading and intelligence. His name has escaped me. He had been in this country ten or fifteen years. I think he was a Polish gentleman, but had lived in Paris much of his time before coming to this country. In some way (as such things will happen) we were led to talk of the story of Peter S. Ney. It seemed that he had made himself acquainted with the prominent parts of the story. It will interest you only to repeat here in substance what he said he had heard in Paris or from Paris since he left the city.

"As I understood him, he said in substance this: In 1853 or 1854, after Louis Napoleon had become firmly seated on the imperial throne of France, a question arose as to the integrity of the account of the execution of Marshal Ney.... Anyway, the story goes that Louis Napoleon became so interested in the matter as to appoint a commission to open the grave of the long-buried marshal. The story goes on to say that no remains were in the decayed coffin, and the evidence was that it had never contained anything."

VARDRY A. MCBEE, LINCOLNTON, NORTH CAROLINA (1890)

"I was a pupil of Peter S. Ney in 1834. There was no man in the country who could compare with him as a teacher. He was facile princeps. He easily gained the love and confidence of his pupils, although he exacted implicit obedience to his command, and was in every respect a very strict disciplinarian. He was quite a large man, tall, erect, of soldierly bearing, and imposing presence. He seemed born to command. All persons regarded him as a man of superior parts, and he exerted a controlling influence wherever he went. . . . He looked like a lion. His countenance, his walk, his movements, his bearing, his general expression and make-up had a decidedly leonine cast. Though he would occasionally drink too much, yet this habit never injured him in the estimation of those who knew him, or, I may say, of the people generally. The great influence which he exerted over the community in which he lived was of a pure, wholesome, and elevating character. He left behind him a name of which any one might well feel proud."

DR. J. R. B. ADAMS, STATESVILLE, NORTH CAROLINA (1886)

"I have been entirely satisfied in my own mind since 1842 that P. S. Ney, who taught school within a few hundred yards of my residence for two years or more, and is now buried in Third Creek Churchyard, was the veritable Marshal Ney. I met him often, and I observed him closely. I never saw a more level-headed man, or one with greater force of character. He took a plain, practical, common-sense view of everything. There was no circumlocution about him. He came directly to the point, and expressed his views (which were rarely wrong on any subject) with exceeding clearness and power. He despised shams of all kinds, and denounced them in pretty severe terms. There was not the shadow of hypocrisy about the man. Everybody felt this, or, with all his strength of mind, he could not have exercised the power over the people which he did. This was simply marvellous. He was a fine specimen of physical manhood, tall, large, and well proportioned, with a manly and majestic bearing. He had a large, broad forehead, bulging out considerably about the eyes. The perceptive faculties were very large. Very heavy, shaggy eyebrows, which gave him a stern and severe-looking countenance, especially as his eyes were uncommonly brilliant and piercing. They seemed to look clear through you. He was a splendid judge of human nature. It didn't take him long to read a person's true character. He avoided crowds, sought only the best company, and was very quiet and reserved in his general demeanor. He did much for the poor, especially poor children. They remember him with deep thankfulness to this day. He had no vices except drinking. He scorned everything that was dishonest or little, though he was pretty abrupt in his manners. . . . He was not only just, but he was merciful. Mr. Lewis Williams, a member of Congress for many years, offered Mr. Ney a good government position in Washington City, but Mr. Ney unhesitatingly declined it. About the year 1842 I met in Alabama a foreigner who called himself Colonel Lamanouski (the name may be incorrectly spelled). He was making a tour of the Southern States, lecturing on Napoleon's campaigns. He told me that he was perfectly convinced, from what he had seen and heard in France and in this country, that Marshal Ney was not executed. He said that he belonged (I think) to the Polish Corps in Napoleon's army, and was well acquainted with Marshal Ney. He said that if the North Carolina school-teacher were Marshal Ney, he could recognize him at a glance. I do not think he ever met him. About the year 1840 Rev. J. M. Wilson, Professor Hugh E. Hall, and Colonel Thomas A. Allison were appointed by the trustees of Davidson College a committee to draw up a device for the college seal. At their request Mr. Ney assisted them. In a few minutes he prepared both the device and the legend. These were very acceptable to the college authorities, and were at once adopted. Those who knew him longest and best were firmly convinced that he was Marshal Ney."

GENERAL W. W. HARLLEE, FLORENCE, SOUTH CAROLINA (1888)

"About the year 1840 . . . the Governor of South Carolina attended a military review of the State troops. A great many persons were present, and it was an occasion of much interest. The governor invited Peter S. Ney to act as an honorary aide-de-camp. Mr. Ney accepted the invitation, and appeared with the governor on the review mounted on a magnificent charger, which had been procured for him. I think he was without doubt the finest-looking man I ever saw. He was well dressed, and his bearing was superb. He was every inch the soldier. His military form and carriage, his easy, graceful horsemanship, his commanding presence attracted every one's attention. Numerous inquiries were made about him, and he really attracted more attention than the governor himself."

DR. ROBERT H. DALTON, LOS ANGELES, CALIFORNIA (1870)

"I began to practise medicine on the 1st day of May, 1827, in Guilford County, N. C., at a place now called Hillsdale. Some time in 1827 or 1828 a gentleman put up at the hotel where I boarded, and remained several days. He purported to be on his way to Raleigh to confer with the governor of the State in relation to writing the history of North Carolina, and we understood that he had been engaged to do the work. He soon seemed to take to my little office, and was much interested in my small new library, composed of a fair selection of standard medical books and a few choice historical, literary, and poetical works. I shall ever remember a remark he made more than once while standing and looking at my books, so nicely arranged in the little case: 'A few books well read are worth thousands kept to ornament the shelves. Know all in these books, young man, and you will be great.' We soon understood that he was a Frenchman, and that his name was Ney, though his language betrayed no brogue, but was clear, chaste, and exceedingly fluent. When talking with me he spoke feelingly of Baron Larrey, Napoleon's great surgeon, and seemed delighted to dwell on his character and exploits, relating many incidents and anecdotes which I have never seen in print, proving his great intimacy with that great man. On evenings at tea and until bedtime we drew him out on subjects involving the history of the French Revolution, and it was very evident that no one but an actual participant in that wonderful drama could have delineated the facts and incidents with such positive clearness and precision; and I am sure that the bitterest enemy of Napoleon and his cause could not have arisen from these discussions with opinions adverse to his honor and his merit. He denied that Napoleon was a tyrant, but represented him as a providential agent of reformation, designed to ameliorate the condition of his people by inaugurating free institutions for France, which could not be done on account of the selfish interest and jealousy of all the crowned heads of Europe, whose very existence depended on the maintenance of absolute government for all the nationalities; that in defence of these just and holy principles he was perpetually assailed by these despotic powers; and for the preservation of his people and their righteous cause he was forced to centralize the powers of the nation to repel invasion; and that for these reasons there never was a time when he could possibly have carried out his views. Hence the empire, with all its semblance of military government.... He was, I think, fully six feet high, neither corpulent nor lean, with a florid complexion and auburn hair. His head was large, and high behind. He wore no beard; and his face, though handsome, showed what are called weather-beaten marks. He was a man of the noblest physique and most commanding appearance I ever saw. I remember well the scar on his head, but I had not the temerity to ask about its cause. In discussing the dynasties of Europe in connection with Napoleon, he seemed to enter into the very essence of their constitutions, and his criticisms made a lasting impression on my mind. Taking him altogether, I am sure he was the finest specimen of humanity, physically and mentally, I ever knew. If he lived till 1854 he must have been very old. I ventured once, by way of ascertaining whether he was Marshal Ney or not, to ask him if he was related to the family of that name. I can never forget his startled look. He gave me an evasive answer, which I took as a rebuke for my impertinence. I have seen and conversed with many great men, but with none greater than Peter Stewart Ney."

MRS. SARAH ANNA (LOCKE) CAMPBELL, JERSEYVILLE, ILLINOIS (1887)

"My maiden name was Sarah Anna Locke. I knew Mr. Ney very well. He often visited my father's house. He was a large man, with a dark red face badly pitted from the smallpox. His nose was very large not a peaked one. He was a swift runner and a fine horseman. When at the house of my father (Major John Locke) he would often pull down my long black hair and say, sometimes with tears, 'It is just like my wife's.' He often talked about his wife and children. According to my recollection, he said he had three sons, and that his wife was living."

Mrs. B. G. Worth, Wilmington, North Carolina (1887)

"My grandfather, Judge Archibald D. Murphey, believed that Peter S. Ney was Marshal Ney. He taught school in Judge Murphey's family, and my mother was greatly attached to him. She thought him one of the kindest and best men that ever lived. Judge Murphey had the highest opinion of his ability and character. He and Mr. Ney were great friends. Mr. Ney would sometimes stroke my sister's hair and say, 'You look just like my wife, with your dark eyes and your long black hair.'"

Hon. David L. Swain, President of the University of North Carolina (1868)

"I have been familiar with the name and handwriting of P. S. Ney (so called) for about forty years. General James Cook, a lawyer, who died in Mocksville, N. C., some years since, whom I knew very familiarly, went to school to Ney forty years ago and was a firm believer in his marshalship, and entertained lofty ideas of his abilities and attainments. More than thirty years ago Judge Murphey employed Ney to copy historical manuscripts and tracts. He was a neat and ready copyist. Pliny Miles had some manuscripts which once belonged to P. S. Ney. I frankly told him that, in my opinion, his hero was not Marshal Ney. Mr. Miles seemed to be firmly convinced that he was."

Giles E. Mumford, Mocksville, North Carolina (1877)

"I was a pupil of Peter S. Ney when he taught one mile north of Mocksville in 1832. . . . When I handed Mr. Ney his mail that morning he stopped writing and opened the Watchman and commenced reading. He always read the poetry and deaths and marriages first. As soon as he opened the paper he became deathly pale, rose from his desk, walked to the middle of the room, threw the paper on the floor, jumped on it with both feet, and stamped it to pieces before saying a word. . . . 'Young Napoleon,' said he, 'is dead, and my hopes are all blasted. I can't go back to France.'"

James McCulloh, Mocksville, North Carolina (1888)

"I knew P. S. Ney. He came to my father's house one day about the year 1834 or 1835. His eyes quickly fell on a picture of young Napoleon

Bonaparte, which was hanging upon the wall. He immediately went to it and stood looking at it intently for some time. When he turned away his eyes were full of tears. 'If that boy had lived,' said he, 'I should not be here.'"

REV. E. F. ROCKWELL, D.D., IREDELL
COUNTY, NORTH CAROLINA (1886)

"When Peter S. Ney was living in this part of the country say from 1830–42 there was a general belief among all classes, especially those who knew him, that he was the celebrated marshal of the First Empire. Indeed, if he was not Marshal Ney, it is very difficult to tell who he was, for Peter S. Ney bore a striking resemblance to Marshal Ney.

"Mr. Ney kept very close here when teaching; corresponded with the National Intelligencer at Washington; had a large sum of money to his credit in the old United States Bank; but he never went to any of the large cities. He could not bear Murat or Grouchy; blamed Napoleon for the Russian campaign and for repudiating Josephine. She and her daughter Hortense were great friends of his wife. His wife, he said, had dark eyes and hair, and was very beautiful. He was athletic, with great power of command, great fascination and discernment of character. When Louis Philippe in 1830 mounted the throne of France, he came near cutting his throat. His friends had great difficulty in quieting him. They had a worse time of it still when young Bonaparte died in 1832. He was greatly attached to Mr. Houston, who had more influence over him than any one else. The manuscripts which P. S. Ney said 'contained something which would astonish the world' were carried off by Pliny Miles, of New York, under the plea of taking them to Europe to be translated, and were never returned. . . . Some time after Mr. Ney came to this country he was at Darlington, S. C., at a hotel, on a cold day, seated by the fire, partly intoxicated. A stranger was present who had travelled extensively, and told the company some things he had seen. He had been at the grave of Marshal Ney. Our Mr. Ney roused up and said, 'You may have been there, but Ney was not there. . . .' It was also reported that some letters came to him through the French consul at Norfolk or some other influential personage at Norfolk. This is a mere rumor, so far as I know."

REV. J. L. GAY, FAYETTE, MISSOURI (1888)

"In 1827 Peter S. Ney taught school in Iredell County, about twenty miles from Salisbury. I was one of his pupils, and I remember him well. He had some hair at the back and on each side of his head, which was of a reddish or sandy color, though it was then turning gray. His lower face was striking: the heavy jaws, the firmly set mouth, the prominent double chin gave him an air of the most determined resolution. He did not look like a Frenchman; had a Saxon or Scottish-Saxon look. Spoke English well, though you could detect a foreign accent. Was fond of music; had concerts in his school. He wore a long bluish-gray broadcloth surtout cut in the old-fashioned transition style that was common in the first quarter of this century. . . . Everywhere we heard that he was a great teacher. Although I had earlier teachers two or three for short terms yet P. S. Ney was the first who really taught me anything worth knowing, or who started me out on the road leading to learning. . . . He was a dull scholar indeed, or a perverse one, who did not learn to write well and did not obtain a fair insight into the wonderful powers of numeral figures. And I gratefully remember, too, his sympathetic interest in our plays and athletic sports; how agile he was at an age (approaching sixty) when other men are usually oppressed with inertia. . . . One day at school one of the older scholars asked him if he were related to Marshal Ney, as he had the same name. 'Yes,' he replied, with some show of annoyance at the question or the questioner 'yes, some connection' a nephew I think he said and turned away, and so abruptly closed the subject. This, with the admission that he had been in the Napoleonic wars and had been wounded in some battle or other, was all that we could get out of him. It began indeed to be surmised that he was none other than Marshal Ney himself; but it was only an idle surmise, that, like thousands of others, was dropped, and so passed out of our minds."

REV. R. H. MORRISON, D.D., FORMERLY PRESIDENT OF DAVIDSON COLLEGE, DAVIDSON, NORTH CAROLINA (1885)

"I knew Peter S. Ney. As far as I could learn, his conduct was upright and marked by propriety except when drinking to intemperance, and even then he seemed to avoid collision with others. There were some points in his behavior so different from the ordinary pursuits of men as rendered it difficult to account for them. He avoided towns and cities and sought schools in the country, and seemed to care for only a bare support, when he might, from his talents and attainments, have obtained much more profitable positions. He also avoided efforts to gain the honors and distinctions in society which learning and integrity often prompt men to seek. He evidently had strong motives to avoid notoriety. He taught school in my neighborhood, and one of my sons went to school to him. He was a fine scholar and a good teacher. He sometimes attended my preaching, and gave the most respectful attention to the services of the sanctuary, as a courteous gentleman always does."

P. H. CAIN, FELIX, DAVIE COUNTY, NORTH CAROLINA (1886)

"I was a pupil of P. S. Ney in 1831. He was the grandest of men. Saw him in the latter part of 1832. He said, 'By Jove! old boy, I came near killing myself since I saw you. The rascals have poisoned young Napoleon, and my hopes of returning to France are forever blasted.' He then spoke of his wife and children; said he once knew what happiness was, but that he should never see his family again; spoke of his wife with a good deal of emotion; had soldiers shot for insulting or outraging ladies; gave me and another student lessons in loading and shooting shot some himself at our target practice; said he and Napoleon's brother-in-law were equally matched in fencing frequently up till ten o'clock at night; that Napoleon made them quit, saying something serious might result from it; said to me and another student at our target practice that if we should ever go into the artillery service to keep well behind our guns when firing. He believed in early marriages; said young people as a rule ought to get married when they are twenty-one years old, but not before. In 1832 Mr. Ney appeared to be sixty-five or seventy years old."

COLONEL C. C. GRAHAM, MEMPHIS, TENNESSEE (1885)

"I saw P. S. Ney sometimes at county musters. When slightly intoxicated he could handle a company or battalion with great skill, showing a fine knowledge of military tactics."

Dr. John A. Allison, Statesville, North Carolina (1887)

"I was well acquainted with Peter S. Ney. He taught school near the residence of my father, Colonel Thomas A. Allison, some three or four years, and I was his pupil the greater part of the time. He boarded at my father's house, or, rather, he was an honored guest, for my father and mother thought so much of him that they would never look upon him as a boarder. Mr. Ney was about five feet eleven inches in height. He was broad and full all the way from the hips up, yet exceedingly well proportioned. He had a fine head, large and roundish, rather long from forehead to back. Forehead large and full, especially near the eyes. Perceptive faculties unusually well developed. He had a magnetic eye. He could just make you love him and fear him and obey him too. Nose large, particularly at the base, and slightly turned up at the end. Lips medium my impression is they were rather thin. Considerable distance between his nose and upper lip. Was very neat in his person and dress. A fine horseback-rider, though he seldom rode a horse. We had a fiery, vicious horse that no one seemed to be able to ride. Mr. Ney mounted him one day and rode him with the utmost ease. Everybody was astonished at his horsemanship. A splendid marksman. He sometimes went out hunting with me. I never saw him miss a squirrel. He would hit him every time.... The best fencer, perhaps, in the whole country. His skill was perfectly marvellous. I have seen splendid swordsmen stand in front of him and try to hit him, but they couldn't touch him. He would play with them as if they were little babies. When he became tired of the fun he would tap them on the side of the head and say it was time to stop. . . . One day, in the winter of 1840 or 1841, Mr. Ney went to Statesville and stayed away three or four days. He seldom went to town, and we were uneasy about him. He finally came back intoxicated, and told my mother that he had been with his son in Statesville. Upon inquiry we found that a young man, evidently a foreigner, well dressed and of good appearance, had been in Statesville for some days past, and that he and Mr. Ney had been constant companions. The young man was very quiet and reserved, and did not tell any one who he was or what was his business. Mr. Ney kept perfectly sober while the man was with him, but as soon as he left he got drunk. He went home, burned up some papers, and was greatly depressed for several days. Mr. Ney had an old hair trunk, in which he kept his papers written in short hand, paintings, drawings, etc. I used to get a glance at them sometimes, though he always kept his trunk locked. He had another trunk which contained his clothing, etc. He was not so particular about this one. My father thought Ney had a sword in his hair trunk. I heard Milus Bailey say that Mr. Ney told him some time in the thirties that he was Marshal Ney. Bailey had somewhere procured a picture of Ney's execution. He showed it to Mr. Ney. Mr. Ney said, 'That is not correct. The positions are wrong, etc. Some day I'll draw it for you. Ney was not shot. I felt safe as soon as I knew that the old soldiers composed the firing party.' I knew Barr, the German, who recognized Mr. Ney as Marshal Ney at a public gathering not far from Statesville. Barr was an old soldier, covered with wounds, and would fight in a minute if any one doubted his word. . . . He [Ney] had a wound on the left side of his head, made, I suppose, by a sabre stroke; also one in his foot. He said to me one day, 'I was in a tight place when I got that wound in my foot.' He made a great point of promptness and punctuality at home and in the school-room. Never late at breakfast; a very early riser, though he sat up late at night reading and writing. His mind was as clear as a sunbeam. He could explain a subject better than any man I ever knew. He was very useful in the neighborhood. He wrote deeds, wills, and other documents for the neighbors, told them how to doctor their horses, how to build bridges, dykes, embankments, flood-gates, etc. Without doubt he was one of the greatest men that have ever lived in this part of the country. My father was firmly convinced that he was Marshal Ney, and so were the most intelligent people of this section."

Frederick Leinster, Statesville, North Carolina (1884)

"I went to school to Peter S. Ney in 1846. He used to call me duke, because my name was Leinster; said he knew the Duke of Leinster, and didn't like him; once had a difficulty with him. It seems to me he said the Duke of Leinster gave him that cut on the head. I know he said he didn't like him, and that there had been some trouble between them."

Mr. James Andrews, Houstonville, Iredell County, North Carolina (1883)

"I knew P. S. Ney for many years. I owned a mill not far from the place where he boarded when he taught school in this part of the country, and he used often to come to the mill as well as to my house and have pleasant and familiar talks with me. One day, in my mill, he took up a handful of wheat out of a hogshead which contained two or three bushels of the grain, and turning to me, said, 'James, if a man had had this much wheat in the Russian campaign, it would have been worth a fortune to him. Men were starving on every hand, and those that were able would mortgage whole estates and give everything they had for a loaf of bread.' He has told me a great deal about his army life, but I cannot remember all that he said. He spoke of the great sufferings which his men endured, and that seemed to hurt him more than anything else. He said that in crossing a certain river I forget the name so many men were killed or wounded or drowned that they almost formed a bridge over which the others could walk. He blamed Napoleon for dividing his army, when the retreat began, into so many separate columns, with two or three days' march between them. He said that it was perfectly ruinous; that the whole army ought to have retreated in one compact body, and to have fought its way directly through. He said that in doing so the army would have encountered many difficulties, but that there were many more difficulties in the other plan of marching in separate columns. He said that he put the stragglers and disbanded men between his main body and the Russians, so that the Russians might fall on them first. It was a desperate measure, he said, but he had to do it, sometimes at the point of the bayonet. . . . Discipline, he said, had to be preserved. . . . He told me more than once, when he had not tasted a drop of strong drink, that he was Marshal Ney, and how he escaped; how the soldiers fired as he gave the command; how the balls passed over him; how he was taken up and secretly conveyed to some point on the coast, where he took passage for America. I well remember the sabre cut on his head. He told me, I think, that he received it at the battle of Waterloo, in the last charge of the Old Guard. The man who wounded him was cut down by one of his aids. He saw Lord Wellington and his staff with his spy-glass. He was so badly hurt that he was left behind couldn't keep up with the army in its retreat. It always gave him pain to speak of Napoleon's defeat at Waterloo. It was like drawing a rasp over a saw. He had wounds, it seemed to me, all over his body. There were prints of horses' hoofs on his legs and breast. He had a wound in the fleshy part of his arm above the elbow. He told me that the surgeon, Larrey, put salt in it. He said that he asked him if that was all he was going to do to the wound. 'Yes,' replied the surgeon, 'I treated the emperor so.' Mr. Ney was a great teacher. His pupils were devoted to him, though he was strict with them, and they advanced rapidly in all their studies. He taught them to be obedient to their parents, and honest and true and merciful in their dealings with their fellow-men. He made an impression upon them which remained throughout life. He was a man of feeling heart. He did a great deal for the poor, especially the poor children of the neighborhood. He taught many of them from year to year without charging a cent for their tuition. His salary was small. He taught for $200 a year and his board. . . . He told me that he could speak the English language when he came to this country; that his mother was a Scotchwoman, and taught it to him in his youth. I think he said, though I am not certain, that his father went to Scotland to escape persecution, and there married a Scotch-woman who was related to a Presbyterian clergy-man. Her maiden name was Stewart, or she was related to some family of that name. He dearly loved his wife and children, though I do not think he gave me their names. He spoke of them often, and said it was sweet to think that some day he should see them again and die among his own people. After the death of Napoleon's son he gave up all hope of going back to France. I felt very sorry for him, for I never saw any one grieve so much. I do not think he ever got over it. He told me that if it were known in France that he was living in the United States, his friends in France, who aided in his escape, would suffer severely, and that his own life would be in danger, for his enemies would not hesitate to hire some one to come over and assassinate him. . . . Mr. Ney was not a religious man, though he was a firm believer in the Bible. Not long before he died he said to me, 'James, hold on to your religion. It is a good thing to have. Don't let it go.' I loved Mr. Ney. Indeed, I feel that it is the greatest privilege and honor of my life to have known such a man."

MAJOR JAMES H. FOOTE, DELLAPLANE, NORTH CAROLINA (1886)

"In the years 1837 and 1838 P. S. Ney was teaching on the farm of Captain Placebo Houston, and it was then I was one of his students. . . . Although he followed teaching as 'a visible means' of support, he was in no want of funds, for it was known that he had credit in the United States Bank at Washington City. His price for teaching was only $200 per session of ten months, including his board. He spent his money freely, but not foolishly; for no man was more charitable than he. If he saw any one, man, woman, or child, in want or distress, he would readily divide with them of what means he had in hand. He would take the poor boys in his school and charge their tuition to himself and have it deducted from his salary. His whole deportment was that of the true gentleman. He had one fault that many great men have that of drinking at times to intoxication; and when drinking was very communicative; when sober he was rather reticent. In 1837 P. S. Ney appeared to be about seventy years old. I think he sometimes wrote his name P. S. M. Ney. These initials, I suppose, stood for Peter Stewart Michael. He often spoke of his wife and children; seemed to have the greatest affection for them. He was a great expert with the sword. When he was teaching at Mocksville (I believe), a French fencing-master came and proposed to Mr. Ney's pupils to teach them the art of fencing. They told him if he would take a tilt with their teacher and hit him they would get him up a big class. This was agreed to, and Mr. Ney was introduced to him. The fencing-master opened his trunk and invited Mr. Ney to select his sword. They repaired to the playground, and after parrying thrusts for awhile, Ney clave the Frenchman's hat in two, just brushing his ear. The professor immediately threw down his weapon and said, 'Boys, you have a master; you have no use for me.' I have heard General James Cook, who was an eye-witness, relate this incident. He never went about large cities; remained far in the interior of the country, and lived in obscurity for some purpose. I do not think he could have been a refugee for crime, one so noble in his bearing, so capable of filling any station in life. Royalty sat upon his brow, and Genius claimed him for her own. I have no doubt he was here for some political offence."

REV. WILLIAM A. WOOD, D.D.,
STATESVILLE, NORTH CAROLINA (1887)

"I knew Peter S. Ney. I was a pupil of his for a considerable time. I was quite young, but I have a very clear and distinct recollection of him. Indeed, it would be almost impossible to forget such a man. I may safely say that I never knew one with a warmer, truer heart, a stronger mind, or more commanding presence. . . . One day, when I was at Davidson College probably in the year 1847 I saw in the library a book entitled, I think, 'Napoleon and his Marshals.' In that book was a fine engraving of Marshal Ney. On the page opposite was a pencil sketch or drawing of Marshal Ney which closely resembled the engraving in the book, and was also a good likeness of Peter S. Ney. Underneath this pencil sketch, in P. S. Ney's handwriting, were the words, 'By Ney himself.' I often looked for the book afterward, searching diligently through the library, with the aid of the librarians, but I could not find it. I can hardly doubt that this great man, for I must call him great, was Napoleon's most famous marshal."

MRS. G. N. BEALE, WASHINGTON, D.C.

"I knew Peter S. Ney; have often played chess with him near Beattie's Ford, N. C. He was very courteous and gentlemanlike, though rather brusque in his manners. One day, when slightly under the influence of wine, he said to Miss Martha Graham, a niece of Governor Graham, 'You look like the Duchess of Argyle.' The Grahams were descended from the Argyle family. Some years ago I attended an entertainment given in this city by a Professor Stoddard. It consisted of a series of movable pictures, representing the principal events, etc., in the life of Napoleon Bonaparte. When the portrait of Marshal Ney appeared upon the canvas I instantly turned toward my husband and said, 'There is Peter Ney, the man I used to play chess with.' 'Why,' said my husband laughing, 'you must be very ancient. You must have been born before the flood.' A few moments after this conversation occurred Professor Stoddard said that the picture which he was then exhibiting was that of Marshal Ney, the 'bravest of the brave.' It was a perfect likeness of Peter S. Ney. Colonel John H. Wheeler observed Mr. Ney closely, and he was satisfied that he was an officer of high rank in Napoleon's army, though he did not think he was Marshal Ney. The only reason he gave for this opinion was that Marshal Ney was an illiterate man, while Peter S. Ney was an accomplished scholar."

Alexander F. Brevard, Machpelah, Lincoln County, North Carolina (October 28, 1892)

"I went to school to Peter S. Ney in 1841, when he taught near Catawba Springs. . . . He told me he was the 'best fencer in the French army with one exception' presumably Murat. One day, when slightly in liquor, he said, 'Some people say I was educated for a Roman Catholic priest. It is a lie. I am the poor old marshal.' Once, when hearing a recitation in history, he described by way of illustration the battle of Waterloo. It was a magnificent description. The old man's eye lighted up, and he appeared truly grand. He gave many incidents connected with the battle which were deeply interesting to the class. At last, when he came to Blücher's arrival, his voice faltered and his eyes moistened. 'Blücher,' said he, putting his hands to his eyes to conceal his emotion 'Blücher ruined everything.'"

H. H. Helper, Mocksville, North Carolina

"I knew Peter S. Ney. He talked at all times with a German brogue."

Dr. Bingham, Mocksville, North Carolina (1889)

"I have often seen a copy of Labaume's 'Russian Campaign' which contained a great many marginal annotations by P. S. Ney. These were very interesting. He would often correct Labaume as to matters of fact connected with the retreat, and would give fuller information as to other points which he considered important, but which were briefly noticed by Labaume. . . . P. S. Ney also wrote in this book a piece of poetry on the Moscow fire. My father had a very high opinion of Mr. Ney's ability and general character. He said Mr. Ney looked like a Scotch bishop that he was too highly educated for Marshal Ney. In other respects he thought he bore a striking resemblance to the great French soldier."

REV. BASIL G. JONES, M.D.,
KINGSTREE, SOUTH CAROLINA (1887)

"When I came from Alabama to Davie County, N. C., in 1829, there was a mysterious person teaching school near Mocksville, calling himself Peter Stewart Ney. He was regarded by the literati and everybody else as a finished gentle man and scholar. He seemed to be perfectly at home in any branch of learning known in that day. He seemed to understand well the Scotch, French, Italian, English, Latin, Greek, Hebrew, Russian, and Polish languages. He said he could read and converse in all of them. He was frequently put to test in at least some of them, as Latin, Greek, French, Scotch, and Hebrew. He was acknowledged by those who professed to understand the Hebrew to be a superior Hebraist.

"Mr. Ney taught at other places. At Mr. Placebo Houston's, in Iredell, the Houstons, Youngs, and others, the most wealthy and respectable citizens of Iredell County, were his pupils; a part of them are still living. Mr. Ney was a man about five feet ten inches high, heavily set, and compactly built; he weighed about one hundred and seventy or one hundred and eighty pounds, and was of extraordinary muscular development. He had every appearance of a large, rough Scottish Highlander, of symmetrical proportions, well adapted to energy and endurance, qualities which Mr. Ney possessed in a high degree. He was more adapted to herculean strength than to agility. His back was straight, shoulders broad and a little stooped, head well balanced, the top bald, the back and sides of the head covered with hair once auburn, but then a little silvered; his nose was straight and very large, with a massive end; his mouth large and broad; lips firm, the under apparently a little thicker than the upper; complexion florid; face full and pitted with smallpox; countenance a little down but stern, thoughtful, and intelligent; his eyes not large, but rather brilliant, indicating a strong, perceptive, and penetrating intellect. One day Mr. Ney received bad news from France. He said his hopes were destroyed. He could never go back. He wept like a child, and large tears found their way rapidly down his pale cheek. While in that condition he could not be trusted alone. He was sick, frantic, and almost ungovernable. During this time the writer and a few others spent a night with him. I never can forget that night. He raved of France, Napoleon, his wife and family, Waterloo,

Moscow, etc.; called for Phesinac [undoubtedly a reference to the Duke of Fezensac, who was Marshal Ney's highly trusted and close aide during the Russia campaign], issued his commands, sketched his past history, gave an account of his birth, connection with the family of the Stewarts, and his relation to the Bonapartes; how he came to be made a marshal of the Empire; how the battle of Waterloo was planned by Napoleon and his Cabinet, etc. Mr. Ney then showed us the wounds or rather scars which he received at Waterloo and elsewhere wounds of precisely the kind described in history. I was a pupil of Mr. Ney in 1831 or 1832. Moral courage, firmness of principle, fixedness of purpose, strength of nerve, indomitable perseverance, honesty and truth, are traits of character which he held in the highest admiration. He used to impress these upon us boys as essential elements of a man. He told me once how he escaped. He said the French people thought Marshal Ney was dead, but he was not. He fell by preconcerted arrangement, as if he were dead; was taken up, disguised, and finally escaped to the United States, the Ancient Fraternity [Masons] aiding in his escape from the first. I never heard Mr. Ney say what became of Phesinac. It seems to me he said Phesinac kept him from being slain at Waterloo, or protected him in some way. His wife, he said, sent him packages he didn't say how."

GEORGE A. MILLER, DAVIE COUNTY, NORTH CAROLINA (1870)

"I was well acquainted with P. S. Ney. From 1833 until his death in 1846. Our intercourse was as familiar as could be between persons of different ages and pursuits. The venerable and dignified deportment of Mr. Ney, his imperial air, his great learning and unexampled scholarship, his perfect acquaintance with the Greek and Latin classics, the modern languages, and especially the history of the French Revolution and every particular in relation to the personal, civil, and military career of the great Napoleon these qualities of mind and person, united to an impenetrable mystery which clung around his own history a mystery which nothing could surprise or remove attracted every one like the secret properties of the magnet. There was a something about the man which once seen seemed to say, 'I dare you to forget me.' . . . We have seen Mr. Ney under all circumstances. We have seen his courage tested, and his face never blanched and his nerves never trembled. . . . We have seen him kiss the portrait of Josephine while the tears of affection and . . . (lines obscured). With the permission of Mr. Foard we examined the papers of Mr. Ney soon after his death. We found any quantity of poetry and prose on all subjects, but nothing to throw light on the object of our search his own life. The longest and most labored production of his mind was a history of the French Revolution written in ciphers (of his own invention), which we could not understand. . . . Mr. Foard told us that a night or two before he died he destroyed all of his more private correspondence, and among them some ship letters lately received from France, which contained valuables."

Mr. A. H. Graham, Bagdad, Texas (1879)

"Peter S. Ney, as he styled himself, came to my father's in Lincoln County, N.C., in 1842, to teach school. He was employed by my father and others for about four years in teaching. He had a sabre wound on his head and numerous gunshot wounds on his body and limbs, and one particularly near the knee-joint, from a musket-ball, part of which he still retained, and at times, in his long walks to and from school, gave him much pain. In 1845 he appeared to be seventy-five or eighty years old. He was well preserved, as he had taken good care of himself. His habits, diet, exercise, cleanliness of person were all conducive to good health. He used Florida water and cologne constantly. Shaved every day. I was his almost daily companion for three years; slept near him, helped him to undress when in his cups. Complexion florid, pale only when sick. Hairs on his arms and legs even of an auburn color. A small eater rarely ate more than two meals a day. Spent most of his time in reading, writing, etc . . . said he received powder burns on his face at Borodino. . . . He had a German brogue. He frequently made use of such words as mon for man, and ye for you, as the Germans use them. In pronouncing algebra, he made the last a sound like r. Spoke much of the excellence of the German language; said it was a great language; seemed to be very fond of it. Spoke it perfectly, as he also did the French and dead languages. I have sat for hours and listened to him tell of his battles and campaigns, especially of the dreadful march from Moscow, and the great battle of Borodino. Also spoke often of Hohenlinden. Said the victory at Borodino was due to him, as Napoleon was too unwell to command in person, but sat astride a cannon the greater part of the day, being afflicted with strangury. Said Lord Wellington saved his life. He feared to make himself known on this account and for his family's sake, as well as for other reasons. As a rule he would not talk about himself except when in wine; but he was rarely intoxicated. He knew what he was talking about. I once saw a letter which he wrote to Wellington. He seemed to be agitated when he wrote it. Said, according to my recollection, that the French Government owed him 60,000 francs. I do not think he sent the letter. Talked about Wellington in a very excited manner. Said he or some of his friends appealed to him in person. Wellington, with his hat drawn down over his eyes, stamped upon the ground, and said with much emphasis, 'I cannot and will not interfere with the laws of the French Government.' Said his friend Rogers in South Carolina was fully acquainted with his history. In 1844 said his wife was still living. Spoke of her with much affection. Said she was a small woman, and very beautiful. For a man of his age he was an excellent and graceful horseman, although he seldom rode a horse. I once saw him ride at full gallop a large, fiery horse, which showed him off to much advantage, and surprised us all very much. This proved to us that he had long been accustomed to the saddle. He used to punish his pupils by pinching their ears. Said that was Napoleon's habit with his officers. My sisters occasionally played 'Bonaparte's Retreat.' Mr. Ney didn't like to hear it sometimes shed tears. I don't think he ever voted or was naturalized. Was a great fencer. Said Murat only was a better swordsman. He often spoke of an adopted child that he rescued during the march from Moscow. He called him Phesnac or Fesnac.[Again, no doubt a reference to Fezenac; it is possible Ney adopted the child and named him after Fezenac.] He appeared to have a greater affection for him than any one of whom I heard him speak not even excepting his wife and children. Always spoke of Phesnac or Fesnac as a youth; called him 'my son.' I think he said Murat cut down the soldier who gave him the sabre wound. Did not say in what battle he received it.[7] I have often seen the manuscript containing an account of his life. He kept it securely in his trunk. In writing it he often consulted Thiers's 'History of the Consulate and Empire.'"

MRS. ELIZABETH P. SLOAN, BRENHAM, TEXAS (1886)

"I was well acquainted with Peter S. Ney. I was his pupil for a considerable time. . . . I have frequently heard him speak of his wife. Said she had an elegant necklace (diamond, I think) which cost several thousand dollars I forget how many. . . . When on horseback, as old as he was, he was grand so erect and rode beautifully."

K. F. HALL, BLACKMER, ROWAN COUNTY, NORTH CAROLINA (1886)

"I saw P. S. Ney several times when he taught near Mocksville. Judge Pearson [chief justice of North Carolina] knew him well. He said to me one day, 'This Peter S. Ney likes whiskey. I believe he is an impostor. I haven't the slightest idea that he is Marshal Ney.' Later Judge Pearson was convinced that he was Marshal Ney. I saw P. S. Ney a short time before he died. He appeared to be very aged. A good fencer. One day a left-handed man was his antagonist. Ney shrank back, and pointing to a heavy sabre scar over the eye, said, 'A left-handed man gave me this scar, or this was made by a left-handed man.'"

GENERAL D. H. HILL, CHARLOTTE, NORTH CAROLINA (1887)

"Many of my acquaintances were pupils of P. S. Ney. . . . The Rev. Mr. Frontis, a native Frenchman, said he never believed Ney to be a French man until he heard him pronounce Augereau. The pronunciation was such, said he, as only a native could give. Ney wouldn't talk French with Frontis, and that excited his suspicions."

MRS. H. M. IRWIN, CHARLOTTE, NORTH CAROLINA (MAY 13, 1887)

"P. S. Ney's mother, according to his assertion to a member of my family, was a Scotchwoman whose name was Isabella Stewart. The way he happened to speak of it was this: he sometimes, at the request of his pupils and other parties, would write acrostics on their names. He would dash off these productions with no apparent effort, give the origin of the name, and state to what language it belonged. In writing an acrostic for a young lady whose name was Isabella, he said, 'I take much pleasure in putting this into verse, as it was the name of my mother,' adding that she was a native of Scotland."

MRS. SALLY NELSON HUGHES, HALIFAX COURT HOUSE, VIRGINIA (1889)

"Peter S. Ney taught school near the residence of my father (Mr. William Nelson), Mecklenburg County, Va., in 1828–29. I was his pupil a great part of the time. He kept a large life-size portrait of Napoleon hanging up in the school-room. He also had a picture of Napoleon's grave at St. Helena. We all thought he was a wonderful man. My father asked him to write an acrostic on the names of the different members of his family. He did so. . . . My youngest sister was named after Mr. Ney's mother Catharine Isabella. Mr. Ney himself asked my mother to let him name her infant child after his mother. She readily granted the request. He was very proud of the honor. It gratified him very much, as he seemed to have great affection for his mother. In the acrostic the different names are connected together in a single piece of composition. . . . He was fond of music, and often played on a flute."

J. W. SANDERS, IREDELL COUNTY, NORTH CAROLINA (1886)

"About the year 1840 Peter S. Ney was recognized as Marshal Ney by John Snyder, of Iredell County. Snyder was a Bohemian German born and raised near Prague. He said he was conscripted by order of Napoleon. . . . He was assigned to Murat's command, and charged in the snowstorm with that renowned marshal on the bloody field of Eylau. . . . He was afterward under Davout, then under various other marshals, including Marshal Ney. Said he had seen Bonaparte (to use his own words) 'hundred times.' Had been in sixteen regular battles, besides several smaller engagements. Napoleon, seeing defection in his German troops, sent them away. . . . Snyder said that after enduring great hardships and suffering he deserted and came to the United States, landing at Charleston, S. C. He afterward settled in Iredell County. Snyder saw P. S. Ney in Statesville about 1840, and immediately recognized him as Marshal Ney. He said he was frightened. He raised his hands and exclaimed: 'Lordy God, Marshal Ney!' P. S. Ney gave him a sign not to talk, and he afterward conversed with P. S. Ney. He said he knew Ney perfectly. Belonged at one time to Ney's command, and was personally acquainted with him. He told me the following incident among many others: On one occasion in a severe battle (I forget the name) Marshal Ney had several horses killed under him. He then walked on foot along the line, animating his desponding troops, with his sword in one hand and a broken standard in the other. Snyder saw that the men were being killed all around him, and he began to dodge at the whistle of the bullets. Ney saw him and tapped him on the shoulder, and said, in German, 'Snyder, the bullets you hear won't kill you.' Snyder said that Ney knew a great many of the private soldiers, and would often go among them and talk to them in his blunt but kind-hearted way. He said Ney's soldiers loved him, and almost worshipped the ground he walked on. He said that the marshal would look out for them as nobody else would. He would see that they had plenty of food and clothing, and that the sick and wounded were properly cared for. He would take the part of any soldier that was abused or imposed upon, and would see that justice was done him. Frederick Barr, one of Napoleon's old soldiers, also recognized P. S. Ney as Marshal Ney. Snyder and Barr were from the same country, and generally spoke the German tongue. They were men of high character, and enjoyed the confidence and esteem of the community in which they lived."

DANIEL SNYDER, STATESVILLE, NORTH CAROLINA (1889)

"I have often heard my father (John Snyder) say that he knew Marshal Ney in Europe; that he had served in Ney's command as a private soldier. When my father saw Peter S. Ney in Statesville about the year 1840, he knew him at once, but he was 'astonished,' he said, 'almost out of his senses.' He had no idea of seeing him. There was a political meeting in Statesville on the day that my father saw Peter Ney. He said when he recognized him as Marshal Ney, Mr. Ney intimated to him to say nothing more, and that after the meeting was over he and Ney had a private talk. I have heard my father say dozens of times that Peter S. Ney was Marshal Ney; that he knew Marshal Ney by sight as well as he knew his own father. Germany was my father's native country, and his people were in good circumstances. He said he knew Marshal Ney personally, as

Marshal Ney was in the habit of going among his soldiers and making the acquaintance of the humblest in the ranks. My father solemnly asserted to his dying day that Peter S. Ney was Marshal Ney."

Dr. James M. Spainhour, Lenoir, North Carolina (1888)

"My father, Noah Spainhour, who died in Caldwell County in 1881, was acquainted with Peter S. Ney. He met him in Rowan County in 1846, a short time before P. S. Ney's death. He said in substance: 'In the summer of 1846 I went to Salisbury, N. C....In passing through Rowan County I lost my way, and asked the first man I met to show me the road to Salisbury. He asked me who I was, and where I lived. I said, "My name is Spainhour, and I live in Caldwell County." "Spainhour, Spainhour" said he, repeating the name slowly and reflectively. "Why, I had some soldiers of that name in my command in Switzerland." "Very probable," I said, "for my family came from Switzerland, and we have several relatives in that country." He then asked me to go home with him; said it was nearly dark, and Mr. Foard, the gentleman with whom he boarded, would be glad to entertain me. I accepted his invitation. After supper he asked me to walk out with him into the grove, not far from the house. I did so, and we had quite a long talk. He said he thought he had three soldiers named Spainhour belonging to his command in Switzerland; that he had a distinct recollection of the name. He then told me that Marshal Ney had command of Bonaparte's troops in Switzerland, and that he was not executed, as history states that he was. He said the arrangement was that the soldiers detailed to execute him were not to fire until they heard the word of command from the marshal himself; that he was to fall while giving the command fire, so that the balls might pass over him. This arrangement was carried out. He was quickly taken up and carried to a neighboring hospital. He then disguised himself, made his way to the coast, and sailed to the United States. He said that when he walked to the place appointed for his execution he had in his left bosom a bag of red fluid resembling blood, and that when he struck his hand upon his heart or breast in giving the command, the bag bursted, and the fluid spurted over his person, etc. I think he also told me that he went on board the boat which carried him to America disguised as a servant, carrying a valise. His clothes did not fit him, and it made him mad. They were too small for him. During the voyage he said he was recognized by an old soldier who had been in the Napoleonic wars, and that when they reached Charleston he remained on board the vessel until the old soldier had gotten off and disappeared. He saw him leave from the cabin window.' I have heard my father make this statement more than once, and I cannot be mistaken as to its substantial accuracy. My father further stated that P. S. Ney told him that Marshal Ney was then living, but he would not say positively that he was Marshal Ney."

VALENTINE STIREWALT, DAVIDSON COLLEGE, NORTH CAROLINA (1894)

"I went to school to P. S. Ney in 1842. He boarded at my father's, and I saw him often sometimes had long talks with him in his room. He was fond of his toddy, and my father gave him a dram every morning for breakfast. He didn't drink much at a time, and he rarely went beyond proper bounds. I appeared to be one of his favorites, and he would occasionally talk to me about his past life. He once told me he was Marshal Ney, and how he escaped. He said that when he marched out for execution he had in his bosom a sack of red fluid, and that when he gave the command to fire he struck the sack with his right hand, and the liquid spurted out on his face and clothing. He fell, and appeared to be dead. He was taken up and carried off, and finally escaped to the United States."

R. A. HENDERSON, ATTORNEY-AT-LAW, TOPEKA, KANSAS

"I was born in England; was educated at the Royal Military College, and served three years in the regular army. My grandfather (Robert Laird) was an English soldier in the Peninsular War and at Waterloo. In the Peninsular War he was a member of the Eighty-eighth Regiment, known as the Connaught Rangers, and at Waterloo he was a sergeant in the celebrated Sixth Inniskillen Dragoons, who were almost annihilated in their charge against the cuirassiers. After the battle of Waterloo he went to France, and remained there with the army of occupation. He was one of the persons representing the English army, appointed to witness the execution of Ney. I have heard him say often that Ney was not executed—that he saw the muskets discharged, saw Ney fall, viewed the body, saw it taken up and carried away, saw it in the hospital, but that Ney was not hurt; that the so-called execution was a farce. He always affirmed this in the most positive manner. Said Ney's fall was not natural, and that the supposed bullet marks upon his person were artificial. I think he also stated that some Prussians were present at the scene. My impression is that he said the guns contained blank cartridges. The report made by the commission, of which he was a member, to the military authorities was this: 'Marshal Ney was not shot.' I may be mistaken as to some minor matters, but the essential facts are as I have given them. My grandfather was a man of approved courage. He had a great many medals which were given to him for gallantry in the Peninsular War and at Waterloo. He was born in Fermanagh, six miles from Inniskillen, Ireland, and was very old when he died. While in the army he kept a private diary, which he bequeathed to me. I have it among my books in Canada. In that diary will be found a confirmation of what I have said and other details of the alleged execution. My grandfather further said that at the time of the so-called execution it was the common talk in the army and elsewhere that Ney was not shot."

CORRESPONDENT OF THE ST. LOUIS *REPUBLIC*, ROCHEPORT, MISSOURI (1891)

"Major Thomas W. Sampson, of Rocheport, gives some very interesting facts in regard to the mysterious Ney which seem to establish the fact conclusively that he was not shot on that dismal and foggy morning when so many brave men fell victims to the merciless decree of the French Council of Peers. Major Sampson states that the late George H. C. Melody, of St. Louis, spent several weeks in Paris, France, in 1845, during the reign of Louis Philippe, King of the French. His Majesty extended to the American commoner many tokens of friendship in recognition of courtesies extended to the king by Mr. Melody in St. Louis during the king's exile years before.

"In the course of a confidential conversation during this visit, Mr. Melody asked Louis Philippe the question: 'Is the statement in history that Marshal Ney was shot true?' The king replied: 'Mr. Melody, I know the fact that you are one of the highest Masons in America. I am known as one of the most exalted Masons in Europe. Marshal Ney held a position among Masons equal to either of us. The prisons were full of men condemned to be shot. These men were daily being marched out to meet their fate. Some other man may have filled the grave intended for Marshal Ney.' Mr. Melody replied very quietly: 'May it please your Majesty, Ney was not shot.'"

Thomas D. Graham, Davidson College, North Carolina (1888)

"I was well acquainted with Peter S. Ney. I helped to nurse him in his last illness. He was sick several days, and I sat up with him every other night. I saw him die, shaved him, and helped to dress him and bury him. He had wounds all over his body. I don't remember how many. He had a scar on the left side of his head, one on his breast, one on his thigh, one on his arm, and one in the calf of his leg. He would ask those who waited on him to rub his leg for the cramp, but to be careful, for there was a ball in the calf of his leg which sometimes gave him pain. He had many other scars, but I have forgotten where they were located or how many there were. Mr. Ney boarded at Mr. Osborne G. Foard's. I often saw him there, and sometimes had long talks with him. He described to me one day the battle of Waterloo drew a plan of it on the sand, marked off the position of the army, also that of the English army; showed me how the battle was conducted, etc. I think he told me that he received the sabre cut on his head at the battle of Waterloo; that he cut down the man who gave him the blow, but broke his own sword in doing so. . . . During his last illness I heard him say four or five times that he was Marshal Ney. He died on the 15th day of November, 1846, about five or six o'clock in the evening. About ten o'clock in the morning Dr. Matthew Locke, his physician, and one of his old pupils, came into the room and said to him, 'Mr. Ney, it pains me deeply to tell you that you have not long to live.' Mr. Ney looked at Dr. Locke and said calmly, 'I know it, Matthew, I know it.' About three o'clock in the afternoon Dr. Locke returned. He was much affected. 'Mr. Ney,' said he, 'you have but a short time to live, and we would like to know from your own lips who you are before you die.' Mr. Ney, perfectly calm and rational, raised himself up on his elbow, and looking Dr. Locke full in the face, said, 'I am Marshal Ney of France.' Two or three hours later he died.

"Archie Foard, a colored man, was present when Mr. Ney told Dr. Locke he was Marshal Ney. Mr. Foard, I think, was also present."

ARCHIE FOARD, CLEVELAND, ROWAN COUNTY, NORTH CAROLINA (1890)

"I belonged to Mr. Osborne Foard. Mr. Peter Ney died there, and I nursed him while he was sick. He was sick, I think, about two weeks. He had rheumatism and pains in his back, with a good deal of inflammation at times. He was very thankful for what I did for him, or for what anybody did for him. He said to me, 'You are very good to me. I will reward you when I get well.' Sometimes he would hug his pillow and say, 'Oh, my wife! my wife!' I felt so sorry for him, for he was just as good to me and the other colored people as any man could be. One day he said, 'Oh, I can't stand it any longer! If I get well I must go back and see my wife and children.' Often when he was in pain he would say, 'Oh, my God!' not 'Oh, my God!' like most people, but, 'Oh, my (me) God!' I heard him say two or three times that he was Marshal Ney. I didn't know who Marshal Ney was, but that is what he said. He had wounds all over him. I don't know how many he had. He was awfully marked up. I used to rub his back. He said it did him a great deal of good, and he would thank me over and over again for it. He wasn't out of his head at any time except a little while before he died. He said not long before he died that he was Marshal Ney."

MRS. OSBORNE G. FOARD, NEWTON, NORTH CAROLINA (1887)

"I knew P. S. Ney when he taught school near Third Creek in Rowan County. I remember him well. He walked rather briskly at all times, even in going about the house. Had small marks or spots on his face, produced, I suppose, by the smallpox. Skin a little rough, though of a healthy hue. Loved fun and jokes when he had nothing to do. A hearty laugher when anything amused him. A great fencer. His sword or stick would fly like lightning. Hawk-looking eyes, with a good deal of white in them. One day when he was sick, he said, 'O France! France! why can't I? No, I must not!'. . . Had a wound on his arm between shoulder and elbow so deep that the flesh appeared to adhere to the bone. He had an Irish brogue, a deep, rolling voice. I have his writing-desk, comb, and knife. He had a fine sword, with the point broken off; but I do not know what became of it. I have seen it often. It was highly polished, as bright as new silver, with a richly ornamented hilt. About one fourth of the sword was broken off. Mr. Ney noticed everything. Mr. Foard used to say, 'What Mr. Ney couldn't see was not worth seeing.' Mr. Foard was very sorry that he allowed Pliny Miles to carry off Mr. Ney's shorthand manuscript. Mr. Foard wrote to Mr. Miles about the document, and he replied that he would return it after awhile. Some months afterward Mr. Foard wrote again to Pliny Miles, but he received no answer to his second letter. . . . I have frequently heard Mr. Foard speak of Mr. Ney's last illness, and of his dying declaration that he was Marshal Ney. He said in substance that not long before Mr. Ney died, Dr. Locke approached his bedside and said, 'Mr. Ney, I have done everything for you that I could do, and it grieves me to tell you that I do not think you can possibly get well. We would like to know who you are before you die.' Mr. Ney answered, 'I might as well tell you. I am Marshal Ney of France.'"[8]

Ney told three people, while on his deathbed, that he was Marshal Ney and repeated it shortly before he died and while he was still lucid.[9] All three later attested to it.

—◦—

P. S. Ney died November 15, 1846. His obituary that appeared in the Charlotte, North Carolina, *Journal* on December 24, 1846, read as follows:

"Died . . . of typhus fever, Peter Stewart Ney, aged about 68 years. Mr. Ney was a native of Scotland, where he received a liberal education; before the completion of which his father emigrated to France.
—One of his pupils."[10]

The administration of his estate showed a positive balance of $16 after payment of debts.[11] He was buried in the graveyard of the Third Creek Presbyterian Church in Cleveland, Rowan County, North Carolina. At the instigation of Lyman Copeland Draper, who was investigating the Marshal Ney/P. S. Ney mystery, his grave was opened by a team of local doctors in 1887 to try to verify whether he was Marshal Ney. They looked especially for evidence that he had been trepanned, as supposedly was Marshal Ney, and for the bullet in his thigh (evidently ignorant of the account that the bullet had passed through his leg and into his horse). They found his skull too deteriorated to determine whether it had been trepanned, and they found no bullet or silver plate allegedly placed in Marshal Ney's skull as a result of his trepanning.[12] Their report is as follows:

> The body of P. S. Ney was exhumed on the 3d day of May, 1887. The physicians present say:
>
> The undersigned physicians wish to state that, according to a previous notice, we did to-day cause to be exhumed the remains of P. S. Ney in the presence of a great number of witnesses, some of them from Washington City, Raleigh, and other parts of the country. We found some of the bones only, and these in a state of such decay that we cannot state positively whether the skull had ever been trepanned or not. We made diligent search for bullets said to have lodged in the body, but found none. We succeeded so far, however, as to ascertain that the skeleton was about five feet ten inches long, and the skull around about the eyes about twenty-four inches in circumference.
>
> (Signed) J. G. Ramsay, M.D.,
> D. B. Wood, M.D.,
> S. W. Stevenson, M.D.,
> James McGuire, M.D.,
> C. M. Pool, M.D.,
> S. W. Eaton, M.D.,
> Thomas E. Anderson, M.D.,
> J. H. Wolff, M.D.,
> J. B. Gaither, M.D."[13]

They reburied the body and erected a tombstone with the following inscription:

IN MEMORY OF
PETER STEWART NEY,
A NATIVE OF FRANCE AND SOLDIER
OF THE FRENCH REVOLUTION
UNDER NAPOLEON BONAPARTE,
WHO DEPARTED THIS LIFE
NOVEMBER 15TH, 1846,
AGED 77 YEARS

In conclusion, the eyewitness accounts show that P. S. Ney, among other things:

- Bore a highly similar, if not exact, physical resemblance to Marshal Ney.
- Was of the same physical constitution and possibly the same approximate height as Marshal Ney.
- Had, with the exception of the head wound, what appeared to be the same wounds that Marshal Ney was known to have.
- Appeared to be the same age as Marshal Ney, although a handful of people judged him to be younger.
- Was an exceptional swordsman and equestrian.
- Had a knowledge of military affairs as well as a military bearing and approach.
- Had detailed knowledge of the Napoleonic campaigns in which Marshal Ney participated.
- Spoke German, French, and English (as did Marshal Ney), plus Latin and Greek (and possibly Hebrew as well as some Polish and Russian, none of which Marshal Ney was recorded as knowing, although he likely knew at least some Latin from his school days).
- On multiple occasions was recognized as Marshal Ney by soldiers who fought under him visiting or living in America.

- Played the flute, as did Marshal Ney, but also composed poetry and acrostics and painted, none of which Marshal Ney was recorded as doing.
- Like Marshal Ney, drank (but unlike him to excess on occasion) and used tobacco in the form of chewing tobacco, while Marshal Ney is known to have smoked cigars.
- Variously claimed his mother was Scottish or Irish, which does not accord with the generally accepted origin of Ney's mother.
- On occasion described his wife and children in accord with Marshal Ney's family and (as will be seen) in detail such as probably only Marshal Ney would have known.
- Exhibited personality traits completely consistent with those of Marshal Ney, as summarized at the end of chapter 8.
- Generally avoided commenting on his origins but, especially when under the influence of alcohol, would freely state he was Marshal Ney and reminisce accurately about details in Marshal Ney's life.
- Was an ardent Bonapartist who hoped to return to France on the accession of Napoleon's son the Duke of Reichstadt.
- Made a deathbed confession that he was in fact Marshal Ney.

So who was P. S. Ney? Either he was (1) a calculating imposter, (2) a delusional imposter who truly believed he was Marshal Ney, or (3) Marshal Ney in fact.

Was Marshal Ney Executed?

To RECAPITULATE, THE P. S. NEY STORY COLLAPSES IF IT CAN BE PROVEN that (1) Marshal Ney in fact was executed on December 7, 1815; (2) because of differences between Marshal Ney and P. S. Ney, they could not have been identical; or (3) there is evidence that P. S. Ney had an identity other than that of Marshal Ney before coming to America.[1]

Let us examine each in turn.

1. DID MARSHAL NEY REALLY DIE ON DECEMBER 7, 1815?

A. *The Execution*

Ney's execution and its immediate aftermath were attended by a great flurry of paperwork. As soon as the cadaver was brought to the Maternity Hospital, a Major Weurbroucq (or Deurbroucq), commanding a cavalry post at the hospital approximately 200 yards from the execution spot, issued a written "certificate of arrival of Ney's corpse." It read, "I the undersigned declare to have received in trust from the Commissioner of police of the Luxembourg quarter the corpse of Michel Ney, marshal of France, condemned to death by the Chamber of Peers, the 6 December, 1815, at half-past eleven at night. . . . This judgment has been executed at half-past nine in the morning, the 7 December, 1815." The certificate contains a postscript: "P.S. The corpse will be delivered up by us to the relatives of the aforesaid Michel Ney, in case they reclaim it, whom we will give a receipt for it."[2]

The stilted wording of the first two sentences of the certificate suggests that they might have been dictated by orders from Rochechouart or

Despinois and designed to confirm the fact of the execution and its legality rather than to confirm the receipt of a corpse identified as that of Ney. Notably, the certificate does not state that Major Weurbroucq viewed the corpse (which arrived covered) and confirmed that it was that of Ney or that Ney was in fact dead. Weurbroucq's ability to confirm the fact (much less the legality) of the execution as stated in the certificate is inapposite since he would have been too far away to witness it in any detail if at all. And then there is the odd postscript, possibly added by Weurbroucq as an afterthought, dealing with disposition of the corpse and containing the time-honored bureaucratic defensive maneuver "we will give a receipt for it."

The adjutant major who commanded the execution squad, St. Bias, also issued a written report to Rochechouart on December 7 providing an official description of the execution:

> I arrived at the ground chosen for the execution, where I arranged the troops, according to the orders that you gave me.
>
> At half past nine the Marshal arrived, he descended from the vehicle near the picket chosen for the execution. He asked me where he should place himself; after having shown him, I proposed to blindfold him and that he kneel, he refused saying that an officer such as him would never kneel and that he had no need of a blindfold; then I gave the command *Peleton Arme* [rough equivalent of "Squad, ready"], at this moment he advanced one step and offered the words "French," "brave" and some other unintelligible words, immediately I commanded "Present, fire." He fell dead immediately, hit by three balls in the head and five or six in the body.
>
> Following my instructions, I left the body there a long quarter of an hour, exposed to the eyes of the public, after which I had it transported to the hospital of the Maternity, where I escorted it with a picket of twenty men that I left there as a guard.[3]

Presumably, Rochechouart reported on the execution to Despinois, for the latter issued his own report in turn on December 7 to Minister of War General Henri Clarke. His report was at once factual and polemical:

The condemned was taken at nine o'clock from the room where he was detained; he got in a vehicle accompanied by two officers of the Gendarmerie, and of the Cure of Saint-Sulpice, of whom he had earlier rejected with a sort of contempt, the consoling ministry, and that he had thereafter re-demanded . . . with evidence of resignation. . . . Conducted to the place of execution by an escort of a detachment of the Royal Grenadiers of Rochejacqelin [*sic*], a picket of Gendarmerie, another picket of mounted National Guard and the company of veteran sub-officers in service at the Luxembourg [Palace], he refused on arriving to kneel and would not permit his eyes to be blindfolded. . . . He dared to protest again his innocence, as if treason, of which he has been found guilty, were not already manifest in the eyes of Europe, as in those of France. . . . The body of the condemned was picked up some moments after the execution and deposited in the Maternity Hospital, to be guarded until an officer of the civil state can process it and hand it over to his relatives. The number of spectators was barely considerable, and the most perfect tranquility reigned all during the night and reigns again in Paris.[4]

The same day, Despinois drafted a report to the Grand Referendar of the Chamber of Peers, Count de Semonville. Apparently, in Despinois' view, the execution had gone so well that now it was time to take credit and line up people for promotions. It read in relevant part,

Charged under my personal responsibility with all the necessary dispositions to ensure the clear and complete execution of the verdict rendered yesterday by the Chamber of Peers against Marshal Ney, I have the honor to inform you that I gave the order to the Maréchal de Camp Comte de Rochechouart, in his capacity as commandant of Paris, to present himself, on the field, at the Luxembourg Palace, to take under his guard the person of the condemned, to direct all the troops, pay attention to maintaining internal and external security. . . . M. de Montigny will be invited, by him and in my name, to continue his functions in the interior of the Palace, and I await with great pleasure his service reports with the Comte de Rochechouart which deserve all your confidence.[5]

In order to obtain the official death certificate, at 3:00 p.m. on December 7, Ney's brother-in-law Charles-Guillaume Gamot and his steward Louis-Frédéric Rayot—not the "officer[s]of the civil state" contemplated by Despinois—made a formal, signed declaration before the Prefecture of the Department of the Seine that Ney was killed at 9:20 that morning.[6] Although it is perhaps normal that a family member and close personal employee would apply for the death certificate, they were not the government functionary stipulated by Despinois, and, in the context of subsequent questions about the execution, they were hardly impartial third-party witnesses to the fact that Ney was indeed dead. And, as noted earlier, Gamot was acknowledged to be part of a conspiracy to free Ney.[7]

B. The Firing Squad

According to an unsigned document in French dated May 2, 1835, that was apparently prepared in response to a request by Ney's son the Second Prince de la Moskowa, who was investigating the circumstances of his father's death, the 12-man firing squad was staffed by the First Company of *sous-officiers vétérans* from the Luxembourg Palace. That document also states that the members of the firing squad "had a great deal of repugnance on their part" for having to shoot Ney and that Adjutant Major St. Bias, who commanded the squad, "was on the point of falling ill—he was very troubled."[8] One contemporary newspaper report, datelined "PARIS, Dec 10 [1815]," that was picked up and run in American newspapers, stated that "[t]he officer commanding the veterans appeared struck dumb" and that Despinois said, "[O]fficer, if you cannot command I will" but that St. Bias remained "silent," upon which Ney himself said, "[S]oldiers do your duty." The article reported that, once shot, Ney fell on his knees and "died instantly" (if one believes that the execution was staged, the fall to his knees arguably could have been to break his fall before tumbling forward and exploding the hidden bladder). Finally, the article reported that St. Bias was thereafter arrested.[9]

Other than the documentary evidence that the 12-man firing squad was composed of four sergeants, four corporals, and four fusiliers from the *Compagnie de sous-officiers vétérans* of the Luxembourg Palace, no one has yet established who really manned the firing squad. Hoyt attempted to identify the individuals but failed. Indeed, his efforts to match the names of soldiers in that unit with the names of persons issued uniforms for guard duty over Ney produced no matches.[10] Some scholars think it is possible that royalists were interposed in the firing squad disguised as *sous-officiers vétérans*, but the evidence for that conclusion is less than compelling.[11] The simple fact is that, based on the evidence available to date, no one knows who composed the firing squad. It could have been anyone. From the available documents, it appears that Rochechouart chose the men following Despinois' orders, but who they in fact were is an open question. Rochechouart, it will be remembered, was Prime Minister Richelieu's man on the scene.

However, for reasons that are not now clear but presumably related to his alleged hesitancy to give the command to fire, concerns arose almost immediately about Adjutant Major St. Bias, who commanded the squad. On December 9, Despinois in a curt note questioned Rochechouart's selection of St. Bias and advised him never to employ him again because he had "lost his head" at the execution.[12] Rochechouart defended his choice, and on January 6, 1816, St. Bias prepared a history of his service record titled "Exposé de la Conduite." In this document, St. Bias reveals that he, like Rochejaquelein, served as a carabinier officer in the Russian campaign of 1812. He did not serve directly under Ney in the Third Corps but was attached to the Second Division of the Second Corps under Marshal Nicolas Oudinot Duke de Reggio. However, like Rochejaquelein, he would have fought in close proximity to Ney and may well have owed his life to his heroic retreat. Much of the tenor of the document suggests that St. Bias is trying to prove his loyalty to the Bourbons. He does not mention his command of the firing squad.[13]

St. Bias received a reward, however. He was granted naturalized French citizenship 16 days later on December 23.[14] St. Bias was to die from unknown causes less than three months after that on March 12, 1816.[15]

C. *The Bullets*

According to official reports, Ney received 11 balls out of 12: one in the right arm, one in the neck, three in the head, and six in the breast. The total in these reports conflicts with St. Bias's report that Ney was struck by "three balls in the head and five or six in the body," for a total of eight or nine bullets.[16] Under St. Bias's count, assuming use of one customary blank, two or three balls would have missed altogether, a surprising result for such a short-range stationary target and perhaps indicative of at least some of the squad "aiming to miss." Either way, the bullets were almost certainly .69-caliber Charleville balls, which would have done massive damage, especially when fired at such a short range. As observed by many people since then, their impact should have caused Ney to fall backward, not pitch forward.

Depending on how close Ney stood to the wall, it as well as the ground may have been splattered with blood. One official report states, "The wall which was in course of construction and the debris were soon covered in his blood."[17] If the wall were covered in his blood, this would be strong evidence that he was in fact executed. However, eyewitness accounts record only blood on the ground where he lay—under and about the body—not on the wall.[18] These observations could be consistent with the burst-bladder theory. Moreover, four days after the execution, a French hussar visited the site and recorded his observations:

> I saw the spot where he fell; the ground there has been turned over, in order to make the traces of his blood disappear. One sees, in the wall, six traces of balls, of which one is at the top; it appears that he who shot there was trembling very much: the marshal was too near the squad for one to be able to miss him. . . .
>
> On the wall, a little below the holes of the balls, was written: "here died the French Achilles." These words had already been effaced, but not sufficiently well that one could not distinguish them.
>
> I searched vainly in the wall to find one of the balls. But I was not the first to have had that idea, and I did not discover any of them. . . .

I returned there several times; the wall has been masoned, so as to make disappear even the slightest traces of his death. Everything that could recall the great d'Elchingen has been carefully effaced.[19]

What does one make of this visual account shortly after the fact? First, it discredits any theory that the firing squad was armed only with blanks. Beyond that, on the one hand, it could mean that five balls passed through Ney's body and struck the wall, with an additional one missing him and flying high. That would have left five balls embedded in his body, assuming use of the customary blank in one musket. On the other hand, it could mean that six balls just missed him because of his well-timed fall and struck the wall while the remaining balls, fired high, missed the wall altogether and went off into the trees beyond. Unfortunately, the hussar did not record the height at which the ball marks stood in the wall, although one assumes they were at an approximately appropriate height or he would have remarked otherwise, as he did as to the one that was visibly high. If Ney did fall before or just as the volley was fired, it would have been a "close-run thing," as the Duke of Wellington said of Waterloo.

Efforts to find the alleged report on the execution to higher British military authorities made by the eyewitness Sergeant Robert Laird of the Sixth (Inniskilling) Dragoons in which he described the execution as a "farce"[20]—or by other British military observers—have proven fruitless. Indeed, the *Waterloo Medal Book*, which is in effect a roll call of Wellington's army at Waterloo and which records the names of all recipients of the Waterloo Medal for having fought at that battle regardless of rank, shows no Robert Laird.[21]

D. Inside the Maternity Hospital
Here things turn very murky indeed. Two contrasting pictures of the scene within emerge. The first is provided by an unidentified police agent in a report dated December 9 stating that hundreds of people viewed the body:

It is quite certain that more than 500 Englishmen have been to see the corpse. Their curiosity seemed out of place to some National Guardsmen, who told them ironically, "But, gentlemen, you should have seen him in Spain; oh, that you did not come to see him ten years ago!". . . Some attentive observers have made observations that have led them to conclude that the English were expecting a movement. Several officers of that nation have affected to bewail Ney and to consider him as a political victim.[22]

Another anonymous police report dated December 9 tracked the first one in reporting a large number of visitors to the hospital and made the additional point that some of the foreigners who viewed the body came to ascertain whether it was Ney or someone else who had been shot, evidence that questions were already arising on this point: "A lot of individuals of note have been to see the body of the Marshal, at the place where it had been deposited. One noticed peers, generals, officers of every nation and persons attached to foreign embassies, who all came to convince themselves that it was really the Marshal who had been shot."[23]

Efforts to verify visitations by such "Englishmen" and other dignitaries have proven fruitless. The dispatches of the British and American embassies in the wake of the execution show no evidence of their personnel having visited the hospital. Nor does the voluminous corpus of memoirs by military and political leaders of the time show evidence of any such visitations. That is not to say they did not occur, just that there is no obviously extant evidence to verify the above statements. More typically, in letters dated December 7, both Wellington and British ambassador Sir Charles Stuart reported Ney's death in a matter-of-fact manner and with no reference to having seen the body to Tsar Alexander I and British foreign minister Castlereagh, respectively.[24]

Therefore, one of the principal arguments that the execution took place, namely that the body was viewed afterward in the hospital by hundreds of people, is based on so far uncorroborated evidence.

Moreover, the recorded impressions of those who did leave records of viewing the body in the hospital are ambiguous. The most reliable—indeed crucial—record is that of one Pelletier, a neighborhood merchant who was on duty with the National Guard. He heard the fusillade from the firing squad and ran to the place of execution. "I saw the Body of the Victim which had just been placed on a simple stretcher," he wrote. "The ground near me was saturated with blood which I hastened to cover with sand with my foot." [He, like the hussar, did not report blood on the wall, only on the ground where Ney fell.] He noted that very few people were about and that "some of the inhabitants of the quarter . . . seemed to re-enter their homes as if frightened." He went on to state that "I followed the stretcher alone, regarding it with a sad meditation." He saw the right arm of "the illustrious victim" fall from the conveyance and nearly touch the ground. "I hastened to replace it under the cloth which covered the corpse, without saying anything." Once in the Maternity Hospital, he lingered. He saw the porters who carried the stretcher "lift the blanket that covered the body" and place it in a "small, dark room." At length, he obtained a viewing. The room was so shadowy that he could not tell whether the color of the coat in which it was dressed was brown or blue ("the obscurity of the cave did not permit seeing well the color"), but he noted that his black vest was buttoned almost to the top and that his chest was pierced by balls. [The fact that the vest was buttoned to the top would have obscured any trunk wounds to the body; Pelletier was evidently reporting bullet holes in the clothing only.] Before he was hustled away and expelled by higher authorities, he had the chance to observe and later describe the wounds: "The noble head of the Marshal was respected and his physical traits did not appear affected at all. . . . One single ball reached the bottom of the right side of his lower jaw without changing the expression of this noble figure, his bust was imposing and seemed to still command respect."[25] This observation conflicts with the above-quoted official reports that three balls struck Ney's head and one struck his neck. How a head and neck that had received four .69-caliber balls fired at point-blank range could not be "affected at all" is a question that has never been answered by ballistics experts. But it needs to be.

In addition, if one is to believe her, Ida Saint-Elme also was in the Maternity Hospital, where a friend had taken her immediately on her having fainted on the execution ground:

When I came to I found myself lying on a narrow iron bedstead, in a room with whitewashed walls. A sister of mercy was at my side. I was being cared for at the Maternity Hospital, whither Belloc had taken me in my unconscious condition. I was still in a very feeble state.

After a space the silence of the hospital was disturbed by a strange commotion. The good sister went out, and returned almost at once, deeply moved. The marshal's body had been brought in to be left in the hospital until burial.

"He wants our prayers; I am going to offer mine," said the sister of mercy. I fell into a violent weeping fit. When Sister Theresa heard of my long attachment for Ney, she mingled her tears with mine at the memory of the hero who had died defenceless. She had lost a brother at the battle of Montereau, and in her heart she bore love of her country and aversion to foreigners and the white [royal] ensign. Kind charitable soul that she was, she contrived to let me gaze upon the marshal's mortal remains. She lent me some of her own garments, and so, in the dress of a sister of mercy, I went with her to kneel at the melancholy bier. Ney looked as if wrapped in placid slumber.[26]

Setting aside the dramatic touch of the *fille du regiment* dressed as a nun, Saint-Elme evidences no indication that the body was not that of Ney or that he was not dead. She was up close ("at the melancholy bier") and knew him well on sight. She also was a self-confessed conspirator. And, like Pelletier, her account of Ney "wrapped in placid slumber" despite having allegedly been hit by 11 .69-caliber balls fired at close range, including four in the head and neck, strains belief.

A third final witness is the anonymous artist who sketched Ney's body stretched out, lounging almost, on a stretcher in the hospital. It was later turned into a print (figure 11.1), several versions of which exist, one with nuns praying at his side and the other with hussars standing near him. The same observations reported above pertain to the depiction: languid, clean, minimal (indeed, in one version, no) bullet damage—a figure peacefully asleep, light beaming down, and the vest not closed but gone

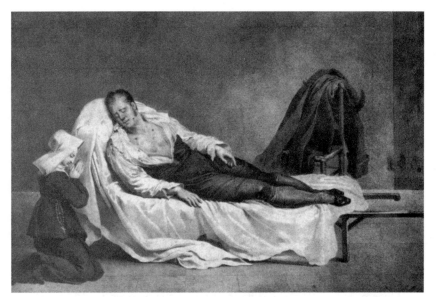

Figure 11.1.   Ney in the Maternity Hospital, based on an eyewitness sketch.
FINE ARTS MUSEUMS OF SAN FRANCISCO, GIFT OF M.H. DE YOUNG.

altogether (and thus inconsistent with Pelletier's eyewitness account). The print may have been designed to "prove" Ney's death to the public, which proof could have benefited either the government or people who theoretically might have rescued Ney. Reportedly, the government sought to repress the print for unclear reasons, so that possibly may eliminate the government as its propagator. The picture was rumored to have been sketched by the commander of a detachment of horse that accompanied Ney to the execution, and there has been speculation that it was drawn by Rochejaquelein,[27] but the matter remains unproven. If it were sketched by Rochejaquelein and if he were part of an escape plot, he arguably would have had a motive to create and disseminate a flattering picture "proving" that it was indeed Ney who was shot. Therefore, even more questions pertain as to this depiction than as to Pelletier's report.

E. The Burial and Inventory

Ney was buried at 6:30 or 7:00 a.m. on December 8, depending on which account one reads. Either way, it was still dark, and the cemetery was closed to the public. His wife did not attend, but his brother-in-law Charles-Guillaume Gamot did. His body was enclosed in two coffins: the inner one of lead and the outer one of oak.[28] Lead-lined coffins were sometimes used for British royals to delay decay of the body, but why this departure from the norm occurred in the case of Ney is unclear. One result of the use of two coffins, including one of lead, may have been to mask the weight (or lack thereof) of their contents.

Ney's burial certificate, dated December 8 at "8 o'clock in the morning," reads as follows:

> I the undersigned, Concièrge de l'Est, acknowledge that there has been delivered to me to-day, at 7 o'clock in the morning, by M. Guibrunet, special director of burial service of the XIIth arrondisement, a body enclosed in a coffin, and which has been declared to me to be that of Michel Ney, deceased on the 7th December, in 1815, rue d'Enfer, house of la Maternité.
>
> I declare also that the body has been buried at the same moment of its delivery to me . . .
>
> [Signed] Asseline[29]

The language "which has been declared to me to be that of Michel Ney" raises the immediate question of "declared by whom?" By Gamot? By Ney's steward Rayot? In any event, Asseline was hardly in a position to verify the identity of the body by opening two heavy, sealed coffins.

On December 27, 1815, Ney's notary Henri Batardy prepared a 211-page official inventory of the marshal's goods, replete with multiple references to his having died at Paris on December 7.[30] This would have been normal procedure to commence the probate of the estate of a wealthy decedent.

F. The Aftermath

Notwithstanding the extraordinary lengths the government went to bury Ney in secrecy, things did not work out quite as intended. *L'Abeille Américaine* reported on August 8, 1816, that the tomb of Ney at Père Lachaise Cemetery was a "subject of veneration" and that the "tombstone is covered with inscriptions that the police erase every night."[31] Apparently, much of the graffiti was antiroyalist in content.

Earlier that year, on June 1, Gamot petitioned the government to reinter the body in a vault that "he had prepared to receive it but on which no monument was to be erected nor any inscription engraved." His request was denied. However, he was persistent and renewed the request, with success the second time. It is hard to imagine why he would have made and then persisted in this request if the grave were empty. On November 27, 1816, the prefect of police in Paris wrote to the minister of police reporting on his execution of the plan. But, as before, the circumstances were shrouded in secrecy. The prefect of police wrote,

> Your Excellency ... asked me to prescribe ... the necessary measures, which should, moreover, be carried out with the greatest secrecy. ... This operation was planned with all the care and executed with all the secrecy that Your Excellency enjoined; by means of precautions taken beforehand, all the preparatory work was done at night by the number of workmen strictly necessary, and on whose discretion one could count the most. The removing of the body and its depositing in a new vault on which there [is] neither monument nor inscription, were done afterwards from six till seven o'clock in the morning by the same workmen, in the presence of only persons necessary, and at eight o'clock the operation was finished, and all traces of the former monument had entirely disappeared; all had been done behind closed doors, and it was not until eight o'clock that the gates of the Cemetery were opened.[32]

Why the need for such secrecy? Was the government that afraid of a dead man? Apparently so, as the grave had become a shrine to anti-Bourbon sentiment. Even with the removal to the new vault, the uninscribed and unmonumental cenotaph became a place for writing "anathemas" and "sarcasms" against the royal family and was removed by the government, eventually to be replaced in 1903 by the present, rather elaborate monument erected by the family.[33] Many years later, in 1886, Marshal Ney's grandson Jules-Napoleon Ney stated that the caskets were opened at the time of the reburial and that bullet holes were "distinctly visible" in the forehead of the skull of Marshal Ney.[34] Jules-Napoleon Ney or "Count Napoleon Ney," as he styled himself, was born in 1849, the illegitimate son of the marshal's oldest son,[35] and was not a firsthand witness to what transpired in 1816, although his father or uncles may have told him what they saw or heard when they themselves were children. In contrast, one of the persons involved in the reinterment at the time in 1816 was reported to have said that the caskets were empty. Neither claim is supported by solid documentary evidence. Why the caskets were opened in 1816 in any case is perhaps the more interesting question. Such a step was hardly necessary for reinterment, and there must have already been questions as to whether Ney was within. Further, such questions continued. Napoleon III, "who had probably heard certain significant rumors," reportedly ordered the coffins opened in 1853 when the tomb was being reconstructed. The conclusion: "No remains were in the decayed casket and apparently it had never contained anything."[36] No corroboration has been found of this story either. Finally, in connection with the erection of the present monument, in 1903, Ney's coffins were reportedly once again opened (why, once again, is a question). A gravedigger named Dumesnil who participated in the project was reported as stating that they were empty.[37] Again, there is no confirmatory evidence. One would have thought that the opening of the coffins in either 1853 or 1903 would have been rather major news picked up by the Parisian newspapers of the time.

After Ney's interment, Gamot was later to be buried in the same vault along with Ney's father-in-law and two of Ney's four sons. One might reasonably ask why they were buried there if it were not in fact Ney's tomb aside from the fact that it is a particularly prestigious burial spot.

Madame Ney was never known to visit her husband's grave. By the time Gamot reinterred him in 1816, Madame Ney had left France for Italy. She returned to France in October 1819. During her sojourn in Italy, she apparently entered into a secret morganatic marriage with Louis d'Y. de Resigny, a former Napoleonic ordnance officer and later a general, in either Milan or the free port of Livorno. It was a religious ceremony only with no civil ceremony. La Moskowa kept her name of Ney and titles. She announced the marriage to her family only on her return to France.[38] The evidence of her remarriage is scanty, but the family, including her sons, appeared to accept it and referred in correspondence to the "good Resigny" and the "excellent Resigny." More to the point, Madame Ney's daughter-in-law called him "the greatest nonentity of beings."[39] On her return to Paris, Madame Ney, who was in straitened financial circumstances, sold the house she shared with Marshal Ney at 74-76 rue de Bourbon and lived thereafter in a series of rented homes in Paris. Although she died in Paris on July 2, 1854, she was buried not with Ney but with her two sisters in the church at Saint-Leu-la-Florêt in the Val d'Oise, some 12 miles north of downtown Paris. It is not known whether de Resigny is buried with her; he is not listed on her tomb.

De Resigny died on October 25, 1857. They had no children. While the facts of the alleged marriage remain shadowy and it may have been, at best, a marriage of convenience, it would nonetheless be odd (if not illegal) for Madame Ney to have remarried if she knew Ney still to be alive and exiled in America. By way of context, Napoleon's second wife, Marie Louise, lived with Count von Neipperg of Austria starting with Napoleon's exile on Elba, but she did not morganatically marry him until after Napoleon's death in 1821.

Despite her apparent remarriage, Madame Ney and her sons labored unceasingly to overturn Ney's conviction. It was a family struggle of monumental proportions, carried out, especially in the early years, when they were under intense scrutiny from the French secret police wherever they went.[40] For example, Ney's second son, Michel-Louis-Félix (called "Aloys"), age 17 at the time, was the subject of a series of secret police reports between August 20 and September 6, 1821, in connection with a plot against the Duke of Wellington.[41] This would have been inconsistent conduct if he had known his father to be alive in America or if he had known Wellington had indeed saved his life. One of the sons was so embittered against Wellington for allegedly not saving his father that he challenged him to a duel. For unclear reasons, the duel never took place (perhaps Wellington deemed him not to be worthy of dueling under the code duello). The secret police reports at the time, of which there were many, portrayed Ney's sons as "dangerous conspirators."[42] Ultimately, in the 1830s, after the accession of Louis Philippe, they succeeded in obtaining a pardon for their father and even a military pension, although not retroactively to the date of the execution. But clearly the tragic injustice done to Marshal Ney cast a long shadow of misery over the family and became their all-consuming obsession for the remainder of their lives. At no time did Madame Ney or the sons evidence any extant indication that they thought the marshal was alive.[43]

G. The Bottom Line

The events of December 6–8, as well as the aftermath, suggest that the greater likelihood is that Ney was killed by the firing squad. But it is not a certainty. Ney stated many times before and during his trial that he wanted to emigrate to America, there is ample evidence of multiple plots under way to free Ney at the time, and the eyewitness accounts are so riven with anomalies that questions arose starting the very day of the execution and have persisted for 200 years. If indeed nearly 500 people viewed the body, this would likely be confirmatory of the execution, although the way the body was displayed in a separate darkened room tends to call into the question the validity of any such viewings, none of which seem to have been recorded by those present save Pelletier and Saint-Elme (neither of whom commented on the alleged hordes of visitors being present to view the body). The likelihood that Ney fell forward on his face when shot and exhibited no traumatic damage from large-caliber bullets and the fact that his vest was kept buttoned to block any view of the details of his chest wounds raise particular unanswered questions that make the execution less than certain.

Although there is no evidentiary "smoking gun" as to who might have been involved in a successful plot to save Ney, if there were one, a string of people who interacted with Ney and the "body" in the days surrounding the execution raises questions. These people include Curate Charles de Pierre; Secretary-Archivist Louis Cauchy; Notary Henri Batardy;

Ney's brother-in-law Charles-Guillaume Gamot; Ney's steward Louis-Frédéric Rayot; Richelieu's proxy general Louis Rochechouart, who apparently picked the firing squad; Colonel Auguste Rochejaquelein; Adjutant Major Frederic St. Bias; and possibly even the firing squad itself.

Despite P. S. Ney's occasional statements that the Duke of Wellington saved him, available evidence does not support the contention that the Duke was involved.[44] The Duke's final word on the matter came on September 1, 1849, a few years before he died, in response to a query from one Miss Angela Burdett-Coutts, who had written him about the Ney affair:

> There is no doubt that Louis XVIII had much cause to complain of Him [Ney]! He received money from the King! Went off with promises of faithful exertion: and betrayed his trust. As a Christian Louis XVIII ought to have pardoned the offence! But a Sovereign is bound to take care that treasonable offences are not repeated! . . .
>
> The treatment of Ney was not a question of indifference! The King could not decide it either as a Christian or according to His Wishes! . . .
>
> I might or might not have had great influence on the decision of the King! I did not interfere in any way! I did not consider it my duty to interfere! . . .
>
> I recollect to have heard of I am not certain that I did not see a letter from Lord Holland on the subject of the execution of Ney! In which he accused me of having permitted that he should be executed because I had not been able to get the better of Him in the field in some affair in Portugal.
>
> There was no foundation for the supposition that such motive could exist! There was no such affair! . . . That is all that I can recollect of the affair of Ney![45]

Wellington may have had his faults, but no one ever accused the Iron Duke of being a liar.

2. COULD MARSHAL NEY AND P. S. NEY
HAVE BEEN THE SAME PERSON?

As is evident from the sketches above of Marshal Ney and P. S. Ney, there were many similarities, both physically and temperamentally. Even a skeptic like Hoyt admitted that he was taken aback by the degree of similarity. In the realm of the physical, these similarities include approximately correct height and age as well as a corresponding body build, facial physiognomy, hair color, eye color, balding pattern, and war wounds (more on that below). Moreover, eyewitnesses recalled P. S. Ney as having a "dimple in the middle his chin."[46] Early portraits, as well as Houdon's bust, of Marshal Ney, all executed from life, show a dimple in the middle of his chin; later portraits do not show the dimple, it perhaps having been eliminated out of vanity. Both Marshal Ney and P. S. Ney were described as having penetrating eyes when aroused or agitated, and it was effectively said of P. S. Ney, as it was explicitly said of the marshal, that "[t]he play of his features strongly expressed the feelings by which he was excited."[47] It is not known if Marshal Ney was marked by smallpox, as was P. S. Ney, although contemporaries would have been likely to have commented on it if he had been; one presumes that portrait painters regularly flattered their subjects on the matter of skin blemishes. It also is possible that some eyewitnesses in America mistook powder burns for smallpox scars.[48]

In the temperamental realm, the similarities included discipline, diligence in study, occasional impetuousness and bursts of temper, antipathy toward England, spontaneous acts of charity, use of tobacco and alcohol, modesty, general indifference to money, mastery of retreats and disguises, a preference for rural over urban areas, and an oft-stated desire by Marshal Ney to emigrate to America. There also were similarities of talent, such as playing the flute, swordsmanship, equestrian skills, probable language abilities, and the fact that P. S. Ney prepared wills and deeds for his neighbors much as a notary would in France. There also are some unexplained differences of talent, as discussed below. Finally, there were similarities of knowledge, including knowledge of Napoleonic campaigns and of Marshal Ney's close family. There are hundreds of strands of evidence, any one of which could prove or disprove that they were the same person. This analysis will focus on the most significant ones.

A. The War Wounds

The record of Marshal Ney's life in service documents at least the following wounds, which appear to match the wounds shown on P. S. Ney's body:

1. Serious gunshot wound to left shoulder[49] at Mayence or Mainz in 1795, which became infected and required extensive recovery.
2. Musket ball into and possibly partially or wholly through thigh at Winterthur in 1799.
3. Bayonet through sole of foot at Winterthur in 1799.
4. Bullet shattering wrist at Winterthur in 1799.
5. Musket ball in neck at Smolensk in 1812.

In addition, Marshal Ney is known to have had these wounds:

6. Musket ball in chest at Mannheim in 1799 (minor wound).
7. Musket ball in shoulder at Schonfeld in 1813.

Furthermore, the French Archives of the Ministry of War contain records showing the following additional wounds borne by Marshal Ney:

8. An unspecified "grievous" wound while entering Stuttgart in 1799.
9. An unspecified wound at the Battle of Lutzen in 1813.
10. A "badly contusioned" bullet wound at the Battle of Leipzig in 1813 (may possibly be the same as the Schonfeld wound).

The documents do not mention any wounds received at the Battle of Waterloo, but then they probably would not have, as Ney fled shortly after Waterloo.[50]

When the three men who attended P. S. Ney on his deathbed dressed his body for burial, they noted, in addition to the large scar on the left top side of his head, wounds in his neck, side, right thigh, wrist, left leg, and foot.[51] These additional wounds appear, at least broadly, to track with the first five known wounds suffered by Marshal Ney listed above. Not only is this a remarkable degree of apparent correlation, but multiple observers commented on the serious wound P. S. Ney had to his upper left arm, which, from their descriptions, is highly consistent with the wound received by Marshal Ney at the same location on his body. Also, the unusual bullet wounds to the wrist and neck and bayonet wound to the foot match wounds that P. S. Ney bore and were noted by observers, although no one stated on which side of the body these were located as to either Marshal Ney or P. S. Ney.

The bottom line is that at least five wounds seem to have matched closely (if not exactly), and both men were covered in a variety of other war wounds that could well have been the same or similar.

But the wound that received the most comment and that poses the largest mystery is the head wound that P. S. Ney bore on the left side of his skull, running from above his eye to his ear, approximately three to four inches long. He ascribed it to a "glancing" saber blow and variously said he received it at Waterloo while fighting either Major General Sir William Ponsonby or the Duke of Leinster.[52] He also said, inconsistently, that he received it in the "last charge of the Old Guard." Efforts to place Marshal Ney near the Duke of Leinster at Waterloo are inconclusive, but it is plausible that Ney was engaged against Ponsonby. Their respective units did clash at Waterloo even if they did not engage in personal hand-to-hand combat. Ponsonby commanded the Second Heavy Cavalry Brigade at Waterloo. He was captured and later killed on the battlefield by Maréchal de Logis François Orban of the Fourth Lancers when his horse became mired in mud.[53] He was not killed by Ney, but it is possible that someone under Ponsonby's command executed a left-handed saber slash across Ney's head and was then killed.

Interestingly, P. S. Ney made extensive annotations in his own hand-writing on his copy of Barry O'Meara's *Napoleon in Exile*, as he did with many other books in his collection. These annotations focused largely on Marshal Ney's actions and perspectives and were cast in the third person (along the lines of "Ney did this, thought that . . ."; in one instance, at pages 117–19 of O'Meara, P. S. Ney indicated in his annotations that he had knowledge of Article 12 of the Capitulation of Paris and Marshal Ney's argumentation based on it in his trial, but that could have been widely known from newspaper coverage of the trial). In the section of O'Meara dealing with the destruction of Ponsonby's brigade, P. S. Ney made no annotations, which is perhaps surprising if that were the action in which he received such a visible wound.[54]

If the wound were inflicted later in the battle during the "last charge of the Old Guard," it would not have been caused by Ponsonby, who by then was dead. As described earlier, the fighting by Ney while leading the Old Guard was so intense that such a wound, if he did receive it, could have been inflicted by anyone. Moreover, Ida Saint-Elme, who claimed to have watched Waterloo from horseback, stated she saw Ney's face "streaming with blood" at the end of the battle, which could have indicated such a wound, although she later records having met with him at the end of June and did not remark about any wounds.[55] Similarly, Ney appeared before the Chamber of Peers just days after Waterloo, and there was no recorded mention of wounds in such a public forum.

Although Ney sought leave from the army in early July to "recover," again possibly indicating wounds, no one seems to have remarked about a head wound. The French edition of the *Trial of Marshal Ney*, published in December 1815, contains a somewhat stylized pen-and-ink drawing of the Marshal (figure 11.2), presumably done at his trial, and it shows no obvious head wound.[56]

Figure 11.2. Ney at his trial. PHOTOGRAPH TAKEN BY AUTHOR OF ILLUSTRATION IN ORIGINAL FRENCH BOOK *PROCÈS DU MARÉCHAL NEY. DEUX-IÈME EDITION. PARIS: MICHAUD, 1815.*

None of the above definitively answers the question of whether he received a serious head wound at Waterloo. On balance, there is no solid contemporary evidence that he did,[57] but that conclusion could change if additional evidence were to come to light.

B. The Skull

Both Marshal Ney and P. S. Ney were noted by contemporaries to have noticeably large heads. When P. S. Ney's body was exhumed in 1887, the doctors conducting the exhumation measured the circumference of his skull. Although the left part of the skull where he bore the head wound had deteriorated, apparently there was enough of the skull remaining to allow a measurement starting at the area of the eyebrows. It measured "about 24 inches" in circumference, according to the doctors' report.

The bust of Marshal Ney produced by Jean Antoine Houdon was life size, as were many other Houdon busts. Houdon was noted for his accurate portrayals. In fact, Houdon's bust of John Paul Jones was used to identify the body discovered in 1905 in Paris and transported to Annapolis for burial at the U.S. Naval Academy.[58] A measurement of the bronze version of Houdon's bust of Marshal Ney, taken at the eyebrows, shows a circumference of 24¼ inches—well within the margin of error for a match.[59]

C. Languages Spoken

It is established that Marshal Ney spoke German and French. It also is likely that, based on his education, he knew some Latin and, based on credible eyewitness accounts, that he spoke at least some English. P. S. Ney spoke English fluently although with what many eyewitnesses variously called a Scots or German accent. That they seemed to confound the two is surprising because North Carolina was the recipient of significant patterns of both Scottish and German emigration, and one would think they would have distinguished between them. There also is contemporary evidence that P. S. Ney knew and probably spoke German and French.[60] He appeared to use French sparingly, to the point that it raised suspicions in the minds of some eyewitnesses in North Carolina as to whether he was in fact French at all. However, as noted above, one resident of French background who himself spoke French was convinced by P. S. Ney's pronunciation of the name "Augereau" that he rendered it in a way that only a native French speaker could.[61] There is no evidence that Marshal Ney knew Greek or other languages attributed to P. S. Ney,[62] although it is plausible that he might have picked up a few words or expressions in Russian or Polish because of his campaigning there. One of the theories behind the assumed identity of P. S. Ney is that he improved his Latin and taught himself Greek and maybe Hebrew during his initial three years under cover in the United States.

The bottom line is that there is largely a match of language abilities but not a perfectly aligned one prior to 1815, but it is possible that Marshal Ney in three years of study could have improved his English and Latin and taught himself Greek and possibly Hebrew.

D. Literary, Artistic, and Other Abilities

P. S. Ney was a multitalented individual. Not only did he play the flute like Marshal Ney, but he also was accomplished in mathematics, including specifically geometry. His extant geometry teaching papers in the Hoyt Collection show an advanced understanding of the discipline that would have come only through university-level study or years of self-instruction.[63] Marshal Ney's familiarity with mathematics and especially geometry remain unknown, although the reasonable assumption would be that he had at least some proficiency based on his decades of practical experience as a soldier and on his propensity for self-instruction.

Two other aspects of P. S. Ney's talents—indeed, of his whole personality—raise more questions. First, he was an inveterate poet who frequently dashed off clever and graceful poems and acrostics with ease and fluidity (he tellingly wrote a poem titled "My Mind Is My Kingdom"). He also authored numerous articles that appeared in local newspapers. His command of the English language was quick, fluent, and devoid of the awkward expressions that one would expect of a nonnative English speaker.

An example of his dexterity with the nuances of the English language is provided by one eyewitness: "He asked me if I was a relative of Alexander McCorkle. I told him that I was a 'nevu.' He remarked that was the right pronunciation and not 'nephu.'"[64] The fact that Ney preferred the traditional, even archaic, pronunciation suggests a classical education in the English language. However, as with most matters involving P. S. Ney, there could be a second interpretation: *neveu* is the French word for "nephew" and the origin of the archaic English pronunciation of the word.

Nonetheless, although this judgment is subjective, P. S. Ney simply knew and used English too well to be anything other than a native speaker of the language.

Many of P. S. Ney's submissions to periodicals offered sometimes lurid commentary on political or social issues. On October 1, 1831, he wrote a letter of such a nature to the 80-year-old former president James Madison. Presumably, he chose Madison because he was the then surviving senior founding father. After apologizing for approaching the former president directly without an introduction and heaping praise on Madison to flatter him, he then played on Madison's known Francophilia and established his own intellectual bona fides by addressing him in French: "*Le Sage attend à demi mot.*" Next, he got down to the point: enlisting Madison's endorsement of a scheme to resettle America's Black population west of the Rocky Mountains "for the future security of the Whites!" accompanied by a gradual emancipation of the people so transported and their future offspring.[65] There is no record that Madison responded to Ney. It is an extraordinary letter and is printed in full in appendix B. It strains the imagination to conceive of Marshal Ney writing such a letter.

P. S. Ney also was an artist of some amateur ability. Eyewitnesses have described his portrait of Napoleon. He continually sketched and scribbled in the margins of his books. He designed the official seal of Davidson College. In one notable case, he allegedly "improved" a picture of Marshal Ney in a book by adding his own version in pencil of the marshal, titling it *Ney By him Self* (figure 11.3). This title could mean it was a rendering of Marshal Ney drawn by himself or a picture of Ney sitting alone. Beneath the printed picture, he wrote in French, "This is not a true likeness; but I am not surprised at it. He was bald. I have not read the book; I have only turned the leaves." *Ney By him Self* resides today in the collection at the library of Davidson College.

In another case, in his personal copy of *The Alhambra*, P. S. Ney drew in pencil profiles of two heads with an undecipherable shorthand annotation.[66] The heads bear a passing resemblance to the head of Marshal Ney that illustrates the 1815 French edition of *Procès du Maréchal Ney* in figure 11.2. It is unclear if they were meant to be self-portraits, influenced by the above-published representation, or profiles of other people. With

Figure 11.3. "Ney By him Self" (supposed sketch made by P. S. Ney c. 1820–1846). DAVIDSON COLLEGE ARCHIVES.

the possible exceptions of *Ney By him Self* and these two heads, there is no known portrait depiction of P. S. Ney.

Whether Marshal Ney had similar literary and artistic abilities is an open question. He was a very guarded man in his private life. Although he wrote and published a military treatise, he exhibited no known talents as a poet or as an artist. He was, however, an exceptionally busy military man and would likely have had little time for such avocations during his career. Those attributes plausibly could have flourished later. All four of Marshal Ney's sons had notable artistic and musical talents; they sang, played the piano, and painted.[67] At least one, Eugène, had literary talents as well and had his works published.

One other aspect of P. S. Ney's talents or personality is worth noting. He frequently wrote in a self-devised shorthand based on the Taylor and Bailey shorthand methods. Because much of it was invented or adapted by Ney, the net effect was to produce an encrypted body of texts. Notwithstanding the existence of some contemporary explanatory keys among the papers in the Hoyt Collection, only some of it can be understood today. A few of his students learned greater or lesser parts of it, but by the time he died most of it was undecipherable. As discussed in chapter 10, on his death he left in his locked chest a lengthy document in shorthand that he said would explain everything and surprise the world. Atop it was a picture of the execution of Marshal Ney. The document went into the hands of his executors in North Carolina, who subsequently entrusted it to a New York antiquarian named Pliny Miles, who said he could decipher it. He took the document but died in 1865 in Malta without having deciphered it. The document is now lost.

Why P. S. Ney wrote in shorthand is a mystery. The practice may have evidenced a secretive and paranoid personality, but he often used the shorthand for mundane observations and comments. At the end of the day, it is one of the more enigmatic quirks of P. S. Ney's character. There is no known evidence that Marshal Ney used shorthand of any kind.

E. Religion and Politics

Marshal Ney, by all appearances, was a conventional but not especially devout Catholic. P. S. Ney is not known to have attended or affiliated with any particular church. One eyewitness stated that he "did not believe in a Saviour, but in an over ruling Providence."[68] He did, however, own a Bible,[69] and on occasion, he broadly commended Christian principles to his students. He lived in largely Presbyterian parts of North Carolina, which arguably could point to his possible Scots background. However, he specifically told eyewitness James F. Johnston that he was "educated for a Catholic priest,"[70] which might be consistent with the education that Marshal Ney received at the Collège des Augustins.

P. S. Ney wrote a poem on May 18, 1831, that sheds some light on his religion and perhaps much more. Titled "Worship the Lord in the Beauty of Holiness," it reads as follows:

> When virgin voices sweetly blend
> With manly tones, and both ascend
> Harmonious on the dulcet air—
> How soothed is then the listening ear!
> Sweet symphonies the heart disarm
> And all our sterner passions charm.
>
> When brooding over former times
> And perils passed in distant climes—
> Defeat and glory all are gone
> Like dreams, before Louisa's tone.
> Harsh thunders of the battle-field
> To soft melodious accents yield.
>
> But when the holy anthem swells,
> That speaks where Christ in glory dwells,
> When Hope and Faith united say:
> "Leave worldly schemes, and come this way."
> Thrones, dynasties, and martial power
> Appear the playthings of an hour
> Seducing, evanescent, vain,
> The phantoms of a worldly brain.

Politically, P. S. Ney was a Whig and an admirer of Henry Clay and Daniel Webster. Although analogies with European political movements are inexact, the Whigs' advocacy of modernization, meritocracy, and the rule of law was not inconsistent with certain attributes of Bonapartism.

F. Bonapartism

If one is to believe Marshal Ney's statements at his trial, his Bonapartism during the Hundred Days was of an accommodationist stripe intended to save France a civil war. His allegiance was to France more than to the man Bonaparte. His statements on these points may have been self-serving and designed to save himself, but there probably was an element of truth in them given the frosty relationship he had with the emperor even after he declared for him in the Hundred Days. It is true that in return for his service over the years Bonaparte had enriched him with very significant *dotations*, or endowments of income-generating lands in conquered territories,[71] but at the end of the day money did not seem to matter that much to Ney. He was a French patriot first and a Bonapartist out of convenience. In contrast, P. S. Ney was a passionate, uncritical Bonapartist whose actions on occasion exhibited a greater commitment to the leader than to his own life. Although Marshal Ney acknowledged suicidal thoughts after Waterloo, it is a subjective judgment but P. S. Ney's Bonapartism does not coincide exactly with that of Marshal Ney.

G. Attitude toward England

As demonstrated by the letter from Marshal Ney quoted in chapter 8, the marshal harbored pronounced sentiments against England. So did P. S. Ney, whom one eyewitness said "bitterly hated England and so expressed himself."[72]

H. Knowledge of Family

P. S. Ney occasionally spoke of his wife. In the recollections of Mary C. Dalton of Houstonville, Iredell County, North Carolina (1885), Ney is described as saying that "his wife was a beautiful woman and had dark eyes and long black hair so long that she could sit on it."[73] Identical comments were recorded in the Campbell and Worth testimonies quoted in chapter 10. Madame Ney did indeed fit the description of being beautiful and having dark eyes. It is possible that P. S. Ney could have known that from having personally seen her in France (although she is not known to have gone on campaign with the marshal) or perhaps having seen the most famous portrait of her by François Gérard dating from circa 1810 (see illustration 10). But in that portrait, she had short hair, which would impeach P. S. Ney's recollections. However, there is in fact another but lesser-known portrait of Madame Ney done when she was a student at Madame Campan's school in which she had long braided dark hair that could easily have reached to her lower back or beyond (see figure 11.4).[74] One might well ask how P. S. Ney could possibly have known this intimate detail. There is no obvious answer.

P. S. Ney also told Mary Dalton that his wife was a "great friend" of Josephine and her daughter Hortense, which was certainly true of Aglaé Ney. Mrs. Dalton further said that she could not remember the name of the wife of P. S. Ney but that it began with the letter "A."[75]

Figure 11.4. Aglaé Auguié and Hortense de Beauharnais by Adèle Auguié while both were students at Madame Campan's. Painting made c. 1800. ART RESOURCE.

Perhaps even more tellingly, when asked why he did not bring his wife to America, P. S. Ney replied with various reasons, including the fact that she was better provided for in France than she would be in America and that "he would not know what to do with her here."[76] The last point is particularly apposite given Aglaé's personality and courtly interests as described above.

But the signals that P.S. Ney allegedly sent were mixed to be sure. Some eyewitnesses thought he said his wife had died (Aglaé in fact outlived P. S. Ney by eight years), and, in one instance, an eyewitness recalled his saying that his wife was living and kept a "house of entertainment" in Paris.[77] In nineteenth-century usage, a "house of entertainment" meant a tavern or a gambling salon—or worse.

Also, Mrs. Dalton recounted how P. S. Ney "said he had four children, used to tell the girls about his boys, never heard him say he had any daughters."[78] This coincides with an accurate description of the four sons Marshal Ney had by Aglaé. Again, how would P. S. Ney have known? And yet, P. S. Ney wrote of his "only" son (see below) and told others that he had one son and two daughters.

Finally, in his poetry, P. S. Ney referred to his wife as "Louise" or the name's English variant "Louisa." This was ostensibly the private name Marshal Ney used for his wife. How would P. S. Ney have known?

I. The Visits of a Son

Chapter 10 recounts eyewitness testimony concerning one or more visits by a person alleged to be P. S. Ney's son. Could this have been a visit by one of Marshal Ney's sons? The answer is, surprisingly, maybe.

In the Hoyt Collection, there is a letter to Dr. Lyman Draper dated September 2, 1886, from Houstonville, North Carolina. The signature page is missing, but it was almost certainly written by a son of Mrs. Mary C. Dalton of Houstonville. It describes two visits by a son of P. S. Ney. The first states, "I do not know how many times I have heard him [Ney] say he saw his son in Va, Soon after he came [to Houstonville] from Va., he related the circumstances to mother. Told her what he said to him—and described his person. My recollection is he had red hair, something like his own."[79]

Documentation in the Hoyt Collection establishes that P. S. Ney was resident in Mecklenburg County, Virginia, in 1828–1829.[80] Mecklenburg County is in south-central Virginia near the North Carolina border. It is a little-known fact that Eugène Ney, the third son of Marshal Ney, born in 1806, visited the United States at least twice: the first time in 1828–1829 and the second time in 1832–1833.[81] On his first visit, he was accompanied by Louis Napoleon Lannes, the Duke of Montebello. Eugène was sickly most of his life and was ill during his 1829 visit to the United States. He stayed with Joseph Bonaparte at Point Breeze in Bordentown, New Jersey, as evidenced by this letter written by Joseph dated Point Breeze, May 20, 1829:

> M. Eugène Ney sent me your letter of March 21, 1828, only a few months ago. He has been for a long time ill in Connecticut. He arrived here quite discouraged by the treatment he was subjected to at the hands of some country doctors. He planned to embark, ill as he was, to return to France. I have urged him not to judge all the doctors of the United States by those who treated him. He has consulted the two most skillful doctors of Philadelphia, who are both friends of mine, and they have assured me of his early recovery. He lives at my house where he finds at least tranquillity, a good atmosphere, and a paternal interest, in commemoration of that brave Marshal Ney that I knew so well in Spain. His son is such as you describe to me: he has love of the arts, the sciences, is pleasant and energetic. I want him to get well again soon, but to stay with me a long time.[82]

The ministrations of Joseph and his doctors must have worked, for several months later, Eugène considered heading south—for Virginia. On July 21, 1829, Charles Jared Ingersoll wrote a letter of introduction for him to President James Madison, who resided in Orange County, Virginia:

> Dear Sir—I have offered this letter of introduction to you to Count Ney son of the Marshal of that glorious name with whose

renown you are familiar—In addition to the associations suggested by it you will find in the bearer a most intelligent, unassuming and interesting young man whom I have ventured to promise at your house the cordial hospitality of American country life dispensed by the patriarch of our political institutions.[83]

Apparently, Eugène did not leave immediately because local newspapers mentioned his presence with Joseph Bonaparte at Saratoga Springs, New York, in mid-August 1829. However, he eventually did travel to Virginia and met with Madison because Madison's docket on Ingersoll's letter ("by Count Ney") indicates that Ney hand delivered the letter to Madison.[84] Where did they meet? A maritime record shows that Count Ney traveled from Charleston to Savannah aboard the steam packet *John D. Mongin*, arriving in Savannah on December 28, 1829 (interestingly, on this leg of his travels, one of his shipmates was Armand d'Otranto, the son of Joseph Fouché, who perhaps was accompanying him).[85] It is thus possible that Eugène Ney met with Madison at Montpelier sometime between late August and early October, when Madison moved to Richmond, Virginia, for a state constitutional convention and where Madison remained until January 1830. This would have resulted in a very leisurely trip indeed by Ney from Virginia to Charleston. More likely, Ney met with Madison in Richmond during the autumn of 1829, as did several other people bearing letters of introduction during this time period. If this is the case, it would have placed Ney within less than 100 miles of P. S. Ney in Mecklenburg County, Virginia, at the time the latter said he met with his son. P. S. Ney himself left Virginia by January 1, 1830. Dalton's description of P. S. Ney's alleged son who visited in 1829 as having red hair matches Eugène.

Eugène Ney visited the United States a second time in 1832–1833. He came first to the French islands off Canada, St. Pierre and Miquelon, and then made his way south. He visited his uncle "Citizen" Genêt at his home near Albany, New York, on the Hudson River before going farther south and eventually reaching the Deep South. He later wrote and published a travelogue based on parts of this trip. It is possible that he passed through North Carolina and could have met with P. S. Ney on this trip (thus arguably constituting the second meeting of P. S. Ney with his son), but he did not write on that aspect of it. Moreover, the eyewitness testimony about the alleged son who visited P. S. Ney in 1834–1835 describes him as having black hair and black eyes. None of the other sons of Marshal Ney other than Eugène is known to have visited the United States.

Eugène Ney enjoyed a diplomatic career that took him to postings in Brazil, Greece, and Italy. He had lifelong health problems and never married. Unfortunately, he died young on October 25, 1845. Both his life and his death are well documented.

J. Variants on the P. S. Ney Story

To complicate the assessment of whether P. S. Ney and Marshal Ney were the same person, three narratives arose concerning Marshal Ney, one of them as early as the 1790s. These stories involved (1) a supposed son of Marshal Ney and/or P. S. Ney named E. M. C. Neyman, (2) a totally separate legend that Marshal Ney was in fact an American named Michael Rudolph or Rudulph, and (3) an escape narrative focusing on Marshal Ney, Napoleon's second cousin Pascal Luciani, and General Lefebvre-Denouettes. The first and last of these stories warrant examination. The second can be dismissed out of hand.

i. E. M. C. Neyman

A respected local medical doctor living in Indiana named Ebenezer M. C. Neyman claimed to be the third son of Marshal Michel and Aglaé Ney.[86] As noted above, he could not have been Eugène Ney, the real third legitimate son of the marshal, whose life and death are amply accounted for by contemporary records.[87]

E. M. C. Neyman claimed to have been born in Paris on February 29, 1808, and to have come to the United States in 1821.[88] However, the 1850 census records for Brown Township, Washington County, Indiana, show an Ebenezer Neyman, physician, aged 35, born in New York (by implication in 1815), together with his wife Elizabeth, aged 27, and son Ebenezer, aged six months. Apparently, in 1860, he was living in Cass, Cedar County, Iowa, as the census for that year records an E. M. C. Neiman, physician, born in 1808 in New York. In contrast, the 1870 census for Saltillo, Brown Township, Washington County, Indiana, shows E. M. C. Neyman, physician, aged 61, born in Pennsylvania (by implication in 1809).[89] The 1880 census for the same place shows his birth as 1809 in Virginia. The 1890 census results were largely destroyed in a fire at the Department of Commerce in Washington, D.C. Finally, the 1900 census for the same place shows his name as Eugene (not Ebenezer) Neyman and his and his parents' birthplaces as France. At one point earlier in his life, in a Jefferson County, Indiana, indenture dated April 22, 1843, he styled himself Ebenezer McNimon and his wife as Elizabeth Neyman.[90] It seems that the facts of his birth—and even his name—were constantly shifting.

In a 1900 newspaper article, the aged Neyman sat down with Weston and two reporters to tell his story. Among other things, he alleged that Marshal Ney's execution was faked; that Ney escaped to England, "aided by powerful friends and passports furnished by the Duke of Wellington," and was befriended by the British pamphleteer and reformer William Cobbett, who "gave him letters to influential people in Baltimore and aided him to cross undetected to this country"; but that he kept his identity secret to protect those who had aided in his escape. Neyman further claimed that he himself came to the United States from France in 1821; that he met several times with P. S. Ney, who helped him financially; and that he served in the U.S. Army Eighth Infantry in the Seminole Wars (1835–1842), "in the expedition against the Mormons" (1857–1858), and in the Mexican War (1846–1848), in which he served under the pseudonym "Neyman."[91]

The author has been able to identify no records showing evidence of Marshal Ney in England, no records that Wellington assisted Ney (indeed quite to the contrary), no records connecting Cobbett with Marshal Ney, no records showing the arrival of Marshal Ney in Baltimore, no records confirming Neyman's arrival in 1821, and no U.S. military service records for Ney, Neyman, or McNimon in the three conflicts cited above (although the Eighth Infantry did fight in the Seminole and Mexican wars). However, the Joseph Smith Papers contain a "license" for Ebenezer M. C. Neyman dated May 30, 1841, signed by Smith, that "receives and ordains" Neyman as an elder in the Church of Jesus Christ of Latter-day Saints.[92] How this license is reconciled with his own statement that he later fought against the Mormons is one of the many mysteries surrounding E. M. C. Neyman.

Records also show E. M. C. Neyman to have been an 1836 graduate of Jefferson Medical College in Philadelphia.[93] He further claimed in various medical licensing documents to have apprenticed under Dr. James Rush (the son of Dr. Benjamin Rush, signer of the Declaration of Independence) in Philadelphia from 1828 to 1835, although, oddly, those documents make no mention of his attending or graduating from Jefferson Medical College and indeed in one case affirmatively state that he did not graduate from medical college, although the records at Jefferson Medical College show him as a graduate.[94]

Whenever and wherever he was born and whatever he called himself or whatever he did, he lived a long life, dying in 1909. His tombstone uses the 1808 birth date and states that he was the son of Marshal Ney. His 1909 Saltillo, Indiana, death certificate, based on information provided to the clerk by Gary C. Neyman (presumably his son or grandson), claims he was born in France and was the son of "Marshal Michael Ney" and "Aglae Louise Auguie." The certificate further states that his father Marshal Ney was born in Wachendorf, Wurtemburg, Germany, thus placing him in an alternate line of descent from Anton (grandfather) and Nicholas (father) Ney, a line of descent proposed by Weston but not accepted by any serious scholar of Marshal Ney's origins.

Neyman first appears in the P. S. Ney story when he arrived in North Carolina to claim P. S. Ney's body in 1876 with the intention of removing it to Indiana, stating not only that P. S. Ney was Marshal Ney and he was his son but also that P. S. Ney had visited him in Indiana, most likely in 1837, where he was recognized by an old Polish officer, Colonel Lehmanowsky, who had been in Napoleon's service.[95] A variant on this tale is that P. S. Ney lived in Indiana with his son shortly after he first arrived in the United States. How P. S. Ney, who by most accounts arrived in the United States in 1816, who was known to be in South Carolina in 1819–1820, and who was thereafter in the South the rest of his life, could have lived in Indiana with E. M. C. Neyman, who arrived only in 1821, is unexplained. In any event, the leaders of the Third Creek Presbyterian Church, where P. S. Ney was buried, refused his request to remove the body.

In Neyman's later life, when the story of a visit to P. S. Ney in North Carolina by his son surfaced, E. M. C. Neyman claimed (decades after the fact) that it was he who visited his father behind the haystack in North Carolina and that at that meeting his father had given him the money to attend medical school.[96] He offered no proof, but he said he had papers that would explain everything that would be released on his death. He died, but no papers were released.

Given the dearth of factual proof surrounding E. M. C. Neyman's claims, it is likely that he was an imposter. There remains some statistical chance that he was a biological son of P. S. Ney (but not necessarily of Marshal Ney). There also is some chance that he may have been the adopted son of Marshal Ney, whom the marshal saved on the retreat from Moscow (an 1808 birth date would roughly correspond for that individual). In this connection, it is perhaps significant that the name "Neyman" is a variant on the name "Nieman," which is the crucial river that Ney and the retreating French crossed, ensuring their passage out of Russia.[97] However, if the latter were the case, it is odd that E. M. C. Neyman named one of his daughters Aglaé after Marshal Ney's wife, who would not have been his mother. Again, the best reading based on currently available evidence is that E. M. C. Ney was an imposter. Why a respected local physician with nothing to gain from such an effort did it is an enduring mystery.

ii. Michael Rudolph

The legend of Michael Rudolph arose as early as the 1790s and appeared in American newspapers as early as 1823 if not before.[98] Rudolph was an American of German descent from Elkton, Maryland, who spoke German. He fought as an officer in the American Revolution under "Light Horse Harry" Lee but then disappeared. The theory was that he emigrated to France, enlisted in the French Revolutionary army, and became Marshal Ney.[99] It was apparently in the context of this legend that Marshal Grouchy was asked in 1819 if Marshal Ney spoke English. Not only is there no credible documentary evidence to support, much less prove, this theory, but his age would not correspond even remotely with that of Marshal Ney (Rudolph was born in 1758). The fact that Ney's military service is amply documented starting in 1787 while Rudolph resigned from the U.S. Army on July 17, 1793, should be dispositive. Despite some superficial similarities between the handwriting of Rudolph and P. S. Ney, this legend can almost certainly be discarded.

iii. The Ney/Lefebvre-Desnouettes/Luciani Escape

This variant on the Ney escape story is more complex and worthy of closer attention. It has the marshal escaping jointly with General Lefebvre-Desnouettes and Napoleon's cousin turned confectioner Pascal Luciani. It is based largely on an affidavit that Luciani's last surviving daughter, Victoria Arnold, provided to Smoot in 1926 when she was 86.[100] The gist of the story is that the unnamed parties who arranged Ney's escape also arranged exits for Lefebvre-Desnouettes and Luciani at the same time and that the three rode through the night to escape Paris (P. S. Ney often recollected how hard he rode 80 miles that night to escape Paris and the fine horse that had taken him), reached Bordeaux after five days, hid there another 12 days, and on December 26 embarked on a ship called *City of Philadelphia* with a cargo of skins for America. Ney traveled disguised as a servant or valet to the other two. Lefebvre-Desnouettes and Luciani disembarked at Philadelphia, and Ney continued on to Charleston, South Carolina, where he arrived on January 29, 1816. The story is replete with details such as that, on arriving at Bordeaux and awaiting boarding, the trio were so hungry that Luciani tried to buy food from a peasant by offering him the gold watch he had worn at Waterloo. Ney objected, saying, "Don't give him your watch—just give him the outer case," which was detachable. Mrs. Arnold testified that her daughter still had the watch minus its outer case. Mrs. Arnold further swore in her affidavit that "Marshall Ney was never executed, but died in North Carolina" and that her father had been in touch with P. S. Ney during his lifetime.[101]

Another detail in this legend is that P. S. Ney brought with him on the ship a handheld military compass in a polished wood case. When he entered the compass at U.S. Customs on arrival, the compass was stolen, leaving only the case. That case as well as a flute he purchased on arrival still exist and are in the collection of the library at Davidson College. The compass case bears the dates 1811 and 1816.[102] The inventory of personal effects that Marshal Ney prepared while incarcerated at the Conciergerie, cited earlier, shows a flute but no compass.

As noted in chapter 10, elements of this story came to light many years before Smoot or even Weston published their books. Those elements first appeared in the form of an interview published in 1874 in the Dayton (Ohio) *Journal* with a man named Philip Petrie, who alleged to have been a Bonapartist soldier turned French sailor on the ship from Bordeaux to Philadelphia. Shortly after getting under way, he halted on deck before the supposed valet.

"It seems to me I ought to know you," he said.

"For whom do you mistake me?"

"For my old commander Marshal Ney."

"Marshal Ney was executed in Paris a fortnight ago," the valet responded, and he returned to his cabin and never left it for the remainder of the voyage.

On reaching Charleston, the valet remained in his cabin until the too-curious sailor had gone ashore. After disembarking, the valet went to a café, where he found himself again face-to-face with the sailor. The sailor greeted him.

"Hello, Marshal Ney."

The man replied immediately, "I am not Marshal Ney. My name is Peter Stewart Ney."[103]

The Petrie story and the legend of the flight by the three men have elements of plausibility but can be proven to be at least partially in error. First, the port of Philadelphia maintained detailed crew lists that are extant for this period. A thorough examination of these records shows no crew man named Philip Petrie or any variant on that name. The records list the crews of all outward bound ships. Although Petrie was alleged to have joined the ship in Bordeaux, once the ship was in Philadelphia and embarked on its onward voyage to another port in America, such as Charleston, he should have been listed with the crew. He was not listed with the crew of any outbound ship from Philadelphia in 1816.[104] This absence renders uncorroborated the account provided by Petrie.

Second, the ever-vigilant French secret police had Lefebvre-Desnouettes under surveillance, and they believed him still to be in the country but plotting to escape via Le Havre. On January 6, 1816, the prefect of police in Paris wrote the mayor of Le Havre that he had given a passport to a M. Bidaut, a 19-year-old commission merchant, for travel from Le Havre to Louisiana. He advised that afterward he learned of Bidaut's "intimate connections" with Lefebvre-Desnouettes and that the purpose of his trip to Le Havre was to help Lefebvre-Desnouettes escape to Louisiana. He asked the mayor to look into it. In a reply letter dated February 6, 1816, the mayor reported on the surveillance he had ordered of Bidaut:

> Mr. Bidaut during his stay in this town and up to his departure on the 28th of the last month on the American ship *Minerve* destined for Louisiana went out very little and only associated with two or three passengers like himself who were lodged in the same hotel. His most habitual walks were along the docks and wharves, he was seen several times at the theater, several times he went to the offices of Messrs. LAHERE, DOREY and LE MAISTRE who were the ship agents with whom he had arranged passage and which are very well known, almost every day he received letters, in general he was little communicative and very reserved in his communications. No indications have given grounds to suspect that he was seeking to assist the ex-general Lefebvre-Desnouettes with whom he had here no contact.[105]

While the prefect of police awaited his response from the mayor, the police complained on January 19 that they were having difficulty maintaining active surveillance, and on February 3, the prefect of the Northern Department in Lille reported to the minister of police in response to an all-points bulletin issued by the minister on January 31 for the arrest of Lefebvre-Desnouettes along with three other fugitive generals. The prefect of the Northern Department reported that "Lefebvre-Desnouettes was for around two months in Aix-la-Chapelle [Aachen] but that he left for Anvers [Antwerp] with a false passport issued by a Prussian commandant. He said in Anvers that he had been offered service in Prussia. He embarked for America on the ship *Zoe*. I believe these facts perfectly certain, without however being officially investigated."[106]

He was correct. The manifest of *Zoe*, contained in the port of Philadelphia maritime records, shows *Zoe* arriving from Antwerp on April 6, 1816, and having as her sole passenger General "Desnotts, Lefebre."[107] He was traveling alone and, unusually for a fleeing Bonapartist, under his actual name. This record demolishes the myth that the three men traveled together.

But could Ney and Luciani have traveled together?

The Philadelphia port records for the first six months of 1816 show five ships arriving from Bordeaux: *Siro* (February 2), *John Howe* (February 29), *Hunter* (March 13), *Susquehanna* (May 1), and *Magnet* (May 4). A thorough search of those port records for ships named *City of Philadelphia*, *Minerve*, and *Ligonier* (the last of these being another rumored name of the escape vessel), as well as reasonable variants on those names, fails to reveal any corroborative information on arrival by ships of those names during the relevant time period, although there was a ship, *Philadelphia*, that arrived in Philadelphia at various times from 1800 to 1810, including once (in 1804) from Bordeaux.

John Howe, the second ship that arrived in Philadelphia from Bordeaux, docked on February 29 (vice January 29 in the legend) following a lengthy 61-day voyage[108] that would have placed her departure from France on December 31, not December 26 as in the legend. She was a 166-ton brig out of Philadelphia co-owned and captained by a Franco-American named Frederick Bousquet, who later in life became the U.S. consul at Cette (modern-day Sete) on the south coast of France. Interestingly, the manifest for *John Howe* (Fig. 11.5) shows two cabin passengers, L. Philippon with "two trunks, beds and bedding" and someone simply identified as "Vallette" traveling with him with "one bag containing his baggage and four gun barrels." There is a further notation on the manifest that in Philippon's "baggage bundle" were "2 fowling pieces, 18 vol. books, 14 [16?] engravings"[109]—an interesting collection of items with which to start out life in the United States, no doubt carried by most immigrants.

Attempts to find subsequent records of "L. Philippon" and "Vallette" in Philadelphia, including through a review of the Philadelphia City Directory, which lists the names and addresses of residents, from 1816 through 1820 shows no Philippons and no relevant Vallettes (as well as no Neys, McNees, or other variants on that name), even though it regularly lists other prominent Bonapartists, such as Joseph Bonaparte, Emmanuel Grouchy, and Henri Lallemand. Could Philippon and Vallette have been aliases? An examination of all the 1816 ship manifests

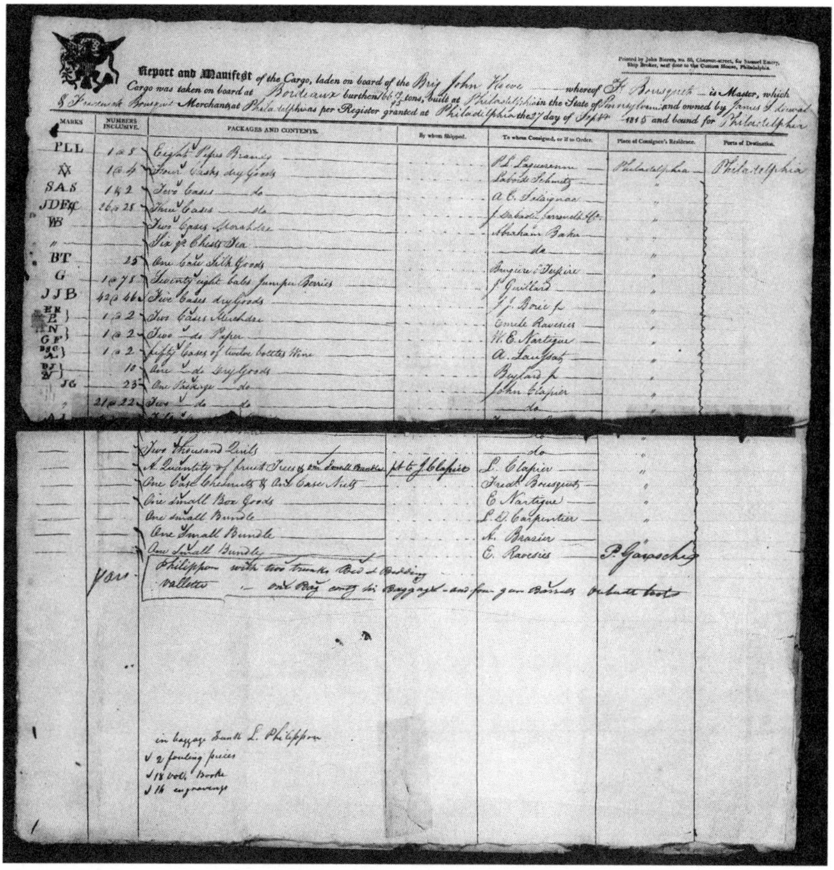

Figure 11.5. Ship's manifest for *John Howe* showing passengers "L. Philippon" and "Vallette," February 29, 1816. PHOTOGRAPH BY AUTHOR OF 1816 DOCUMENT IN HISTORICAL SOCIETY OF PENNSYLVANIA.

in the port records of Philadelphia shows no arriving passenger named Luciani. Was "L. Philippon" an alias used by Pascal Luciani? Ney allegedly traveled disguised as a valet, and the name of the notary for whom he worked as a young man was Vallette.

All coincidences? Maybe. Maybe not.

If "Philippon" were an alias, it was a name steeped in some irony. General Armand Philippon was a Bonapartist officer who served under Vandamme and was governor of Badajoz. He capitulated to the British and was taken to England. From there, he made a daring escape and, returning to France, broke his parole. A hero to the French, he was a blackguard to the British.

The Charleston port records commence only in 1820, which was the year after P. S. Ney was first seen in South Carolina, but a review of those records for 1820 shows no evidence of the arrival of a Ney, McNee, Nieman, Niebourg, or any of the other obvious variants on the name. A daily local newspaper, the *Charleston Courier*, reported in detail on ship arrivals, however, often listing the names of passengers who disembarked at the busy port of Charleston. A review of its reporting from January 24 through May 10, 1816,[110] shows neither any of the above-named ships nor any passengers bearing the above names arriving at Charleston from Bordeaux or Philadelphia. It does report the January 30, 1816, arrival of the British ship *Mary*, sailing from Liverpool and Kinsale, Ireland, carrying as passengers "Messrs. McGill, Mulligan, O'Neil and *Stewart*" (emphasis added).[111] However, there is nothing to link this Stewart with P. S. Ney.

Despite this lack of explicit evidence as to Charleston, there are indications that *John Howe* continued southward after stopping in Philadelphia. The *Charleston Courier* on May 8, 1816, contains a May 4 notice that the "brig John Howe, Bouquet, Bordeaux" was cleared at Savannah (however, an examination of the Charleston shipping reports in the same newspaper from January 24 through May 10 fails to show an entry by the ship at Charleston).[112] Further, a newspaper article dated August 8, 1816, reports the arrival of *John Howe* of Philadelphia from Savannah (the article is unclear at which port she was arriving, but it appears to be either Philadelphia or New York).[113] Moreover, an article from the previous year reported on *John Howe* voyaging from New Orleans with a cargo of cotton bound for Bordeaux but having put into New York in distress.[114] Thus, there was a pattern of *John Howe* including a southern leg on her voyages, and it is conceivable that she put into Charleston en route to Savannah in 1816. However, at this stage, the part of the story that holds that P. S. Ney continued on to Charleston after landing in Philadelphia cannot be corroborated. This lack of corroboration in turn possibly may support Hoyt's theory that P. S. Ney was in fact in or around Philadelphia after his initial arrival in the United States and came to South Carolina only in 1819.[115]

K. Colonel Lehmanowsky

Colonel John Jacob Lehmanowsky (1773 [1776?]–1858) was born in Warsaw, Poland, the son of a Jewish father and a French mother. His father was a chemist, and Lehmanowsky was well educated. He went to France to study medicine and converted to Christianity while at university. He became wrapped up in the French Revolution and joined the French Revolutionary army in 1793. He fought in many campaigns, including on the Iberian Peninsula and in Russia, often under Marshal Ney's command. He later claimed to have fought in more than 200 engagements and to have been wounded 14 times.[116] He bore a highly visible saber scar across his cheek. Serving under the surname "Lehman," he rose through the ranks of the Polish lancer regiments in that army. As of July 23, 1814 (some two months after the first exile of Napoleon), his service record shows him as a major in the Ninth Polish Lancers. When he was promoted to colonel is unclear, but it may have been during the Hundred Days of Napoleon's return from exile.

Based on his own uncorroborated account of his life (which may have been embroidered), he was captured by the Bourbons in the wake of Waterloo, imprisoned at the same facility as Ney (presumably La Conciergerie), and sentenced to be shot on December 8, 1815, the day after Ney.[117] The night before he was scheduled to be executed, a sympathizer smuggled him a file hidden in a cake. He used the file to remove an iron grill in a window, and he escaped by an improvised rope made of bed blankets. When challenged by a guard outside the prison, he instructed the guard, "Do your duty." The guard, who knew him, let him pass. Although pursued by the authorities, he evaded them and ultimately made his way to America.

He claimed to have been in the United States as early as 1816 and to have married Maria Salomé Halter in Philadelphia in 1819. While this may be true, there is scant evidence of his early years in America. If true, he and his family returned to Europe and then came back to America, for port records show that he arrived in New York on August 27, 1822, aboard the ship *Packet* from London, as confirmed by that ship's manifest, which describes him as "J. Lehmanouskey," age 46 and a "late officer of the French army." It also describes him as being 6 feet 2 inches tall and having a "dark complexion, brown hair, [illegible word] walk, scar on left cheek."[118] The manifest appears to but does not definitively show him to be accompanied by a 27-year-old woman whose name is illegible and a three-year-old girl named "Annetta." It separately but definitively shows at the end of the manifest that he was accompanied by his "infant" son "Louis Lehmanouskey."

Operating initially under the surname "Lehman," Lehmanowsky struggled in the early 1820s to make a living in and around New York and Philadelphia as an instructor of fencing and European languages. He moved to Washington, D.C., where in 1824–1825 he taught French at Columbian College. He subsequently held a political appointment at the Post Office Department in Washington. Not only was he impecunious, but his wife's health was delicate, and he had the added burden of caring for his brother Louis, who had escaped from slavery under the Turks but was a broken man. Lafayette, who was a friendly acquaintance, purportedly gave him $1,000. Using this money and some other funds, Lehmanowsky moved west and eventually settled at Knightstown, Indiana, where he raised his children. His wife Maria died there, and he married a woman much younger than himself by whom he had yet more children.

On October 5, 1836, Lehmanowsky was ordained a Lutheran pastor. He served a circuit in rural Indiana and traveled the state preaching. He also gained fame as a lecturer on the Napoleonic Wars. He traveled all over the United States giving well-received talks on the empress Josephine, Napoleon, and his own roles in the various wars. It was during one of these trips in 1842 that Dr. J. R. B. Adams met him in Alabama and discussed Marshal Ney. While in St. Louis, Missouri, on a later lecture tour in 1849, a daguerreotype was taken of Lehmanowsky (figure 11.6). One of the few surviving photographs of a Napoleonic officer, it shows a striking-looking man.

Lehmanowsky told Dr. Adams in 1842 that he had not seen Marshal Ney but would instantly recognize him if he did. According to Lehmanowsky's family, this is exactly what occurred shortly thereafter. In a 1900

Figure 11.6. Colonel John Jacob Lehmanowsky of the 9th Polish Lancers. MISSOURI HISTORICAL SOCIETY.

interview, Lehmanowsky's daughter Mrs. Nicholas Reising explained what happened:

> It was either in 1843 or 1844. We were seated on the front porch at our old home in Knightstown, when an aged man of powerful build came along the walk, and my father, Col. J. J. Lehmanowsky, of France's famous Old Guard, marked from afar his majestic bearing. My father was before Toulon with Napoleon . . . and later became one of his aids [*sic*]. . . . With Grand Marshal Ney he covered the retreat from Moscow, and again with Ney . . . he made the last stand of the Old Guard on the plain of Waterloo. . . .
>
> As I was saying, we were on the porch of our old Knightstown home when an aged man came along the walk. He seemed to be looking for some house. As he neared our home his face lit up with a smile. My father jumped to his feet, ran out and grasped him in his arms and they hugged and kissed each other and probably cried.
>
> I was only six years old at the time and my brother Martin . . . was only a little older, but we both remember the scene as though it were only a week ago instead of over a half century ago. The stranger was Grand Marshal Ney of France. He stayed at our home over night and he and my father sat up almost until morning talking.

In making the above statements, Mrs. Reising acknowledged that "anyone who raises a voice against the old story that Ney was executed back in the Luxemburg gardens meets with disapproval."[119]

Mrs. Reising also stated in the interview that her father included the story of the meeting in an autobiography that he wrote but that the manuscript mysteriously disappeared after he sent it to a publisher for printing.

Mrs. Reising's account of the meeting with Marshal Ney was repeated by her granddaughter Christine A. Reising in a letter to *Time* magazine published on September 21, 1936.[120] In that letter, she said she often heard her grandmother speak of the incident, and she added the detail that her grandmother had said that Lehmanowsky and Ney "talked in French" when they met. She also stated that "not until the gentleman had gone the next day did her father [Lehmanowsky] tell certain members of the family that their guest was none other than Marshal Ney but that the secret must not be revealed to anyone."

Can this story ever be corroborated? Probably not, but there it is, laid out by seemingly credible witnesses—Lehmanowsky's daughter and granddaughter.

L. The Royal Pardon of 1830

Skeptics of P. S. Ney's authenticity have argued that he was free to return to France by virtue of King Louis Philippe's ordinance of August 26, 1830, which "annulled all condemnations pronounced after July 7, 1815 for political offenses."[121] The decree was published widely in the United States and would almost certainly have been known to P. S. Ney. The problem with this expansive reading of the ordinance is that the actual text is more ambiguous and is susceptible to divergent readings. The relevant portion of the decree states, "Article First. The judgments, decisions and adjudications rendered, either in France or the colonies, by royal courts, assize courts, courts of criminal justice, provostal courts, military commissions, courts martial and other ordinary or extraordinary jurisdictions, because of political acts, from the 7th of July, 1815, to this day, shall cease to be effective."

The problems are twofold. First, although the Chamber of Peers might arguably be an "extraordinary jurisdiction," there is no definition of that term in the ordinance, and the Chamber of Peers is not specifically enumerated in Article 1 as a covered court.

Second, Marshal Ney was convicted of violating the Military Convention of July 3, 1815, which predated the July 7 trigger date, even though his conviction itself postdated the trigger date.[122] This should not have been an impediment to application of the pardon to Ney, but it might have raised a question in the mind of an overly cautious refugee. There also is the interesting question of how a dead person could have his decease "cease to be effective."

In any case, the wording of the decree may have been sufficiently ambiguous so as not to provide adequate comfort to an exiled Ney to spur him to risk his life by a return to France. That this may plausibly have been the case is underscored by P. S. Ney's comments as recorded in an affidavit dated March 17, 1927, by Edmond P. Graham, son of Dr. Thomas D. Graham of Iredell County, North Carolina, who attended P. S. Ney in his final illness and death. Although Edmond was born in 1866 some 20 years after P. S. Ney's death and never personally knew P. S. Ney, he obviously was attesting to stories passed on by his father. According to Graham, "A few days prior to" P. S. Ney's final illness and death, he received a letter that he opened and read. He said it was from his wife. "He wept saying 'My wife has written to me to come home—that I have been pardoned.' Ney then said: 'Old Ney is not going—I am afraid it is a trap.'"[123]

If this incident occurred in 1846 shortly before he died, this would have been very late notice indeed of the 1830 pardon. More likely, it occurred earlier (P. S. Ney was in fact in or around Iredell County, North Carolina, in 1830) and may help to explain P. S. Ney's particularly dramatic reaction on the death of Napoleon's son in 1832. It is evident that P. S. Ney did not trust the 1830 pardon for whatever reason and that he believed he could safely return to France only if a Bonaparte were on the throne. The fact that a number of high-profile Bonapartist refugees took advantage of the pardon and returned to France seemed to make little impression on him.

M. Practical Questions

In addition to the above factors, several practical questions demand answers. First, if P. S. Ney were afraid for his safety and felt the need for an alias, why did he retain the surname "Ney"? Surely, that choice fooled no one and only drew attention to him as the purported refugee marshal. Second, Marshal Ney was known to have contemplated living with his kinsman Edmond-Charles "Citizen" Genêt near Albany, New York. Similarly, his final escape plan to the United States called for him to stay with the Pontalba family in New Orleans. If Marshal Ney escaped to America, why did he not do either? There is no record of P. S. Ney calling on or staying with either Genêt or the Pontalbas, and there is probably a reason why he did not: they would have recognized him not to be the marshal. Indeed, in 1896, in the immediate aftermath of the publication of Weston's book, George Clinton Genêt, the sole surviving son of "Citizen" Genêt, wrote an article in which he expressly disavowed P. S. Ney. Among the reasons he cited were a lack of similarity in the handwriting of the two Neys and the 1832 visit by Eugène Ney to Genêt's father, during which it was apparently evident that he "never heard of this alleged Duke of Elchingen." Genêt also stated tantalizingly in the article that "Ney was offered an opportunity to escape, but he refused." He provided no further explanation of or authority for this statement.[124]

N. The Citizenship "Report"

One of the most probative pieces of evidence that P. S. Ney was not Marshal Ney is a "report" that P. S. Ney submitted to South Carolina authorities in March 1820 in connection with a prospective application for U.S. citizenship. The document, possibly (but maybe not) in P. S. Ney's handwriting and signed by him, still exists.[125] It reads in relevant part,

> I, Peter Stewart Ney, do hereby Report myself to you and notify my sincere desire and intention of becoming a Bona fide citizen of the United States of North America.
>
> I was born in Sterling Shire [*sic*] Scotland Ano 1787 subject to H. Britannic Majesty, Emigrated from Britain.
>
> My intention is to reside in Marlborough Dist. So. Carolina.
>
> [Signed] Peter Stewart Ney[126]

Ney submitted the "report" early in his sojourn in the United States and before the Marshal Ney narrative began to take hold. It was, moreover, consistent with the more or less contemporary statements of Archibald D. Murphey, one of his early sponsors (and Hoyt's ancestor), who wrote in a letter dated August 22, 1827 to Colonel William Polk, "I wrote to you that I had engaged a Gentleman to assist me in the Military Part of the Work in which I am engaged. I was misinformed as to his Character. He is not a Frenchman, but a well educated, intelligent Scotsman by Birth, who did not go to the Continent Untill he was eighteen Years of Age. His name is

Ney, and he was recommended to me as the Relative of Marshal Ney. He tells me he is not a Relative. He has been a good deal in Service."[127]

The "report" would be dispositive of the question of P. S. Ney's origins unless it contained a lie. The "report" was made pursuant to Section 2 of the naturalization law of 1802. Despite significant research by Hoyt, he was never able to locate (1) his declaration of intention made on oath before a court, as required by the first condition of Section 1 of the naturalization law of 1802; (2) his oath of allegiance, also made before a court, as required by the second condition of that section; or (3) a court order or judgment admitting him to citizenship, as required by the third condition of that section and by the act of March 22, 1816. Accordingly, Hoyt concluded that Ney never became naturalized, although his name appeared on the voting list of 1825 for Rowan County, North Carolina. Hoyt speculated, "Perhaps Ney gave up the idea of getting naturalized because a declaration of intention under a fictitious name would be invalid."[128]

Moreover, under U.S. naturalization law at the time, he would have to have formally renounced all foreign allegiances to become a U.S. citizen. Marshal Ney made clear at numerous points that he would never renounce his French citizenship and even refused to allow his counsel to argue at his trial that he was not French because his birthplace had ceased to be in France.

An alternative interpretation of why P. S. Ney might have held himself out to be a Scot during his first decade in the United States is that he would have felt the need to live under an alias because of a genuine fear of assassination but that, as he became more comfortable about his safety in remote rural areas of America and as he was increasingly recognized as Marshal Ney, he grew lax in maintaining the alias, especially when under the influence of drink.[129] The example of Joseph Bonaparte living under an alias when initially in the United States is perhaps instructive on this point.

Finally, P. S. Ney misspelled "Stirlingshire" in the "report." This was not the kind of mistake that P. S. Ney commonly made, especially on a legal document, thereby suggesting that he possibly may not have been a Scot, who surely would have spelled correctly the shire of his birth.

Thus, even one of the most dispositive pieces of evidence as to P. S. Ney's origin can be examined critically—if hypothetically—at the end of the day.

O. The Forensic Handwriting Analyses

Weston engaged a handwriting expert from New York to compare the writing of Marshal Ney and P. S. Ney in connection with his 1895 book. The expert concluded that they were the same. Two subsequent examinations by other experts (including one with the Secret Service) reached the same conclusion. Then, in 1952, Hoyt engaged three French forensic handwriting experts from the Court of Appeal and the Tribunal of the Seine to review the work of the prior analysts and to examine de novo a large sampling of the written works by both Marshal Ney and P. S. Ney. They examined scores of documents from each person, including some 38 signed by Marshal Ney and 13 signed by P. S. Ney. To cite but two of the many examples of their analysis, not only did they find that Marshal Ney formed the initial stroke of the capital "N" in his name in a Gothic (i.e., German) manner, which P. S. Ney did not, they also concluded that P. S. Ney's formation of the letter "e" in his name was done in an English manner that was unknown to Marshal Ney. Their exceptionally thorough and detailed report is devastating to any theory that the two men were the same. Their conclusion reads, "The three experts, unanimously, are of opinion that the above described documents of Peter Stewart Ney do not emanate from the same hand as those of Michel Ney, the Marshal of the Empire."[130] Unless forensic handwriting analysis has materially changed since 1952, their conclusions remain the final word based on forensic handwriting analysis: the two Neys were different people.

P. Other Approaches

Modern tools for cracking the Marshal Ney/P. S. Ney enigma are unfortunately of no help. DNA analysis would be an obvious avenue. Marshal Ney is not known to have any living descendants, his last heir seemingly having died in 2006. However, a purported lock of Marshal Ney's hair exists. On June 20, 2012, the reputable Parisian auction house of Binoche et Giquello auctioned a number of Ney family items, including a framed lock of Ney's reddish-brown hair, allegedly cut "at the place of execution." The provenance states that its ownership was not known from 1815 to 1855, when it was acquired by a Parisian picture dealer. He sold it to Marshal Ney's fourth and youngest son in 1855, and it passed down through the family until the last Ney heir died in 2006. At the auction, the lock of hair went for 1,600 euros. Other personal items of Ney, such as portraits, medals, and uniforms, went for much more significant sums. The provenance says the lock was possibly cut by the National Guardsman Pelletier when he visited the body at the Maternité right after the execution.[131] This is doubtful, as Pelletier's account shows that he saw the body only at a distance. More likely would have been Ney's brother-in-law Gamot, his steward Rayot, one of the attending nuns, or even Ida "La Contemporaine" Saint-Elme. On the other side of the DNA equation, P. S. Ney's body was so badly decomposed when it was disinterred that recovering any useful DNA to conduct a test would be most unlikely.

Apart from its potential DNA value, the lock of hair has other possible relevance to the question at hand: assuming it is genuine, why would anyone have cut it if Ney were not in fact dead?

Another line of approach might be to apply text analysis software to examine the writings of each man. However, the exemplars of Marshal Ney's writing are in French, while P. S. Ney's are almost all in English or Latin, so a comparison of words and word structures would be most difficult if not impossible.

Q. The Bottom Line

Both P. S. Ney and Marshal Ney bore physical and personality resemblances that were remarkable, inducing a long line of eyewitnesses to think they were the same person. In addition, on occasion, P. S. Ney exhibited intimate knowledge of Marshal Ney's family. In some instances, P. S. Ney had talents that were not visible in Marshal Ney in his life as a soldier in Europe, but they plausibly could have been cultivated once he fled to the United States if indeed he did flee to the United States. P. S. Ney's Bonapartism was seemingly more passionate and uncritical than the marshal's. All that said, the citizenship "report" and 1952 forensic handwriting analysis—unless convincingly rebutted— present major obstacles to concluding that they were the same person. Additionally, if accurate, Rochechouart's statement (discussed in note 9) that Ney fell on his back when executed would tend to discredit the burst bladder theory.

But these conclusions are only the beginning—not the end—of the mystery of P. S. Ney.

3. DID P. S. NEY HAVE AN IDENTITY OTHER THAN THE MARSHAL BEFORE 1815?

With this question, the analytical model collapses. We now come to what is perhaps the greatest mystery of all: if he were not Marshal Ney, who was P. S. Ney?

A. Treaty of Amiens and Service in the French Army

If one accepts the 1827 statement of Archibald D. Murphey that P. S. Ney was a well-educated Scot who first went to France with his father at age 18 and if one accepts 1787 as his birth year as stated in the "report," that would mean that he went to France in 1805. This is highly unlikely for the following reasons. Prior to the Treaty of Amiens of March 1802, British subjects were prohibited by law from traveling to France and had been so barred since the Revolution in 1789. Even allowing for the occasional exception or scofflaw—and, of course, the "damned elusive" Scarlet Pimpernel—there was effectively no cross-Channel travel. Accordingly, by the time of the Treaty of Amiens, there was considerable pent-up curiosity about and demand for travel to France. The treaty opened France to British travel, and thousands of Britons took advantage of it to go to France. Fortunately for the historical record, both the U.K. government and the French police kept close tabs on the British visitors. It was a veritable cavalcade of peers, members of Parliament, soldiers, businessmen, intellectuals, adventurers, and scoundrels. Based on these records, which were collected and published in 1904 by John Goldworth Alger in *Napoleon's British Visitors and Captives 1801–1815*, it is possible to know the identities of thousands of British who went to France during the thaw in relations offered by the treaty. None of them appears to be an obvious match for the profile of P. S. Ney, even assuming that "Ney" was not the name he used at the time. This is especially so in the matter of his purported service in the French army. There were a few instances of service by Irish expatriates in the French army. A good example is William Tone, the son of the Irish nationalist T. Wolfe Tone, who went to France with his father in 1796 (from Philadelphia, thus avoiding the ban on travel from the United Kingdom), served in Napoleon's army, fought at Waterloo, and then returned to America (he was not P. S. Ney, however, as both his life and early death in America are well recorded). Moreover, the respite provided by the Treaty of Amiens was short lived. By May 1803, Britain and France were back at war with one another. With few exceptions, Napoleon interned all British subjects in various cities around France, especially Verdun, for the duration of the hostilities. They were not serving in Napoleon's army and, it is probably safe to say, not pleased with Napoleon's action in interning them. The logical conclusions to draw from this background are that (1) it is highly unlikely P. S. Ney went to France in 1805; (2) if he went to France, it was more likely in 1802–1803; (3) if he were 18 at the time, that would place his birth year at 1784 or 1785, not 1787 as stated in the "report"; and (4) it is unlikely he served in the French army if his going to France were in this time frame because he would have been interned. However, if one accepts an earlier birth year for P. S. Ney, such as 1769 (being the birth year of Marshal Ney), it would be plausible for him to have gone to France at age 18 in the last several years of the ancien régime, to have stayed, and to have served in Napoleon's army. Hoyt examined the rosters of Bonaparte's "Irish Regiment" and found a Peter McNee born in Cork in 1790, but he would not appear to be a match for P. S. Ney because of his place and date of birth.

B. The Scots Candidates

Years of research on the question of P. S. Ney's true identity led Hoyt to conclude that the person who called himself P. S. Ney may have been one Peter McNee, born of apparently modest origins in 1787 and baptized on February 3, 1788, in Fintry, Stirlingshire, Scotland. According to the baptismal records, his father was "John McCnee" or McNee and his mother "Isbal Stewart." The parents were apparently originally from Balquhidder, Perthshire, where they were married and had three children before moving to Fintry, where their son Peter was born. Based on the 1787/1788 birth date, modern genealogical data bases show that this son might have been one of two people, neither of whom could have been P. S. Ney. The first was a Peter McNie (the records use this spelling interchangeably with McNee and McCnee; for example, the Balquhidder marriage records name his putative father as "John M'Nie"). He appears to have grown up to be an innkeeper in Gargunnock, less than 10 miles up the road from Fintry. He died on June 26, 1847, at age 59, thus having been born in 1787–1788. The second and less likely candidate is a Peter McNee baptized on February 2, 1788, in Port of Menteith, Perthshire, which borders on Stirlingshire. He is shown in the 1871 census as a retired farmer, age 83. He died in Port of Menteith on April 1, 1877.[132] Hoyt apparently did not see the records of the innkeeper in Gargunnoch or the farmer in Port of Menteith.

But, even assuming the above were not the case, there are other problems with Hoyt's Peter McNee. Although P. S. Ney often said his mother was named Stewart, he also said her name was Catharine or Catharine Isabella, not Isbal, and, as seen in chapter 10, he even wrote an acrostic on the name Catharine for an acquaintance who named her daughter Catharine after his mother. In addition, Peter McNee would have been 18 years younger than Marshal Ney, surely a sufficient age gap to have raised questions in the scores of eyewitnesses who believed him to be the marshal. Eighteen years is a significant gap; it is hard to envision a 32-year-old passing himself off as a 50-year-old, which is what P. S. Ney would have been doing under this theory when he first became known in 1819. Although some people who knew him thought he looked "somewhat younger" than the marshal might look, the overwhelming bulk of those who commented on his age (Gaither, Gay, Cain, Foote, and Graham) all placed him squarely within a close date range that would have been appropriate to the known birth date of Marshal Ney.[133] The fact that Peter McNee's 1788 baptism date almost coincides with the 1787 birth date on P. S. Ney's citizenship "report" is puzzling. It can be read two ways: (1) that it confirms he was really born in 1787 because he would not have lied to the court and he would not have fooled the court as to his age when he appeared before it to complete the citizenship process or (2) that he was lying about his age and never completed the citizenship process because he could not continue to deceive the court as to his age and identity.

Moreover, the Peter McNee theory failed to gain traction when Hoyt tried to establish what McNee did from 1787 to 1820. It was not for want of trying. He undertook to trace him through the descendants of the McNee family (under several spellings) and in the records of Scottish academic institutions. He searched the muster rolls of the British army, especially those involved in the Peninsular War (in which the young Peter McNee might have fought), but neither of the two Peter McNees he identified on those rolls was born in Stirlingshire. In short, the academic and army records produced nothing relevant. Again, the probable reason was that he was running an inn in Gargunnock.

Finally, there is something wrong both with the Scottish soldiers identified by Hoyt and with the Peter McNee baptized in Fintry, Scotland. The Scottish soldiers named McNee or McNie flagged by Hoyt were rank-and-file. For example, one such McNee is shown in the pay records at the Public Records Office in London as a private in the 91st Foot doing depot garrison duty in Glasgow in 1804–1817.[134] However, a Private Peter Mcnee [*sic*] did receive a Waterloo Medal for having fought at the battle of Waterloo.[135] Both the two soldier Peter McNees discussed above and the Peter McNee, son of a farmer, baptized at Fintry in 1788, do not square with what is so glaringly obvious about P. S. Ney: the latter was simply too smart, well educated, and sophisticated to match the profiles of those candidates. Like some of them, he may have served in the Napoleonic Wars, but he almost certainly would have been at least a sergeant and more likely an officer and possibly a well-placed one at that. He also was reported to be an expert horseman and swordsman, which most enlisted foot soldiers and farmers were not.

Expanding the analytical framework in Scotland beyond the names Ney, McNie, Stewart, and variants thereof, an examination of the ScotlandsPeople database shows some 237 Catharine or Isobel Stewarts or Stuarts (with the usual variants on those names) who married in Scotland between 1765 and 1795.[136] Of these, only a handful were in Stirlingshire. An even smaller number of these are recorded in the baptismal records as being a parent to a son born during this time frame. None of these sons born in Stirlingshire is listed in the *Waterloo Roll Call*. The broader list contained in the *Waterloo Medal Book*, which includes enlisted men, shows two possible matches for sons named Peter born of the above women. The first is a Private Peter Stewart of the 92nd Highlanders.

However, he is recorded as having settled in Banff, Scotland, and lived to an old age. The second is Private Peter Wright of the 95th Regiment of Foot. However, the Peter Wright shown in the ScotlandsPeople database was born on July 30, 1776, in Callander, Perthshire, not Stirlingshire—albeit close to the border between Perthshire and Stirlingshire. He may well be the Peter Wright who died at age 70 on January 14, 1847, at Stirling.

Likewise, attacking the mystery through P. S. Ney's supposed wife named Louisa, there were some 95 women named Louisa who are recorded as having married in Scotland between 1785 and 1816 (which would be a reasonable suppositional range of dates for P. S. Ney to have married). Of these, only one was in Stirlingshire, and she was not married to a husband named Ney or Stewart (or any variants thereof). Three in other counties were marriages with military officers. None of them matches with P. S. Ney because they either are not listed as having fought at Waterloo or had subsequent careers that are documented.

It may be noteworthy that a number of eyewitnesses recalled that P. S. Ney often spoke warmly about his mother but never spoke about his father. This raises the question of whether he might have been an illegitimate son who was raised by his mother. Under this scenario, without knowing his father's name, it is impossible to trace who he might be. A review of the above records for a single mother named Stewart or Stuart with a son produces no matches.

However, there are three further (albeit remote) possibilities. First, interestingly, for unstated reasons, Draper asked a number of eyewitnesses to compare a photograph of the Scots peer James Bruce, the Eighth Earl of Elgin (1811–1863), with their memory of P. S. Ney. Most found them similar but noted some differences, generally finding P. S. Ney to have been more martial in appearance. Bruce's father, the Seventh Earl Thomas Bruce (1766–1841) (of the Elgin Marbles fame), studied in France before the French Revolution, married for the first time at the then advanced age of 31, was interned by Napoleon in France with the collapse of the Peace of Amiens, and died in Paris many years later. Might he, as a young man, have been P. S. Ney's father? The author has been unable to find any unequivocal link between the two.

Second, P. S. Ney told at least one eyewitness that "his mother was connected with a family of Stuarts who lived in Scotland, not far from the residence of Sir James Graham."[137] The reference to Sir James Graham almost certainly was to Sir James Graham, Second Baronet Graham of Netherby (1792–1861), who was First Lord of the Admiralty and later Home Secretary. Some scholars have interpreted the reference to be to John de Graeme, who had a castle near Fintry, Scotland.[138] However, John de Graeme, who lived in the thirteenth century, was not P. S. Ney's prominent contemporary Sir James Graham, to whom he no doubt was referring.

The Second Baronet's mother was Lady Catharine Stewart (1765–1836), daughter of John Stewart, the Seventh Earl of Galloway, who married Sir James Graham (1761–1824), First Baronet Graham of Netherby, in 1785. The Second Baronet lived at his castle Netherby, in Arthuret, Cumbria, bordering Scotland. Lady Catharine Stewart's father, the Seventh Earl of Galloway, lived about 40 miles away at Wigtown, Dumfries and Galloway, Scotland (none of these locations is in or near Stirlingshire). John Stewart, the Seventh Earl of Galloway, apparently had a sister named Lady Catharine Stewart, who was born circa 1750 (and died 1799?) and about whom almost nothing is known. She disappeared from the records, leaving no evidence of a marriage or death, which is uncharacteristic for a member of the peerage. Might P. S. Ney have been the illegitimate son of this Lady Catharine Stewart who was a member of the Stewarts who lived near Sir James Graham? As with the Elgins, the connection is attenuated at best and there is no evident concrete proof to link either her or her niece Lady Catharine Stewart Graham with P. S. Ney.[139]

Third, a branch of the Stewart family of Balquhidder, Perthshire, settled at Cheraw, Marlborough District, South Carolina, in the 1760s.[140] On September 14, 1819, one Peter Stewart arrived in Philadelphia as a passenger, alone and without family, on the ship *Nancy* from London.[141] The ship's manifest showed him as bringing "1 Box & bedding, 5 Boxes, 1 Portmanteau, Numerous empty casks, bowles [*sic*], sundry cooking utensils, provisions and sea stores."[142] It will be recalled that P. S. Ney had a large trunk or portmanteau and that he took up his first teaching post at Cheraw, Marlborough District in the "early fall" of 1819, which presumably would have allowed time to travel by sea from Philadelphia to South Carolina soon after his arrival on September 14. Examining the 1820 Philadelphia City Directory, it is evident that this Peter Stewart did not linger in Philadelphia (the two Peter Stewarts, one a long-standing resident of Plumstead, Bucks County, and the other with wife and children, are distinguishable from the newly arrived Peter Stewart). Could it be that P. S. Ney was a Stewart of Balquhidder who arrived in 1819, not 1816, and traveled to South Carolina to join relatives who lived in the exact spot of his first teaching post? Unfortunately, beyond the presence of both Balquhidder Stewarts and P. S. Ney in Cheraw, Marlborough District, there is nothing definitive to link this 1819 emigrant with P. S. Ney, with the Balquhidder Stewarts, or with prior service in the Napoleonic Wars. Furthermore, a review of the Balquhidder baptismal records shows no Peter Stewart between 1765 and 1790.

Accordingly, it is virtually impossible to document a birth in Scotland for the man who called himself P. S. Ney.

C. Did P. S. Ney Serve as an Officer in the British Army?

A French historian who examined the mystery in 1935, René Arnaud, likewise could not pin down who P. S. Ney really was. However, based on various statements by P. S. Ney about the Napoleonic campaigns, he concluded, "All this happened as if he had seen it himself but on the English side." He explained, "Such is the case in the story of the battle of Albuera in 1811, in his calling the battle of Moskva *Borodino*, in his recollections of the words spoken by Wellington at Waterloo while he was waiting for Blücher, and the very fact that he detested Wellington could be another proof—that he served Wellington."[143]

It is an interesting theory if one accepts that P. S. Ney was not the marshal. However, an examination by the author of the available British Army Lists for 1811–1812, 1814, and 1816–1820 (there was no 1815 edition available) identifies at least six Peter Stewarts or Stuarts as officers and no Neys, McNees, or McNies or variants thereof.[144] Of the six Peter Stewarts or Stuarts, most are accounted for in the historical record, and none evidences any likelihood of being P. S. Ney. A similar review by the author of British Army and Royal Navy officers' records at the U.K. National Archives for the relevant period produced no valid matches for Peter Ney, Peter Stuart (Stewart), Peter McNee, or Peter McNie.

Finally, a thorough review of the lists of officers who fought in all British regiments at Waterloo contained in the *Waterloo Roll Call*, which also annotates their lives after the battle, shows a few who went on half pay soon after the battle or otherwise disappeared from the historical record. Although several had the surname "Stewart," none of them bore the first name "Peter" or convincingly can be associated with P. S. Ney.[145]

D. The Huguenot Candidate

The documents in the Hoyt Collection also show French police reports on a Protestant minister named Pierre Née from Mézières-en-Drouais who had gone to Paris to study medicine and was arrested in May 1816 by the Bourbon government as a Bonapartist. He escaped from the police,[146] but further research showed him to have died in Mézières in 1856.[147]

E. Further Speculation

Hoyt also looked for evidence of the arrival of P. S. Ney/Peter McNee in the United States and of his naturalization but found nothing. At the end of the day, Hoyt concluded, albeit speculatively, that the man who called himself P. S. Ney was a fugitive from justice or a refugee from disgrace, perhaps a deserter from the British army or a murderer. He also speculated that he might have been involved in political unrest in Scotland in the period from 1808 to 1817 and was forced to flee to America and that he initially lived in Philadelphia.[148] Hoyt furthermore believed that he did not come to America with the intention of passing himself off as Marshal Ney. His acquaintances in the United States at first assumed that he was a nephew of Marshal Ney, but he was increasingly identified as the marshal himself. In the latter part of his life when his age was not as obvious, he did nothing to dispel the notion and indeed encouraged it when he drank.[149]

An examination by the author of the British Newspaper Archive from 1805 through 1820 for variants on the names "Peter Ney," "Peter Stewart," and "Peter Stuart" similarly failed to find any convincing matches that could account for P. S. Ney.[150]

As a result, there is no hard evidence that would definitively account for the prior life of the man who called himself P. S. Ney, and the known candidates do not match P. S. Ney in terms of his personality, bearing, or accomplishments.

At the end of the day, P. S. Ney's masterful deception has proven as unsolvable as it has proven enduring. He remains, to this day, the self-described "atom floating on the atmosphere of chance."

However, the French historian René Arnaud had another insight: P. S. Ney had "an imagination of persecution which manifested itself in his frequent changes of residence and the constant fear of the assassins which 'the king of France would send to kill him if his retreat were known.'" Arnaud concluded that P. S. Ney was "a sick man."[151] It is possible that the head wound that P. S. Ney sustained might have traumatized and unbalanced him, but this supposition is speculative.

Despite all of the uncertainties outlined above, one cannot quite come to the conclusion that P. S. Ney was a calculating imposter. If he were not Marshal Ney, he may have been delusional on the subject. The likelihood that he believed he was Marshal Ney is borne out by his reported final words before dying. Several hours after making the deathbed confession while in a lucid state that he was in fact Marshal Ney, he went into a state of delirium that lasted a short while before he died. According to eyewitness testimony, his last words, spoken in delirium, were "Bessières is dead, and the Old Guard is defeated; now let me die."[152] Marshal Jean-Baptiste Bessières, a great favorite of Napoleon, was the commander of the cavalry in the Grande Armée. He was elevated to the Marshalate at the same time as Ney. He served with Ney in Iberia and on the Russian campaign (although his correspondence with Ney was far more limited than that of certain other generals and marshals, to judge from the records in the Archives Nationales). He was killed by a cannonball to the chest on May 1, 1813, while reconnoitering the defile of Rippach the day before the Battle of Lutzen. Ney was at his side, talking to him in the familiar "*tu*" at the time he was killed.[153] His younger brother, Brigadier General Bertrand Bessières, publicly defended Ney when he was on trial after Waterloo. The Old Guard was Napoleon's praetorian guard of tall, handpicked veterans. Ney led and fought with them until they disintegrated in the last desperate hour as the sun set over Waterloo.

That these would be the final words of P. S. Ney while delirious and dying is either additional proof that he was Marshal Ney or evidence that he believed he was the marshal even if he were not.

——————

The French Revolutionary Declaration of the Rights of the Man and of the Citizen, promulgated in 1789, promises liberty, equality, and property. In contrast, the American Declaration of Independence aspires to life, liberty, and the pursuit of happiness. The last of these attributes—happiness—is a peculiarly American concept. Europe did not promise happiness, nor did it deliver it.

Whether Marshal Ney died facedown or on his back off the rue d' Enfer on December 7, 1815, or 31 years later in rural North Carolina, the result was equally tragic. He either died or was exiled for no reason, and either way, not only a man but also a wife and family suffered grievously. Among P. S. Ney's handwritten papers is a poem to his son, written on the latter's birthday, November 26, 1840. From its content, there can be little doubt that Ney in fact wrote it for his son. The birth date coincides with no known birth dates of the four Ney sons[154] or of E. M. C. Neyman. The poem starts out with two shorthand symbols. The first shorthand symbol means "young" or "young man." The other remains undeciphered. The poem reads,

> for my son [two shorthand symbols]
> on his birthday Nov 26, 1840
>
> Son of my heart—my only child—
> A violet in this lonely wild—
> My comfort and my glory thou—
> My pride—Now, manhood on thy brow
> Begins to dwell with feature high
> Delightful to a mother's eye—
> Hope whispers thou shalt ever be
> An honor to thyself and me.

Thy principles of virtue bright
Shall ever guide thee to the right
And point thee with unerring reach
To action worthy of esteem.
Son of my love my precious mind
Would gladly know what is designed
For Now by fate It cannot be—
Yet my fond hopes are fixed on thee.
My darling boy—I can't believe
Thy future actions will deceive.[155]
My bosom's hope—But well I know
The num'rous snares that lurk below
To lure thy thoughtless mind astray
Be firm my son let seasons sway
And piety direct thy way—
Through fleeting life—& thou shall be
An honor to thyself and me.

P. S. Ney

Such was the heartbreaking sadness of the detritus of the Napoleonic Wars that washed up on the shores of America.

But the waltz of Marshal Ney's family with America did not end there. Seventy-one years after Marshal Ney died, on a drizzly October 28, 1886 the Frenchman Frédéric Auguste Bartholdi stood on a dizzying perch high above New York City's harbor. Fifteen years earlier, the Alsace-born Bartholdi had lost his homeland, which, following Marshal Ney's birthplace in Lorraine, had been snatched by Germany from the France for which Ney, facing the firing squad, viewed himself as having fought and about to die.

Bartholdi drove the final rivets into his behemoth copper creation, the Statue of Liberty Enlightening the World, a gift from the French people, on Bedlow's Island in New York Harbor, a site chosen by General William Tecumseh Sherman. Bartholdi removed the giant French

Tricolor that covered the face of the statue. This was the signal for "an enthusiastic outburst of the steam-whistles from the flotilla anchored in front of the island, and a national salute from the ships of war, drowning completely, by the volume of the sounds the strains of the Marseillaise from the band."[156] The cannon salvos and uproar lasted a full 15 minutes.

On a podium 305 feet below the diadem on her head, in front of the large stone pedestal built with 120,000 one-dollar subscriptions from ordinary American citizens, President Grover Cleveland led the U.S. delegation. Count Ferdinand de Lesseps, the aged genius behind the Suez Canal, headed the 16-member official French delegation, consisting of senators, deputies, navy and army officers, government officials, and prominent citizens.

Special Ambassador W. A. Lefaivre delivered the address on behalf of the French government. Speaking in English, he said,

> The republics of the past were debased by hostility to foreigners, by arbitrary and brutal power, and by slavery. Even in the modern world, liberty was during long ages the monopoly of privileged castes or races. Far different is our liberty, which relies upon the equality of rights and duties for all citizens, which secures for each the same protection and extends to all a maternal solicitude without distinction of birth, wealth, opinion or color. Consequently, this symbol, which we inaugurate today is not a chimerical allegory. . . . It means, in brief . . . the union of all peoples, through the study of science, the respect of the law, and sympathy for the weak. Yes, such are the truths which our Statue of Liberty is proclaiming. Such are the rays which beam from her torch to illuminate the whole world. Among the thousands of Europeans who are daily conveyed to these hospitable shores, no one will pass before this glorious emblem without immediately perceiving its moral greatness, and without greeting it with respect and thankfulness.[157]

On the podium, as a member of the French delegation, sat the president of the Société de Géographie Commerciale. He was a soldier, world explorer, adventurer, and author. His stocky frame and penetrating blue-gray eyes were those of the Prince of Moscow, the Duke of Elchingen, the "Bravest of the Brave." The program for the ceremony listed his name: "Mr. Napoléon Ney."

He was the Marshal's illegitimate grandson.

Appendix A

Principal U.S. Foreign Policy Decision Makers Responsible for France, 1809–1823

President	Secretary of State	Minister to Paris
James Madison (March 4, 1809–March 4, 1817)	James Monroe (April 2, 1811–March 3, 1817)	Gen. John Armstrong (June 30, 1804–September 14, 1810)
		Jonathan Russell, *Chargé* (September 14, 1810–July, 1811 (arrival of J. Barlow)
		Joel Barlow (February 27, 1811–December 26, 1812)
		William H. Crawford (April 9, 1813–April 22, 1815)
		Henry Jackson, *Chargé* (April 22, 1815–July 9, 1816)
James Monroe (March 4, 1817–March 4, 1825)	John Quincy Adams (September 22, 1817–March 3, 1825)	Albert Gallatin (July 16, 1816–May 16, 1823)

Letter from P. S. Ney to
Former President James Madison

Respected Sir, 1 Oct. 1831

The honour of an introduction to the revered Mr. Madison has not been my happy lot. The subject of this intrusion shall be briefly expressed. "Le Sage entend à demi mot." And it shall be à *demi mot*. You, respected Sir, already Stand at the head, the very head of American Patriots. You have it in your power to transcend them all! The step is a bold One—but it requires only one hour of your prolific pen to accomplish your elevation. Neither Tariff, nor Nullification, nor State, nor Federal sovereignty is the object of this "*demi Mot*," but what is infinitely more important than either, to the permanent happiness of this Union and the subjects thereof. In a word, it is the future security of the *Whites*! Your powerful mind can at once grasp the whole subject. Your wisdom and sage habit of thought can readily devise the means, and point out to the States and General Government acting in concert & mutual compromise for their Common welfare, the mode of dislodging the tremendous incubus, which now sits on their bosom. I mean Negro Slavery! Recent events confirm the long established axiom, "That *Men* submit no longer to slavery & degredation [*sic*] than circumstances compel them—" & that hope and desperation will prompt to the most sanguinary and woeful attempts at revenge or vindication enough.

What I propose for your consideration is this. Let the U. S. territory *West* of *the* Rocky *Mountains* be appropriated by Mutual Consent of the States for the colonization of the Sable population of U.S. Let the period for the commencement of gradual emancipation & its equitable details, be fixed by the States and Congress &c. at 1832–33, –34, or such time as their collective wisdom may deem meet. Let the *child Unborn* be the subject of emancipation and emigration, after a proper servitude to redeem its raising &c. in such proportions as may be agreed on by the proper authorities. Say every 3d. or 5th. Slave &c *per annum*.

The African Colonization Society, may, in the mean time, pursue *their* noble object in view. This drain over the Rocky Mountains will be tenfold, and efficient to keep down the procreation in the States, and its inevitable consequence, if such a plan be not adopted. Enough for you My dear & revered Sir. I have gone over *un demi Mot*. Permit me merely to suggest one idea more. You I fear will call it *selfish*—But what are we all but selfish beings! He who leads the <van> in this affair will be immortalized! Yes Sir, immortalized.

Your name is already high on the Roll of fame; but this Scheme recommended by you, in the clear and irrefutable Style of your Pen, will place your name on the *Apex* of that Pyramid of American glory & humanity produced to last forever.

God grant & that you may comprehend my "demi mot," & that your health & inclination may prompt you to fill *one sheet* for the consideration of those whom it so deeply concerns.

P. S. NEY.

Notes

Chapter 1
1. Alessandro Barbero, *The Battle: A New History of Waterloo* (New York: Walker and Company, 2003), 290.
2. Quoted in ibid., 291.
3. Ibid.
4. Ibid., 292.

Chapter 2
1. This appears to be an exact quotation from Joseph Bonaparte. See James K. Paulding, "An Interview with Napoleon's Brother," *Harper's Magazine* 131, no. 776 (November 1915): 818. A three hour interview with Joseph Bonaparte was conducted and memorialized in 1825 by James K. Paulding, who later became secretary of the navy in the Van Buren administration. However, it was not published until much later. See also Clarence Edward Noble Macartney and Gordon Dorrance, *The Bonapartes in America* (Philadelphia: Dorrance and Company, 1939) (hereinafter Macartney and Dorrance, *Bonapartes in America*), 79.
2. Andrew Roberts, *Napoleon: A Life* (New York: Viking, 2014), 771 (hereinafter Roberts, *Napoleon*).
3. For an insightful account of Fouché's machinations, see Rand A. Mirante, *Medusa's Head: The Rise and Survival of Joseph Fouché, Inventor of the Modern Police State* (Bloomington, IN: Archway Publishing, 2014), 178 et seq. (hereinafter Mirante, *Medusa's Head*).
4. Anonymous, *Life of Lafayette* (Boston: Light & Horton, 1835), 113–14; see also Roberts, *Napoleon*, 772.
5. Roberts, *Napoleon*, 771.
6. René Savary, "Duke of Rovigo," in *Memoirs*, vol. 4, pt. 2 (London, 1828), 111 (hereinafter Savary, *Memoirs*). Savary's *Memoirs* contain what is probably the most comprehensive and readable account of Napoleon's flight and eventual entrapment by the British. He was an eyewitness to and participant in the events; even discounting for the inevitable instances of self-serving presentation, it is a gripping read. For another good,

accessible online study, see https://shannonselin.com/2015/06/why-didnt-napoleon
-escape-to-the-united-states.

Passports, normally issued by the country from which emigration occurred, were in
common use in European countries at this time. They effectively allowed the holder to
depart the country and claim the protections of the issuing state of which the holder was
a citizen or subject. Entry to the United States was wide open. Visas were not required
for entry, and U.S. diplomats did not commonly issue them to foreigners except as an
accommodation and on request. The practice of regular visa issuance had its roots much
later in the Chinese Exclusion Act of 1882.

As John Quincy Adams, the American minister to London at the time, lamented
in his diary on July 1, 1815, "Every body of every country had a right to go to America
without needing my consent. I had no right to prevent anyone from going." [John
Quincy Adams, *Diaries*, vol. 29, July 1, 1815 (Boston: Massachusetts Historical Society,
2004), online version at http://www.masshist.org/jqadiaries/php (hereinafter, all volumes
collectively, Adams, *Diaries*), 282].

7. Roberts, *Napoleon*, 773, citing Elizabeth Wormeley Latimer, ed., *Talks of Napoleon
at St. Helena with General Baron Gourgaud* (Chicago: A. C. McClurg, 1903) (hereinafter
Latimer, *Talks*).

8. Antoine Marie Chamans Lavallette, *Memoirs of Count Lavalette* (London, 1835),
327–28.

9. Savary, *Memoirs*, 112.

10. Guillaume Joseph Roux Peyrusse, *1809–1815: Mémorial et archives de M. Le Baron
Peyrusse* (Carcassonne, 1869), 317. The reference is to Alexander Humboldt's *Personal
Narrative of Travels to the Equinoctial Regions of America*, which was first published in
French in 1807.

11. Inès Murat, *Napoleon and the American Dream*, trans. Frances Frenaye (Baton Rouge:
Louisiana State University Press, 1981) (hereinafter Murat, *Dream*), 18. See also Savary,
Memoirs, 140.

12. Savary, *Memoirs*, 121.

13. Ibid., 117.

14. J. S. Reeves, *The Napoleonic Exiles in America, 1815–1819*, Johns Hopkins University
Studies in Historical and Political Science, vol. 23 (Baltimore: Johns Hopkins University
Press, 1905) (hereinafter Reeves, *Exiles*), 537.

15. Savary, *Memoirs*, 121.

16. John Gurwood, ed., *The Dispatches of Field Marshal the Duke of Wellington, during
His Various Campaigns in India, Denmark, Portugal, Spain, the Low Countries, and France,
from 1799 to 1818*, vol. 12 (London: John Murray, 1838), 515.

17. Mirante, *Medusa's Head*, 183–84, quoting communication of F. Marshall, Esq., to
Wellington, reproduced in Arthur Wellesley, Duke of Wellington, and A. R. W. Wel-
lington, eds., *Supplementary Despatches, Correspondence and Memoranda, of Field Marshal
Arthur, Duke of Wellington, K. G.*, vol. 10 (London: John Murray, 1843), 601.

18. Sir Frederick Lewis Maitland, *The Surrender of Napoleon* (Edinburgh: William
Blackwood & Sons, 1904) (hereinafter Maitland, *Surrender*), 21, quoting letter dated
July 7, 1815, from Rear-Admiral Sir Henry Hotham to Captain Frederick Lewis Mait-
land aboard HMS *Bellerophon*.

19. Savary, *Memoirs*, 134–35.

20. Ibid., 138–39.

21. On July 3 and 4, the Maritime Prefect worked to provision the two ships for the voyage to America, indicating that a breakout was contemplated. The provisions included two cows, three goats, stuffed partridges, 140 dozen wrapped eggs, 300 bottles of Bordeaux, 16 bottles of Jamaican rum, 30 bottles of Medoc, 2 bottles of Madeira, and 60 bottles of champagne. The emperor, it seemed, was to travel in some style. See *Nouvelle Revue Retrospective*, January–June 1895 (Paris, 1895), 420 et seq.

22. Savary, *Memoirs*, 149–50.

23. Latimer, *Talks*, 14.

24. George Foster Emmons, *The Navy of the United States* (Washington, DC: Gideon & Co., 1853) (hereinafter Emmons, *Navy*), 184 and 188. See also George Coggeshall, *History of the American Privateers, and Letters-of-Marque, during Our War with England in the Years 1812, '13 and '14* (privately printed, 1856) (hereinafter Coggeshall, *Privateers*), which contains numerous references to successful captures by the privateer *Pike* of Baltimore. Emmons lists *Ludlow* as "missing at the end of the war," and there is a record of a *Ludlow* privateer being wrecked at Riverhead Beach near Boston on January 22, 1815. She was not the same ship. There also is in other records a listing for a 207-ton privateer brig *Ludlow*, out of Portsmouth, New Hampshire, under Captain Joseph Mudge, who was an active privateer captain during the War of 1812. According to Alfred Mudge, *Mudge Memorials* (Boston: Alfred Mudge & Son, 1868), 218, Captain Joseph Mudge sailed to France on this *Ludlow* at the end of the War of 1812 "and brought home the first news of the Allies having entered Paris." She is also mentioned in Coggeshall and is the correct ship. As made clear in newspaper reports from 1815, she was under Captain Joseph Mudge's command.

25. Karthaus and Hurxthal owned a number of Baltimore-based privateers, including *Bordeaux Packet*, whose captain was one George Lee. The U.S. consul at Bordeaux, William Lee, who figures prominently in this story, had a younger brother, born in 1784, named George Lee. It is possible that he was her captain, in which case William Lee's connections with the Baltimore privateering community would have been a family affair.

26. Halsey Dunning, *In Memoriam: A Tribute of Respect to the Late Capt. Joel Vickers, for Nearly Seventy Years a Resident of Baltimore* (Baltimore: John W. Woods, 1860), 10–11, and John Philips Cranwell and William Bowers Crane, *Men of Marque: A History of Private Armed Vessels Out of Baltimore during the War of 1812* (New York: W. W. Norton & Co., ca. 1940) (hereinafter Cranwell and Crane, *Men of Marque*), 294 et seq.

27. See generally Cranwell and Crane, *Men of Marque*, 295 and 390.

28. Ibid., 298–99, describes how on August 22, 1814, *Pike* was chased by but outran a British war brig, HMS *Primrose*, but then ran aground on Tybee Shoals near Savannah, Georgia. Unable to float her, some of the crew offloaded the gold she was carrying in a boat and escaped. The next morning, *Primrose* moved in, seized, and burned *Pike* and took the remaining crew prisoner. How this could be is unclear, as there are contemporary records from 1815 of *Pike*, out of Baltimore and commanded by Captain Vickers, as being the ship that almost rescued Napoleon. It appears likely that the authors may have conflated *Pike* with the much smaller coastal lugger privateer *General Pike*, also out of

Baltimore, as the ship that ran ashore on Tybee Shoals and was captured and destroyed. See Emmons, *Navy*, 178.

29. The Portuguese minister to the United States, José Corrêa da Serra, described Baltimore at the time as rivaling New Orleans as the "new Algiers" because of its privateering activities. See Rafe Blaufarb, *Bonapartists in the Borderlands* (Tuscaloosa: University of Alabama Press, 2005) (hereinafter Blaufarb, *Borderlands*), 249, endnote 5.

30. Edmond Jurien de la Gravière, "L'Amiral Baudin," in *Les Gloires maritimes de la France* (Paris: Plon, 1888) (hereinafter Gravière, *Baudin*), 96 et seq. (translation by the author).

31. Maitland, *Surrender*, 20.

32. Ibid., 21.

33. Gravière, *Baudin*, 96 et seq. (translation by the author).

34. Latimer, *Talks*, 16–17.

35. Roberts, *Napoleon*, 774.

36. W. H. Ireland, ed., *The Napoleon Anecdotes* (London: C. S. Arnold, 1822), 136.

37. Maitland, *Surrender*, 22–23.

38. Ibid., 24.

39. Savary, *Memoirs*, 155 et seq.

40. Ibid., 150.

41. There was considerable American shipping at Bordeaux at the time. In addition to these five ships, which departed together, some 12 American ships remained in the harbor. These included *Susquehannah, Hunter, Tontine, Cosmopolite, Commerce* (on which Joseph Bonaparte escaped), *Balize, Ariadne, Missouri, Bliss, Manlius, Maria Theresa,* and *South Carolina.* See New York *Evening Post*, August 18, 1815.

42. Gravière, *Baudin*, 96 et seq. (translation by the author).

43. Maitland, *Surrender*, 25.

44. There also was an effort by several French naval officers to outfit a small *chasse-marée* vessel for the purpose of transporting Napoleon. Although some of Napoleon's belongings were loaded, the plan was abandoned because the small boat would have been incapable of sailing across the Atlantic to America without stopping to be reprovisioned.

45. Gravière, *Baudin*, 96 et seq. (translation by the author).

46. Latimer, *Talks*, 16.

47. Charles Jared Ingersoll, *History of the Second War between the United States of America and Great Britain*, 2nd ser., vol. 1 (Philadelphia: Lippincott, Grambo & Co., 1852) (hereinafter Ingersoll, *Second War*), 371.

48. Maitland, *Surrender*, 25.

49. Louis-Joseph-Narcisse Marchand, *In Napoleon's Shadow*, ed. Proctor P. Jones (San Francisco: Proctor Jones Publishing Company, 1998), 283–84.

50. Ingersoll, *Second War*, 373.

51. Roberts, *Napoleon*, comes down squarely on the side of stomach cancer.

52. The original Baudin letter containing Lee's handwritten notation is in the William Lee Letters collection at the Columbia University Rare Book and Manuscript Library, call no. MS#0761.

53. See Bertrand Clausel, *Justificatif de la Conduite Politique de M. Le Lieutenant-Général Comte Clausel* (Paris: Chez Pillet, 1816).

54. *Nouvelle Revue Retrospective*, July–December 1899 (Paris, 1899), 3–4 (translation by the author).

55. *L'Abeille Américaine*, vol. 5, October 20, 1817, 192 (translation by the author).

56. New York *Evening Post*, August 18, 1815. Other records show "Joel Vickers" as both an owner and an officer of *Pike* during the War of 1812 under Captain Henry Bolton. See http://www.1812privateers.org/United%20States/menofmarque01.htm. Joel Vickers was indeed a resident of Baltimore. It appears that he assumed command after Bolton, at least on this particular voyage following the cessation of hostilities in the War of 1812 and the end of *Pike*'s role as an active privateer. He was thus misidentified by the New York paper as "Samuel Vickers." Captain Joel Vickers (August 14, 1774–December 2, 1860) was the son of Benjamin Vickers and Rachel Roberts of Kent County, Maryland, on the Eastern Shore, although one source states he was a native of Cecil County, Maryland. He moved to Baltimore after marrying Ada Beck, also of Kent County. He lived a long and useful life as a Baltimore shipowner and was a pillar of the Presbyterian Church in Baltimore.

57. *Niles' Weekly Register*, August 19, 1815, 425.

58. New York *Evening Post*, August 18, 1816.

59. Ibid.

60. *Weekly Raleigh Register*, August 25, 1815. See also *Carlisle Weekly Herald*, August 17, 1815: "The Ludlow shortly after sailing was boarded by a British frigate and very strictly searched, even to the persons of the crew for Buonaparte, who it was thought might be concealed or disguised on board."

Chapter 3

1. Mary Lee Mann, ed., *A Yankee Jeffersonian: Selections from the Diary and Letters of William Lee of Massachusetts* (Cambridge, MA: Harvard University Press, 1958) (hereinafter Mann, *Lee*), 12, February 16, 1796 entry.

2. Ibid., 13, February 18, 1796, entry.

3. Ibid., 21, March 6, 1796, entry.

4. Ibid., 25, March 28, 1796, entry.

5. Ibid., 26, March 31, 1796, entry.

6. Ibid., 35–37, January 7–February 6, 1797, entries.

7. Ibid., 40–41, May 18–19, 1797, entries.

8. Ibid., 44, 46, May 23, 1797, entry.

9. In gratitude and admiration, Lee named his second son Thomas Jefferson Lee.

10. Technically, it appears that Lee functioned as U.S. commercial agent in Bordeaux and that the post was not upgraded to a consulate until Lee left and his successor took office in 1816. However, Lee performed consular functions and was broadly known as the U.S. consul, so he will be accorded that title here.

11. Jefferson's Memorandum Books, vol. 2, Accounts with Legal Records, 1803, 1103. See also June 14, 1803, letter from Jefferson to Lee acknowledging receipt of the above wines and a Perrot & Lee invoice dated August 22, 1803.

12. David B. Matten, ed., *The Papers of James Madison: 2 April–31 August 1804*, Secretary of State Series, vol. 7 (Charlottesville: University of Virginia Press, 2009), 91–92.

13. "To James Madison from William Lee (Abstract), 12 May 1805," *Founders Online*, National Archives, last modified November 26, 2017, http://founders.archives.gov /documents/Madison/02-09-02-0390. (Original source: Mary A. Hackett, J. C. A. Stagg, Mary Parke Johnson, Anne Mandeville Colony, Angela Kreider, and Katherine E. Harbury, eds., *The Papers of James Madison: 1 February 1805–30 June 1805*, Secretary of State Series, vol. 9 [Charlottesville: University of Virginia Press, 2011], 343.)

14. Mann, *Lee*, 75.

15. Ibid., 82–83.

16. Ibid., 108.

17. Ibid., 130. Lee was very much a family man, as revealed in his correspondence. He adored his wife, Susan, and was a caring and engaged father to his children.

18. Ibid., 133.

19. White House Historical Association, "After the Fire," *White House History*, no. 35 (Summer 2014).

290. Mann, *Lee*, 171.

21. David B. Mattern, J. C. A. Stagg, Mary Parke Johnson, and Anne Mandeville Colony, eds., *The Papers of James Madison: 4 March 1817–31 January 1820*, Retirement Series, vol. 1 (Charlottesville: University of Virginia Press, 2009), 227.

22. Mann, *Lee*, 135.

23. Ibid., 140.

24. See William Lee's Memorandum Book for the year 1811 in the Lee-Palfrey Families Papers, Library of Congress.

25. Mann, *Lee*, 136–37.

26. Ibid., 143.

27. It was not the only such letter. Another letter, dated May 24, 1812, marked "Confidential," survives. That letter concludes, "Be pleased, Sir, to present my respects to Mrs. Madison. I hope the things I sent her by the *Constitution* were approved of." Ibid., 159–62.

28. See January 1813 letter from Talleyrand to Lee thanking him for helping to arrange the sale to him of Barlow's wine. William Lee Letters collection at the Columbia University Rare Book and Manuscript Library, call no. MS#0761.

29. "William Lee to James Monroe, ca. 30 August 1813 (Abstract)," *Founders Online*, National Archives, last modified November 26, 2017, http://founders.archives.gov/docu ments/Madison/03-06-02-0559. (Original source: Angela Kreider, J. C. A. Stagg, Jeanne Kerr Cross, Anne Mandeville Colony, Mary Parke Johnson, and Wendy Ellen Perry, eds., *The Papers of James Madison: 8 February–24 October 1813*, Presidential Series, vol. 6 [Charlottesville: University of Virginia Press, 2008], 578–80.)

30. Angela Kreider, ed., *The Papers of James Madison: 1 July 1814–18 February 1815*, Presidential Series, vol. 8 (Charlottesville: University of Virginia Press, 2015), 356, 411–13.

31. The book also contained a chapter endorsing the Bourbons, which Lee described as having been inserted at the insistence of the newly installed Bourbon government.

32. *L'Abeille Américaine*, vol. 5, October 23, 1817, 238, noted that the book "was read all over Europe."

33. Mann, *Lee*, 180, letter dated October 25, 1816.

34. Ibid., 167, letter dated March 12, 1815.

35. The one exception is a file copy in French and in the handwriting of a scribe but dated and signed by Lee in his own handwriting, addressed to "Monsieur le Compte." This letter, which was not included in Mann's compendium of Lee's papers and which has never been published, is curious on several fronts. First, the recipient is not identified by name anywhere in the letter, but a separate letter from Lee to Monroe dated December 26, 1815, makes clear it was to Count Jean-Antoine Chaptal, Napoleon's brilliant and talented minister of agriculture, commerce, and industry. Second, the month of the date in Lee's handwriting at the head of the letter is illegible. However, the same separate letter clarifies that it was written at the end of 1815 and notes ship departures during the early months of 1816. This timing fits with Lee's own departure from Bordeaux in 1816, a plan mentioned in the letter. Third, the ostensible purpose of the letter is to facilitate Count Chaptal's departure for America. The letter reads in relevant part, "The newspapers have apprised that you have the intention of visiting the United States of America and that you are disposed to make it happen. . . . Permit me in that case . . . to choose Bordeaux for the place of your departure, to offer you my services in procuring a passage for you and . . . the embarkation of your effects. We have in the port some superb American ships which will depart after the middle of the present month up to the 1st of March." Fourth, Lee proposes that the count accompany him and his family on the voyage: "I propose, myself, to charter toward this time there a ship to return in my [illegible] with all my family. We would be, Mr. the Count, extremely flattered to work toward all together to advance [illegible] you the rigors of the passage." Fifth, Lee reiterates his offer to help and reveals the true purpose of the letter—inducing the count to emigrate by holding out the prospect of American citizenship for the count: "if it arrives that you [illegible] your country to establish your stay the Congress of the United States will certainly have the honor to count you among its citizens; it will hasten to offer you letters of naturalization." Finally, the letter concludes with elaborate flatteries (e.g., "You would be the benefactor of my nation and of the new world") designed to entice the recipient to settle permanently in the United States (translation by the author). Chaptal politely declined Lee's offer and remained in France. If Lee had succeeded in convincing Chaptal to emigrate, it would have been quite a coup in that Chaptal played a leading role in the industrialization of France, including development of the Grenelle gunpowder works, and he would have been a major strategic asset to the United States.

36. Jackson, a British-born medical doctor who taught in Georgia, was a protégé of Crawford. He stayed on in Paris as chargé for one year after Crawford departed.

37. Letter dated February 16, 1816, to Madison, in Mann, *Lee*, 178. Letter dated February 18, 1816, to Monroe, Dispatches from U.S. Consuls, 1789–1906, T-164, U.S. National Archives and Records Administration (hereinafter NARA).

38. Letter dated September 28, 1815, from the Honorable Jonathan Dayton to Lee, Dispatches from U.S. Consuls, 1789–1906, Bordeaux, T-164, NARA.

39. Mann, *Lee*, 159.

40. Instructions dated September 10, 1816, from Monroe to Gallatin, Diplomatic Instructions from the Secretary of State to U.S. Ambassadors, M-77, roll 3, vol. 8, NARA. See also instructions dated November 26, 1816, from Monroe to Gallatin, Diplomatic Instructions from the Secretary of State to U.S. Ambassadors, M-77, roll 3, vol. 8, NARA. It tells much about the United States at this date that such a small incident that would be dismissed out of hand today caused much introspection on the subject of fundamental American values and, in Monroe's words, "a crisis between the two governments." A few passages from Monroe's lengthy September 10, 1816, instructions to Gallatin give the flavor: "From the nature of our Institutions it is not perceived that it would have been practical under any circumstances, to have removed Mr. Skinner from office for the cause alledged [sic]. The peremptory tone, however, with which it has been demanded, renders it utterly impossible. If a Foreign Minister can dictate measures to the United States, especially in a case so intimately connected with the vital principles of their government, then Independence is gone. . . . This case admitted of no compromise."
41. Murat, *Dream*, 62.
42. Letter dated September 9, 1816, from William Lee to President James Madison, Dispatches from U.S. Consuls, 1789–1906, Bordeaux, T-164, NARA.
43. Mann, *Lee*, 180–82, letter dated October 25, 1816.
44. Harry Ammon, *James Monroe: The Quest for National Identity* (New York: McGraw-Hill, 1971), 534.
45. Mann, *Lee*, 215.
46. *Ibid.*, 231.
47. Stanislaus Murray Hamilton, ed., *The Writings of James Monroe*, vol. 4, *1803–1806* (New York: G. P. Putnam's Sons, 1900) (hereinafter Hamilton, *Monroe*), 15–16.
48. Ibid., 98–99.
49. Letter dated June 25, 1814, from Monroe to Crawford, Diplomatic Instructions from the Secretary of State to U.S. Ambassadors, M-77, roll 2, vol. 7, NARA.
50. Letter dated May 11, 1815 from Monroe to Adams, Diplomatic Instructions from the Secretary of State to U.S. Ambassadors, M-77, roll 2, vol. 7, NARA.
51. Hamilton, *Monroe*, vol. 5, *1807–1816*, 330.
52. Letter dated April 15, 1816, from Monroe to Gallatin, Diplomatic Instructions from the Secretary of State to U.S. Ambassadors, M-77, roll 3, vol. 8, NARA. It is fair to note that this disparagement of Napoleon came 10 months after his fall and that Monroe was dealing with the realpolitik of seeking good relations with the new regime.
53. Letter dated July 9, 1815, from Jackson to Monroe, Dispatches from U.S. Ministers and Ambassadors, 1785–1906, T-1, NARA.
54. British press reports written in conjunction with the 200th anniversary of Waterloo in 2015 that this dispatch was written June 18 are erroneous based on the clear dating of the letter, which is in Jackson's handwriting, as July. Moreover, on June 18, Napoleon was still fleeing the battlefield and was a full five days away from requesting passports. Those reports' interpretation of the dispatch that Jackson was attempting to arrange asylum for Napoleon are also erroneous, as discussed in the text.
55. Letter dated September 27, 1815, from Jackson to Monroe, Dispatches from U.S. Ministers and Ambassadors, 1785–1906, T-1, NARA.

56. Letter dated July 1, 1815, from Chancellor Peters to Monroe, Dispatches from U.S. Consuls, 1789–1906, Bordeaux, T-164, NARA.

Chapter 4

1. Professor Rafe Blaufarb makes a thorough and credible effort in his *Bonapartists in the Borderlands.* This detailed study of the French colony in America provides the single best treatment of the émigrés' political, martial, and settlement activities in the American interior.

2. Murat, *Dream*, 30.

3. Blaufarb, *Borderlands*, 19.

4. A. Roger Ekirch, *American Sanctuary: Mutiny, Martyrdom and National Identity in the Age of Revolution* (New York: Pantheon Books, 2017), 147, citing François-Alexandre-Frédéric, Duke de La Rochefoucault-Liancourt, *Travels through the United States of America* (1799).

5. A second and much smaller wave of emigrants came from France itself during the height of the Reign of Terror. Most of them eventually returned to France. For a full treatment of this wave of refugees, see François Furstenberg, *When the United States Spoke French: Five Refugees Who Shaped a Nation* (New York: Penguin, 2014). Afterward, there was the occasional political refugee, such as General Jean Victor Marie Moreau and Jean-Guillaume Baron Hyde de Neuville, who had found themselves on the outs with Napoleon (Hyde de Neuville, whose father was English, went on to become King Louis XVIII's minister in Washington and the scourge of the Bonapartist émigrés in the United States).

6. There is a long history of French emigration to the United States. Even Georgetown in the District of Columbia sheltered Napoleon's would-be assassin, the nobleman-turned-priest Joseph Pierre Picot de Limoëlan, who, with two confederates, unsuccessfully tried to blow up Napoleon's carriage with a barrel bomb as the first consul and Josephine were en route to the Paris debut of Joseph Haydn's oratorio *The Creation* on Christmas Eve 1800. Although the bomb failed to kill Napoleon, it wreaked havoc on the vicinity, killing nine people, including a girl whom the conspirators paid a few *sous* minutes before to hold the reins of the horse pulling the cart on which the bomb was hidden. Only her feet were found afterward. De Limoëlan fled and eventually escaped to the United States, where he earned money as a painter of portrait miniatures. Apparently, remorse led him to the seminary to study for the priesthood. On his ordination, he became known as Father de Clorivière. He went on to help endow and expand Georgetown Visitation Convent and School, one of the oldest girls' schools in the United States. He is buried in a crypt beneath the convent's chapel. See John Kelly, "Buried beneath Georgetown: A Priest Who Tried to Kill Napoleon," *Washington Post*, July 21, 2019, C3.

7. J. Jefferson Looney, ed., *Papers of Thomas Jefferson*, Retirement Series, vol. 9 (Princeton, NJ: Princeton University Press, 2012) (hereinafter Looney, *Jefferson Papers*), 693–96. The three "very remarkable men" were pianist Denis Germain Étienne, oboist Peter Gilles, and the latter's son, a cellist. They did indeed give concerts up and down the East Coast, and all three settled in the United States. Ibid.

8. *L'Abeille Américaine*, vol. 5, December 4, 1817, 338.

9. Blaufarb, *Borderlands*, 41–42.

10. Murat, *Dream*, 74.

11. Roberts, *Napoleon*, 15.

12. Reeves, *Exiles*, 640.

13. Ingersoll, *Second War*, 375–76.

14. See, e.g., Reeves, *Exiles*, 536. This is unlikely. The author suspects that some authors may have conflated his issuance of a passport for the U.S. citizen Carret with similar action for Joseph. The fee Joseph paid for his passage was roughly comparable to the "tips" Napoleon gave to his mistresses for a night of pleasure. See Roberts, *Napoleon*, 361.

15. Ingersoll, *Second War*, 377.

16. *L'Abeille Américaine*, vol. 5, July 1817, 16.

17. "Commodore Lewis" was almost certainly Commander, aka "Commodore," Jacob Lewis (1764–1824), who was a privateer active during the War of 1812 out of New York. Why he would have recognized Joseph Bonaparte is unclear. He may have been presented to him in Paris earlier in his career. Moreover, his brother Thomas Lewis resided in Bordeaux and knew William Lee, so there may have been a connection through him. However, there was another man broadly known as "Commodore Lewis": Commodore Louis/Lewis Warrington, the illegitimate son of General Rochambeau's nephew and aide-de-camp Captain Louis Francois Bertrand Dupont d'Aubevoye, Comte de Lauberdière (some said he may have been Rochambeau's illegitimate son). He was born of an American mother in Williamsburg, Virginia, in the wake of Rochambeau's march to Yorktown. He attended the College of William & Mary and had a distinguished naval career, serving briefly, in 1844, as secretary of the navy. He also operated out of New York with distinction at the time but as a U.S. Navy officer rather than as a privateer. This latter Lewis would have been only 33 years old at the time (although already a captain) and the former Lewis 54, so it is likelier the former Lewis if he were visiting his presumably grown son in New York. Also, "Commodore" Jacob Lewis appears to have owned property near Perth Amboy that Joseph visited.

18. Letter from Richard Rush dated September 13, 1815, to Commodore Lewis, Rush Collection, Letters 1812–1847, Historical Society of Pennsylvania (hereinafter HSP), AM 13520.

19. Ibid., letter from Madison to Monroe, September 15, 1815.

20. Ibid., letter from Rush to Madison, September 17, 1815.

21. Murat, *Dream*, 24.

22. Ibid., 70.

23. Emmanuel Grouchy, *Memoires du Maréchal Grouchy*, vol. 5 (Paris: E. Dentu, Libraire-Editeur, 1874) (hereinafter Grouchy, *Memoires*), 6 et seq.

24. Looney, *Jefferson Papers*, 13.

25. See, e.g., letter from Charles Lallemand from Baltimore dated April 2, 1804, writing in the third person: "*Il n'est pas tenté de rester aux États-Unis et va partir pour New Yorck, où il se mariera, puis reviendra en France,*" Hoyt Collection, ser. 2, fol. 108.

26. Murat, *Dream*, 108.

27. Savary, *Memoirs*, vol. 4, pt. II, 192 et seq.

28. *L'Abeille Américaine*, vol. 3, July 18, 1816, 223–24, and September 12, 1816, 350.
29. Ibid., May 23, 1816, 89.
30. Ibid., September 12, 1816, 351–52.
31. Sir Walter Scott, *Life of Napoleon Buonaparte, Emperor of the French*, vol. 3 (New York, J. & J. Harper, 1827), 46. See also R. M. Johnston, *In the Words of Napoleon: The Emperor Day by Day* (Lionel Levanthal Books/Frontline Books, 2015), 409.
32. Blaufarb, *Borderlands*, 9.
33. Von Steuben adopted Walker and another aide and made them his heirs, leading to rampant speculation at the time about the nature of their relationship with the baron.
34. Blaufarb, *Borderlands*, 10.
35. *L'Abeille Américaine*, vol. 3, August 22, 1816, 303.
36. Blaufarb, *Borderlands*, 11.
37. *L'Abeille Américaine*, vol. 3, May 16, 1816, 74. See also Blaufarb, *Borderlands*, 10.
38. NARA M425, available online at https://www.familysearch.org/search/collection /1908535.
39. *L'Abeille Américaine*, vol. 3, May 16, 1816, 74, and July 18, 1816, 223–24.
40. Blaufarb, *Borderlands*, 11-12.
41. Luciani's father was Madame Mère's first cousin.
42. https://archive.org/details/philadelphiadire1820phil.
43. James Edward Smoot, *Marshal Ney before and after Execution* (Charlotte, NC: Queen City Printing Company, 1929) (hereinafter Smoot, *Before and after the Execution*), 251–57.

Chapter 5
1. It is virtually impossible to calculate accurately what this would be worth in today's dollars. At the time, one franc was worth approximately 20 U.S. cents, which, adjusted for inflation, would render a total current cash value of about $15 million. This probably understates the value given the lifestyle that Joseph Bonaparte maintained in the United States, and, in any event, he possessed jewelry and art that were of incalculable value.
2. Important Napoleonic refugees continued to pour into Philadelphia during 1816–1817. In addition to Lieutenant General Charles Lallemand on April 23, 1817, *L'Abeille Américaine* recorded on July 31, 1817, the arrival of General Joseph-René Vandamme: "General Vandamme, one of the most generous defenders of his country, has arrived from Amsterdam in Philadelphia. This brave military man is happily sheltered from the attacks of legitimacy [meaning by the royalists]."
3. Murat, *Dream*, 26.
4. Ibid., 31.
5. According to a study by *Forbes* magazine, Girard was the fourth wealthiest man ever to live in the United States when his personal wealth is measured as a percentage of U.S. gross domestic product. Those ahead of him were John D. Rockefeller, Cornelius Vanderbilt, and John Jacob Astor. Girard was wealthier than Andrew Carnegie or Bill Gates in this study. See https://www.forbes.com/asap/1998/0824/032.html.
6. E. M. Woodward, *Bonaparte's Park and the Murats* (Trenton, NJ: MacCrellish & Quigley, 1879), 35.

7. Charlemagne Tower, "Joseph Bonaparte in Philadelphia and Bordentown," *Pennsylvania Magazine of History and Biography* 40, no. 4 (1918): 308.

8. Looney, *Jefferson Papers*, 694.

9. *L'Abeille Américaine*, vol. 3, May 30, 1816, 101.

10. Ibid., vol. 3, August 8, 1816, 268.

11. Macartney and Dorrance, *Bonapartes in America*, 101–2.

12. Daniel Preston, ed., *The Papers of James Monroe*, vol. 1 (Westport, CT: Greenwood Press, 2003), 53.

13. Macartney and Dorrance, *Bonapartes in America*, 109; Patricia Tyson Stroud, *The Man Who Had Been King: The American Exile of Napoleon's Brother Joseph* (Philadelphia: University of Pennsylvania Press, 2005), 59; Murat, *Dream*, 33.

14. Macartney and Dorrance, *Bonapartes in America*, 85.

15. Helen Berkley, *A Sketch of Joseph Buonaparte*, Godey's Magazine and Lady's Book, Vol. XXX (Philadelphia: Louis A. Godey, Jan.-June 1845), 187.

16. Murat, *Dream*, 43–44.

17. Thomas Birch, *Catalogue of valuable paintings & statuary, the Collection of the late Joseph Bonaparte, Count de Survilliers: to be sold at public sale on Wednesday & Thursday, September 17th and 18th, 1845, at the mansion in Bordentown, New Jersey*, items 58 and 59 (listed as "Head of a Turk" and "Similar subject"). The Rubens *Two Lions and a Fawn* is item 14. It sold for the then-high sum of $2,300. How Joseph brought these works of art and furniture to the United States is unclear. As described above, he barely escaped France by being rowed to a waiting ship. Presumably, he sent for these items or acquired them separately after he was in America. Interestingly, the author found no contemporary (or subsequent) allegations that they were looted art, so it appears that Joseph acquired them legitimately on the market, possibly with proceeds derived from the sale of his jewels.

18. Owen Connelly, *The Gentle Bonaparte: The Story of Napoleon's Elder Brother* (New York: Macmillan, 1958) (hereinafter Connelly, *Gentle Bonaparte*), 42, 44, and 53.

19. Macartney and Dorrance, *Bonapartes in America*, 99.

20. Murat, *Dream*, 42–43.

21. Ibid., 43–44. The author cannot help but note the resemblance of the interior decor of Point Breeze to that of the Duke of Wellington's London residence, Apsley House. The resemblance was probably not entirely coincidental because the majority of Wellington's collection of paintings came from the Spanish Royal Collection, rescued from a fleeing Joseph Bonaparte after the Battle of Vitoria in northern Spain. In addition, Wellington, perhaps oddly for a member of the Protestant Ascendancy in Ireland, displayed portraits of Catholic prelates and, even more surprisingly, portraits of Napoleon and Joseph Bonaparte. His home even boasted a more-than-full-scale Canova statue of a naked Napoleon titled *Mars the Peacemaker* executed in white marble.

22. Macartney and Dorrance, *Bonapartes in America*, 91.

23. Surviving plants on the property from his time likely include several willow oaks, an ash tree, and the remains of an orchard. In addition, the rather formal two-story federal gatehouse dating from circa 1816 still stands on the edge of the property.

24. There also was a tunnel, remnants of which still exist, leading from Joseph's house to the bluff overlooking Crosswicks Creek. It was long rumored to have been meant to serve as a means of escape if Joseph had to flee (it would have led to his oared barge, which would have spirited him quickly downriver to Philadelphia and the protection of Stephen Girard). More likely, its use, though uncertain, was more utilitarian, although Joseph reportedly maintained a personal bodyguard for some years out of fear of assassination.

25. Murat, *Dream*, 34.

26. *L'Abeille Américaine*, vol. 3, September 19, 1816, 364 (translation by the author).

27. James Grant Wilson, *The Life and Letters of Fitz-Greene Halleck* (New York: D. Appleton and Company, 1869), 519–20.

28. *L'Abeille Américaine*, vol. 3, September 5, 1816, 336 (translation by the author).

29. Joseph Bonaparte letter dated October 1, 1815, to LeRoy, Bayard et Cie. referencing Carret as his purchasing agent. Gratz Collection (HSP), box 32, folder 22. See also Joseph Bonaparte letter dated August 17, 1825, to William Bayard Jr. with instructions relating to Carret, Gratz Collection (HSP), box 32, folder 22.

30. Joseph Bonaparte letter dated June 8, 1826, to LeRoy, Bayard & Cie., Gratz Collection (HSP), box 32, folder 22.

31. Joseph Bonaparte letters dated June 18, 1824, and June 16, 1826, to LeRoy, Bayard & Cie., Gratz Collection (HSP), box 32, folder 22.

32. Roberts, *Napoleon*, 785.

33. Ibid., 705–6.

34. Another version of the story has her living at Lamberton, New Jersey, where she was known as "Mrs. Horton."

35. Connelly, *Gentle Bonaparte*, 292.

36. Ibid.

37. Murat, *Dream*, 39.

38. *L'Abeille Américaine*, vol. 3, May 16, 1816, 78–80 (translation by the author). Interestingly, the May 2, 1816, edition of the same paper states, "It is believed, in the environs of Bayonne, that Lefebvre-Desnouettes and Drouet d'Erlon, are still in the country, under various disguises. The gendarmerie make the strictest searches for them" (translation by the author).

39. The location of the house was 245 South 6th Street on the east side of fashionable Washington Square. The house was demolished in the 1960s. He also may have owned a house at 244 Lombard Street. See Kathleen A. Foster and Kenneth Finkel, *Captain Watson's Travels in America* (Philadelphia: University of Pennsylvania Press, 1997), 319, and Bill Double, *Philadelphia's Washington Square* (Charleston, SC: Arcadia Publishing, 2009), 108.

40. From Thomas Jefferson to Emmanuel Grouchy, May 23, 1821, Founders Online, National Archives, last modified June 13, 2018, http://founders.archives.gov/documents/Jefferson/98-01-02-2078.

41. See December 25, 1816, letter from Grouchy to Mrs. William Lee, William Lee Letters collection at the Columbia University Rare Book & Manuscript Library, call no. MS#0761.

42. Murat, *Dream*, 70–71.
43. Marshal Emmanuel de Grouchy, *Memoires du Maréchal Grouchy*, vol. 5 (Paris: E. Dentu, 1874), 62.
44. Ibid., 63 (translation by the author).
45. Ibid., 63–64 (translation by the author).
46. Ibid., 64 (translation by the author).
47. Ibid., 67–68 (translation by the author).
48. Ibid., 213 (translation by the author).
49. Grouchy letter dated September 4, 1821, to Charles Jared Ingersoll, Charles Jared Ingersoll Collection (HSP), box 1, folder 11.
50. Murat, *Dream*, 177–78.
51. *L'Abeille Américaine*, vol. 3 August 8, 1816, 272 (translation by the author).
52. Murat, *Dream*, 61.
53. One might posit that Joseph Bonaparte and Marshal Grouchy were exceptions to this characterization, the former because he had nobility of character and the latter because he had nobility of blood.

Chapter 6
1. Murat, *Dream*, 47.
2. Ibid., 55.
3. Ibid., 48.
4. See Rob Mann and Diana DiPaolo Loren, "Keeping Up Appearances: Dress, Architecture, Furniture, and Status at French Azilum," *International Journal of Historical Archeology* 5, no. 4 (December 2001): 281–307.
5. See Laurence J. Kenny, "The Gallipolis Colony," *Catholic Historical Review* 4, no. 4 (January 1919): 415–51.
6. It was also known variously as the Colonial Society of French Emigrants, the French Agricultural and Manufacturing Society, the French Emigrant Association, and the Tombigbee Association.
7. *L'Abeille Américaine*, vol. 3, August 22, 1816, 292–94. See also Blaufarb, *Borderlands*, 42 et seq.
8. Mann, *Lee*, 159.
9. *L'Abeille Américaine*, vol. 4, January 9, 1817, 203–5.
10. Murat, *Dream*, 30.
11. See, e.g., *L'Abeille Américaine*, vol. 4, November 14, 1816, 70, and January 2 and 23, 1817, 205–7 and 239–40, respectively.
12. Blaufarb, *Borderlands*, 46.
13. *L'Abeille Américaine*, vol. 4, January 9, 1817, 206–7.
14. For a thorough discussion of these efforts, see Blaufarb, *Borderlands*, 46 et seq.
15. For those wishing to delve more deeply into the complex geopolitical factors, Blaufarb, *Borderlands*, provides a thoughtful and analytical treatment at 49 et seq.
16. *Columbian Centinel*, January 11, 1817, and *Niles' Weekly Register*, August 8, 1818.
17. *L'Abeille Américaine*, vol. 5, August 28, 1817, 112.
18. See, e.g., *L'Abeille Américaine*, vol. 5, October 30, 1817, 245.

19. See letter he wrote from Philadelphia to a Mr. Barber dated November 11, 1818, in the manuscript collection of the HSP.
20. Murat, *Dream*, 86–87.
21. Blaufarb, *Borderlands*, 117.
22. Ibid., 125.
23. *L'Abeille Américaine*, cited in Murat, *Dream*, 61.
24. On the Vine and Olive settlement generally, see Blaufarb, *Borderlands*; Murat, *Dream*; and Kent Gardien and Betje Black Klier, *Champ d'Asile* (The Handbook of Texas, Texas State Historical Association Online, https://tsaonline.org/handbook/online /articles/uec02) (hereinafter Gardien and Klier, *Champ d'Asile*). See also Reeves, *Exiles*, 560–65.

Chapter 7

1. Adams, *Diaries*, vol. 30, September 22, 1817, 257.
2. Ibid., September 22, 1817, 258.
3. Ibid.
4. Blaufarb, *Borderlands*, 78.
5. Ibid., 79.
6. For a complete description of these documents, see Reeves, *Exiles*, 571 et seq.
7. Blaufarb, *Borderlands*, 82.
8. Adams, *Diaries*, vol. 30, September 24, 1817, 258.
9. Ibid., September 26, 1817, 258.
10. Letter from John Quincy Adams to James Monroe, September 27, 1816, Library of Congress, James Monroe Papers: Series I, General Correspondence, 1758–1839; March 17, 1815—June 3, 1818 (reel 6).
11. Adams, *Diaries*, vol. 30, September 27, 1817, 258.
12. Ibid., September 28, 1817, 259.
13. For the content of Lee's report, see Reeves, *Exiles*, 585–88.
14. Blaufarb, *Borderlands*, 82.
15. Reeves, *Exiles*, 595.
16. Adams, *Diaries*, vol. 30, October 6, 1817, 262.
17. Ibid., October 20, 1817, 264.
18. José Corrêa da Serra was not only a churchman but also an accomplished philosopher, scientist, diplomat, and wit. He was one of Washington's great Enlightenment characters, widely popular and a good friend of Thomas Jefferson.
19. Adams, *Diaries*, vol. 30, November 9, 1817, 271.
20. Ibid., November 10, 1817, 271–72.
21. Ibid., November 21, 1817, 276.
22. Ibid., December 3, 1817, 281.
23. Reeves, *Exiles*, 589.
24. Adams, *Diaries*, vol. 30, January 21, 1818, 299.
25. Ibid., January 22, 1818, 300–301.
26. Ibid., January 23, 1818, 301.
27. Reeves, *Exiles*, 599–600.

28. Blaufarb, *Borderlands*, 63 and 100.

29. Reeves, *Exiles*, 603–604, citing the somewhat fictionalized account by one of the French party who used the pseudonym Just Girard.

30. It is unclear what Henri Lallemand's recent bride—or her uncle Stephen Girard—thought of Henri's decampment. Although Girard had apparently extended a $4,000 letter of credit for the benefit of the expedition, he was far from a major financial backer of it.

31. Reeves, *Exiles*, 604, citing Hartmann and Millard, *Le Texas, ou Notice historique sur le Champ d'Asile* (Paris: Béguin et al., 1819).

32. Adams, *Diaries*, vol. 30, March 18, 1818, 322.

33. Ibid., 321.

34. Reeves, *Exiles*, 603, fn. 2.

35. NARA, M 40, Adams to George Graham, June 2, 1818.

36. Reeves, *Exiles*, 605–6.

37. Just Girard, *Adventures of a French Captain at Present a Planter in Texas, Formerly a Refugee of Camp Asylum*, trans. Lady Blanche Murphy (New York: Benziger Bros., 1878) (hereinafter Girard, *Adventures*), 62.

38. For example, Murat, *Dream*, 132.

39. Girard, *Adventures*, 72.

40. Gardien and Klier, *Champ d'Asile*.

41. Reeves, *Exiles*, 607–8. See also *L'Abeille Américaine*, vol. 5, May 11, 1818.

42. Ibid., 616, citing L. F. L'Heritier, *Le Champ d'Asile, Tableau topographique et historique du Texas (publié au profit des Réfugiés)* (Paris, 1819), 18.

43. Girard, *Adventures*, 84.

44. Blaufarb, *Borderlands*, 110–11.

45. Ibid., 111–15.

46. See June 1829 letter from Joseph Bonaparte to Bayard and related letter from Bonaparte to Charles Lallemand at "193 Warrick Street, New York" at the HSP.

47. Shannon Selin blog, http://shannonselin.com/2014/05/general-charles-lallemand-invader-texas.

48. http://old-new-orleans.com/NO_College_d_Orleans.html, citing *The Picayune's Guide to New Orleans* (1903).

49. Murat, *Dream*, 137.

50. Ibid., 139.

51. For an excellent exposition on this phenomenon, see Orlando Figes, *The Europeans: Three Lives and the Making of a Cosmopolitan Culture* (New York: Henry Holt and Company, 2019).

Chapter 8

1. Sometimes his name is spelled "Peter Stuart Ney," but he most often spelled his middle name "Stewart," so that spelling is used here.

2. See, e.g., Raleigh (NC) *Sentinel*, November 9, 1867, 1.

3. James Augustus Weston, *Historical Doubts as to the Execution of Marshal Ney* (New York: Thomas Whittaker, 1895) (hereinafter Weston).

4. For example, Smoot, *Before and After the Execution*, and LeGette Blythe's fictionalized *Marshal Ney: A Dual Life* (New York: Stackpole Sons, 1937).

5. Dorothy Mackay Quynn, "Destination: America Marshal Ney's Attempt to Escape," *French Historical Studies* 2, no. 2 (1961): 232 (hereinafter Quynn).

6. John Mitchell, "Southern Mythology and Marshal Michel Ney" (BA diss., University of North Carolina, Asheville, 2003) (hereinafter Mitchell), 2.

7. A second repository of material relating to Marshal Ney and P. S. Ney is the Draper Manuscript Collection at the State Historical Society of Wisconsin. Lyman Copeland Draper was a mid- to late-nineteenth-century amateur scholar who investigated the Ney mystery, among many other subjects, and his papers are housed in the collection. Like Hoyt, he never committed his conclusions to publication.

8. George V. Taylor, "Scholarship and Legend, William Henry Hoyt's Research on the Ney Controversy," *South Atlantic Quarterly* 49, no. 3 (Summer 1960) (hereinafter Taylor), 5.

9. The ensuing profile of Ney's career and character is based primarily on Weston, A. Hilliard Atteridge, *The Bravest of the Brave* (London: Methuen & Co., 1912) (hereinafter Atteridge), and A. Bulos, *Memoirs of Marshal Ney* (Philadelphia: E. L. Carey and A. Hart, 1834), vols. 1 and 2 (published by Ney's family) (hereinafter Bulos)—all sources more than 100 years old. Harold Kurtz, *The Trial of Marshall Ney* (London: Hamish Hamilton, 1957), is also a useful English-language biography, especially on his later years. The profile of Ney in this chapter does not purport to be a dispositive, scholarly biography of Ney, although such a biography in English is probably long overdue. Even the existing French biographies of Ney are curiously limited. The *Memoirs* of Marshal Ney, originally published in France in 1833, stop at the end of his diplomatic mission to Switzerland, reportedly because of royalist pressure at the time of its publication. Henri Bonnal's *La Vie Militaire du Maréchal Ney* (Paris: Librairie Chapelot, 1914) stops after the Peninsular campaign. Neither biography is particularly insightful as to Ney's character or personal habits. See also J. Lucas-Dubreton, *Le Maréchal Ney* (Paris: Fayard, 1941). Ney's 12 major campaigns would include the Rhineland; Switzerland; the Rhine; the Danube; planned invasion of England; Ulm and Austerlitz; Jena, Eylau, and Friedland; Iberia; Russia; Dresden and Leipzig; the campaign of France and abdication; the Hundred Days and Waterloo. This breakdown is subjective but generally accords with the approach taken by Atteridge. Other historians have counted up to 20 campaigns in which Ney participated. In 1815, the *Times* of London credited him with "50 pitched battles" and "more than 500 combats." "Expose in Justification of Marshal Ney," *Times* of London, September 6, 1815 (hereinafter "Expose in Justification of Marshal Ney").

10. "When Marshal Grouchy was in this country in 1819 he was asked this question: 'Could Marshal Ney speak the English language?' 'Certainly he could,' replied Grouchy. And he mentioned that on one occasion, in the early years of the French Revolution, when he and Ney served together in the same army, some English prisoners were taken, and that Ney talked with them in their own language. General Lallemand, of the French army, also said that Ney understood the English language" (Weston, 285). One can only speculate why Grouchy and Lallemand were asked when they were in the United States if Ney spoke English; was it because there already were suspicions he was in the United

States? The context might also have been suspicions that an American soldier named Michael Rudolph was in fact Marshal Ney, as discussed in the final chapter of this book.

11. Weston also produces evidence that his mother might have been a woman named Catharine Rossman. Although that possibility has not been conclusively refuted, most historians concur that she was Margaret Groevelinger based on Ney's baptismal record.

12. Napoleon graduated from Brienne at 15, and he studied for one further year at the Royal Military Academy before being commissioned at age 16. Ney studied at the Collège des Augustins until he was 13 and then apprenticed as a notary/lawyer for two further years of study or professional formation, leaving for the workplace at 15. Napoleon was better educated than Ney but not markedly so.

13. Weston, 4.

14. Ney's 1788 enlistment records show him at the equivalent of 5 feet 9⅝ inches tall. However, he was only 19 at the time and could have grown another inch or so. During his lifetime, Marshal Ney was viewed as a tall man by his contemporaries. However, he was described at his trial in 1815, at age 46, as being 1 meter 73 centimeters in height, which is the equivalent of just over 5 feet 8 inches tall. See Taylor, 26–27. This was still taller than the average soldier of the day, but the basis for and accuracy of this measurement are unclear, and it is at odds with his enlistment measurement. It nonetheless suggests a possible discrepancy between the height of Marshal Ney and that of P. S. Ney.

15. These descriptions of Ney are all taken from Bulos, 34. See also Atteridge, 5.

16. Bulos, 6–7.

17. Weston, 5.

18. Ibid.

19. Ibid., 6.

20. Bulos, 76.

21. Ibid., 152–53.

22. Ibid., 153.

23. Ibid., 153–54.

24. For a comprehensive list of Ney's assignments and promotions, see Archives Nationales, *Fonds du Maréchal Ney et de sa Famille (1753–1923)*, 137AP/1-137AP/31, Inventaire de 137AP, Historique du Producteur, Etats des Services de Michel Ney, etc.

25. Bulos, 196.

26. Weston, 11–12.

27. Bulos, 255–56.

28. Atteridge, 13, quoting Bulos.

29. Bulos, 266.

30. Ibid., 272–73.

31. The listing at the Archives Nationales places him with the Army of the Danube in April 1799, but he clearly saw service in Switzerland.

32. Bulos, 292–93.

33. Ibid., 312.

34. Weston, 19.

35. Although there are many references to her name as "Aglaé Louise" and she was commonly known as "Aglaé," the name on her tomb is "Louise Aglaé."

36. Genêt was infamous because his primary mission was to press the Washington administration to accept France's interpretation of its 1778 treaties with the United States so as to allow France to establish privateer bases in the United States to attack British ships and to recruit an army of U.S. citizens to invade Spanish Louisiana and Florida in derogation of the U.S. policy of neutrality in the war between France and Britain. He also tried to extract a single complete payment of the U.S. Revolutionary War debt to France to help pay for these schemes. In his short tenure, "he insulted the sovereignty of America, exacerbated the tensions between Republican supporters of France and Federalist supporters of Great Britain, and ignored every protocol of diplomacy foreign ministers were expected to obey." See Carol Berkin, *A Sovereign People: The Crises of the 1790s and the Birth of American Nationalism* (New York: Basic Books 2017), 81–82. The Washington administration eventually requested his recall but because he feared execution by the Revolutionary government in Paris generously allowed him to remain in the United States. He became an American citizen, avoided politics, and resided in upstate New York.

37. Weston, 272.

38. George Clinton Genêt, "Mme. Campan's Contemporary Account," *The Century* 52, no. 3 (July 1896) (hereinafter Genêt, "Campan"), 420.

39. Moreau lived near Trenton, New Jersey, from 1806 to 1813. President Madison offered him command of U.S. troops at the outset of the War of 1812. He was at first amenable but then decided to return to Europe when he heard of the destruction of the Grande Armée in 1812. It proved to be a fatal choice, as he was killed in combat at Dresden later in 1813.

40. Ida Saint-Elme, *Memoirs of a Contemporary*, trans. Lionel Stracy (New York: Doubleday, Page & Company, 1902) (hereinafter Saint-Elme), 112–13.

41. Ney's letters are something of a rarity, so those that Saint-Elme includes in her memoirs are noteworthy and on occasion provide rare glimpses into Ney's private thoughts and character. For example, in a letter dated August 1800 from his headquarters at Neuburg when he was commander of the Army of the Rhine, Ney reveals both a grasp of political reality and a certain volubility and emotion that he allows to get the better of him. Writing of negotiations with the Austrians, he says, "Everyone believes we are to have peace, but I do not. I am persuaded that England will attempt the impossible to induce the Austrians to make another effort in this campaign. Their false pride is very likely to get the better of them and cause them to make that mistake. It seems difficult to convince these vain people that the French troops will continue to beat them whenever and wherever we attack them. I should recommend them to consider the thing carefully, to let us go back to the Rhine, and to sign a treaty of peace. Otherwise, we might easily, without much ado, go to Vienna. I would gladly give up the rest of my life to fight the execrable English, to compel those tigers whom human nature abhors to acknowledge the power of France, and to give her back what they impudently stole and tore away from her in violation of the rules of war. For I remember that these gentlemen are never as dangerous on the battlefield as when they are engaged in political strife or in criminal attempts to overthrow all social order—so long as it be to the greater glory of their own selves" (Saint-Elme, 97–98). The Austrians ultimately reconsidered their

prospects and entered into a peace agreement with France. So much for the notion that Ney was a semiliterate buffoon. He was, however, passionate, as evidenced by his comments on the English.

42. Ibid., 225.

43. Roberts, *Napoleon*, 640.

44. The life-size bust, executed in plaster, still exists in the collection at Versailles. Around 1840, an exact copy was produced in bronze.

45. Atteridge, 156.

46. Bulos, 33.

47. Atteridge, 5.

48. Weston, 36 et seq. The reference is to the Austrian General Karl Freiherr Mack, who was subsequently known as "the Unfortunate Mack."

49. Cited by Weston, 38.

50. The Hôtel Beauharnais was occupied by the Prussians after Waterloo and remains the German ambassador's residence to this day. Two Napoleonic stone eagles still perch atop the pillars of its entrance gate.

51. Mitchell, 5, citing Smoot, 3, and correspondence between Smoot and the Masonic temple in Paris contained in the Davidson College archives.

52. Weston, 42.

53. See generally ibid., 45–46.

54. Atteridge, 195.

55. The following description of Ney's actions in the Russian campaign, including quotations unless indicated otherwise, is taken from Weston, who quotes extensively from an unidentified and undated nineteenth-century English translation of Ségur's *Expedition to Russia*. Also of immense interest is the journal kept by Ney's one-time aide-de-camp Lieutenant General M. De Fezensac, *A Journal of the Russian Campaign of 1812* (London: Parker, Furnivall and Parker, 1852).

56. Weston, 53.

57. Weston, 202–3, citing Ségur's *Expedition to Russia*. Some versions of this story refer to the child as an "infant," but this may be a mistranslation of the French *enfant*, meaning a child.

58. Atteridge, 232.

59. Raymond Aimery de Montesquiou-Fezensac (1784–1867) was a relative of Pierre de Montesquiou d'Artagnan of Three Musketeers fame. Like Ney, he enlisted as a common soldier, rose through the ranks, and eventually became both a lieutenant general and a duke.

60. Atteridge, 233.

61. Wrede and his Bavarians were allies of Napoleon until 1813, when he switched sides, joined with the Austrians, and tried to block Napoleon's return to France. Napoleon fought and beat him.

62. Atteridge, 239.

63. Ibid., 242–43.

64. According to Madame Campan, the Peninsular and Russian campaigns had personally cost Ney 600,000 francs and had left him with the country estate at Courdreaux as his only major asset. See Genêt, 420.

65. Atteridge, 267.
66. *Court and Camp of Bonaparte*, quoted in Weston, 81.
67. Ibid., 82.
68. Atteridge, 307–8.
69. Weston, 84–85.
70. The possible significance of Ney's proximity to and likely personal engagement with Ponsonby's charge is explained in chapter 11.
71. The possible significance of this saber cut is also explained in chapter 11.
72. Atteridge, 327.
73. Ibid., 327–29.
74. "Expose in Justification of Marshal Ney."
75. Genêt, 420.
76. Napoleon presented Ney with an elaborate golden snuffbox. The snuffbox was looted from Ney's baggage in the immediate aftermath of Waterloo. It still exists and is in the collection of the Green Howards Regimental Museum in the United Kingdom. See http://waterloo200.org/200-object/marshal-neys-snuffbox.

Chapter 9

1. Dispatch from Jackson to Monroe, July 12, 1815, NARA M-24, roll 19, vol. 16.
2. See Mirante, *Medusa's Head*, 185–86.
3. Letter from Ney to Fouché, June 29, 1816, Archives Nationales, *Fonds du Maréchal Ney et de sa famille (1753–1923)*, 137AP, AF/IV/1934, pièce 23. At this point, Ney was probably in Paris. As related by Madame Campan, his château at Courdreaux was eventually occupied by Prussian soldiers who stripped it bare. They loaded their wagons with all its furniture, books, and other belongings, but their commanders decided to sell the lot instead of steal it. The Neys' furnishings were offered for sale at giveaway prices in the nearby market town of Châteaudun. Not a single local would bid on them out of respect for the marshal. After the troops left, they gathered the furnishings up and returned them to the château, Madame Ney losing in the process only one volume out of her "very beautiful library." Genêt, "Campan," 420–21.
4. Why this name was chosen is unclear. However, Neuberg or Neubourg in French was Ney's headquarters in Bavaria on the Danube in 1800.
5. Saint-Elme, *Memoirs*, 230.
6. Quoted in M. K. Ney, *The Marshal and the Myth* (Morgantown, PA: Mastoff Press, 2001), 161.
7. Michel Ney, *Report of the Trial for High Treason and Attempts against the Safety of the State* (Paris: Gaglianis, 1815) (hereinafter Ney, *Report of the Trial*), 26.
8. For a detailed discussion of Ney's flight and arrangements to escape to America, see Quynn, "Destination," 232–41.
9. Letter from Count Angles, Minister of State, Prefect of Police, to the Minister of General Police, December 8, 1816, Archives Nationales, *Fonds du Maréchal Ney et de sa famille (1753–1923)*, 137AP, F/7/6800, dossier 924.
10. Papers Relating to Marshal Ney's Imprisonment and Trial, 1815–1817, Hoyt Collection, ser. 2, fol. 162.

11. Saint-Elme, *Memoirs*, 230.

12. Mirante, *Medusa's Head*, 203, citing Pierre, *Ney: Procès politique à la réhabilitation du "Brave des braves" de 1815 à 1991.*

13. Letter from Duke of Wellington to E. Cooke, December 1815, Wellington's Dispatches, Hoyt Collection, ser. 2, fol. 201.

14. Ney, *Report of the Trial*, 13.

15. Ibid., 23. This provides an interesting insight into Ney's motivation for remaining in France.

16. Ibid., 10–11.

17. Michel Ney, *Procès du Maréchal Ney, Deuxième Edition* (Paris: Michaud, 1815), 17.

18. Antoine Lavallette, *Memoirs of Count Lavallette* (London: Gibbings and Company, 1894) (hereinafter Lavallette, *Memoirs*), 218–19. See also undated inventory of Ney's personal possessions in La Conciergerie, Hoyt Collection, ser. 6, reel 20, and ser. 2, fol. 158; see also Archives Nationales 137AP/16, pièce 156. The involvement of the three Englishmen in Lavallette's escape is well documented because they were found out and tried by the French government. On Bruce's relationship with Madame Ney, see Taylor, "Scholarship and Legend," 23, citing some 50 letters that passed between them during 1814–1817 and subsequently published by the Bruce family in Ian Bruce, *Lavallette Bruce: His Adventures and Intrigues before and after Waterloo* (London: Hamish Hamilton, 1953).

19. Kurtz, *Trial*, 273.

20. Lavallette, *Memoirs*, 206.

21. See documents in Hoyt Collection, ser. 2, fol. 117.

22. Saint-Elme, *Memoirs*, 232.

23. Letter from Stuart to Castlereagh, November 6, 1815, Documents in the Public Record Office, London, 1815, Hoyt Collection, ser. 2, fol. 202.

24. *Times* of London, November 10, 1815.

25. André Dupin, *Memoires de M. Dupin* (Paris: Plon,1855) (hereinafter Dupin, *Memoires*), 42–43.

26. The king had explicitly used it to justify the saving of a bridge in Paris. This fact did not come out until after the trial.

27. Letter from Ney to Wellington, November 13, 1815, Hoyt Collection, ser. 2, fol. 202, 233–35.

28. Extract from the *Procès Verbal* of a Conference between the Plenopotentiaries, etc., November 16, 1815, Documents in the Public Record Office, London, 1815, Hoyt Collection, ser. 2, fol. 202, 233; see also Extract of a Letter (from an Evening Paper) Paris, *Times* of London, November 16, 1815.

29. Letters from La Maréchale Ney to the Prince Regent and Earl of Liverpool, November 13, 1815, Documents in the Public Record Office, London, 1815, Hoyt Collection, ser. 2, fol. 202, 231–33.

30. Additional Note, November 14, 1815, Documents in the Public Record Office, London, 1815, Hoyt Collection, ser. 2, fol. 202, 231–32.

31. Letter from Stuart to Castlereagh, November 13, 1815, Documents in the Public Record Office, London, 1815, Hoyt Collection, ser. 2, fol. 202.

32. Letter from Wellington to Ney, November 15, 1815, Hoyt Collection, ser. 2, fol. 116.

33. Extract from the *Procès Verbal* of a Conference between the Plenopotentiaries, etc., November 16, 1815, Documents in the Public Record Office, London, 1815, Hoyt Collection, ser. 2, fol. 202, 233.

34. Letter from Stuart to Castlereagh, November 16, 1815, enclosing letter from La Maréchale Ney to Stuart of the same date, Documents in the Public Record Office, London, 1815, Hoyt Collection, ser. 2, fol. 202, 236–38.

35. Wellington Memorandum, November 19, 1815, The Duke of Wellington, ed., *Supplementary Despatches, Correspondence and Memoranda of Field Marshal Arthur Duke of Wellington, K.G.*, vol. 10 (London: John Murray, 1843), 694–96.

36. Saint-Elme, *Memoirs*, 233. Davout was one of Napoleon's ablest marshals. He was the original commander of the rear guard on the retreat from Moscow until Napoleon replaced him with Ney. Still, Davout remained devoted to Ney, in whom he recognized a fellow loyalist to France and sought to avert his condemnation.

37. *Times* of London, November 21, 1815.

38. Letter from Stuart to Castlereagh, November 23, 1815, Documents in the Public Record Office, London, 1815, Hoyt Collection, ser. 2, fol. 202. The references are to Marshal Charles-Pierre-Francois Augereau and Generals Augustin Daniel Belliard, Pierre David Edouard de Colbert-Chabanis, Philippe-Antoine d'Ornano (Napoleon's second cousin who was the next year to marry the emperor's former mistress Marie Walewska), Toussaint Campi, Gilbert Desiré Joseph Bachelu, and Pierre François Xavier Boyer. It is unclear whether Augereau was active or complicit in the plot. He was not arrested.

39. It also was the view of the American general Winfield Scott, who was in Paris and who wrote James Monroe on November 18, 1815, "The Council of War assembled for the trial of Marshal Ney decided a few days since against its competency. He is now before the Chamber of Peers and will no doubt be condemned, for the Duke de Richelieu, has in an official Speech, told the chamber that nothing less will satisfy his majesty, or his allies. All the ministers & generals of the allies attend the trial, to overawe the accused, & the better to ensure his conviction. To witness the execution, tickets for places are already granted." See "Enclosure: Winfield Scott to James Monroe, 18 November 1815," *Founders Online*, National Archives, https://founders.archives.gov /documents/Jefferson/03-09-02-0248-0002. (Original source: J. Jefferson Looney, ed., *The Papers of Thomas Jefferson: September 1815 to April 1816*, Retirement Series, vol. 9 [Princeton, NJ: Princeton University Press, 2012], 390–93.)

40. Ney, *Report of the Trial*, 83.

41. Ibid., 55 and 83.

42. Anonymous, *Journal de Service extraordinaire ordonné pour la guarde du Maréchal Ney* (1815), Hoyt Collection, ser. 2, fol. 117 (translation by the author).

43. Letter from Richelieu to Decazes dated only "This Sunday morning," Hoyt Collection, ser. 2, fol. 117 (translation by the author).

44. Letter dated November 27, 1815, from Lord Bathurst, Foreign Office, London to Sir Charles Stuart, British Embassy, Paris, Hoyt Collection, ser. 2, fol. 116.

45. See letter dated December 2, 1815, from Count de Noué, sub-prefect of Soissons to Minister of War Clarke and letter dated December 4, 1815, from Marshal Count

Grundler, commander of the Aisne subdivision of the First Military Division to Lieutenant General H. Despinois, commander of the First Military Division in Paris on the
same subject, Archives Nationales, 137AP/16, items 145 and 146.

46. See Archives Nationales, Dossier personnel du maréchal Ney, 2nd ser., no. 12,
137AP/1-137AP/20, Archives du maréchal Ney.

47. Dupin, *Memoires*, 46–47.

48. Ney, *Report of the Trial*, 111–13.

49. See generally Weston, *Historical Doubts*, 104–5.

50. *Notes & Queries*, vol. 6, no. 160, November 20, 1852, 481; see also Alphonse de la
Martine, *History of the Restoration of Monarchy in France*, vol. 8 (London: George Bell &
Sons, 1891) (hereinafter de la Martine, *History of the Restoration*), 320.

51. Weston, *Historical Doubts*, 110 et seq.

52. Hyacinthe François Joseph Despinois (1764–1848) had been a French Revolutionary general, but Napoleon removed him from battlefield command because of his lack-
luster performance. Following his service involving the execution of Marshal Ney, the
Bourbons promoted and ennobled him in 1816. Unfortunately, he left no memoirs.

53. See *La Quotiedienne*, December 8, 1815, Hoyt Collection, ser. 2, fol. 122. Rochechouart had spent many years in the service of Tsar Alexander I of Russia before returning to France.

54. Comte de Rochechouart, *Souvenirs*, 2nd ed. (Paris: Librairie Plon, 1892), 52 et seq.

55. Ibid., 434–37 (translation by the author).

56. The dispositions at Borodino are confusing, but the basic order of battle is given at
www.napolun.com/mirror/napoleonistyka.atspace.com. It appears that the carabiniers
were integrated with the cavalry and not under Ney's direct command, but they fought
closely with Ney in and around the Shevardino Redoubt.

57. Bruno Belhoster, *Augustin-Louis Cauchy: A Biography* (New York: Springer-Verlag,
1991), 5.

58. Extract from the report of M. Laisne, Inspector General of Prisons, December 7,
1815, Archives Nationales, F-7 6683, Hoyt Collection, ser. 2, fol. 121, translated from
the French.

59. Comte de Rochechouart, *Memoirs*, trans. Frances Jackson (New York: E. P. Dutton
& Company, 1920) (English version of Rochechouart's *Souvenirs*) (hereinafter Rochechouart, *Memoirs*), 329–30.

60. de la Martine, *History of the Restoration*, 325–26.

61. *Niles' Weekly Register*, February 3, 1816.

62. See Atteridge, *Bravest*, 366–67: "The Abbe de St. Pierre . . . had a record of courageous devotion to duty under conditions even more trying than those amid which Ney
had won his name of the "bravest of the brave." Before the Revolution the Abbe had
been one of the Sulpician community. In the days of the Terror he had remained hidden
in Paris. He had said Mass in garrets and cellars for little groups of the faithful. He had
gone disguised to the bedsides of the sick and dying. He had ventured to the very steps
of the guillotine to give the last blessing and absolution to Catholics on their way to
death. For months he had carried his life in his hands, and after the Concordat, refusing
a higher position, he had become Cure of St. Sulpice and re-organized the great parish."

63. Facsimile of note taken from Comte de la Bedoyère, *Le Maréchal Ney* (Paris: Calmann-Lévy, 1902) (hereinafter de la Bedoyère, *Le Maréchal*), 286, translated from the French, Hoyt Collection, ser. 2, fol. 120.

64. Rochechouart, *Memoirs*, 330.

65. Ibid.

66. Ibid., 330–31.

67. Saint-Elme, *Memoirs*, 234–35.

68. See Hoyt Collection, ser. 2, fol. 170.

69. Rochechouart, *Memoirs*, 331.

70. Saint-Elme, *Memoirs*, 235.

71. Rochechouart, *Memoirs*, 332.

72. The exact location of Ney's execution is not obvious today because of substantial rearrangement of the streets in the 1850s and more than 200 years of urban development. However, Rochechouart provides some geographical context: "I received a verbal order [presumably from Despinois] to make the arrangements between the Observatory and the gate of the garden of the Luxembourg, facing a wall, which is still standing, at the left as you go out of the garden. The police had learned that there would be an attempt at a rescue near Grenelle.... A few hundred yards from the iron gate of the Luxembourg, in the Avenue de l'Observatoire, the procession stopped." Rochechouart, *Memoirs*, 331–32. Rochechouart thus implies but does not expressly state that the procession moved through the garden of the Luxembourg Palace to what is now the Avenue de l'Observatoire. It probably took this route because Despinois' explicit orders quoted above were for it to proceed through the Luxembourg garden and because at the time the Avenue de l'Observatoire ran directly from the Luxembourg garden to the place de l'Observatoire (before southward expansion of the Luxembourg garden). The London *Times* reported it as using this route at the time. The conventional view is that the execution spot was at or near the spot where François Rude's bronze statue of Ney, with right arm and sword raised and exhorting his troops to follow, stood when first erected in the place de l'Observatoire. See, e.g., J. A. Galignani and W. Galignani, *Galignani's New Paris Guide for 1872* (Paris: Galignani and Co., 1872), 329. The statue was erected in 1853 and unveiled in the presence of Napoleon III. As stated in the 1872 *Galignani's Guide*, it stood beside the garden of the Closerie des Lilas, a public dance garden on the east side of the place de l'Observatoire. The wall against which Ney was executed bordered the dance garden. However, the statue is currently on the west side of the place de l'Observatoire. In point of fact, the statue was originally erected on the east side of the place de l'Observatoire (on the actual execution spot) but was moved in 1892 to allow construction of a train line. The matter is made all the more confusing because the statue currently is next to the garden of a famed café called the Closerie des Lilas patronized by Ernest Hemingway and Vladimir Lenin, among others. The café is named for the dance garden that stood on the opposite side of the place de l'Observatoire. Rochechouart thus places the execution ground on the left or east of the Avenue de l'Observatoire, as one faces south, several hundred yards from the Luxembourg garden gate. This would be approximately where Rude's statue of Ney originally stood. In today's Paris, the execution site would be more or less where the RER Port-Royal commuter train station now stands.

The only problem with this location is that Lieutenant General Hyacinth Despinois, who planned the details of the execution that were carried out by Rochechouart and who expressly chose the site for the execution, writing on the day of the execution to Minister of War Clarke, places the execution on the boulevard d'Enfer: "J'ai l'honneur de rendre compte à Votre Excellence que l'arrêt de la Chambre des Pairs, portant condamnation de l'ex-maréchal Ney à la peine de mort, a reçu son exécution aujourd'hui 7 courant, à neuf heures et quart du matin *sur la partie du boulevard d'Enfer située entre le jardin du Luxembourg et l'Observatoire*" (emphasis added). See letter from Despinois to Clarke quoted in full at de la Bédoyère, *Le Maréchal*, 502. Despinois thus unequivocally places it on "the part of the boulevard d'Enfer situated between the Luxembourg garden and the Observatoire." The former boulevard d'Enfer is today's boulevard Raspail. The boulevard d'Enfer was a ring road that ran alongside the ancient city wall and terminated in a customs collecting post at the end of the boulevard. See https://fr.wikipedia .org/wiki/Passage_d'Enfer. It does not run between the Luxembourg garden and the Observatoire. It in fact runs a short distance from but south and west of these two sites. It is distinctly *not* the Avenue de l'Observatoire. However, the confusion thus sown by Despinois is readily solved by looking at pre-1850s maps of Paris, such as Ambroise Tardieu's 1839 Plan de Paris. It shows a separate rue d'Enfer (the vestigial northern end of which is today's rue Henri Barbusse) running to the east of the Luxembourg gardens and then bending into the place de l'Observatoire before continuing southward on the other side of the intersection, so that it is indeed exactly "situated between the Luxembourg garden and the Observatoire" and squares with Rochechouart's account of the execution spot. Almost certainly, Despinois was referring to the rue d'Enfer when he said the boulevard d'Enfer. Perhaps not entirely coincidentally, François Rude, the sculptor of the Ney statue, lived and died at 17 rue d'Enfer.

Despinois' choice of the intersection of the rue d'Enfer and the place de l'Observatoire was evidently driven by expediency. By avoiding the Plaine de Grenelle, the usual military execution ground near Les Invalides, Despinois hoped to dispose of the matter quickly, discreetly, and without an anticipated attempt by Ney's supporters to free him.

Note that Rochechouart's *Memoirs* were published in 1857 and that he stated above that the wall was still standing. Early photographs taken in the 1850s show the wall behind Rude's statue. A later, clearer photograph dating from the 1880s shows the same wall and is included as figure 9.3.

73. Archives Nationales, BB/11/150/B, dossier 8034 B2.

74. Rochechouart, *Memoirs*, 332–33.

75. Extract from the report of M. Laisne, Inspector General of Prisons, December 7, 1815, Archives Nationales, F-7 6683, Hoyt Collection, ser. 2, fol. 121 (translated from the French).

76. *Niles' Weekly Register*, February 3, 1816.

77. Saint-Elme, *Memoirs*, 235–36.

78. According to eyewitnesses, during these 15 minutes, the body lay undisturbed with two exceptions. First, an unidentified male civilian approached the body, dabbed his handkerchief in the blood-soaked ground, and walked away. Second, a mounted Dutch

officer in the service of Tsar Alexander I who had witnessed the execution spurred his horse forward and had it jump over the body before riding off. Reportedly, when the tsar heard of this incident, he dismissed the officer from the Russian army because of the disrespect he had shown. Neither of these incidents is relevant to the question of whether the execution was real. More relevant were the absences of a coup de grâce and of a doctor's death certificate.

79. Genêt, "Campan," 422.

80. Report of Cauchy, December 7, 1815, Hoyt Collection, ser. 2, fol. 121 (translated from the French). Note that Cauchy states that the place de l'Observatoire was the place designated for the execution.

81. The domed building with a spire in the background behind the wall in the painting also appears in other, earlier prints depicting the execution. Most likely, it is the cupola of the nearby Church of Val de Grâce. It would not appear to be l'Observatoire, which has no spire and which is farther away. Indeed, one might question how much detail Arago could have seen from the somewhat distant Observatoire. The painting, which is now viewed by many as a masterpiece, debuted to mixed reviews. Critics panned it as derivative of Edouard Manet's *Dead Toreador* (1864). Marshal Ney's grandson objected to its representation of the marshal dressed like a "clerical schoolmaster." Not only is that criticism ironic in light of the emergence of P. S. Ney, but the marshal was in fact so dressed at his execution.

82. Genêt, "Campan," citing Madame Campan, 421.

83. See report from Count Angles, Minister of State, Prefect of Police, to the Minister of General Police, November 24, 1816, Archives Nationales, *Fonds du Maréchal Ney et de sa famille (1753–1923)*, 137AP, F/7/6799, dossier 851. It is not clear what type of "relations" the report alleged.

84. The tomb is located in Division 29 high up in the hilly cemetery, precariously perched at the intersection of two *chemins*, or walkways. The current iteration of the tomb, executed in granite, dates to 1903. It is at once inviting and forbidding. Its back and sides sweep like sheltering wings, inviting entry, but entry is impossible because the front is blocked by bollards looped with heavy metal chains. Somehow, the ambiguity is appropriate given the context. Ney's father-in-law, who died in September 1815, is buried in the tomb, as are various of Ney's children. Ney's wife, the Maréchale, is not buried there. This area in Père Lachaise became known as the preferred burial place for Napoleon's senior military and political leaders. One of the tomb's neighbors is the final resting place of Jean-Jacques-Régis de Cambacérès, Duke of Parma, Napoleon's immensely talented, grossly fat, and openly gay right-hand man who effectively ran French domestic affairs while Napoleon was away campaigning. Despite some efforts to preserve and commemorate important tombs, most of the tombs in the crowded cemetery are crumbling in decay. The wear and tear of 200 years leads the visitor to speculate that in another 200 years, there will be little left. *Sic transit gloria mundi.*

85. See, e.g., *La Quotidenne* and *Le Constitutionnel*, both December 8, 1815. The latter reports Ney's last words as more closely resembling those reported by Madame Campan: "I protest before God and the country against the judgment that condemned me. I appeal to humanity, to posterity, to God: *Vive la France!*" Hoyt Collection, ser. 2, fol. 122.

86. See, e.g., Weston, 44, where P. S. Ney explained his escape: "He then told me how he escaped. He said he was tried and condemned to be shot, and was apparently shot, and that his countrymen thought he was a dead man. 'Louis XVIII,' said he, 'was full of revenge. He ordered that some of my old soldiers, whom I had often led into battle, should be my executioners. The thing was so revolting to Frenchmen that a plan was formed for my escape. The officer appointed to superintend my execution told one of my friends to apply to the king for my body for interment. He did so, and the necessary permission was granted. I was told to give the command fire, and to fall as I gave it. I did so. The soldiers, who had previously been instructed, fired almost instantly, the balls passing over my head and striking the planks or wall behind. I was pronounced dead, hastily taken up, put into a carriage, and driven off to a neighboring hospital. That night I was disguised and left for America.'" No extant eyewitness account of the execution, however, has Ney give the order to fire, and only one has the body placed in a carriage for transmittal to the hospital, while all others have him conveyed on a stretcher.

87. See, e.g., Pascal Cazottes, "Did Marshal Ney Die in America?," www.napoleonic society.com/english/neya.htm.

Chapter 10

1. Hoyt Collection, ser. 2, fol. 134. In addition to the note and lawsuit for $43.83, there is a 1821 note from Ney for $20.

2. See https://southcarolinagoddess.tumblr.com/post/161967728826/so-im-working-on -my-next-blog-post-about-peter. This entry alone leaves little question that P. S. Ney was a singular man.

3. *Mecklenburg Jeffersonian*, November 30, 1841.

4. The 49 testimonials contained in this chapter are redacted from the many more in Weston, 135–226. Weston does not provide detail on how he collected the testimonials. Apparently, many of them came from materials in the Draper MSS. He dates many of them, and they run from the 1870s into the 1890s. Some appear to have been written by the testators, but others appear to have been transcribed interviews or summarized letters. The repetition of a few key phrases ("said he," "equaled but not excelled," and so on) and the repeated use of semicolons in particular suggest that Weston himself transcribed and/or edited them. However, the author has no reason to suspect that they are not genuine or in the main accurate as to what the testators said. But see James R. Garfield, "Doubts Concerning the Execution of Marshal Ney," *Wisconsin Magazine of History* 2, no. 3 (March 1919): 352–53 (https://www.jstor.org/stable/4630178), in which unnamed workers at the State Historical Society of Wisconsin responded to an inquiry from Mr. Garfield by stating that Weston visited the Draper collection and used the Draper manuscripts and "in some cases altered and extracted to give support to the conclusion the author wished to deduce." One contemporary who had studied under P. S. Ney, Judge Victor Barringer, called Weston "credulous." It is therefore possible (if not likely) that Weston to a degree cherry-picked information in the process, but, if so, that still does not mean that the sources he cites are necessarily false.

5. Other eyewitnesses expressly stated that he did not know Hebrew. See, e.g., October 1, 1885, letter to Lyman Draper from unidentified author, probably Mary C. Dalton,

stating that Ney knew Latin and Greek but not Hebrew (although, confident of his intellect, Ney boasted that he could probably learn it with study). Draper MSS 1RR72.

6. There is no definition of this word in either English or French. It is unclear what it means. It possibly might be a misspelling of the archaic English verb *bedote*, meaning "to deceive" or "to fool." As a word used by Shakespeare, it was the type of word that P. S. Ney characteristically might have deployed.

7. If Murat did cut down his assailant, the incident did not happen at Waterloo, as Murat was not present at Waterloo.

8. In addition to the eyewitness accounts detailed by Weston, Smoot in his 1929 book *Marshal Ney before and after Execution* adds documented additional ones, all supportive of the thesis that P. S. Ney was in fact Marshal Ney.

9. See Buffalo *Sunday Morning News*, May 29, 1887, 2.

10. Hoyt Collection, ser. 2, fol. 145.

11. Hoyt Collection, ser. 2, fol. 146.

12. The supposition that Marshal Ney was trepanned and that he bore a silver plate in his head is suspect. The author has been unable to find any contemporary corroboration of such an operation on Marshal Ney, and his portraits show no evidence of it. The 1887 exhumation was instigated largely by Lyman Draper in pursuit of the silver plate as evidence. Draper's basis for thinking that Ney had a silver plate in his head from a trepanning is unclear.

13. An effort to open P. S. Ney's grave again in July 1936 for the same purpose apparently came to naught.

Chapter 11

1. Taylor, "Scholarship and Legend," 5.

2. Certificate of arrival of Ney's corpse at the hospital of La Maternité, December 7, 1815, Hoyt Collection, ser. 2, fol. 121 (translated from the French).

3. Report of the superior officer commanded to execute the judgment of Marshal Ney, December 7, 1815, Hoyt Collection, ser. 2, fol. 120 (translation by the author). Note that the receipt for the corpse states that the police brought it to the hospital. St. Bias states that his soldiers brought it. Perhaps the soldiers accompanied the police who carried the stretcher.

4. Report dated December 7, 1815, from Despinois to Clarke, Hoyt Collection, ser. 2, fol. 120 (translation by the author).

5. Report dated December 7, 1815, from Despinois to the Count de Semonville, Hoyt Collection, ser. 2, fol. 121 (translation by the author).

6. See death certificate of Ney, extract from the register of death certificates, year 1815, 12th Mayoralty, No. 4 Registry Office, Register 128, No. 736, available in the Hoyt Collection, ser. 2, fol. 123.

7. Gamot died in 1820 while writing a book defending Ney's performance at Waterloo. Rayot died in 1847.

8. Document dated May 2, 1835, Hoyt Collection, ser. 2, fol. 104 (translation by the author).

9. See Chambersburg, Pennsylvania *Democratic Republican*, vol. 1, issue 16 (February 20, 1816), 3. The article may be less than credible because it misspells Despinois' name and because it claims that only five out of 16 bullets fired struck Ney, which is almost certainly more bullets than the 12-person firing squad would have discharged. Also, based on the historical record, it is uncertain whether Despinois was present at the execution. Nonetheless, it provides an interesting gloss on the conduct of St. Bias. The article's assertion that Ney fell on his knees is consistent with the assumption that he fell forward when shot, although Taylor, in "Scholarship and Legend," quotes Rochechouart as writing in the original manuscript of his memoirs that he "fell on his back" (8). Oddly, and in contrast, both the original French edition and later English translation of Rochechouart's *Souvenirs* merely state that he fell without reference to his position. If the eyewitness Rochechouart was accurate in stating that Ney fell on his back, this would almost certainly puncture the theory of the blood-filled bladder. However, Rochechouart did not complete his memoirs until 1857. He was by then old and may have had a faulty recollection or even a motive for stating that Ney fell on his back, such as to discredit the escape theories that had been circulating since the very day of the execution.

10. The government kept detailed records of the expenses of Ney's trial and execution, which were ultimately billed to Ney's estate. Interestingly, these records show the receipt by Alexandre Cauchy, the second son of Secretary Archivist Louis Cauchy, of reimbursements for transcribing work and rental of vehicles. See document titled "Advances for the Trial of Marshal Ney," Hoyt Collection, ser. 2, fol. 162.

11. See, e.g., Taylor, "Scholarship and Legend," 19–22.

12. Rochechouart, *Souvenirs*, 441.

13. *Exposé de la Conduite*, in the handwriting of St. Bias, January 6, 1816, Hoyt Collection, ser. 2, fols. 140–144 (translation by the author).

14. Archives Nationales, BB/11/15/B, dossier 8034 B2.

15. See Hoyt Collection, ser. 2, fol. 163.

16. A different count was provided by the U.S. legation in Paris when Draper asked them to investigate the bullets in 1888. Their count, presumably based on discussions with French officials, was three in the head and three in the body. Draper MSS 2RR73. If this figure is accurate, it evidences an even higher miss rate, with five or almost half of the squad improbably missing their target.

17. Genêt, 422. *L'Abeille Américaine* reported, from a distance and probably rhetorically, on July 18, 1816, "The pressure with which the crowd takes itself each day to the grounds where Ney was shot have made it necessary for the police to make disappear the vestiges of this horrible execution. The wall on which were imprinted the last drops of blood that the hero of Moscow shed for the country has been re-covered with plaster" (218).

18. See, e.g., eyewitness account by Pelletier recounted in Taylor, "Scholarship and Legend," 11.

19. "Notes d'un officier du 5e hussards," in *Révue retrospective, réceuil de pièces interessantes et de citations curieuses*, Nouvelle serie . . . juillet-décembre, 1890 (Paris, 1891), 362–70, cited in Taylor, "Scholarship and Legend," 10.

20. See Henderson testimony in chapter 10.

21. See *Waterloo Medal Book*, UK National Archives MINT 15/112/7. No "Robert Laird" is listed under the Sixth (Inniskilling) Dragoons or any other unit that fought at Waterloo.

22. Anonymous police report, December 9, 1815, Archives Nationales, F7 6683, cited in Taylor, "Scholarship and Legend," 12. The reference to a "movement" presumably means an effort to save Ney from execution.

23. Anonymous police report, December 9, 1815, Archives Nationales, F7 6683, cited in Taylor, "Scholarship and Legend," 12. Apparently, questions arose almost immediately. In papers filed by Tench Coxe, clerk of the Court of General Quarter Sessions at Philadelphia on September 15, 1817, it was stated, "It was impossible to get the French public to believe that Ney had really been killed in the execution, and nearly to this day we have had fresh stories recurring of the real Ney being discovered in America." M. K. Ney, *The Marshal and the Myth* (Morgantown, PA: Masthof Press, 2001), 164.

24. Letter from Wellington to Tsar Alexander I, December 7, 1815, UK Public Record Office, F.O. 146/4, Hoyt Collection, ser. 2, fol. 202; letter from Stuart to Castlereagh, December 7, 1815, Hoyt Collection, ser. 2, fol. 202.

25. Pelletier, "*Notes d'un temoin oculaire des premiers instants après la mort du Maréchal Ney...*," Archives Nationales, *Fonds du Maréchal Ney et de sa Famille (1753–1923)*, 137AP/16, pièce 162 and preface, 7 (translation by the author). Pelletier's account was evidently written in 1835 and had been solicited by Ney's son, the second Prince de la Moskowa, when gathering information on his father's death. See Taylor, "Scholarship and Legend," 11.

26. Saint-Elme, *Memoirs*, 236.

27. For example, Weston, 123.

28. *La Quotidienne,* December 8, 1815, Hoyt Collection, ser. 2, fol. 123.

29. Hoyt Collection, ser. 2, fol. 122.

30. The document, *Inventaire après decès du maréchal Ney*, is in the Archives Nationales. *Minutes et reportoires du notaire Henri Batardy, 23 novembre 1799–8 juin 1836* (étude CXVII), MC/ET/CXVII/989-MC/ET/CXVII/1163. MC/ET/CXVII/16-MC/RE /CXVII/20-MC/RS//1075. Among other things, the inventory confirms the birth date of Ney's third son, Eugène, as being September 12, 1806, and documents the extensive and sophisticated contents of Ney's wine cellar, thus confirming his use of wine. The collection also has a logbook in which Batardy recorded his official acts by chronological date. Neither March 7 nor December 7, when he is known to have met with Ney on important matters, contains any entries relevant to Ney, although a December 1 entry under the heading "Obligation," meaning obligation or bond, records Madame Ney undertaking to act as proxy for her husband but without stating to what purpose.

31. *L'Abeille Américaine*, vol. 3, August 8, 1816, 243.

32. Letter dated November 27, 1816, from the prefect of police to the minister of police, Archives Nationales, F7-6683, Hoyt Collection, ser. 2, fol. 129.

33. Taylor, "Scholarship and Legend," 16.

34. "Marshal Ney's Grandson," New York *World*, November 1, 1886, 3, cited in Taylor, "Scholarship and Legend," 15. The exact wording of Ney's statements, as printed in the newspaper in 1886, is as follows:

M. Ney has been greatly surprised during the last few days to note the vast amount of interest displayed in the United States concerning the fate of his illustrious grandfather and to a representative of THE WORLD alluded to the well-known story frequently published in the American press, according to which the celebrated Marshal succeeded in escaping to the United States, and after spending many years in South Carolina as a school-teacher finally died in 1846 at Charleston [*sic*]. M. Ney absolutely denied the truth of the above story and likewise designated as unfounded the assertion that if the coffin of the Marshal at the Paris Cemetery of Pere-La-Chaise were opened it would be found empty.

"It is perfectly absurd," said M. Ney. "When my grandfather's remains were finally [in 1816] transferred to their last resting place at Pere-La-Chaise the coffin was opened and the bullet-holes in the forehead were distinctly visible." As to the romance widely published in this country according to which Major Michael Rudolph of Lee's legion in our Revolutionary War, went from this country to France, joined the French army and became the great Marshal [see discussion of the Rudolph legend below], M. Ney asserts that the mother of the grandfather was the daughter of the well-known Paris banker M. Augue [*sic*].

Several comments on the above statements. First, Napoleon Ney was not an eyewitness to the exhumation in 1816. Second, it is difficult to conceive how bullet holes would have been "distinctly visible" in the forehead when three .69-caliber bullets were fired at point-blank range into his head, which would surely have left more damage than visible holes. Third, the answer provided by Ney to the question concerning the Rudolph legend is inapposite and a non sequitur. Fourth, his response is incorrect. Aglaé was Marshal Ney's wife, not his mother. It makes one wonder if Napoleon Ney knew what he was talking about or if the journalist was competent in transcribing what he did say or both.

35. Archives Nationales, *Fonds du Maréchal Ney et de sa famille (1753–1923)*, preface, 12. Jules-Napoleon Ney was adopted by one Simon Ney but recognized as the illegitimate son of Marshal Ney's oldest son, the Second Prince of Moscow. He did not, however, accede to any of his titles.

36. Charles Holland Kidder, "The Mystery of Marshal Ney," *Muncey's Magazine*, vol. 13, 1895, 281. However, the U.S. legation at Paris provided a different conclusion in responding to Draper's inquiries in 1888, again presumably after consulting with French authorities. They advised that Ney's remains were not removed when the tomb was constructed in 1853. That would mean that the only time they were removed and examined, if at all, prior to 1888 was in 1816.

37. See https://www.senat.fr/evenement/archives/D26/execution_et_rehabilitations /la_legende_aux_etats_unis.html.

38. See Hoyt Collection, ser. 2, fol. 197.

39. Archives Nationales, *Fonds du Maréchal Ney et de sa famille (1753-1923)*, Preface, 10; see also numerous materials in Hoyt Collection, ser. 2, fols. 196–198.

40. See, e.g., *Extrait du Rapport de M. le Préfet du Département du Ht. Rhin, en date de 2 Novembre 1826*, reporting that "the sons of Marshal Ney, especially the two oldest, always speak against France with great exasperation and that the oldest said haughtily in

public that his greatest pleasure was, during the course of his military career, being able to revenge rigorously the death of his father." Archives Nationales, F7-6683; Hoyt Collection, ser. 2, fol. 137 (translation by the author).

41. Archives Nationales, *Fondes du Maréchal Ney et de sa famille (1753–1923)*,137AP/16, pièces 172–77.

42. See Archives Nationales, *Fonds du Maréchal Ney et de sa Famille (1753–1923)*, 137AP/21, dossier 10.

43. Both of Ney's lawyers, Berryer and Dupin, wrote memoirs, and they too showed no indication that they thought he had survived.

44. Broader rumors that Wellington saved Marshal Ney were attributable to statements made in Sir William Fraser's *Words on Wellington* (London: John C. Nimmo) 1889, 123–27, based on an account of the execution by purported eyewitness Quentin Dick. Fraser was a colleague and friend of the Duke of Wellington, and Dick was an Anglo-Irish member of Parliament who was in Paris at the time. Fraser believed that the execution was a staged fake based on Dick's account. Dick stated that Ney fell forward "on his face" when he was shot. But he also stated, inaccurately, that the "weather was perfect" and that the Luxembourg Gardens were filled with "children and nursery maids." Further, he stated that Ney's body was removed in a fiacre rather than by a stretcher—a point on which no other eyewitness concurred. Consequently, Dick's version is suspect.

45. Letter dated September 1, 1849, from the Duke of Wellington to Angela Burdett-Coutts, Hoyt Collection, ser. 2, fol. 140.

46. See, e.g., September 21, 1886, letter from M. H. Brandon to Lyman Draper, Draper MSS 4RR82-1.

47. Bulos, *Memoirs*, 34.

48. See eyewitness testimony of A. H. Graham, in chapter 10, which describes powder burns on the face of P. S. Ney that he claimed were received at the Battle of Borodino.

49. See letter from the Minister of War to Dr. J. Edward Smoot dated April 24, 1928, in Smoot, *Marshal Ney*, 396.

50. Ibid., 396–97.

51. See Buffalo *Sunday Morning News*, May 29, 1887, 2.

52. Among the several inconsistencies attending P. S. Ney's explanation of this wound is Mary C. Dalton's explicit recollection that he said he received it at the Battle of Ligny on June 16, 1815. Ligny was a Franco-Prussian engagement and an overture to the Battle of Waterloo. Marshal Ney was not at Ligny, being otherwise engaged at Quatre Bras. See letter dated August 31, 1885, from Mary C. Dalton to Lyman Draper, Draper MSS 2RR7.

53. See http://waterloo200.org/200-object/sword-sir-william-ponsonby.

54. See page 327 of P. S. Ney's personal copy of O'Meara's *Napoleon in Exile* in Hoyt Collection, ser. 2, fol. 192A.

55. Saint-Elme, *Memoirs*, 223 and 227.

56. The portrait contains what appears to be a faint blemish, perhaps something more, near the left top of his head, which is where P. S. Ney's wound was located. However, it does not appear to be part of the engraving.

57. In 1888, Draper also asked the U.S. legation in Paris to investigate whether Marshal Ney had a head wound. The response was that the legation was unable to find out about the wound but that it was "not believed to have existed." Draper MSS 2RR73.

58. Charles Henry Hart and Edward Biddle, *Memoirs of Jean Antoine Houdon: The Sculptor of Voltaire and Washington* (Philadelphia: privately printed, 1911), 125 et seq.

59. Measurement courtesy of Mr. Charles Clark, owner of the bust. The portrayal by Houdon shows no evidence of either smallpox or trepanning.

60. See Smoot, *Marshal Ney*, 348–49.

61. René Arnaud, *The Death and Resurrection of Marshal Ney* (typescript draft of article contained in the Hoyt Collection and translated from the French, 1935) (hereinafter Arnaud, "Resurrection"), 30. The article appears to have been published in *Annales politiques et littéraiares*, 52e anné, no. 2545–53e année, no. 2547 (December 25 1935–January 25, 1936).

62. Hoyt Collection, ser. 2, fols. 190 and 191.

63. See documents with marginal notes by P. S. Ney in Hoyt Collection, ser. 2, fol. 190.

64. Letter from M. L. McCorkle to Lyman Draper, February 26, 1887, Draper MSS 8RR38.

65. "Peter Stewart Ney to James Madison, 1 October 1831," *Founders Online*, National Archives, http://founders.archives.gov/documents/Madison/99-02-02-2447.

66. Hoyt Collection, ser. 2, fol. 186.

67. Archives Nationales, *Fonds du Maréchal Ney et de sa Famille (1753–1923)*, 137AP, preface, 11.

68. Letter from Mary C. Dalton to Lyman Draper, July 16, 1885, Draper MSS 2RR2.

69. Letter from Daniel J. Murphey to Lyman Draper, June 29, 1887, Draper MSS 8RR159.

70. Letter from James F. Johnston to Lyman Draper, July 20, 1886, Draper MSS 1RR130.

71. Archives Nationales, *Fonds du Maréchal Ney et de sa Famille (1753–1923)*, 137AP/18; pièces 24–85 show landholdings in Parma, Hanover, Westphalia, Warsaw, and, most important, the Po region of Italy worth an income well in excess of 700,000 francs.

72. Letter from Dr. W. C. Ramsay to Lyman Draper, September 23, 1886, Draper MSS 2RR58.

73. Weston, 155.

74. An additional portrait, often alleged to be of Aglaé Auguié circa 1800 before she married, shows a young lady in a white dress in park-like setting with shoulder-length dark hair. However, the sitter in the portrait does not strongly resemble Aglaé and possibly is one of her sisters.

75. Letter from Mary C. Dalton to Lyman Draper, August 31, 1885, Draper MSS 2RR7.

76. Ibid.

77. Letter from Dr. W. C. Ramsay to Lyman Draper, September 23, 1886. Draper MSS 2RR58.

78. Letter from Mary C. Dalton to Lyman Draper, August 31, 1885, Draper MSS 2RR7.

79. Letter to Lyman Draper, September 2, 1886, Hoyt Collection, ser. 2, fol. 150.

80. See letter written by P. S. Ney from Abbyville, Mecklenburg County, Virginia, dated August 7, 1828, saying that he will leave at Christmas when his teaching engagement ends but that he could stay longer, as well as letter evidencing his continuing presence there on June 8, 1829. Hoyt Collection, ser. 2, fol. 139.

81. It is also possible that he visited the United States in 1821. There is a record of a letter of introduction for him to American general Marinus Willett from Lafayette that reads as follows:

> Paris, Aug. 6, 1821.
> My Dear Willet:—It is fitt that I should introduce to our Senior Revolutionary Commander, a son of the illustrious and unfortunate Marshal Ney—who intends to visit the United States—I am to thank you my dear friend for the introductory letters I note and then receive, and doubly rejoice at every opportunity to Hear from You and to offer the best wishes and tender regards of your affectionate brother soldier, Lafayette.
> Col. Willet,
> New York,
> By Eugene Ney. 58 Broome St.
> Source: *Wofford College Journal*, no. 9, May/June 1900, 13.

It is not known if Eugène in fact made that visit. He would have been only 15 years old at the time.

82. Hoyt Collection, ser. 2, fol. 242.

83. "Charles J. Ingersoll to James Madison, 21 July 1829," *Founders Online*, National Archives, http://founders.archives.gov/documents/Madison/99-02-02-1845.

84. E-mail to author from Angela Kreider, editor, *Papers of James Madison*, University of Virginia Press, September 13, 2018.

85. The Savannah *Georgian*, December 28, 1829.

86. Smoot, *Marshal Ney*, 301–3.

87. See, e.g., letter from Madame Ney to her son Eugène in Athens dated January 1, 1836, in the Gratz Collection at the HSP. Eugène could not have been serving in the French embassy at Athens and graduating from medical school in Philadelphia at the same time.

88. Smoot, *Marshal Ney*, 301–3 and 203.

89. See census documents in Hoyt Collection, ser. 2, fol. 147.

90. See April 22, 1843, indenture, Hoyt Collection, ser. 2, fol. 145.

91. Chicago *Inter Ocean*, January 7, 1900, 27.

92. See https://www.josephsmithpapers.org/paper-summary/license-for-ebenezer -neyman-30-may-1841/1.

93. Smoot, *Marshal Ney*, 317.

94. See, e.g., Affidavit of a Legal Practitioner upon License Signed by E. M. C. Neyman of Saltilloville, Washington County, Indiana, on July 13, 1897.

95. This statement conflicts with the testimony of Dr. J. R. B. Adams in chapter 10, which suggests that Colonel Lehmanowsky had never met P. S. Ney when Adams met Lehmanowsky in 1842. As discussed below, this situation may have soon changed.

96. Smoot, *Marshal Ney*, 392–93. See also letter from Neyman at https://digital.lib.ecu .edu/24079#?c=0&m=0&s=0&cv=3&xywh=678%2C588%2C2936%2C3014.

97. Other versions of the adopted child story have Ney calling him Fezensac after his trusted one-time aide-de-camp.

98. See Marilou Alston Rudulph, "The Legend of Michael Rudulph," *Georgia Historical Quarterly*, 45, no. 11 (December 1961): 312–13. For an early newspaper account, see *American Watchman and Delaware Advertiser*, August 15, 1823, 1.

99. See, e.g., "Michael Ney, Otherwise Michael Rudolph," *Southern Literary Messenger* 13 (January 1847). See also "Marshal Ney an American," *The Carolina Watchman*, March 12, 1847. As recounted in these and other sources, the would-be U.S. minister to France Charles Cotesworth Pinckney, while there in the mid-1790s, learned of an American officer fighting in General Kléber's German Legion in the Army of Italy. Later, General Charles Lallemand believed Rudolph to be Ney and noted that Ney's detractors in the officer corps disparaged him as a "foreign tobacco merchant" (Elkton was at the time a tobacco-producing and tobacco-shipping region).

100. Some skeptics have suggested that Smoot may have "helped" the aged Mrs. Arnold with the affidavit.

101. Smoot, *Marshal Ney*, 251 et seq. See also Arnaud, "Resurrection," 5–6.

102. Smoot, *Marshal Ney*, 161–62, 338. They are currently in the collection of Archives and Special Collections Library at Davidson College.

103. Arnaud, "Resurrection," 5–6.

104. See Index to Port of Philadelphia Chronological List of Crews 1789–1880, 1816, Maritime Records Port of Philadelphia, HSP; see also Port of Philadelphia, Alphabetical List of Masters and Crews 1798–1880, 1816, Maritime Records Port of Philadelphia, HSP, and Port of Philadelphia Arrivals and Clearances, sec. III, vol. 4, 1811–1816, Outbound Philadelphia to Charleston, HSP. The Chronological List of Crews does show a sailor named "Peleg Ney" in 1815 (sec, IV, vol. 25, 157), but he appears to have no link to P. S. Ney or Marshal Ney. Lyman Draper tried unsuccessfully to locate Petrie about 10 years after the article appeared.

105. Letter from the prefect of police, First Division, First Bureau, Paris, to mayor of Le Havre, January 6, 1816, and letter from mayor of Le Havre to prefect of police dated February 6, 1816, Hoyt Collection, ser. 2, fol. 126 (translation by the author).

106. Report from the prefect of the Northern Department to the minister of police, February 3, 1816, Hoyt Collection, ser. 2, fol. 126 (translation by the author).

107. Michael H. Tepper, ed., *Passenger Arrivals at the Port of Philadelphia 1800–19* (Baltimore: Genealogical Publishing Co., 1986) (hereinafter Tepper, *Arrivals*), 912.

108. New York *Evening Post*, March 1, 1816.

109. NARA M425, https://www.familysearch.org/search/collection/1908535. A subsequent arrival on November 4, 1816, of *Magnet* shows a Miss Philoppon as a passenger. Ibid.

110. These dates were chosen as a likely time frame because the ship could hardly have made a transatlantic crossing to Philadelphia and then Charleston sooner than January

24 and because May 10 should have allowed sufficient time for *John Howe* to have unloaded in Philadelphia following arrival on February 29 and continued on to Charleston, if indeed she did so. She clearly continued on to Savannah in early May.

111. *Charleston Courier*, January 31, 1816, 2.

112. The microfilm records of the *Charleston Courier* at the Library of Congress are in places barely legible, so this conclusion should be qualified.

113. New York *Evening Post*, August 8, 1816.

114. Ibid., August 25, 1815.

115. The author's efforts to link P. S. Ney with Charleston or Marshal Ney through an examination of the extant primary source records of the Second Bank of the United States at the HSP also proved fruitless. It will be recalled that the eyewitness testimonial in chapter 10 by Mary C. Dalton stated that P. S. Ney had a $10,000 account at the Bank of the United States and that she had seen a letter he had written to bank president Nicholas Biddle concerning the account when he was concerned that the bank may fail or be closed. Ney explained that "his friends placed it there for his benefit; but he was able to take care of himself and hoped he would never have to call for any of it." Letter from Mary C. Dalton to Lyman Draper, August 3, 1886, Draper MSS 2RR20. The surviving Second Bank records, contained in the McAllister Collection (McA MSS 012) of the Library Company of Philadelphia on deposit with the HSP, are far from complete, but they contain no Ney material (although they do contain Joseph Bonaparte material, among others). Another major deposit of Second Bank of the United States primary source documents at NARA (Record Group 53, Records of the Bureau of Public Debt) relate mainly to public debt and currency issuance by the bank.

Nicholas Biddle was appointed president of the Second Bank in 1822 and held that office until March 3, 1836, when it lost its federal charter, though he continued as president of its state-chartered successor until 1839. Biddle was a prolific correspondent, and his papers are housed in the Manuscript Division at the Library of Congress. They fall into two main categories relevant to this search: the Letter Books he maintained when he was president of the Second Bank of the United States and General Correspondence. Biddle corresponded with Americans both great and small and kept copies. The author examined the entire Letter Books from 1823 to 1836 and the General Correspondence from 1833 through 1840 but was not able to identify any letter from or to P. S. Ney (in the General Correspondence, there was the occasional anonymous letter, e.g., the letters from "One in the Know" or a letter written under a pseudonym, such as "Brutus," but these tended to deal with policy issues rather than account inquiries).

116. *People's Advocate* (Boston), June 5, 1843.

117. If this is true, it is unclear why the Bourbons would have wanted to bother to try to execute a field-grade officer recently promoted to colonel. The author has been unable to corroborate the story of Lehmanowsky's trial, sentence, or escape.

118. Year: *1822*; Arrival: *New York, New York*: Microfilm Serial: *M237, 1820–1897*; Microfilm Roll: *003*; Line: *4*; List Number: *425*.

119. South Bend (Indiana) *Tribune*, December 13, 1900, 8.

120. *Time*, vol. 28, issue 12, September 21, 1936, 6.

121. Taylor, "Legend and Scholarship," 16–17.

122. See letter from Despinois to Minister of War Clarke at Hoyt Collection, ser. 2, fol. 167.

123. Smoot, *Marshal Ney*, 312.

124. See Genêt, "Campan," 416–17.

125. If it is in P. S. Ney's handwriting, it is a highly stylized and formal version of his handwriting, complete with flourishes. In fact, it bears little resemblance to other surviving samples of his handwriting. Possibly, it was written by a court clerk or another party.

126. Report by P. S. Ney dated March 1820, Hoyt Collection, ser. 2, fol. 133.

127. Letter from Archibald D. Murphey to Colonel William Polk, August 22, 1827, in W. H. Hoyt, ed., *Letters of Archibald D. Murphey*, vol. 1 (Raleigh, NC: E. M. Uzzell & Co., 1914), 361–62.

128. Typed note by Hoyt, dated February 27, 1949, Hoyt Collection, ser. 3, fol. 242.

129. However, this interpretation begs the question of why he would keep the name "Ney" if he wanted the protection of a genuine alias. Unfortunately, there is no clear answer to that question.

130. See report dated May 13, 1952, Hoyt Collection, ser. 2, vol. 8. The three French experts also examined the earlier reports and dismissed two of them, including the one cited by Weston, as "affirmations without proof."

131. For the auction catalog, see www.binocheetgiquello.com/catalogue/12321. No extant eyewitness account of the execution records that anyone cut the hair while the body lay on the execution ground.

132. See ancestry.com at https://www.ancestry.com/search/?name=peter_mcnee&event =_stirlingshire-scotland-united+kingdom_5354&birth=1788&birth_x=1-0-0 as well as the British government–sponsored site at www.scotlandspeople.gov.uk. Additional research by the author shows that one John M'Nie married Isabel Stewart in Balquhidder, Perthshire, Scotland, on December 24, 1774. In a possible prior marriage, the records interestingly also show that John McNie married Catharine Ferguson, also in Balquhidder, on February 14, 1767. Although issue from both of these marriages are recorded in the Balquhidder baptismal records, no son Peter is shown (bearing in mind that Hoyt's Peter McNee was born at Fintry, Stirlingshire, after the family moved there). If P. S. Ney's statement is correct that he was born in Stirlingshire, one might logically ask if there were other people named Peter McNie or McNee born in Stirlingshire between 1765 and 1795. There were none that the author has been able to identify, although the ScotlandsPeople website records show three, all born in Port of Menteith, Perthshire, near Stirlingshire: (1) Peter McNee, son of James McNee and Janet McKieson, baptized on August 20, 1781; (2) Peter McNee, son of John McNee and Agnes McKieson, baptized on March 10, 1769; and (3) Peter McNee, son of Peter McNee and Agnes Stewart, baptized on April 30, 1780. These three would be in addition to the Peter McNee who was baptized on February 2, 1788, in Port of Menteith and died on April 1, 1877, and who is discussed above (the Port of Menteith records also show a Peter McNee marrying Jean Stewart on February 6, 1770, but they show no son Peter from this marriage). None of the above three individuals has a mother named Catharine or Isabel, so they are unlikely to be P. S. Ney. While the records show the death of Peter McNee, born in 1769, they do not show the deaths of the other Peter McNees in

(1) and (3) above, thus raising the possibility that they left Scotland. Notwithstanding her forename of "Agnes," the last name of "Stewart" for the mother of Peter McNee in (3) above born in 1780 cannot help but raise an eyebrow. Unfortunately, the author has been unable to find further information on this Peter McNee.

133. Taylor conveniently ignores these eyewitnesses when trying to make the case that P. S. Ney was born in 1787.

134. Hoyt Collection, ser. 2, fol. 183.

135. According to the *Waterloo Medal Book*, he served in Captain A. Ross's Company No. 8 of the First Battalion of the 91st Regiment of Foot (Argyllshire Highlanders). The *Waterloo Roll Call*, 245–46, does not show a Captain A. Ross in the 91st. This Peter McNee was probably the same McNee of the 91st whom Hoyt identified as on garrison duty in Glasgow for much of the Napoleonic Wars.

Separately, the Royal Artillery Pensions Register 1815–1818 shows the 1816 discharge for a pension of one Peter McNie, who enlisted as a gunner in the Royal Horse Artillery in 1806. See UK National Archives WO 69/618/5235. He likely would have seen service in the Peninsular War. He is recorded on the regimental rolls of the Fourth Battalion on duty in Quebec, Canada, in 1813. See Royal Regiment of Artillery-Capt. John Caddy Company in the Fourth Battalion, UK National Archives WO 10/976. Although the Royal Horse Artillery fought at Waterloo, of the 5,536 members thereof who were awarded the Waterloo Medal, there is no Peter McNie. One wonders why. Of all the British soldiers named McNie or McNee, this one raises the most questions: close to 10 years of service (almost certainly including in combat), familiarity with North America, exposure to French speakers, possible knowledge of mathematics learned in the artillery service, and discharge in the same year that P. S. Ney supposedly came to America. Alas, he must be eliminated because, courtesy of the Royal Artillery Museum, an Admission Book from the Royal Hospital Chelsea shows the 1816 discharge of Gunner Peter McNie, born in Greenock, Lanarkshire, and a plasterer by trade, service number 2866, with a total service of nine years, 183 days. He was discharged from the army because he was blind in both eyes.

Additionally, the *Waterloo Medal Book* also shows a Peter Stewart as a private in Captain Robert Winchester's Company of the 92nd Regiment of Highlanders (Gordon Highlanders). The 92nd took particularly heavy casualties in fierce fighting at Quatre Bras immediately preceding Waterloo. However, this Private Peter Stewart is likely the same Private Peter Stewart of the 92nd who was born at Mortlach, Banffshire, Scotland, in 1793 (and thus too young to be P. S. Ney). Moreover, he was discharged at the Royal Hospital Chelsea at age 34 in 1827 following some 20 years of service. See UK National Archives WO 97/1013/102. He thus could not have been P. S. Ney. So the matter remains a mystery, and, as pointed out elsewhere, there remains a wide gap between any enlisted soldier and the educated man who P. S. Ney was.

136. The online ScotlandsPeople database, while extensive, is not complete because it covers only records of the Church of Scotland, "other churches" that later merged with the Church of Scotland and the Roman Catholic Church. It implicitly does not include records for the Scottish Episcopal Church, the Church of England, or others.

137. Statement of Mrs. D. H. Hill, Charlotte, NC (1894), quoted in Weston, 209.

138. Specifically, Taylor, "Scholarship and Legend," 32–33.

139. The October 25, 1773 will of Alexander, the Sixth Earl of Galloway, who would have been the father of the Lady Catharine Stewart born circa 1750, provides no clues. UK National Archives, PROB 11/995/19.

140. https://www.chuckspeed.com/balquhidder/history/Stewart_Clan_Magazine_%20 References_to_Baldorran_Stewarts.html. The presence of Balquhidder Stewarts in Cheraw raises the obvious question of whether there was a link between them and Isbal Stewart, the wife of Hoyt's John McNee and mother of Peter McNee, who was apparently from Balquhidder. The Balquhidder Stewarts descended from an illegitimate branch of the royal house of Stewart and were generally middling landholders in Scottish society. The Cheraw Stewarts were founded by one of this family, Patrick Stewart, Laird of Ledcreich, Balquhidder (1697–1772), and his wife Elizabeth Menzies. While possibly distantly related to Isbal Stewart, there were no obvious close ties between them. Moreover, as discussed above, based on his birth date, the only likely candidate for Isbal Stewart's son Peter McNee died an innkeeper in Gargunnock, Stirlingshire, Scotland. The implication is that if P. S. Ney were related to the Cheraw Stewarts (and that relationship led him to Cheraw), he would have been from somewhere other than Balquhidder or even Stirlingshire.

141. See Pennsylvania Passenger and Crew Lists 1800–1882, NARA M425-Philadelphia, 1800–1882, microfilm #029, list no. 204.

142. www.findmypast.com/record?id=US/PASS/PA/004719581.

143. Arnaud, "Resurrection," 61–62.

144. Great Britain, War Office, *A List of the Officers of the Army and of the Corps of Royal Marines*, vols. 1814 and 1816–1820. Of the officers identified in British army records, two stand out as potential candidates. First Lieutenant and Adjutant Peter D. Stewart of the Royal Artillery was promoted to second captain on May 21, 1815, shortly before Waterloo. See www.findmypast.co.uk/transcript?id=GBM/BARM/PROM/21909. However, he is not listed in the *Waterloo Roll Call* and therefore probably did not fight at Waterloo. Moreover, he is recorded as dying in his native Prince Edward Island, Canada, on November 1, 1867. Second, army records also show a Peter Stewart promoted to lieutenant on November 23, 1815, while a member of the First Royal Regiment of Veterans and serving as the adjutant of the York Depot at Chelsea (he had previously served on half pay as adjutant of an unnamed recruiting district). The records also show him as being discharged on February 7, 1816, the same year that P. S. Ney allegedly emigrated to the United States. See www.findmypast.co.uk/transcript?id=GBM/WO121 /121057666, www.findmypast.co.uk/transcript?id=GBM/BARM/PROM/24614, and www.findmypast.co.uk/transcript?id=GBM/BARM/PROM/24280 (assuming the three records pertain to the same Stewart despite the latter two spelling the name as "Stuart"). However, there is no evidence that he fought at Waterloo, and the Army records show him having been born in 1771 in Perthshire, not Stirlingshire, so it is unlikely that he was P. S. Ney.

145. These include Lieutenant George Stewart of the First (Royal Scots) Regiment of Foot, who was wounded at Waterloo and went on half pay March 25, 1816; Lieutenant Ronald Stewart of the 52nd (Oxfordshire) Regiment of Foot, who went on half pay in

1816; and Lieutenant John Stewart of the 69th (South Lincolnshire) Regiment of Foot, also wounded at Waterloo, who went on half pay in 1816.

146. See Hoyt Collection, ser. 2, fols. 127 and 166. The police report described him as "very dangerous."

147. Taylor, "Scholarship and Legend," 34.

148. See, generally, ibid., 33–35.

149. See Hoyt's typewritten notes in the Hoyt Collection, ser. 3, fol. 242.

150. The Perthshire *Courier* reported on April 2, 1812, on a reward of 20 guineas for a militia deserter named Peter Neish, a weaver from Auchterarder, Perthshire. However, his physical description in the article does not match that of P. S. Ney. More intriguing was Peter Stewart or Stuart, Esq., a Scottish-born publisher of a London newspaper, *The Oracle*, who was arrested by the House of Commons for libel in 1805, went bankrupt in 1809, was appointed British consul at Le Havre (Havre de Grace) in August 1814, and was "ordered to quit his post and return to England" with his family by Foreign Secretary Lord Castlereagh in May 1815. See, e.g., Bristol *Mirror*, May 20, 1815, and *Corbett's Weekly Political Register*, December 29, 1819. The reasons for his recall are not known, but they must have been controversial given his very short tenure at post. He was known to have republican sympathies and would have been U.S. Consul William Lee's British analogue at Le Havre from 1814 to 1815. His social standing, probable education, literary abilities, and professional interest in newspapers and political commentary all would square with known attributes of P. S. Ney. However, he was the older brother of Daniel Stewart, also a newspaper publisher, who was born in 1766 (see *Dictionary of National Biography*, vol. 55, 75), so he would have been older than P. S. Ney. Also, there is nothing to suggest that he fought in the Napoleonic Wars or disappeared after his recall from Le Havre. Finally, there is a record of his having died on January 31, 1829. See *Morning Post*, February 9, 1829.

151. Arnaud, "Resurrection," 63.

152. Weston, 296.

153. www.tambours-bgha.org/la-gazette/portraits/la-mort-de-jb-bessieres.

154. The exact birth dates are known for all of Ney's sons. If P. S. Ney's poem were to commemorate the accession to manhood of Eugène, it would have been a case of arrested development, as he was 34 years old in 1840.

155. This is a particularly telling comment, evidently contrasting his aspirations for his son's conduct with his own.

156. Anonymous, *Inauguration of the Statue of Liberty Enlightening the World* (New York: D. Appleton and Company, 1887), 31.

157. Ibid., 35–36.

Bibliography

Resources

American Philosophical Society, Philadelphia, PA
Archives Nationales de France, Paris, Fonds du Maréchal Ney et de sa Famille (1753–1923), 137AP
Athenaeum of Philadelphia, Philadelphia, PA
Columbia University Library, New York, NY
Davidson College Library, Davidson, NC
Historical Society of Pennsylvania (HSP), Philadelphia, PA
Library Company of Philadelphia, Philadelphia, PA
Library of Congress (LOC), Washington, DC
Lyman Copeland Draper Manuscripts, 1735–1890, State Historical Society of Wisconsin (available at the LOC, Manuscript Reading Room, Microfilm 17,881-134P [reels 113–15])
Maryland Historical Society (MHS), Baltimore, MD
National Archives and Records Administration (NARA), Washington, DC
New York City Public Library, New York, NY
United Kingdom National Archives, Kew, UK
University of North Carolina, Southern History Collection, William Henry Hoyt Papers, Chapel Hill, NC
University of North Carolina, Southern History Collection, Richard F. Little Papers, Chapel Hill, NC

Partial List of Newspapers and Periodicals

Carlisle Weekly Herald (Carlisle, PA)
Chambersburg *Democratic Republican* (Chambersburg, PA)
Charleston Courier (Charleston, SC)
Columbian Centinel (Boston, MA)
Corbett's Weekly Political Register (London, UK)
Evening Post (New York, NY)
Indianapolis *News* (Indianapolis, IN)

Inter Ocean (Chicago, IL)
Journal (Charlotte, NC)
L'Abeille Américaine (Philadelphia, PA)
La Quotiedienne (Paris, France)
Le Constitutionnel (Paris, France)
Mecklenburg Jeffersonian (Charlotte, NC)
Morning Post (London, UK)
National Intelligencer (Washington, DC)
New York *Columbian* (New York, NY)
Niles' Weekly Register (Baltimore, MD)
People's Advocate (Boston, MA)
Perthshire Courier (Perthshire, Scotland)
Philadelphia Gazette (Philadelphia, PA)
Savannah *Georgian* (Savannah, GA)
South Bend Tribune (South Bend, IN)
Time (New York, NY)
Times of London (London, UK)
Washington Post (Washington, DC)
Weekly Raleigh Register (Raleigh, NC)
Wofford College Journal (Spartanburg, SC)
The World (New York, NY)

Books, Articles, and Online Sources

Adams, John Quincy. *Diaries*. Boston: Massachusetts Historical Society, 2004. www .masshist.org/jqadiaries/php.

Alger, John Goldworth. *Napoleon's British Visitors and Captives 1801–1815*. Edinburgh: T. & A. Constable, 1904.

Ammon, Harry. *James Monroe: The Quest for National Identity*. New York: McGraw-Hill, 1971.

Anonymous. *Inauguration of the Statue of Liberty Enlightening the World*. New York: D. Appleton and Company, 1887.

———. *Journal de Service extraordinaire ordonné pour la guarde du Maréchal Ney* (1815).

———. *Life of Lafayette*. Boston: Light & Horton, 1835.

———. "Michael Ney, Otherwise Michael Rudolph." *Southern Literary Messenger* 13 (January 1847).

Arnaud, René. *The Death and Resurrection of Marshal Ney*. Unpublished monograph translated from the French original, 1935.

Atteridge, A. Hilliard. *The Bravest of the Brave*. London: Methuen & Co., 1912.

Barbero, Alessandro. *The Battle: A New History of Waterloo*. New York: Walker and Company, 2003.

Bedoyère, J., Comte de la. *Le Maréchal Ney*. Paris: Calmann-Lévy, 1902.

Belhoster, Bruno. *Augustin-Louis Cauchy: A Biography*. New York: Springer-Verlag, 1991.

Belmontet, Louis. *Biographical Sketch of Joseph Bonaparte, count de Survilliers*. London: J. Ridgway, 1834.

Berkin, Carol. *A Sovereign People*. New York: Basic Books, 2017.

Berkley, Helen. *A Sketch of Joseph Buonaparte*. Godey's Magazine and Lady's Book, January–June 1845. Philadelphia: Louis A. Godey.

Berryer, Pierre-Nicolas. *Souvenirs de M. Berryer*. Paris: Ambroise Dupont, 1839.

Bertin, Georges. *Joseph Bonaparte en Amérique*. Paris: Libd. de la Nouvelle revue, 1893.

Birch, Thomas. *Catalogue of valuable paintings & statuary, the Collection of the late Joseph Bonaparte, Count de Survilliers: to be sold at public sale on Wednesday & Thursday, September 17th and 18th, 1845, at the mansion in Bordentown, New Jersey.*

Blaufarb, Rafe. *Bonapartists in the Borderlands*. Tuscaloosa: University of Alabama Press, 2005.

Blennerhassett, Sir Rowland. "The Execution of Marshal Ney." *National Review* 37 (March–August 1901).

Blythe, LeGette. *Marshal Ney: A Dual Life*. New York: Stackpole Sons, 1937.

Bonnal, Henri. *La Vie Militaire du Maréchal Ney, duc d'Elchingen, prince de la Moskawa*. Paris: Librairie Chapelot, 1914.

Brugger, Robert J., et al., eds. *The Papers of James Madison: 2 April–31 August 1804*. Secretary of State Series, vol. 7. Charlottesville: University of Virginia Press, 2005.

Bulos, A. *Memoirs of Marshal Ney*. Vols. 1 and 2. Philadelphia: E. L. Carey and A. Hart, 1834. (Published by Marshal Ney's family.)

Cazottes, Pascal. "Did Marshal Ney Die in America?" www.napoleonicsociety.com/english/Neya.htm (accessed November 3, 2019).

Chamans, Antoine Marie Comte de Lavalette. *Memoirs of Count Lavalette*. London: Gibbings and Co., 1894.

Clarke, T. Wood. *Emigrés in the Wilderness*. New York: The Macmillan Company, 1941.

Clausel, Bertrand. *Justificat de la Conduite Politique de M. le Lieutenant-Général Comte Clausel*. Paris: Chez Pillet, 1816.

Coggeshall, George. *History of the American privateers, and letters-of-marque, during our war with England in the years 1812, '13 and '14*. Privately printed, 1856.

Compton, Piers. *Marshal Ney*. London: Metheun & Co., 1937.

Connelly, Owen. *The Gentle Bonaparte: The Story of Napoleon's Elder Brother*. New York: Macmillan, 1968.

Cooper, William J. *The Lost Founding Father, John Quincy Adams and the Transformation of American Politics*. New York: Liveright Publishing Corporation, 2017.

Cranwell, John Philips, and William Bowers Crane. *Men of Marque: A History of Private Armed Vessels Out of Baltimore during the War of 1812*. New York: Norton, 1940.

Cunningham, John T. *The Good Mr. Bonaparte*. Trenton, NJ: New Jersey Tercentenary Commission, 1963.

Dalton, Charles. *The Waterloo Roll Call; with Biographical Notes and Anecdotes*. 2nd ed. Leopold Classic Library, 2016. (Reprint of the original; London: Eyre and Spottiswoode, 1904)

Deléry, Simone de la Souchère. *Napoleon's Soldiers in America*. Gretna, LA: Pelican Publishing Company, 1998.

Double, Bill. *Philadelphia's Washington Square*. Charleston, SC: Arcadia Publishing, 2009.

Dunning, Halsey. *In Memoriam: A Tribute of Respect to the Late Capt. Joel Vickers, for Nearly Seventy Years a Resident of Baltimore*. Baltimore: John W. Woods, 1860.

Dupin, André. *Memoires de M. Dupin*. Paris: Plon, 1855.

Ekirch, A. Roger. *American Sanctuary: Mutiny, Martyrdom and National Identity in the Age of Revolution*. New York: Pantheon Books, 2017.

Emgarth, Annette H. *French Philadelphia: Tours of Penn's City Exploring French Influence and Presence*. Philadelphia: Philadelphia Council for International Visitors, 1976.

Emmons, George Foster. *The Navy of the United States*. Washington, DC: Gideon & Co., 1853.

Fezensac, Lieutenant General M. de. *A Journal of the Russian Campaign of 1812*. London: Parker, Furnivall and Parker, 1852.

———. *Souvenirs Militaires de 1804 à 1814*. Paris: Dumaine, 1870.

Figes, Orlando. *The Europeans: Three Lives and the Making of a Cosmopolitan Culture*. New York: Henry Holt and Company, 2019.

Foord, Edward. *Napoleon's Russian Campaign of 1812*. Boston: Little, Brown, 1915.

Foster, Kathleen A., and Kenneth Finkel. *Captain Watson's Travels in America*. Philadelphia: University of Pennsylvania Press, 1997.

Fraser, Sir William. *Words on Wellington*. London: John C. Nimmo, 1889.

Furstenberg, François. *When the United States Spoke French: Five Refugees Who Shaped a Nation*. New York: Penguin Press, 2014.

Galignani, J. A., and W. Galignani. *Galignani's New Paris Guide for 1872*. Paris: Galignani and Co., 1872.

Gardien, Kent. "The Splendid Fools: Philadelphia Origins of Alabama's Vine and Olive Colony." *Pennsylvania Magazine of History and Biography* 104 (1980).

Gardien, Kent, and Betje Black Klier. *Champ d'Asile*. Handbook of Texas. Austin: Texas State Historical Association. https://tsaonline.org/handbook/online/articles/uec02 (accessed September 12, 2020).

Garfield, James R. "Doubts Concerning the Execution of Marshal Ney." *Wisconsin Magazine of History* 2, no. 3 (March 1919).

Genêt, George Clinton. "A Family Record of Ney's Execution, Containing Mme. Campan's Contemporary Account" (from manuscript of Jeanne Louise-Henriette Genêt Campan). *The Century* 52, no. 3 (July 1896): 415–22.

Girard, Just. *Adventures of a French Captain at Present a Planter in Texas, Formerly a Refugee of Camp Asylum*. Translated by Lady Blanche Murphy. New York: Benziger Bros., 1878.

Gravière, Edmond Jurien de la. "L'Amiral Baudin." In *Les Gloires maritimes de la France*. Paris: Plon, 1888. (Drawing on manuscript by Charles Baudin, *Memories of My Youth 1784–1815*.)

Great Britain, War Office. *A List of the Officers of the Army and of the Corps of Royal Marines*. Vols. 1811–1812, 1814, and 1816–1820. London: War Office.

Grouchy, Marshal Emmanuel de. *Memoires du Maréchal Grouchy*. Vol. 5. Paris: E. Dentu, 1874.

Gurwood, John, ed. *The Dispatches of Field Marshal The Duke of Wellington, during his Various Campaigns in India, Denmark, Portugal, Spain, the Low Countries, and France, from 1799 to 1818*. Vol. 12. London: John Murray, 1838.

Hamilton, Stanislaus Murray, ed. *The Writings of James Monroe*. Vol. 5, *1807–1816*. New York: G. P. Putnam's Sons, 1900.

Hart, Charles Henry, and Edward Biddle. *Memoirs of Jean Antoine Houdon, The Sculptor of Voltaire and Washington*. Philadelphia: privately printed, 1911.

Houssaye, Henri. *1815: La Seconde Abdication-La Terreur Blanche*. Paris: Perrin, 1905.

Hoyt, William Henry, ed. *Papers of Archibald D. Murphey*. Vol. 1. Raleigh, NC: E. M. Uzzell & Co., 1914.

Ingersoll, Charles Jared. *History of the Second War between the United States of America and Great Britain*. 2nd ser., vol. 1. Philadelphia: Lippincott, Grambo & Co., 1852.

Ireland, W. H., ed. *The Napoleon Anecdotes*. London: C. S. Arnold, 1822.

Jefferson, Thomas. *Jefferson's Memorandum Books, Volume 2: Accounts, with Legal Records and Miscellany, 1767–1826*. Edited by James A. Bear and Lucia C. Stanton. Princeton, NJ: Princeton University Press, 1997. doi:10.2307/j.ctt1m3p0pn (accessed September 14, 2020).

Johnston, R. M. *In the Words of Napoleon: The Emperor Day by Day*. London: Lionel Levanthal Books/Frontline Books, 2015.

Kenny, Laurence J. "The Gallipolis Colony." *Catholic Historical Review* 4, no. 4 (January 1919): 415–51.

Kidder, Charles Holland. "The Mystery of Marshal Ney." *Muncey's Magazine* 13 (1895).

Kreider, Angela, ed. *The Papers of James Madison: 1 July 1814–18 February 1815*. Presidential Series, vol. 8. Charlottesville: University of Virginia Press, 2015.

Kurtz, Harold. *The Trial of Marshall Ney*. London: Hamish Hamilton, 1957.

Latimer, Elizabeth Wormeley, ed. *Talks of Napoleon at St. Helena with General Baron Gourgaud*. Chicago: A. C. McClurg, 1903.

Lee, William. *Les États-Unis et L'Angleterre*. Bordeaux: P. Coudert, 1814.

Lillard, Stewart. *Here Come the Russians*. Morrisville, NC: Lulu Press, 2017.

Looney, J. Jefferson, ed. *Papers of Thomas Jefferson: September 1815 to April 1816*. Retirement Series, vol. 9. Princeton: Princeton University Press, 2012.

Lucas-Dubreton, J. *Le Maréchal Ney*. Paris: Fayard, 1941.

Macartney, Clarence Edward Noble, and Gordon Dorrance. *The Bonapartes in America*. Philadelphia: Dorrance and Company, 1939.

Maitland, Sir Frederick Lewis. *The Surrender of Napoleon*. Edinburgh: William Blackwood & Sons, 1904.

Mann, Mary Lee, ed. *A Yankee Jeffersonian: Selections from the Diary and Letters of William Lee of Massachusetts*. Cambridge, MA: Harvard University Press, 1958.

Mann, Rob, and Diana DiPaolo Loren. "Keeping Up Appearances: Dress, Architecture, Furniture, and Status at French Azilum." *International Journal of Historical Archeology* 5, no. 4 (December 2001): 281–307.

Marchand, Louis-Joseph-Narcisse. *In Napoleon's Shadow*. Edited by Proctor P. Jones. San Francisco: Proctor Jones Publishing Company, 1998.

Martine, Alphonse de la. *History of the Restoration of Monarchy in France*. Vol. 3. London: George Bell & Sons, 1891.

Matten, David B., et al., eds. *The Papers of James Madison: 4 March 1817–31 January 1820*. Retirement Series, vol. 1. Charlottesville: University of Virginia Press, 2009.

Mirante, Rand. *Medusa's Head: The Rise and Survival of Joseph Fouché, Inventor of the Modern Police State*. Bloomington, IN: Archway Publishing, 2014.

Mitchell, John. "Southern Mythology and Marshal Michel Ney." (Senior thesis submitted to the Faculty of the Department of History, University of North Carolina at Asheville, November 21, 2003.)

Morgan, J. B. *Marshal Ney*. London: Arthur Baker Limited, 1958.

Mudge, Alfred. *Mudge Memorials*. Boston: Alfred Mudge & Son, 1868.

Murat, Inès. *Napoleon and the American Dream*. Translated by Frances Frenaye. Baton Rouge: Louisiana State University Press, 1981.

Ney, M. K. *The Marshal and the Myth*. Morgantown, PA: Masthof Press, 2001.

Ney, Marshal Michel. *Military Studies*. Translated by G. H. Caunter. London: Bull and Churton, 1834.

———. *Procès du Maréchal Ney*. Deuxième Edition. Paris: Michaud, 1815.

———. *Report of the Trial for High Treason and Attempts against the Safety of the State*. Paris: Gaglianis, 1815.

Notes and Queries. Vol. 6, no. 160 (November 20, 1852).

Nouvelle Revue Retrospective. January–June 1895. Paris, 1895.

Nouvelle Revue Retrospective. July–December 1897. Paris, 1897.

Nouvelle Revue Retrospective. July–December 1899. Paris, 1899.

Paulding, James K. "An Interview with Napoleon's Brother." *Harper's Magazine 131*, no. 776 (November 1915).

Peyrusse, Guillaume Joseph Roux. *1809–1815: Mémorial et archives de M. Le Baron Peyrusse*. Carcassonne: Labau, 1869.

Preston, Daniel, ed. *The Papers of James Monroe*. Vol. 1. Westport, CT: Greenwood Press, 2003.

Quynn, Dorothy Mackay. "Destination: America: Marshal Ney's Attempt to Escape." *French Historical Studies* 2, no. 2 (Autumn 1961).

Raciti, James J. *Stephen Girard: America's Colonial Olympian, 1750–1831*. Santa Fe, NM: Sunstone Press, 2015.

Reeves, J. S. *The Napoleonic Exiles in America, 1815–1819*. Johns Hopkins University Studies in Historical and Political Science, vol. 23. Baltimore: Johns Hopkins University Press, 1905.

Roberts, Andrew. *Napoleon: A Life*. New York: Viking, 2014.

Rochechouart, Comte de. *Memoirs*. Translated by Frances Jackson. New York: E. P. Dutton & Company, 1920.

———. *Souvenir*. Deuxième ed. Paris: Librairie Plon, 1892.

Rochejaquelein, Marie-Louise-Victoire de la, Marquise de. *Memoires de la Marquise de la Rochejaquelein*. Paris: Dentu, 1848.

Rudulph, Marilou Alston. "The Legend of Michael Rudulph." *Georgia Historical Quarterly* 45, no. 11 (December 1961): 309–28.

Saint-Elme, Ida. *Memoirs of a Contemporary*. Translated by Lionel Strachey. New York: Doubleday, Page & Company, 1902. (Original French edition published 1827.)

Savary, René, Duke of Rovigo. *Memoirs*. Vol. 4, pt. 2. London: Henry Colburn, 1828.

Scott, Sir Walter. *Life of Napoleon Buonaparte, Emperor of the French*. Vol. 3. New York: J. & J. Harper, 1827.

Ségur, Count Philippe-Paul de. *Histoire de Napoléon et de la grande-armée pendant l'année 1812*. Paris: Baudouin, 1824.

———. *Napoleon's Russian Campaign*. Translated by J. David Townsend. Boston: Houghton Mifflin, 1958.

Selin, Shannon. "Why Didn't Napoleon Escape to the United States?" https://shannon selin.com/2015/06/why-didnt-napoleon-escape-to-the-united-states (accessed November 3, 2019).

Smoot, James Edward. *Marshal Ney before and after Execution*. Charlotte, NC: Queen City Printing Company, 1929.

Stephen, Sir Leslie. *Dictionary of National Biography*. Vol. 55, London: Smith, Elder and Company, 1898.

Stroud, Patricia Tyson. *The Man Who Had Been King: The American Exile of Napoleon's Brother Joseph*. Philadelphia: University of Pennsylvania Press, 2005.

Taylor, George V. "Scholarship and Legend, William Henry Hoyt's Research on the Ney Controversy." *South Atlantic Quarterly* 59, no. 3 (Summer 1960).

Tepper, Michael H., ed. *Passenger Arrivals at the Port of Philadelphia 1800–1819*. Baltimore: Genealogical Publishing Co., Inc., 1986.

Tower, Charlemagne. "Joseph Bonaparte in Philadelphia and Bordentown." *Pennsylvania Magazine of History and Biography* 40, no. 4 (1918).

Unger, Harlow Giles. *Lafayette*. Hoboken, NJ: John Wiley & Sons, 2002.

Waterloo Medal Book. UK National Archives. MINT 15/112/7.

Webster, Constance A. "Documenting Cultural Landscapes: The French Influence in New Jersey." *Landscape Journal* 15, no. 2 (Fall 1986).

Wellington, The Duke of, K. G. *Supplementary Despatches, Correspondence and Memoranda of Field Marshal Arthur Duke of Wellington, K. G.* Edited by his son The Duke of Wellington, K. G. Vol. 10. London: John Murray, 1843.

Weston, James Augustus. *Historical Doubts as to the Execution of Marshal Ney*. New York: Thomas Whittaker, 1895.

Wilson, James Grant. *The Life and Letters of Fitz-Greene Halleck*. New York: D. Appleton and Company, 1869.

Wood, Gordon S. *Friends Divided*. New York: Penguin Press, 2017.

Woodward, E. M. *Bonaparte's Park and the Murats*. Trenton, NJ: MacCrellish & Quigley, 1879.

Acknowledgments

THE GENESIS OF THIS BOOK WAS A SERIES OF SHORT BIOGRAPHICAL PRO-
files I wrote on residents of Georgetown in Washington, D.C., during the
period 1816–1817. Checking in the newspapers of that period, I chanced
on a report of the Philadelphia wedding of Stephen Girard's niece
attended by the king of Spain, Marshal Grouchy, General Lallemand,
and others. Immediately realizing that the guest list was an abbreviated
version of Napoleon's order of battle for Waterloo, I was surprised to learn
that these people were in the United States and suspected that therein lay
a story. So my research began.

Shortly thereafter, at the wedding of the daughter of an old friend,
Allen Barringer, I fell into a conversation with Napoleonic scholar Rand
Mirante, also a long-standing friend. He alerted me to the controversy
surrounding Marshal Ney and P. S. Ney. Suddenly, the shape of the book
formed in my mind, and I was off to the races, writing even as I researched.
It is hard to describe the thrill of holding in one's hands original letters
written by Napoleon, Marshal Grouchy, the prince and princess of Moscow, and others from this colorful cast of characters. Only toward the end
of the process did I discover that Allen Barringer's great grandfather and
great-great uncle were students of P. S. Ney in the 1830s (the latter, Judge
Victor C. Barringer, thought that P. S. Ney's French was weak and that he
was not Marshal Ney).

I started the book with no impression one way or the other about
Marshal Ney. During the course of my research and writing, I came to
respect and even like him as a man of virtue.

I wish to thank Rand Mirante for giving me the inspiration for this book and for reading and critiquing the manuscript in draft form. His comments helped immeasurably. I also wish to thank my agent Roger Williams, especially for stepping in and taking ownership of this project when my long-standing agent Joe Vallely died in an untimely fashion just days after receiving the manuscript. Thanks also to Jonathan Kurtz and Jessica McCleary at Prometheus Books/Rowman & Littlefield, as well as to Vally Sharpe, who more than once rescued me from seemingly intractable formatting issues with the manuscript. I found the staff at the Wilson Library at the University of North Carolina, the Historical Society of Pennsylvania, the Library of Congress, and the National Archives, among others, all to be knowledgeable and helpful.

Finally, I wish to thank my dear wife Beth for accompanying me all over the United States and to France while I conducted my research and for acting as my sounding board (and sanity check) as I constantly tested theories and leads about the Marshal Ney/P. S. Ney mystery. This book is dedicated to her in love and gratitude.

Index

Page references for figures are italicized.

About the Author

Thomas E. Crocker is a graduate of Princeton University and Columbia Law School. He is a former U.S. diplomat and for many years was a partner in a large U.S. law firm, where he specialized in international trade issues. He also is the author of *Braddock's March* (2009), an award-winning history of General Edward Braddock's expedition at the start of the French and Indian War.